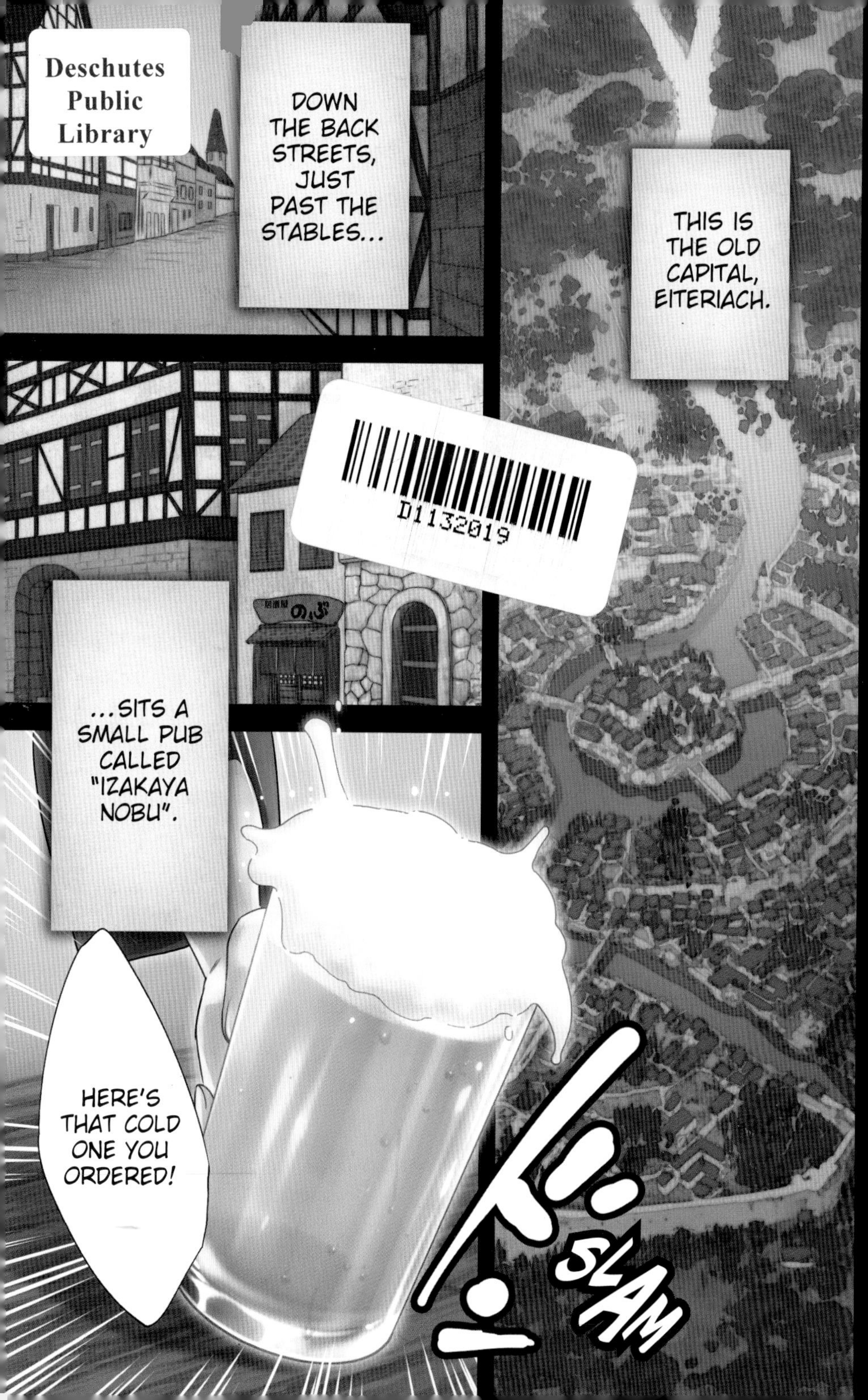
THIS IS THE OLD CAPITAL, EITERIACH.
DOWN THE BACK STREETS, JUST PAST THE STABLES...
...SITS A SMALL PUB CALLED "IZAKAYA NOBU".
HERE'S THAT COLD ONE YOU ORDERED!
SLAM

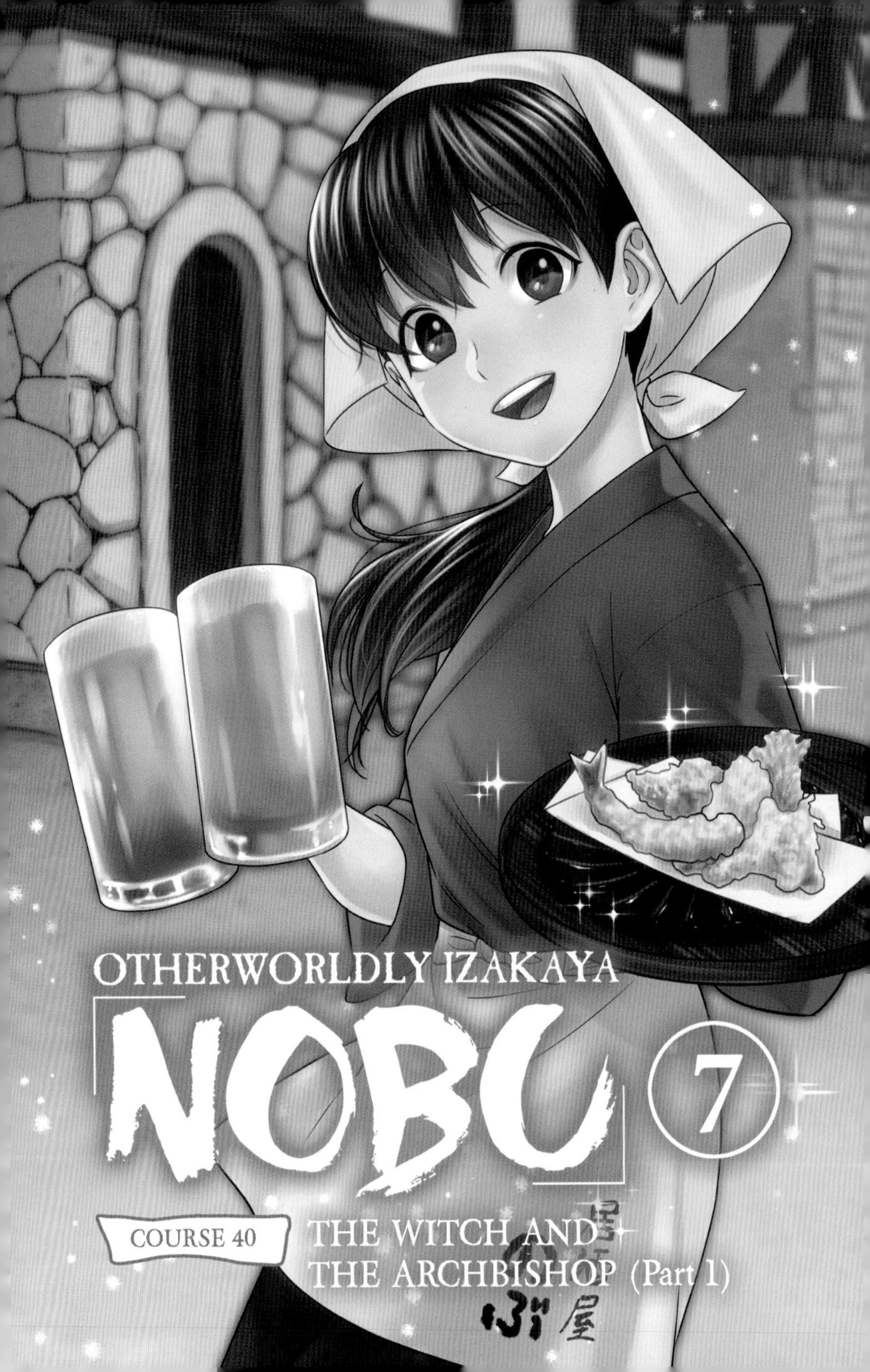
OTHERWORLDLY IZAKAYA
NOBU
7
COURSE 40
THE WITCH AND
THE ARCHBISHOP (Part 1)

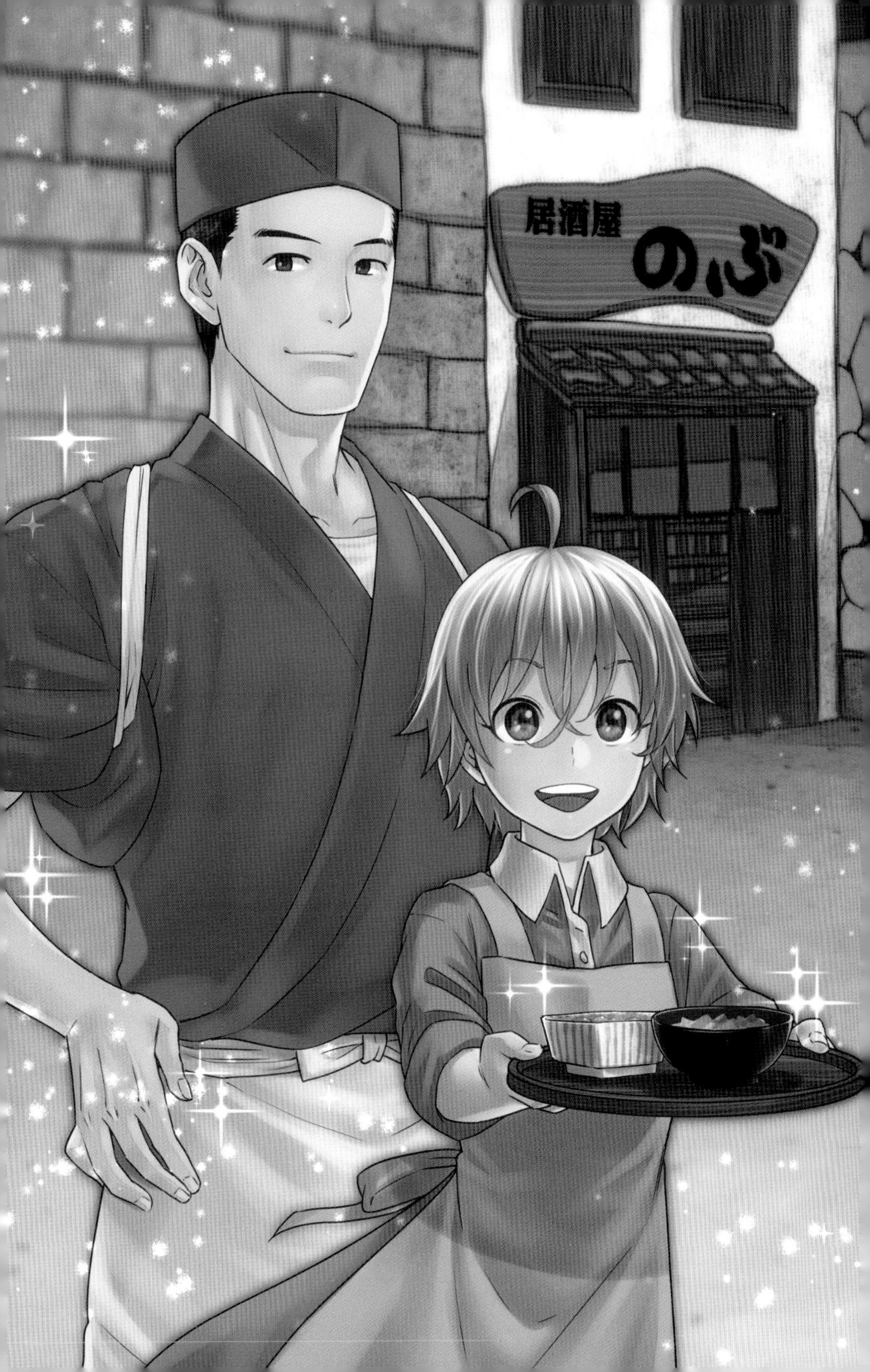
居酒屋
のぶ

MENU

OTHERWORLDLY IZAKAYA

NOBU

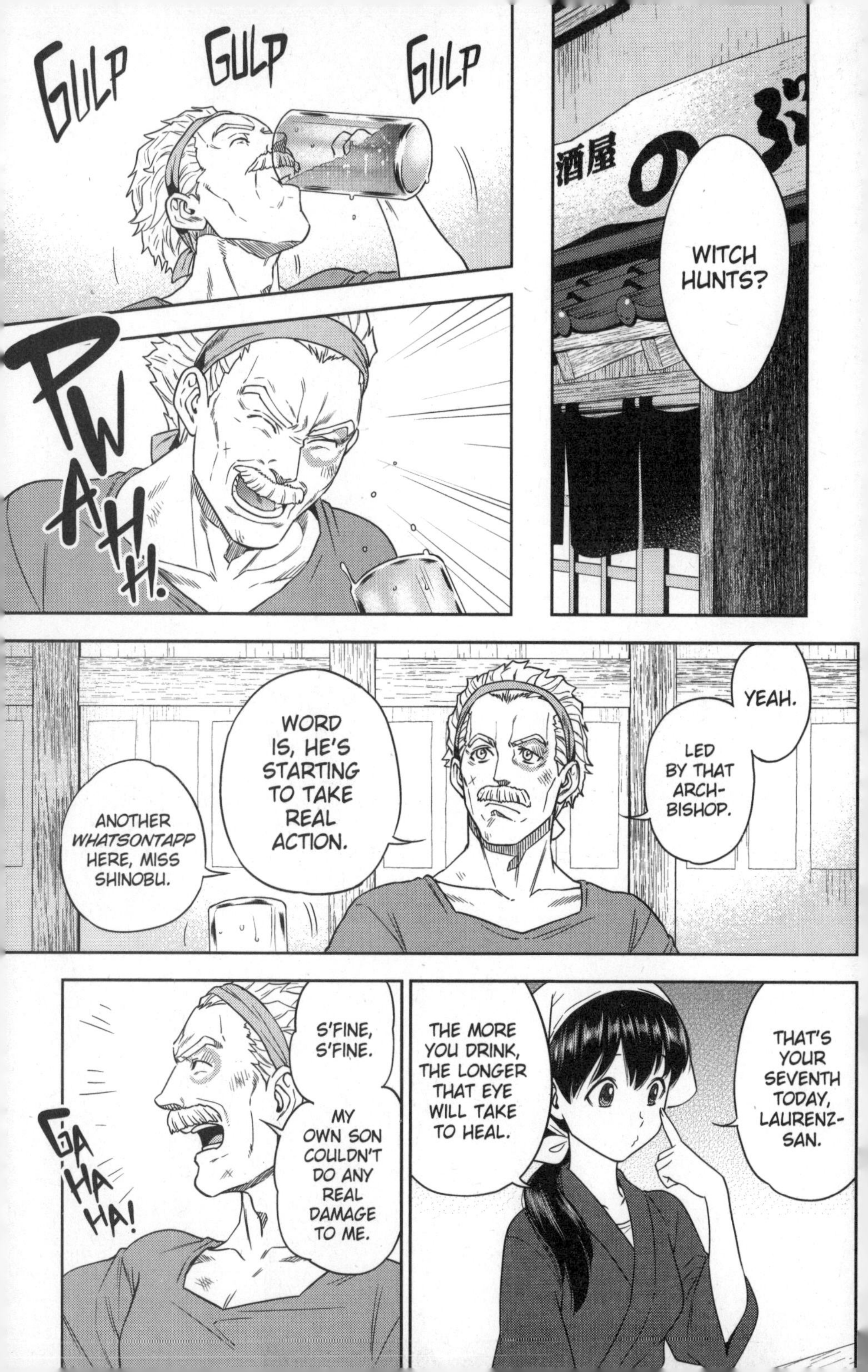
酒屋 のぶ
WITCH HUNTS?
GULP GULP GULP
PWAHH.
YEAH.
LED BY THAT ARCH-BISHOP.
WORD IS, HE'S STARTING TO TAKE REAL ACTION.
ANOTHER *WHATSONTAPP* HERE, MISS SHINOBU.
THAT'S YOUR SEVENTH TODAY, LAURENZ-SAN.
THE MORE YOU DRINK, THE LONGER THAT EYE WILL TAKE TO HEAL.
S'FINE, S'FINE.
MY OWN SON COULDN'T DO ANY REAL DAMAGE TO ME.
GAHAHA!

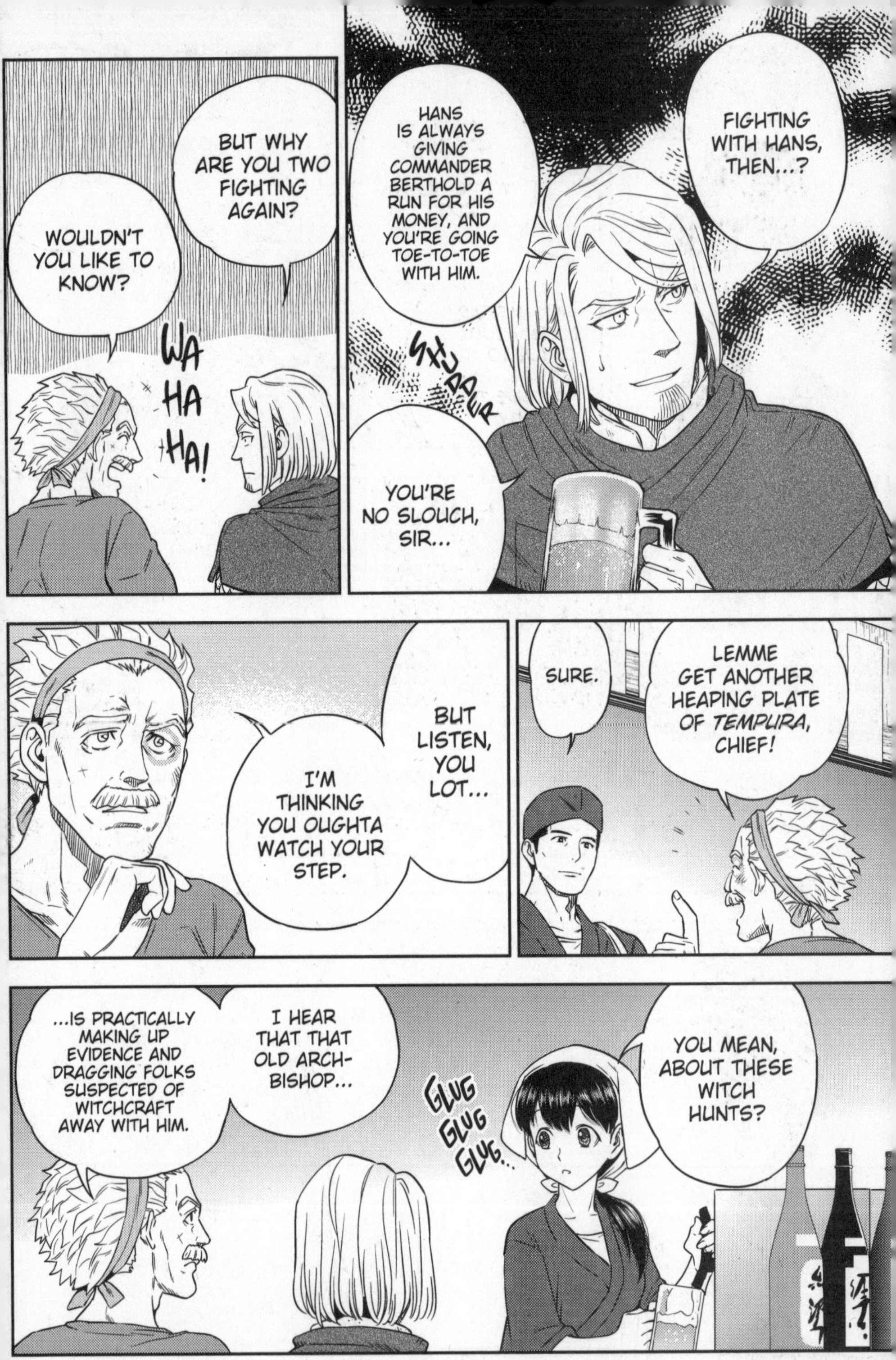
FIGHTING WITH HANS, THEN...?
HANS IS ALWAYS GIVING COMMANDER BERTHOLD A RUN FOR HIS MONEY, AND YOU'RE GOING TOE-TO-TOE WITH HIM.
SHUDDER
YOU'RE NO SLOUCH, SIR...
BUT WHY ARE YOU TWO FIGHTING AGAIN?
WOULDN'T YOU LIKE TO KNOW?
WA HA HA!
LEMME GET ANOTHER HEAPING PLATE OF *TEMPURA*, CHIEF!
SURE.
BUT LISTEN, YOU LOT...
I'M THINKING YOU OUGHTA WATCH YOUR STEP.
YOU MEAN, ABOUT THESE WITCH HUNTS?
GLUG GLUG GLUG...
I HEAR THAT THAT OLD ARCH-BISHOP...
...IS PRACTICALLY MAKING UP EVIDENCE AND DRAGGING FOLKS SUSPECTED OF WITCHCRAFT AWAY WITH HIM.

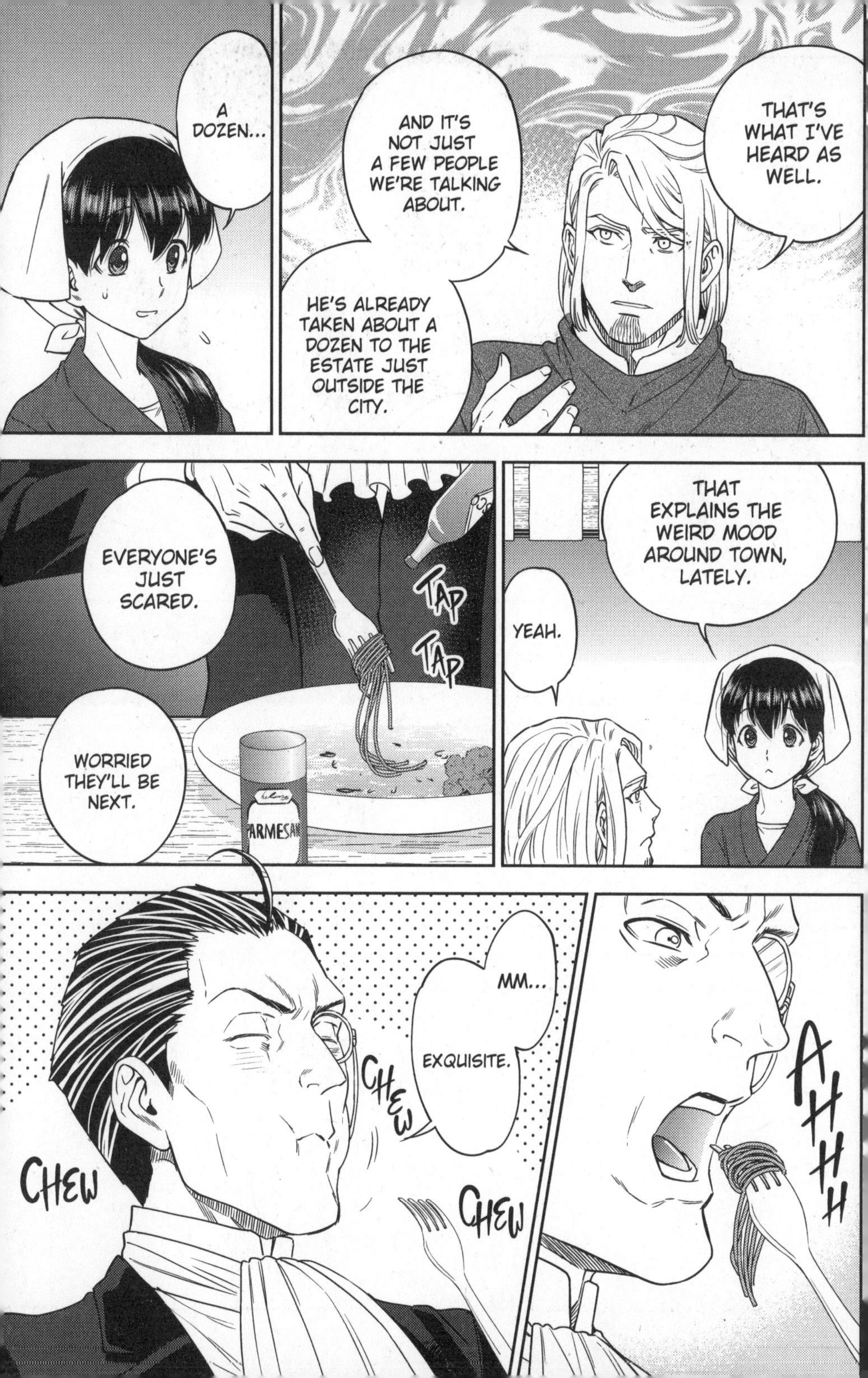
THAT'S WHAT I'VE HEARD AS WELL.
AND IT'S NOT JUST A FEW PEOPLE WE'RE TALKING ABOUT.
HE'S ALREADY TAKEN ABOUT A DOZEN TO THE ESTATE JUST OUTSIDE THE CITY.
A DOZEN...
THAT EXPLAINS THE WEIRD MOOD AROUND TOWN, LATELY.
YEAH.
EVERYONE'S JUST SCARED.
TAP
TAP
WORRIED THEY'LL BE NEXT.
AHHHH
MM...
EXQUISITE.
CHEW
CHEW
CHEW
CHEW

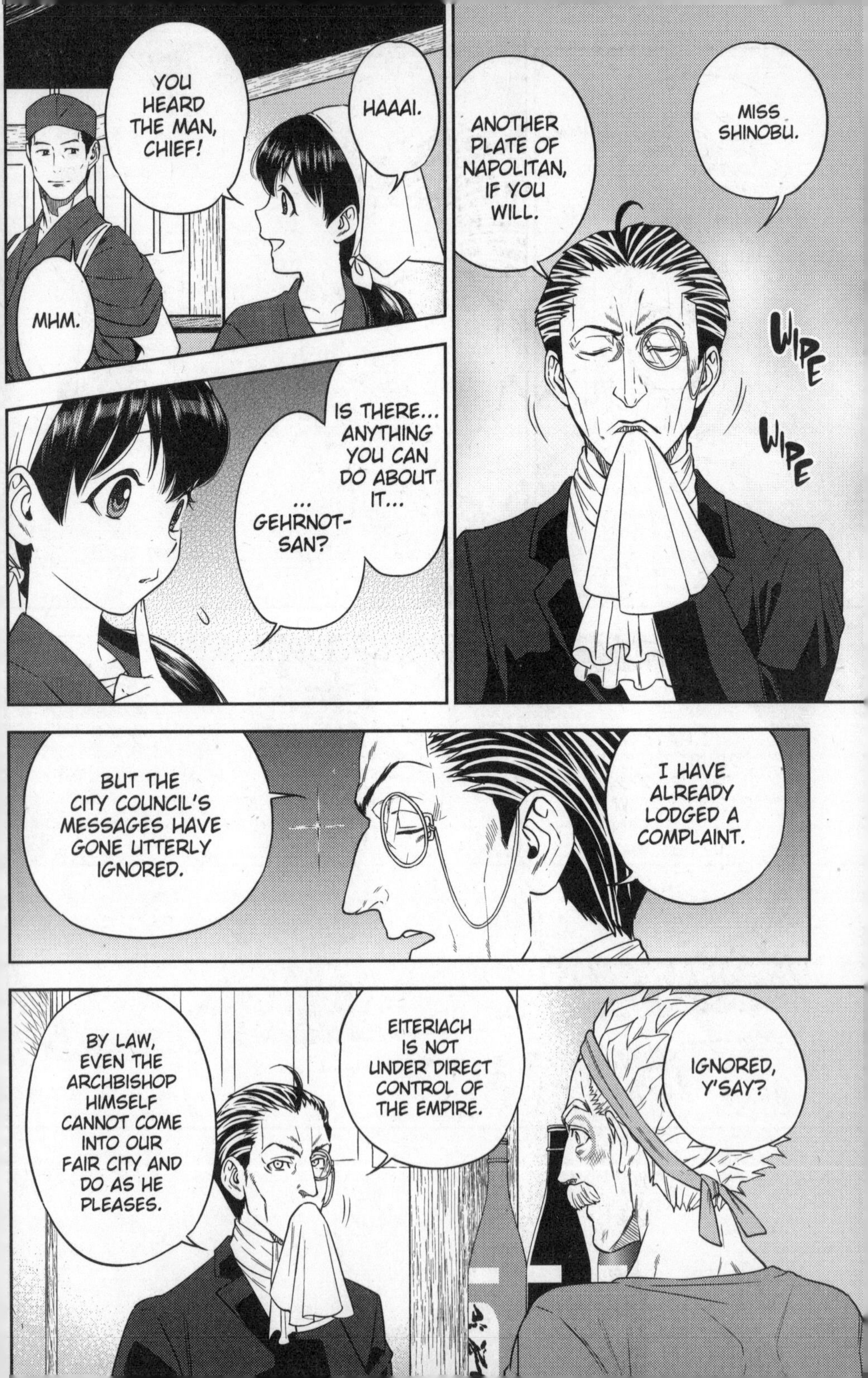
MISS SHINOBU.
ANOTHER PLATE OF NAPOLITAN, IF YOU WILL.
WIPE
WIPE
HAAAI.
YOU HEARD THE MAN, CHIEF!
MHM.
IS THERE... ANYTHING YOU CAN DO ABOUT IT...
... GEHRNOT-SAN?
I HAVE ALREADY LODGED A COMPLAINT.
BUT THE CITY COUNCIL'S MESSAGES HAVE GONE UTTERLY IGNORED.
IGNORED, Y'SAY?
EITERIACH IS NOT UNDER DIRECT CONTROL OF THE EMPIRE.
BY LAW, EVEN THE ARCHBISHOP HIMSELF CANNOT COME INTO OUR FAIR CITY AND DO AS HE PLEASES.

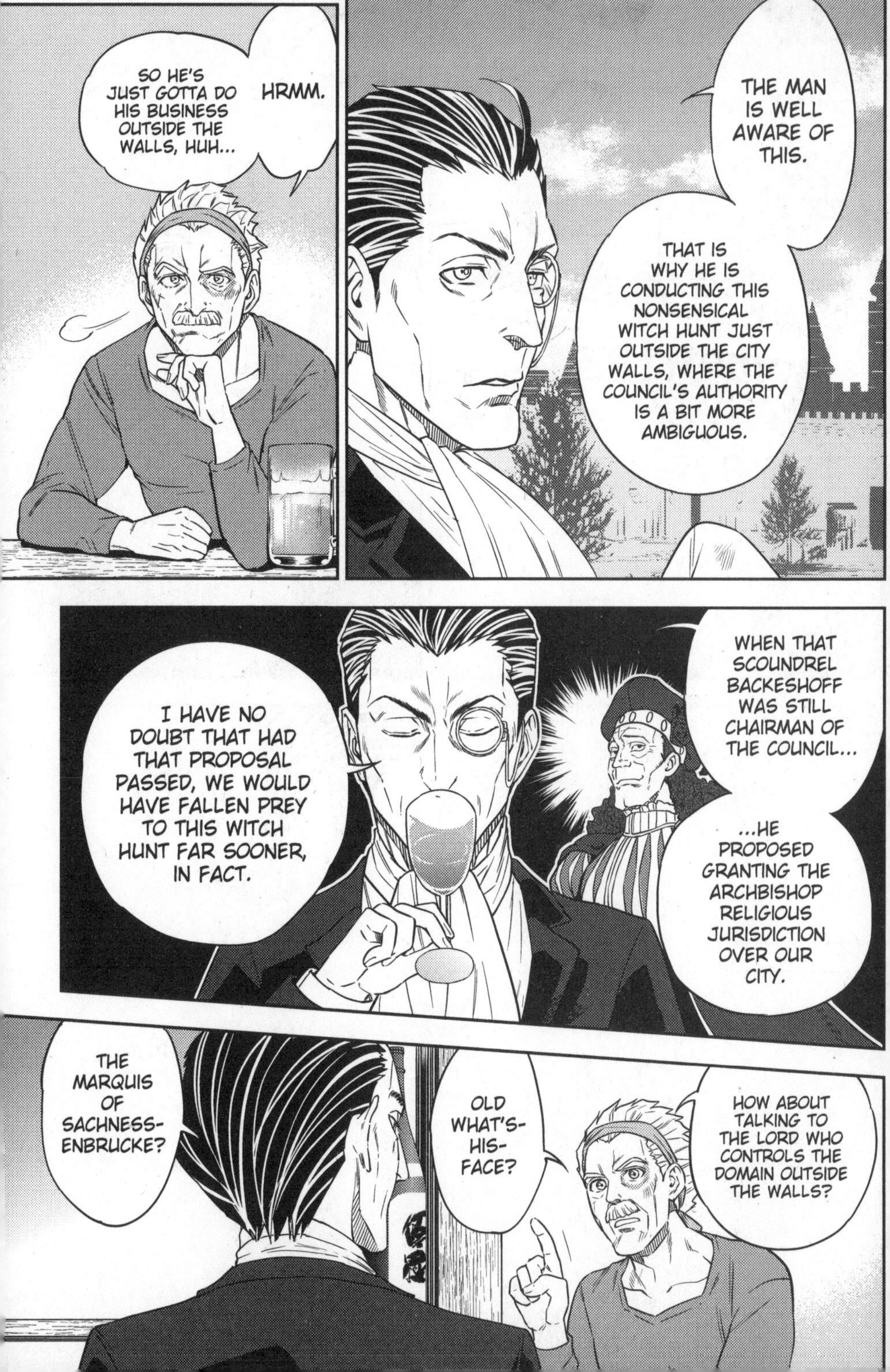
THE MAN IS WELL AWARE OF THIS.
THAT IS WHY HE IS CONDUCTING THIS NONSENSICAL WITCH HUNT JUST OUTSIDE THE CITY WALLS, WHERE THE COUNCIL'S AUTHORITY IS A BIT MORE AMBIGUOUS.
SO HE'S JUST GOTTA DO HIS BUSINESS OUTSIDE THE WALLS, HUH... HRMM.
WHEN THAT SCOUNDREL BACKESHOFF WAS STILL CHAIRMAN OF THE COUNCIL...
...HE PROPOSED GRANTING THE ARCHBISHOP RELIGIOUS JURISDICTION OVER OUR CITY.
I HAVE NO DOUBT THAT HAD THAT PROPOSAL PASSED, WE WOULD HAVE FALLEN PREY TO THIS WITCH HUNT FAR SOONER, IN FACT.
HOW ABOUT TALKING TO THE LORD WHO CONTROLS THE DOMAIN OUTSIDE THE WALLS?
OLD WHAT'S-HIS-FACE?
THE MARQUIS OF SACHNESS-ENBRUCKE?

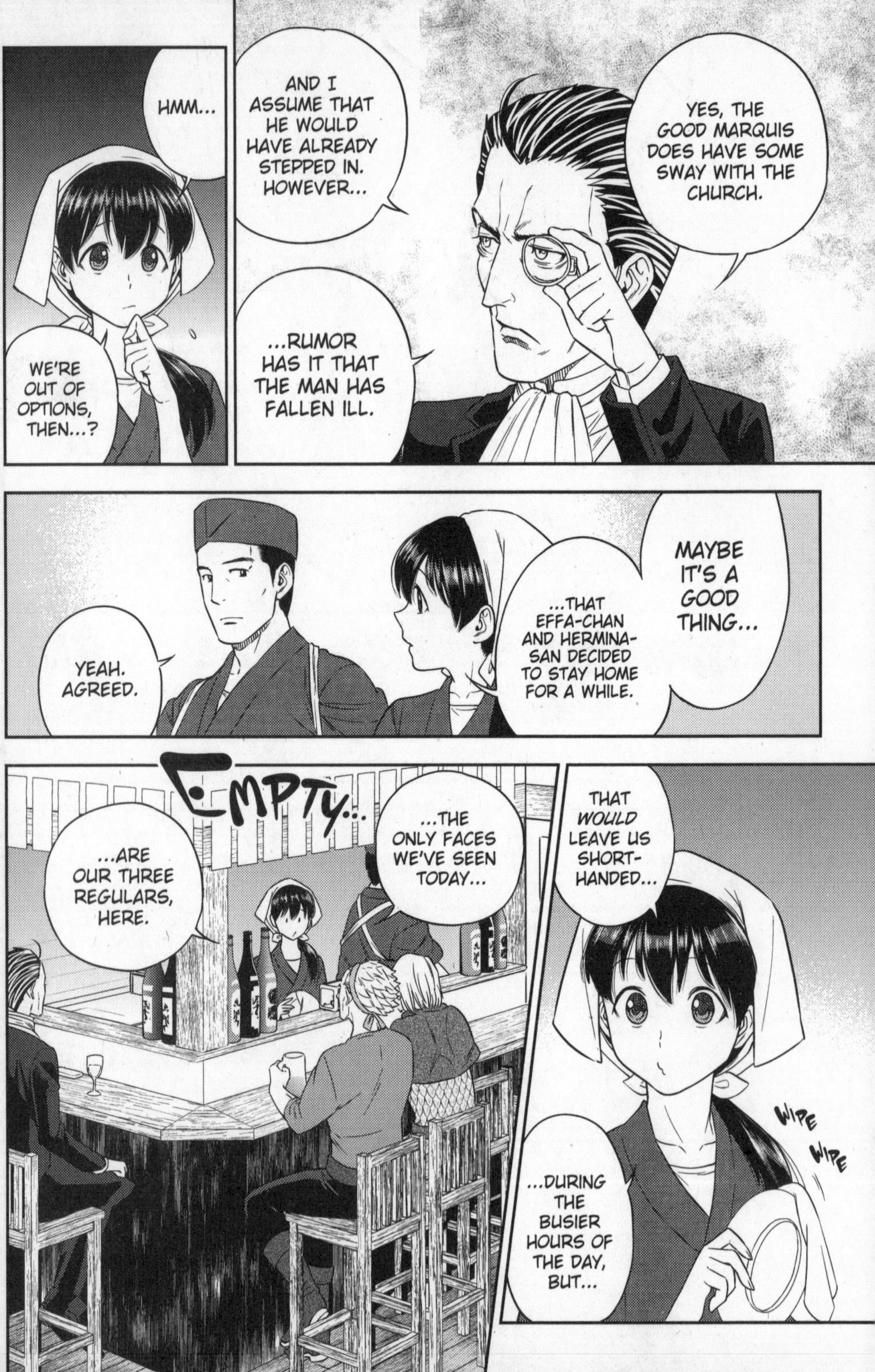
YES, THE GOOD MARQUIS DOES HAVE SOME SWAY WITH THE CHURCH.
AND I ASSUME THAT HE WOULD HAVE ALREADY STEPPED IN. HOWEVER...
...RUMOR HAS IT THAT THE MAN HAS FALLEN ILL.
HMM...
WE'RE OUT OF OPTIONS, THEN...?
MAYBE IT'S A GOOD THING...
...THAT EFFA-CHAN AND HERMINA-SAN DECIDED TO STAY HOME FOR A WHILE.
YEAH. AGREED.
THAT *WOULD* LEAVE US SHORT-HANDED...
...DURING THE BUSIER HOURS OF THE DAY, BUT...
WIPE
WIPE
EMPTY...
...THE ONLY FACES WE'VE SEEN TODAY...
...ARE OUR THREE REGULARS, HERE.

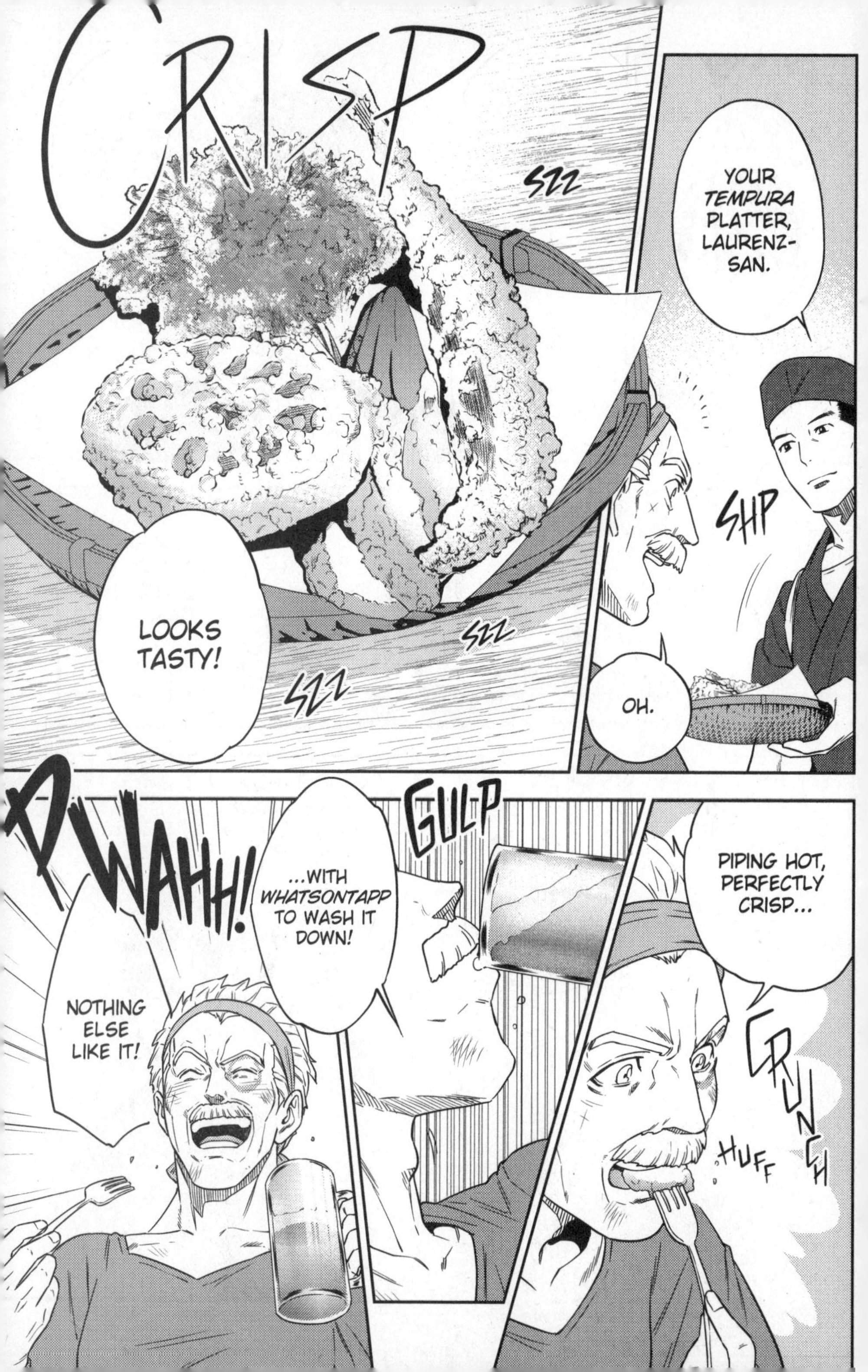
YOUR TEMPURA PLATTER, LAURENZ-SAN.
SHP
OH.
CRISP
SZZ
LOOKS TASTY!
SZZ
SZZ
PIPING HOT, PERFECTLY CRISP...
CRUNCH
HUFF
GULP
...WITH *WHATSONTAPP* TO WASH IT DOWN!
PWAHH!
NOTHING ELSE LIKE IT!

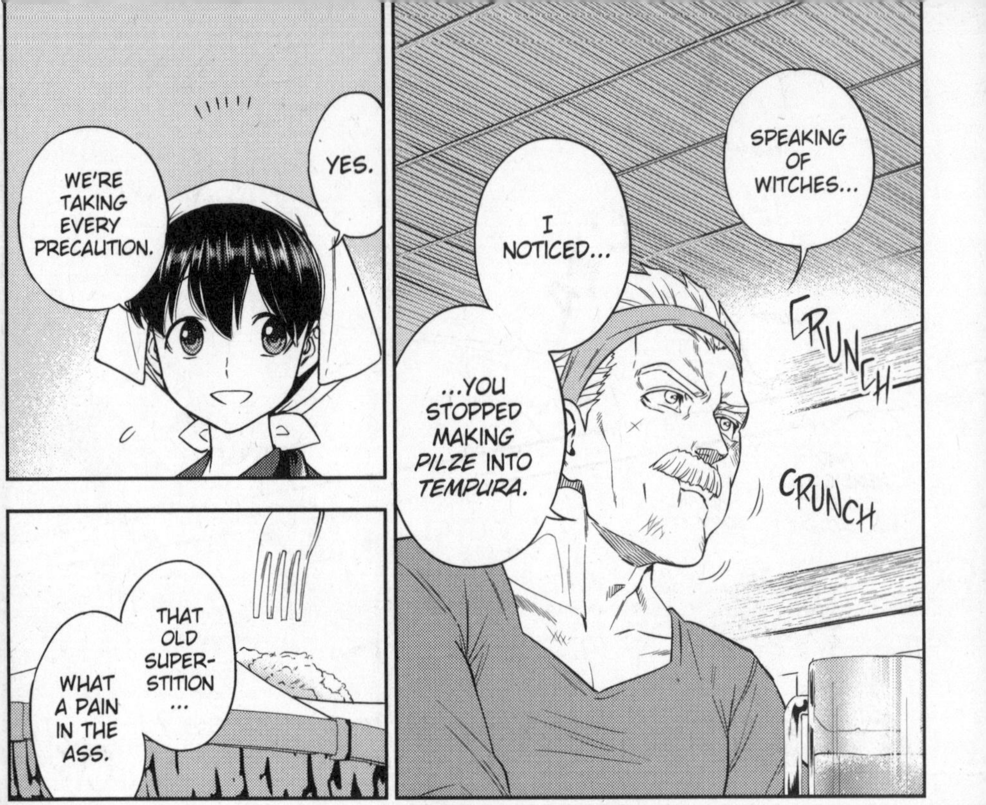
SPEAKING OF WITCHES...
CRUNCH
I NOTICED...
...YOU STOPPED MAKING *PILZE* INTO *TEMPURA.*
CRUNCH
YES.
WE'RE TAKING EVERY PRECAUTION.
THAT OLD SUPER-STITION...
WHAT A PAIN IN THE ASS.

**PILZE* IS GERMAN FOR MUSHROOMS

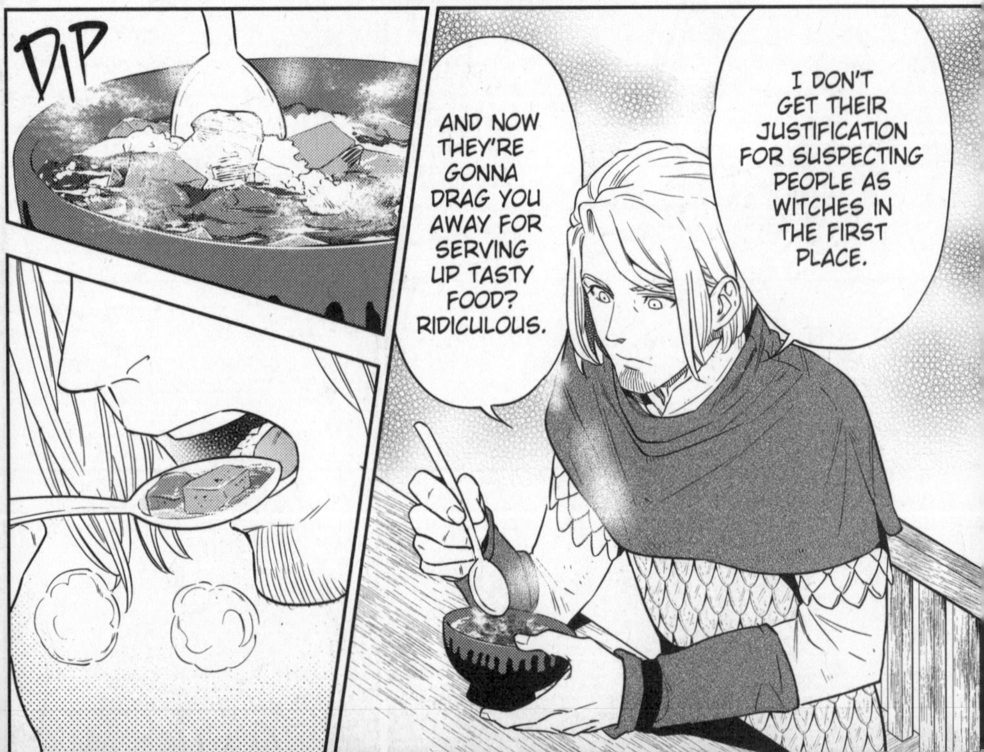
I DON'T GET THEIR JUSTIFICATION FOR SUSPECTING PEOPLE AS WITCHES IN THE FIRST PLACE.
AND NOW THEY'RE GONNA DRAG YOU AWAY FOR SERVING UP TASTY FOOD? RIDICULOUS.
DIP

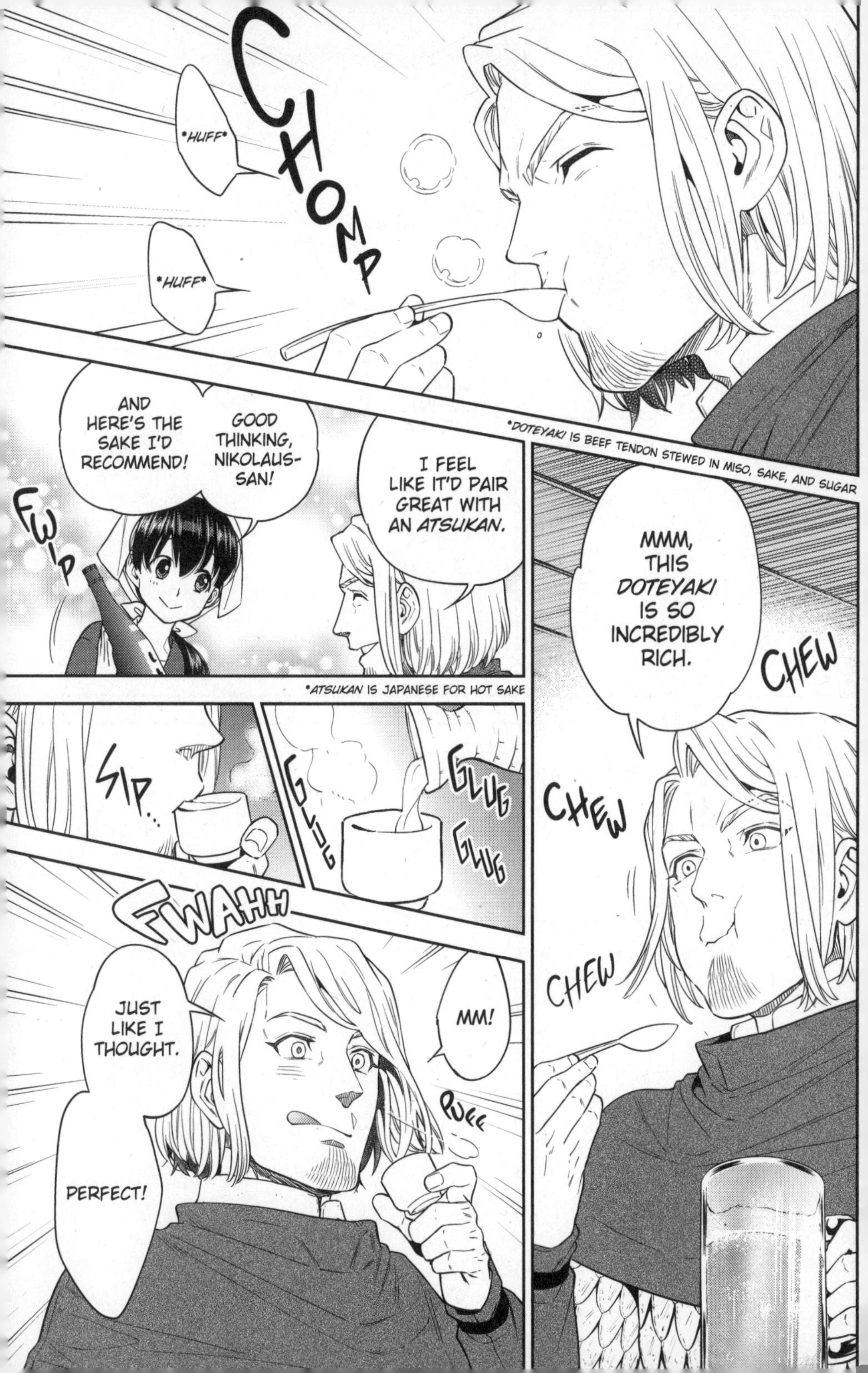
CHOMP
HUFF
HUFF
*DOTEYAKI IS BEEF TENDON STEWED IN MISO, SAKE, AND SUGAR
MMM, THIS DOTEYAKI IS SO INCREDIBLY RICH.
CHEW
CHEW
CHEW
I FEEL LIKE IT'D PAIR GREAT WITH AN ATSUKAN.
GOOD THINKING, NIKOLAUS-SAN!
AND HERE'S THE SAKE I'D RECOMMEND!
FWIP
*ATSUKAN IS JAPANESE FOR HOT SAKE
GLUG
GLUG
GLUG
SIP...
FWAHH
MM!
JUST LIKE I THOUGHT.
PERFECT!
PUFF

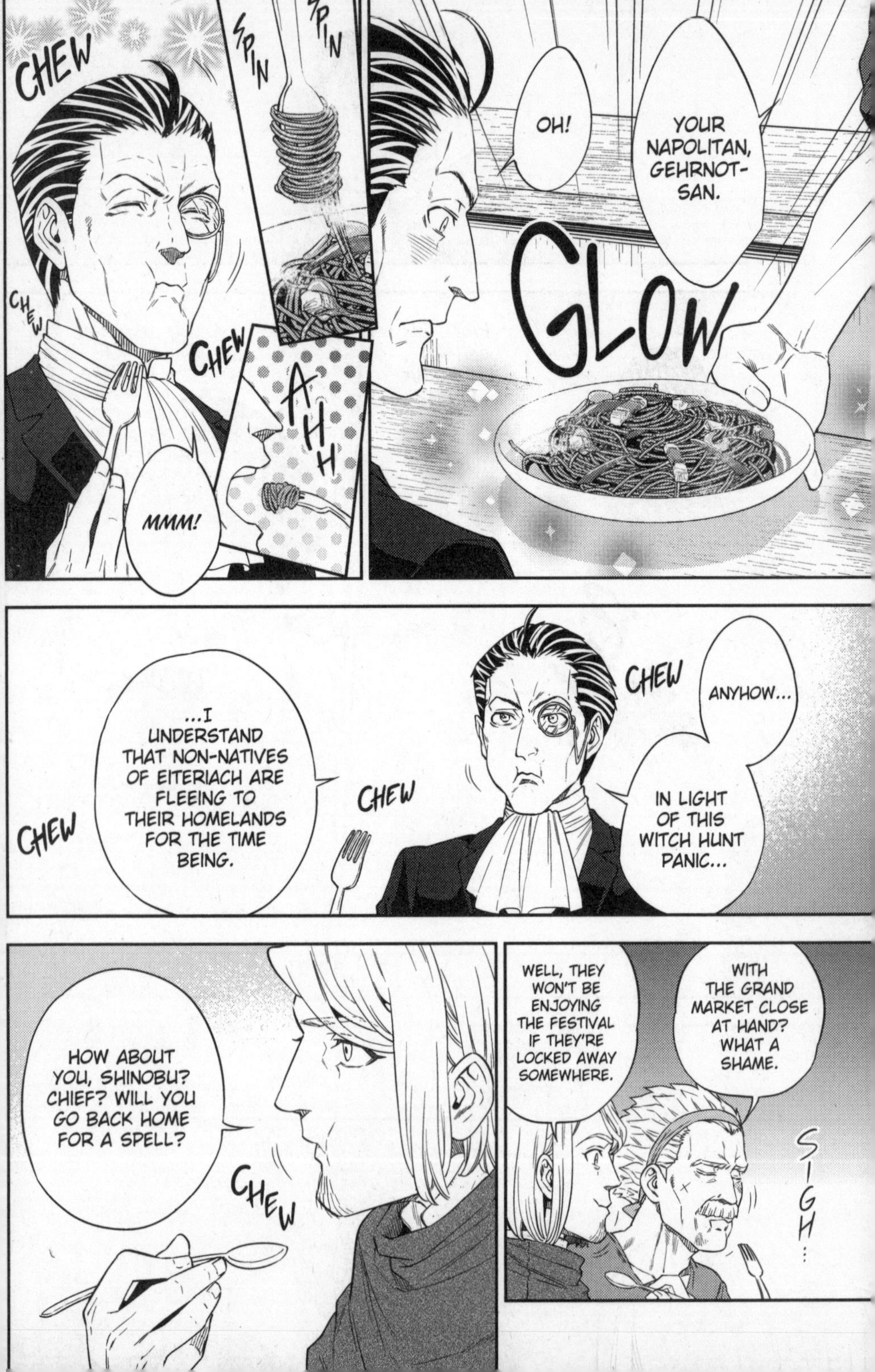
YOUR NAPOLITAN, GEHRNOT-SAN.
OH!
GLOW
SPIN SPIN
AHH
CHEW
CHEW
CHEW
MMM!
CHEW
ANYHOW...
IN LIGHT OF THIS WITCH HUNT PANIC...
CHEW
...I UNDERSTAND THAT NON-NATIVES OF EITERIACH ARE FLEEING TO THEIR HOMELANDS FOR THE TIME BEING.
CHEW
WITH THE GRAND MARKET CLOSE AT HAND? WHAT A SHAME.
WELL, THEY WON'T BE ENJOYING THE FESTIVAL IF THEY'RE LOCKED AWAY SOMEWHERE.
SIGH...
HOW ABOUT YOU, SHINOBU? CHIEF? WILL YOU GO BACK HOME FOR A SPELL?
CHEW

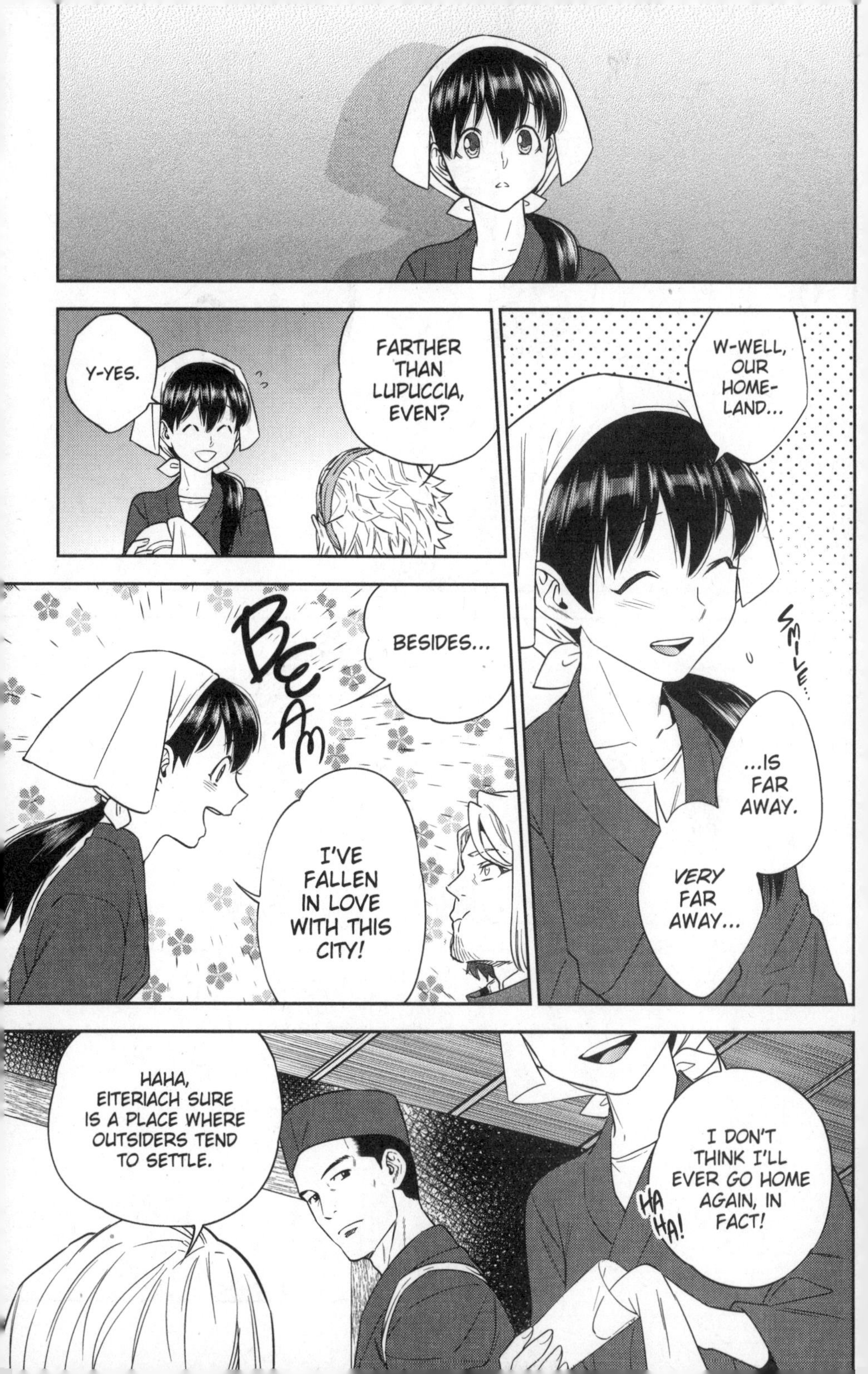
W-WELL, OUR HOME-LAND...
SMILE...
...IS FAR AWAY.
VERY FAR AWAY...
FARTHER THAN LUPUCCIA, EVEN?
Y-YES.
BESIDES...
BEAM
I'VE FALLEN IN LOVE WITH THIS CITY!
I DON'T THINK I'LL EVER GO HOME AGAIN, IN FACT!
HA HA!
HAHA, EITERIACH SURE IS A PLACE WHERE OUTSIDERS TEND TO SETTLE.

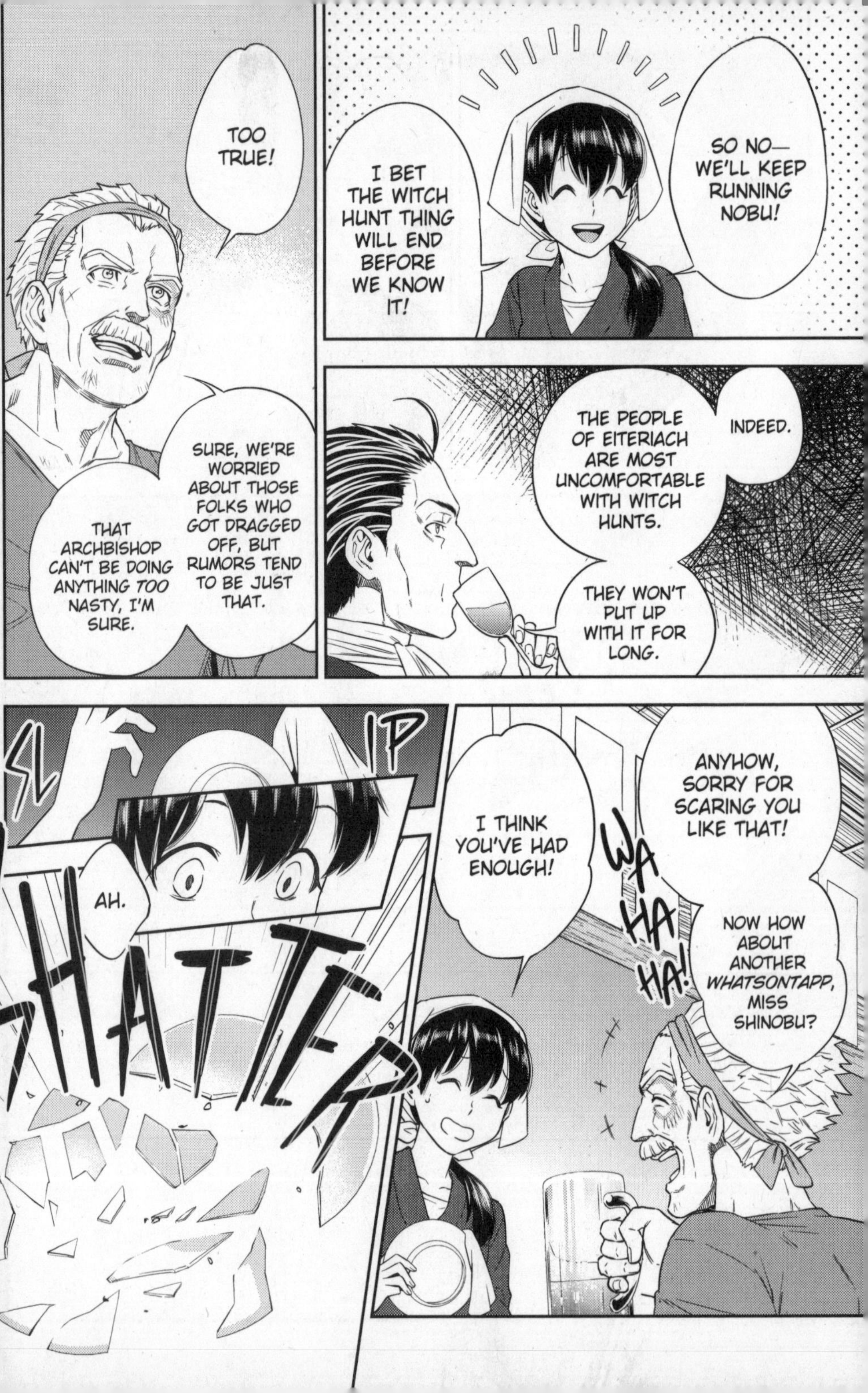
SO NO— WE'LL KEEP RUNNING NOBU!
I BET THE WITCH HUNT THING WILL END BEFORE WE KNOW IT!
INDEED.
THE PEOPLE OF EITERIACH ARE MOST UNCOMFORTABLE WITH WITCH HUNTS.
THEY WON'T PUT UP WITH IT FOR LONG.
TOO TRUE!
SURE, WE'RE WORRIED ABOUT THOSE FOLKS WHO GOT DRAGGED OFF, BUT RUMORS TEND TO BE JUST THAT.
THAT ARCHBISHOP CAN'T BE DOING ANYTHING *TOO* NASTY, I'M SURE.
ANYHOW, SORRY FOR SCARING YOU LIKE THAT!
WA HA HA!
NOW HOW ABOUT ANOTHER *WHATSONTAPP*, MISS SHINOBU?
I THINK YOU'VE HAD ENOUGH!
SLIP
AH.
SHATTER

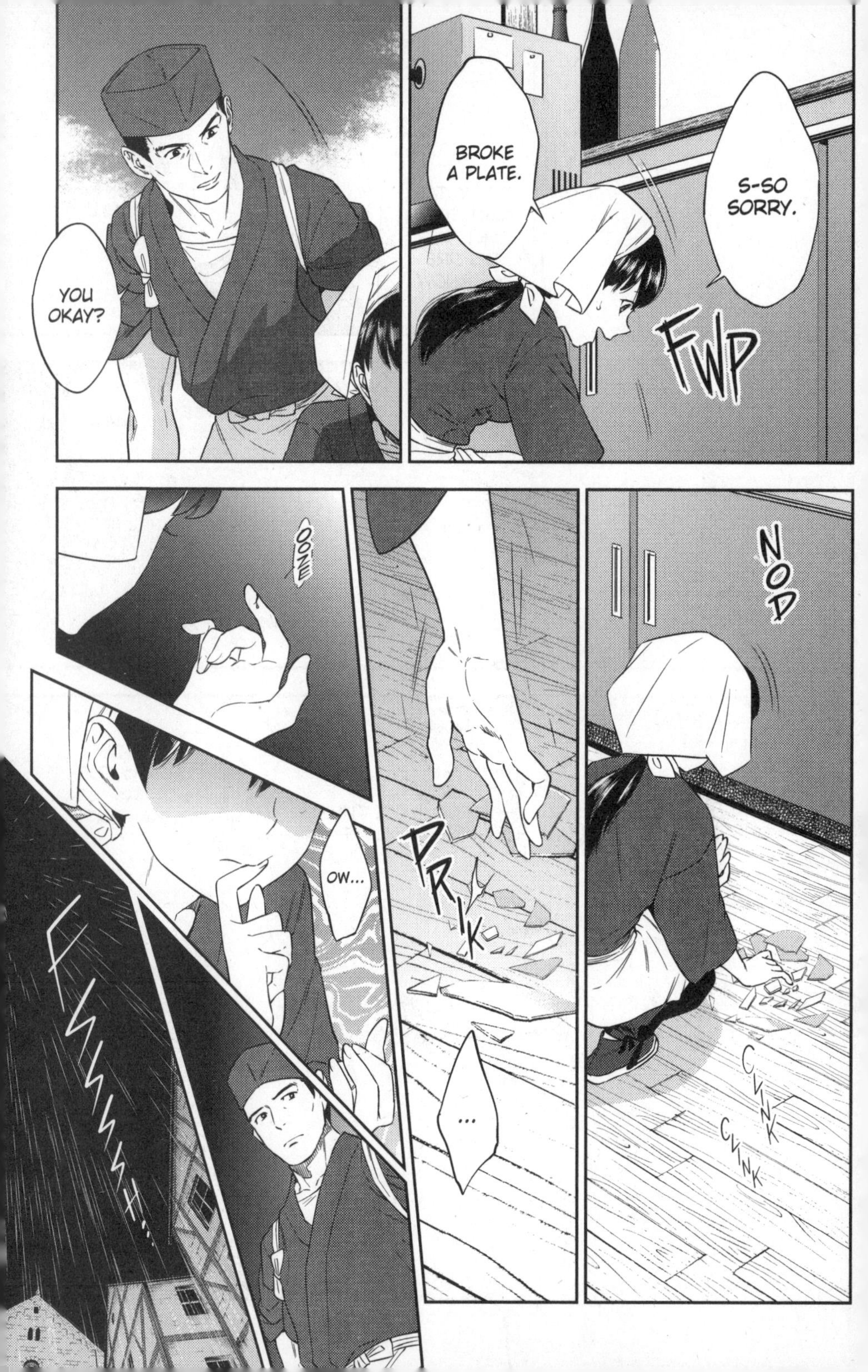
S-SO SORRY.
BROKE A PLATE.
FWP
YOU OKAY?
NOD
CLINK
CLINK
PRIK
...
OOZE
OW...
FSSSSSH...

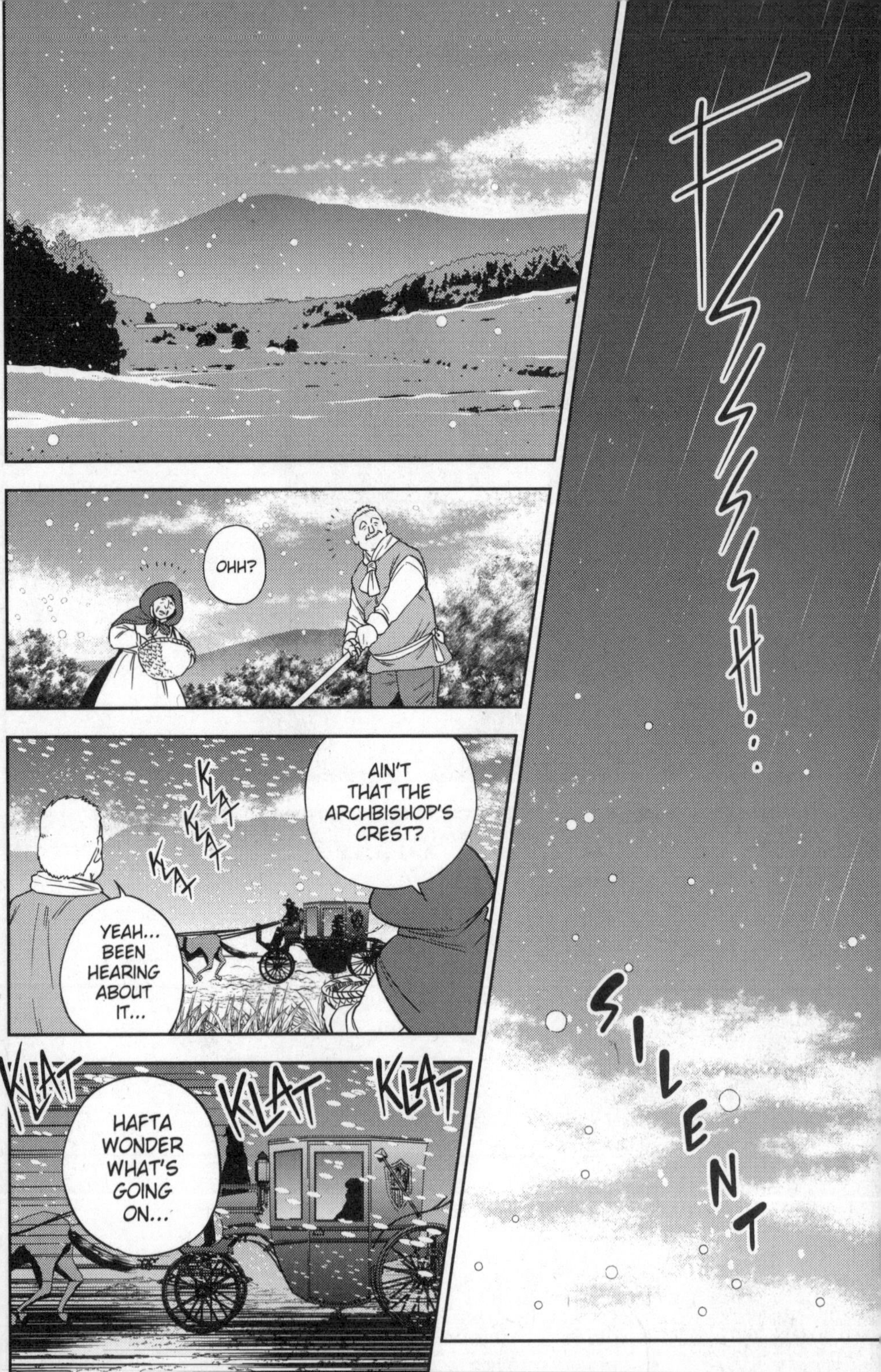
FSSSSH...
SILENT
OHH?
AIN'T THAT THE ARCHBISHOP'S CREST?
KLAT KLAT KLAT
YEAH... BEEN HEARING ABOUT IT...
KLAT
KLAT
KLAT
HAFTA WONDER WHAT'S GOING ON...

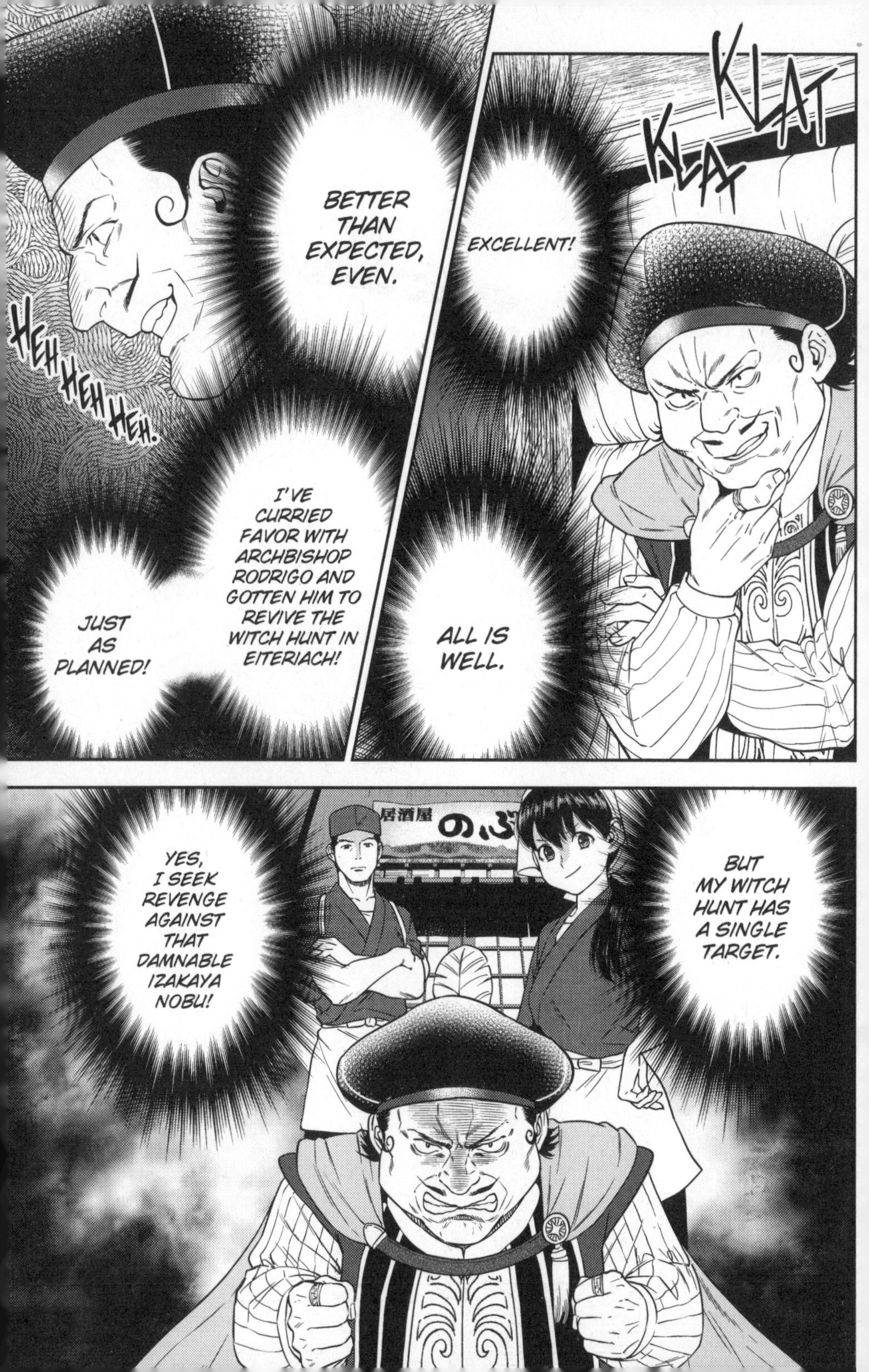
KLAT KLAT
EXCELLENT!
ALL IS WELL.
BETTER THAN EXPECTED, EVEN.
HEH HEH HEH.
I'VE CURRIED FAVOR WITH ARCHBISHOP RODRIGO AND GOTTEN HIM TO REVIVE THE WITCH HUNT IN EITERIACH!
JUST AS PLANNED!
BUT MY WITCH HUNT HAS A SINGLE TARGET.
居酒屋 のぶ
YES, I SEEK REVENGE AGAINST THAT DAMNABLE IZAKAYA NOBU!

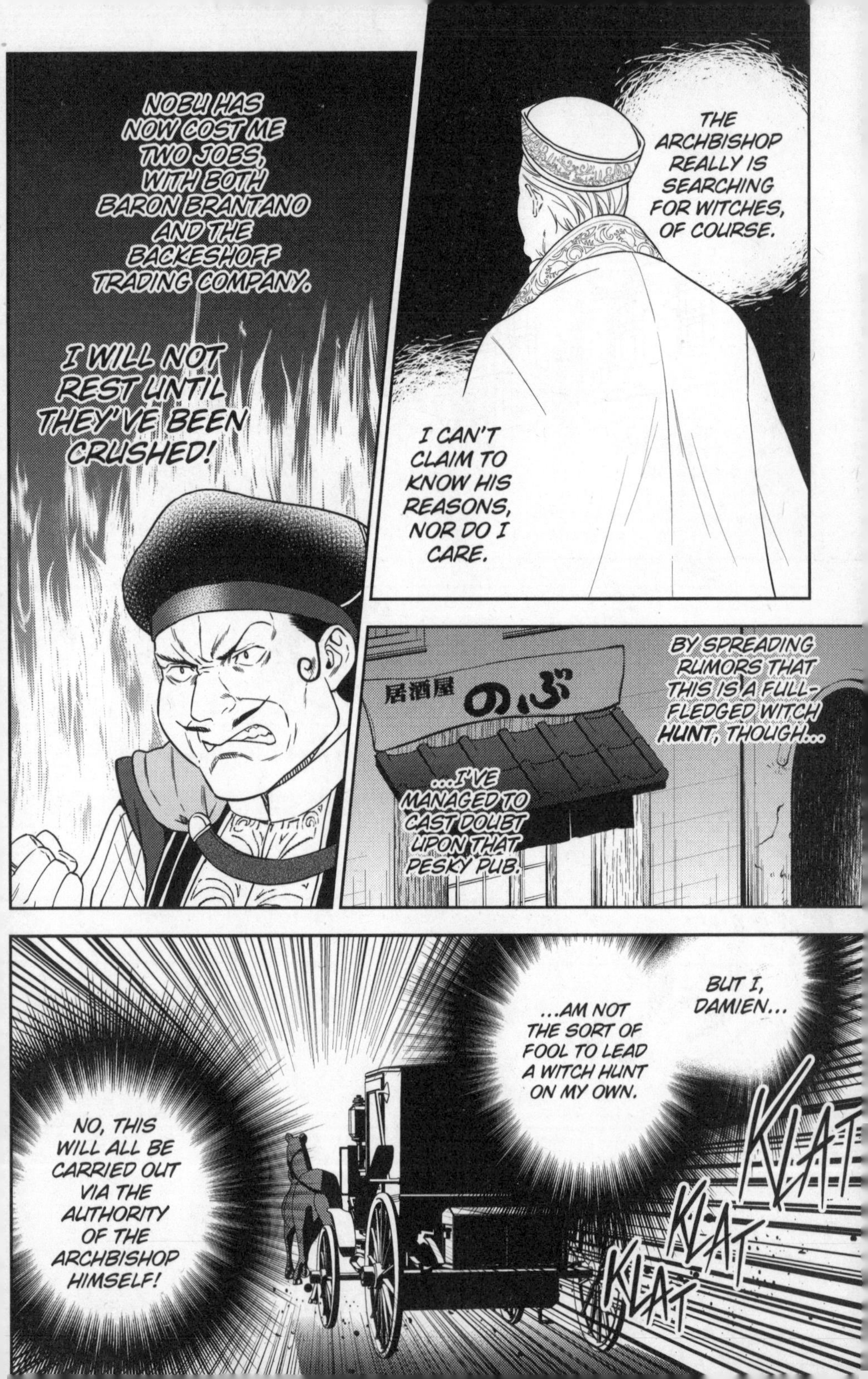
THE ARCHBISHOP REALLY IS SEARCHING FOR WITCHES, OF COURSE.
I CAN'T CLAIM TO KNOW HIS REASONS, NOR DO I CARE.
BY SPREADING RUMORS THAT THIS IS A FULL-FLEDGED WITCH HUNT, THOUGH...
居酒屋 のぶ
...I'VE MANAGED TO CAST DOUBT UPON THAT PESKY PUB.
NOBU HAS NOW COST ME TWO JOBS, WITH BOTH BARON BRANTANO AND THE BACKESHOFF TRADING COMPANY.
I WILL NOT REST UNTIL THEY'VE BEEN CRUSHED!
BUT I, DAMIEN...
...AM NOT THE SORT OF FOOL TO LEAD A WITCH HUNT ON MY OWN.
KLAT
KLAT
KLAT
NO, THIS WILL ALL BE CARRIED OUT VIA THE AUTHORITY OF THE ARCHBISHOP HIMSELF!

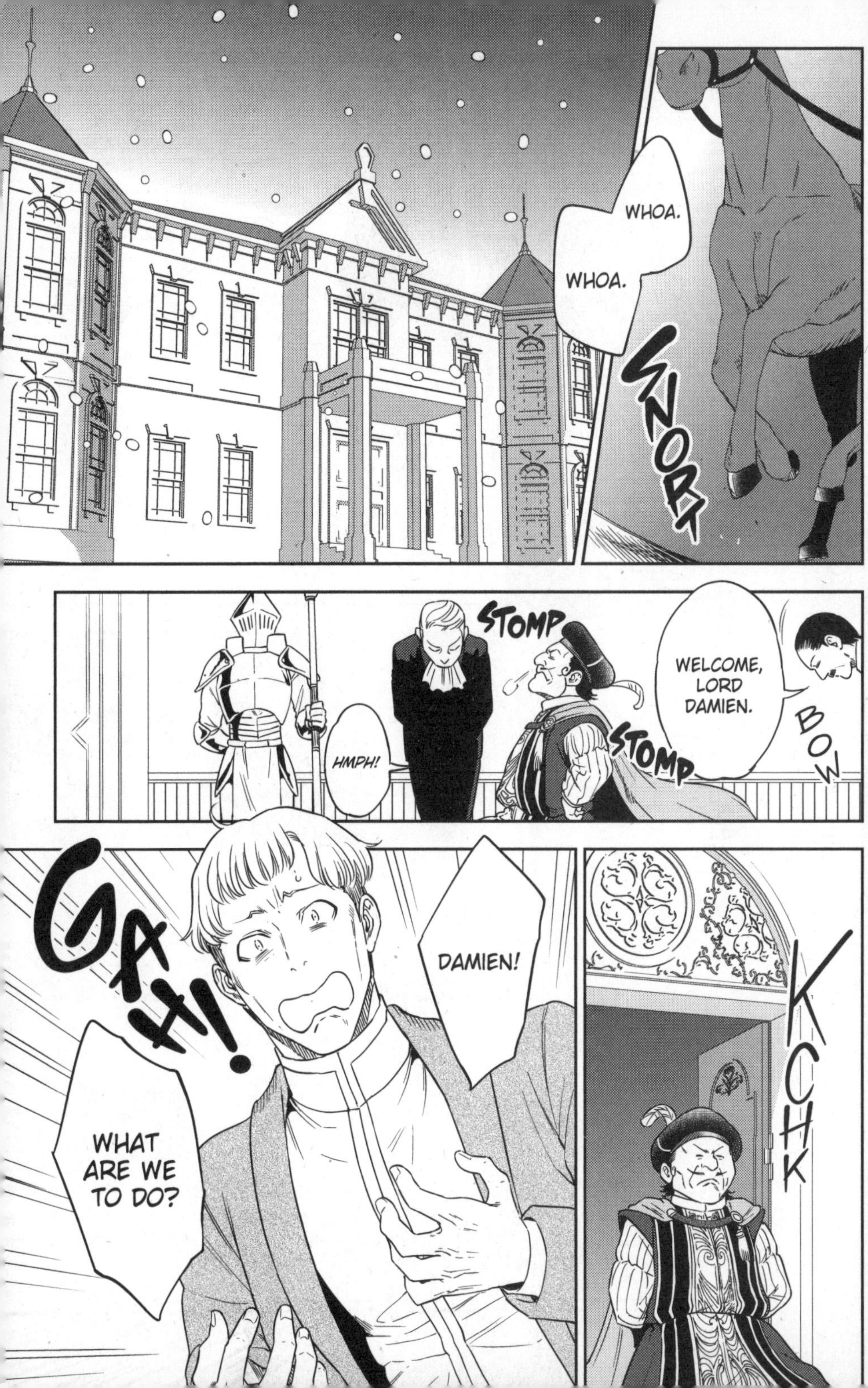
WHOA.
WHOA.
SNORT
WELCOME, LORD DAMIEN.
BOW
STOMP
STOMP
HMPH!
KCHK
DAMIEN!
GAH!
WHAT ARE WE TO DO?

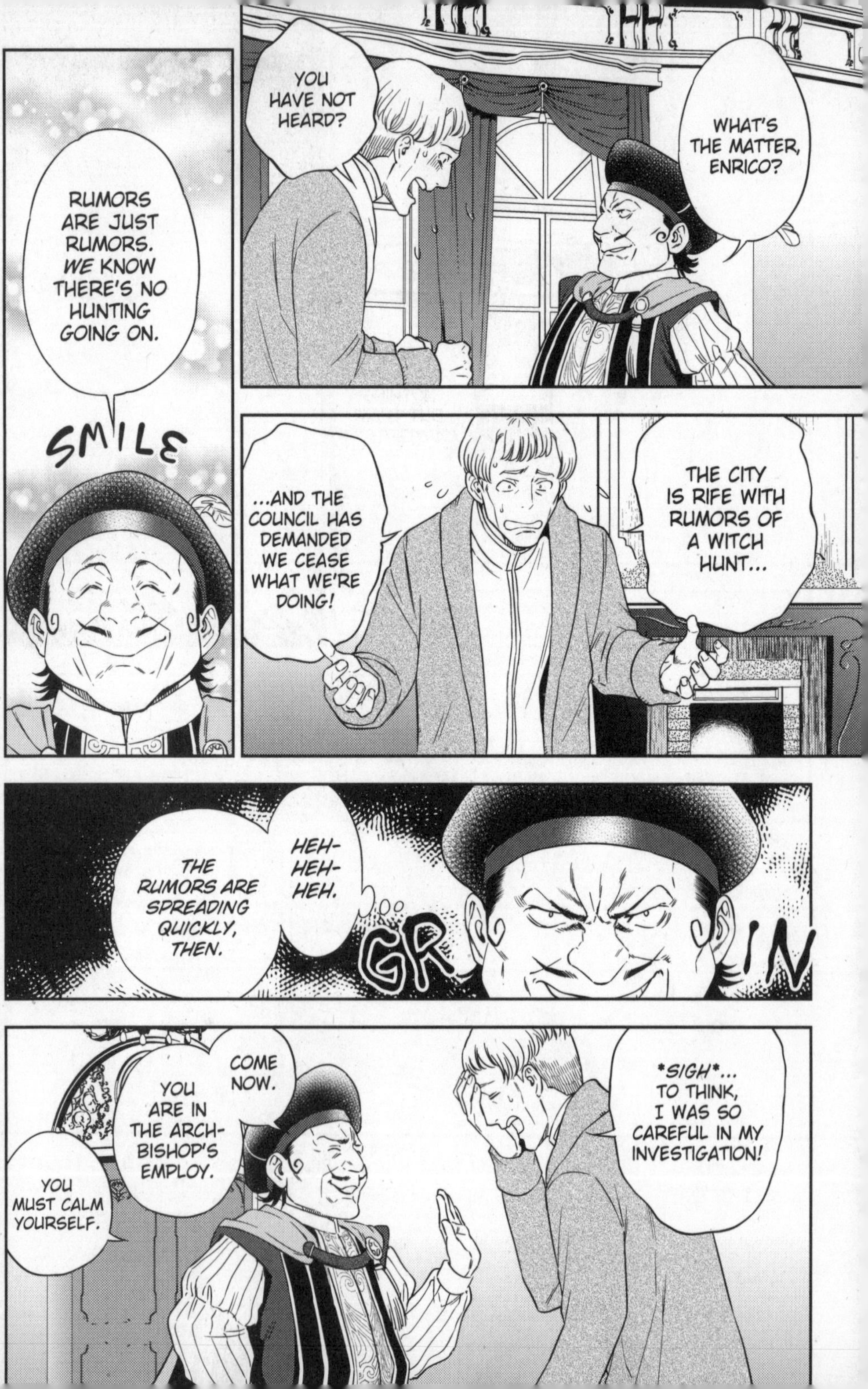
WHAT'S THE MATTER, ENRICO?
YOU HAVE NOT HEARD?
THE CITY IS RIFE WITH RUMORS OF A WITCH HUNT...
...AND THE COUNCIL HAS DEMANDED WE CEASE WHAT WE'RE DOING!
RUMORS ARE JUST RUMORS. *WE* KNOW THERE'S NO HUNTING GOING ON.
SMILE
HEH-HEH-HEH.
THE RUMORS ARE SPREADING QUICKLY, THEN.
GRIN
SIGH... TO THINK, I WAS SO CAREFUL IN MY INVESTIGATION!
COME NOW.
YOU ARE IN THE ARCH-BISHOP'S EMPLOY.
YOU MUST CALM YOURSELF.

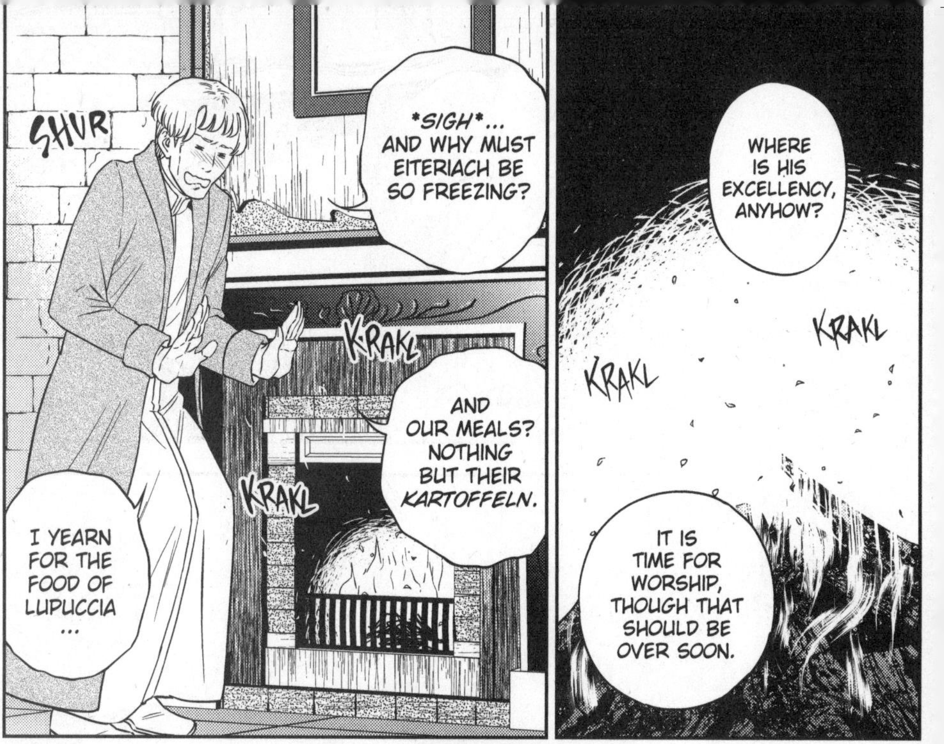
WHERE IS HIS EXCELLENCY, ANYHOW?
KRAKL
KRAKL
IT IS TIME FOR WORSHIP, THOUGH THAT SHOULD BE OVER SOON.
SHUR
SIGH... AND WHY MUST EITERIACH BE SO FREEZING?
KRAKL
AND OUR MEALS? NOTHING BUT THEIR KARTOFFELN.
KRAKL
I YEARN FOR THE FOOD OF LUPUCCIA ...

*KARTOFFELN IS GERMAN FOR POTATOES

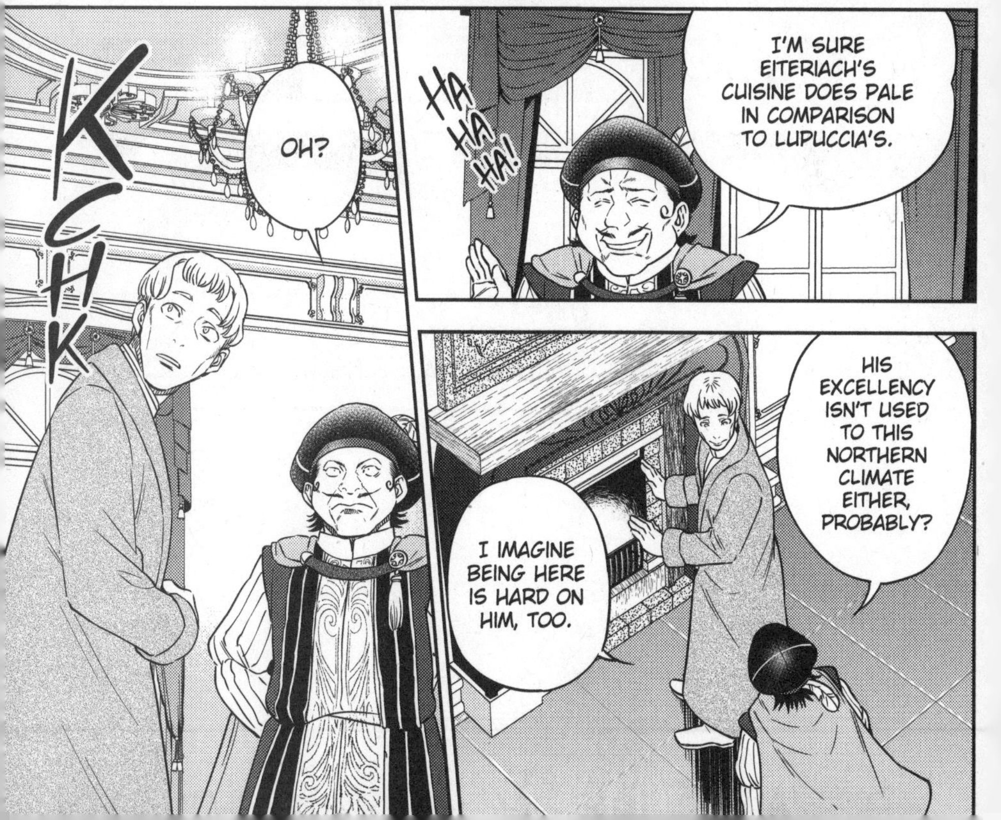
I'M SURE EITERIACH'S CUISINE DOES PALE IN COMPARISON TO LUPUCCIA'S.
HA HA HA!
HIS EXCELLENCY ISN'T USED TO THIS NORTHERN CLIMATE EITHER, PROBABLY?
I IMAGINE BEING HERE IS HARD ON HIM, TOO.
OH?
KCHK

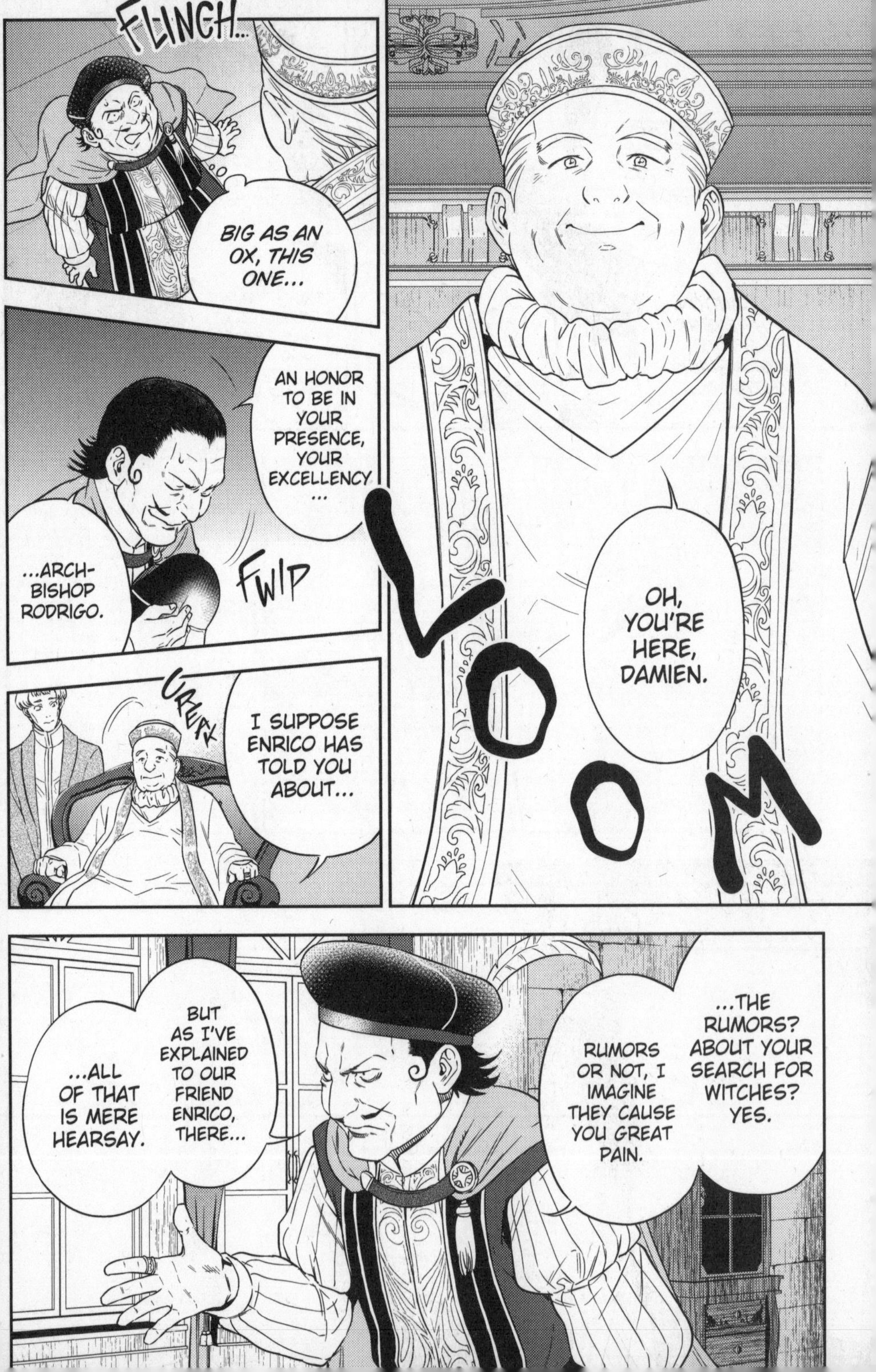
LOOM
OH, YOU'RE HERE, DAMIEN.
FLINCH...
BIG AS AN OX, THIS ONE...
AN HONOR TO BE IN YOUR PRESENCE, YOUR EXCELLENCY...
...ARCH-BISHOP RODRIGO.
FWIP
CREAK
I SUPPOSE ENRICO HAS TOLD YOU ABOUT...
...THE RUMORS? ABOUT YOUR SEARCH FOR WITCHES? YES.
RUMORS OR NOT, I IMAGINE THEY CAUSE YOU GREAT PAIN.
BUT AS I'VE EXPLAINED TO OUR FRIEND ENRICO, THERE...
...ALL OF THAT IS MERE HEARSAY.

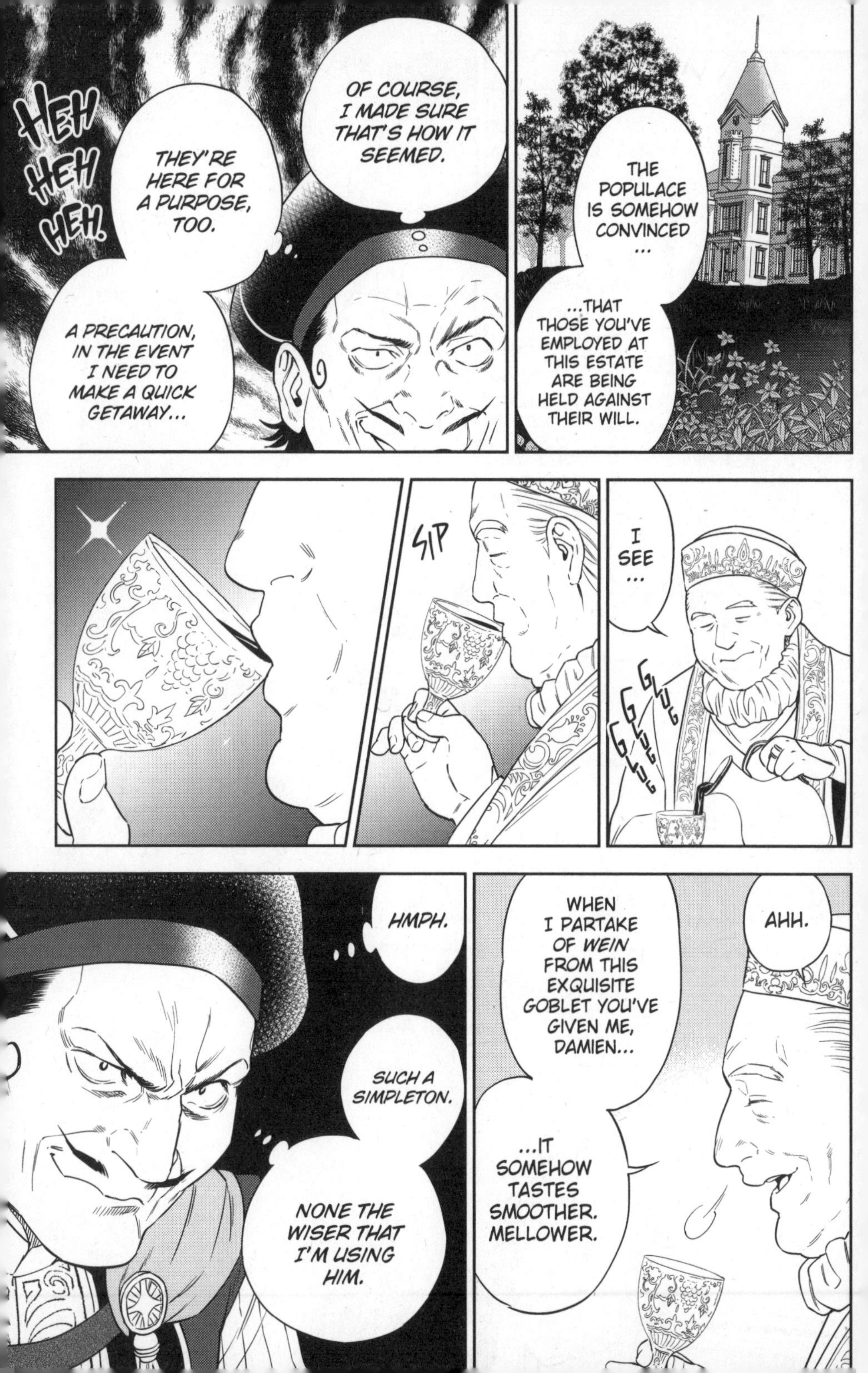
THE POPULACE IS SOMEHOW CONVINCED ...
...THAT THOSE YOU'VE EMPLOYED AT THIS ESTATE ARE BEING HELD AGAINST THEIR WILL.
OF COURSE, I MADE SURE THAT'S HOW IT SEEMED.
THEY'RE HERE FOR A PURPOSE, TOO.
HEH HEH HEH.
A PRECAUTION, IN THE EVENT I NEED TO MAKE A QUICK GETAWAY...
I SEE ...
GLUG GLUG GLUG
SIP
AHH.
WHEN I PARTAKE OF *WEIN* FROM THIS EXQUISITE GOBLET YOU'VE GIVEN ME, DAMIEN...
...IT SOMEHOW TASTES SMOOTHER. MELLOWER.
HMPH.
SUCH A SIMPLETON.
NONE THE WISER THAT I'M USING HIM.

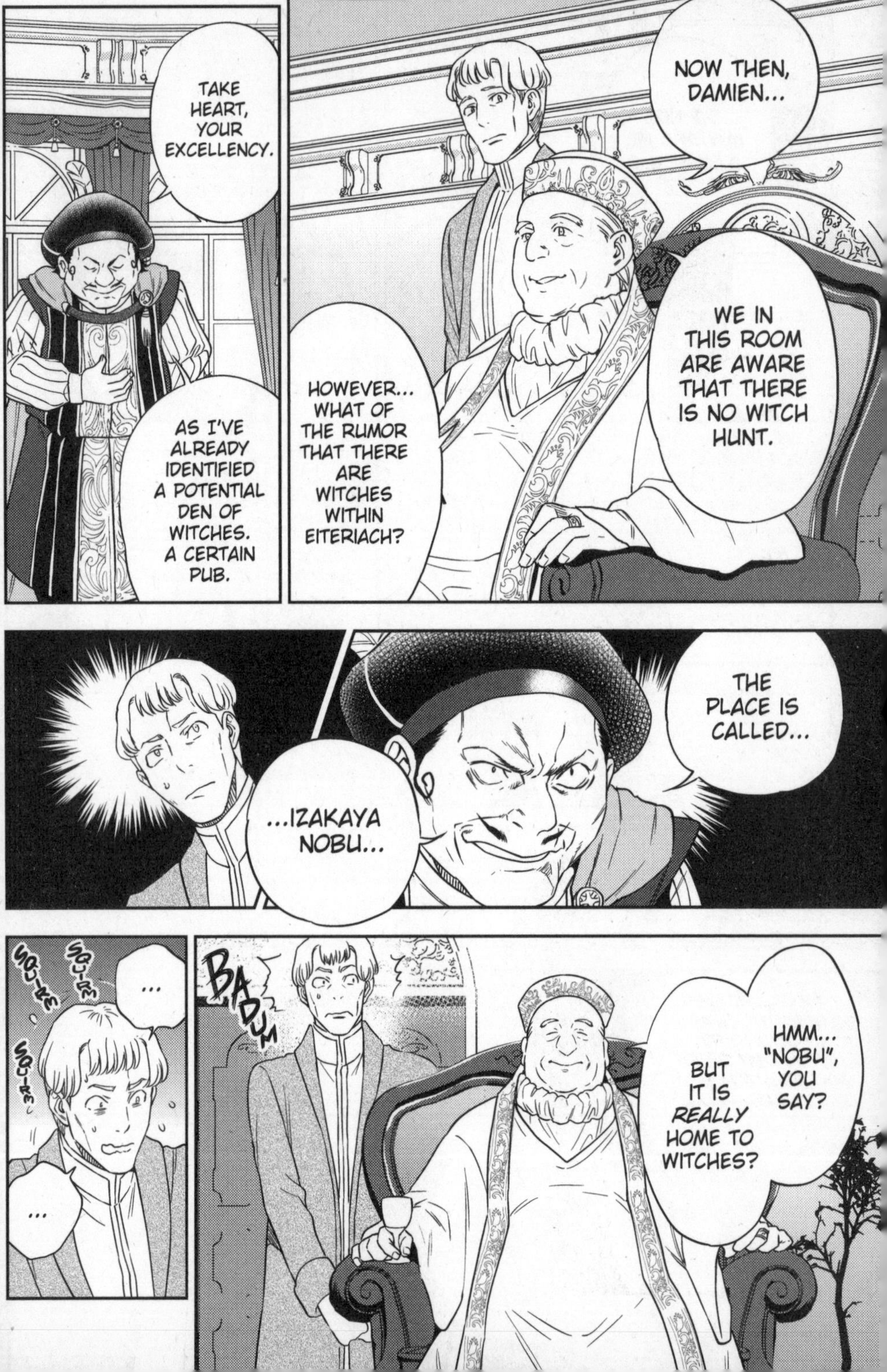
NOW THEN, DAMIEN...
WE IN THIS ROOM ARE AWARE THAT THERE IS NO WITCH HUNT.
HOWEVER... WHAT OF THE RUMOR THAT THERE ARE WITCHES WITHIN EITERIACH?
TAKE HEART, YOUR EXCELLENCY.
AS I'VE ALREADY IDENTIFIED A POTENTIAL DEN OF WITCHES. A CERTAIN PUB.
THE PLACE IS CALLED...
...IZAKAYA NOBU...
BADUM
HMM... "NOBU", YOU SAY?
BUT IT IS *REALLY* HOME TO WITCHES?
...
SQUIRM
SQUIRM
SQUIRM
...

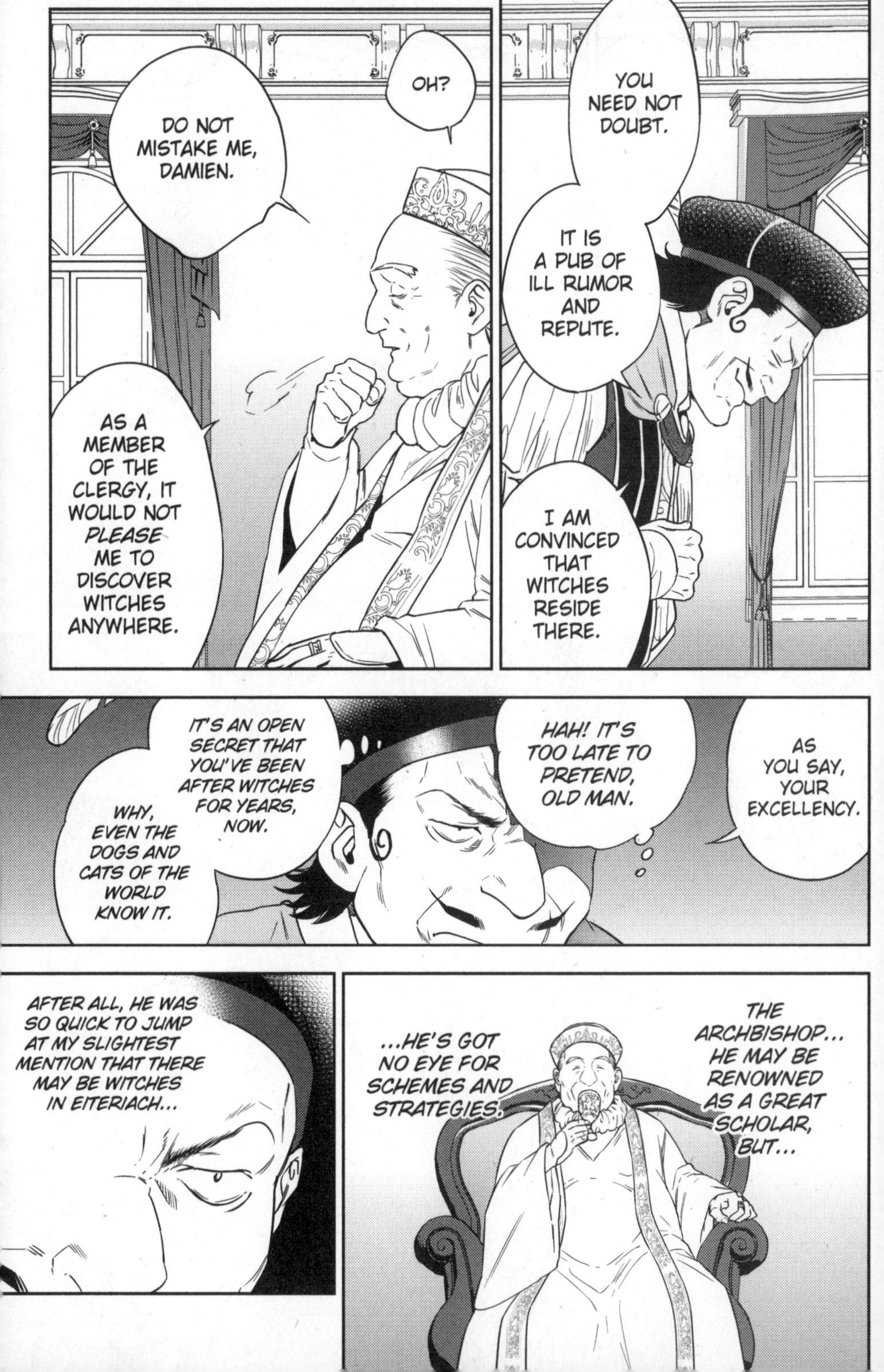
YOU NEED NOT DOUBT.
IT IS A PUB OF ILL RUMOR AND REPUTE.
I AM CONVINCED THAT WITCHES RESIDE THERE.
OH?
DO NOT MISTAKE ME, DAMIEN.
AS A MEMBER OF THE CLERGY, IT WOULD NOT *PLEASE* ME TO DISCOVER WITCHES ANYWHERE.
AS YOU SAY, YOUR EXCELLENCY.
HAH! IT'S TOO LATE TO PRETEND, OLD MAN.
IT'S AN OPEN SECRET THAT YOU'VE BEEN AFTER WITCHES FOR YEARS, NOW.
WHY, EVEN THE DOGS AND CATS OF THE WORLD KNOW IT.
THE ARCHBISHOP... HE MAY BE RENOWNED AS A GREAT SCHOLAR, BUT...
...HE'S GOT NO EYE FOR SCHEMES AND STRATEGIES.
AFTER ALL, HE WAS SO QUICK TO JUMP AT MY SLIGHTEST MENTION THAT THERE MAY BE WITCHES IN EITERIACH...

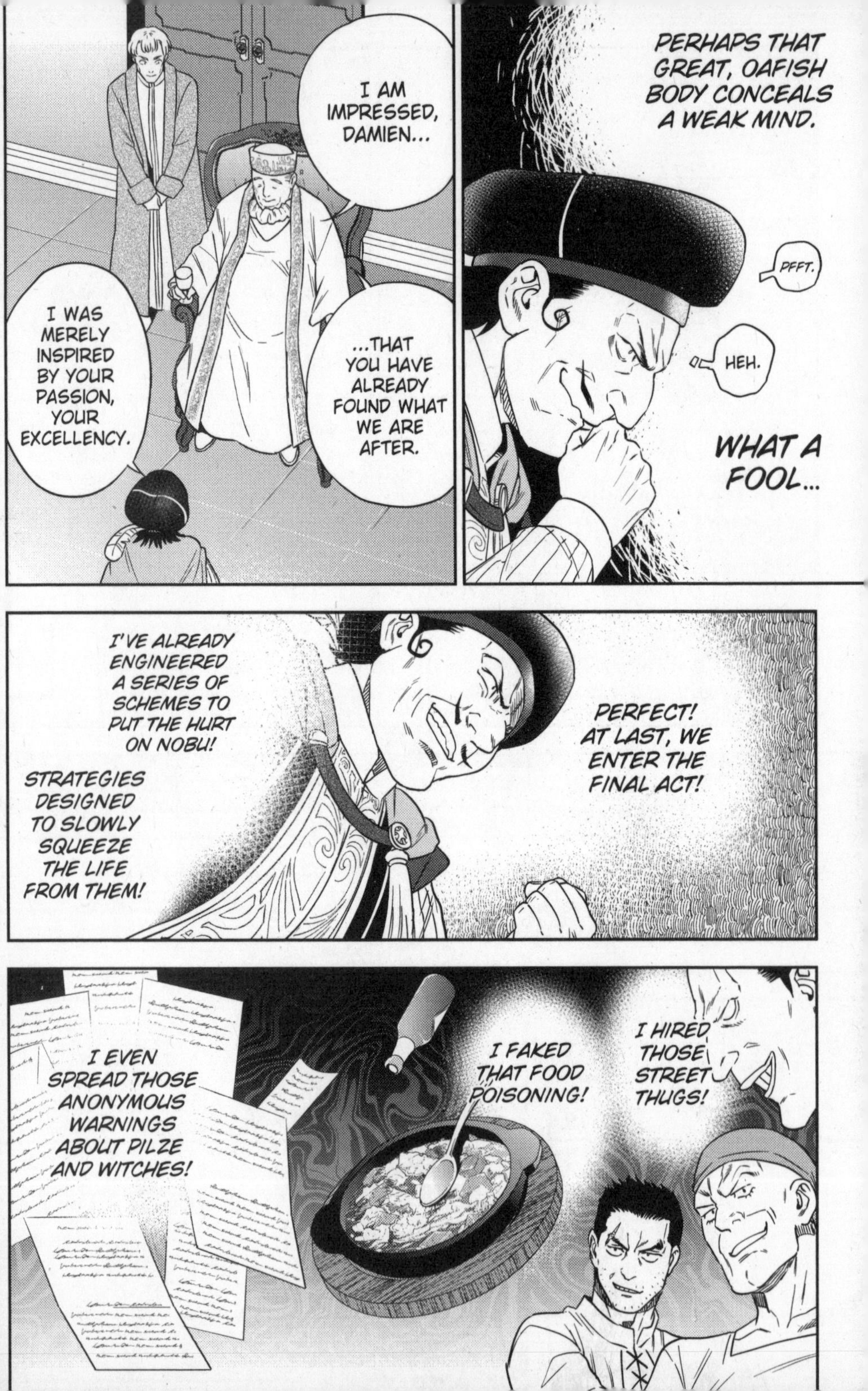
PERHAPS THAT GREAT, OAFISH BODY CONCEALS A WEAK MIND.
PFFT.
HEH.
WHAT A FOOL...
I AM IMPRESSED, DAMIEN...
...THAT YOU HAVE ALREADY FOUND WHAT WE ARE AFTER.
I WAS MERELY INSPIRED BY YOUR PASSION, YOUR EXCELLENCY.
PERFECT! AT LAST, WE ENTER THE FINAL ACT!
I'VE ALREADY ENGINEERED A SERIES OF SCHEMES TO PUT THE HURT ON NOBU!
STRATEGIES DESIGNED TO SLOWLY SQUEEZE THE LIFE FROM THEM!
I HIRED THOSE STREET THUGS!
I FAKED THAT FOOD POISONING!
I EVEN SPREAD THOSE ANONYMOUS WARNINGS ABOUT PILZE AND WITCHES!

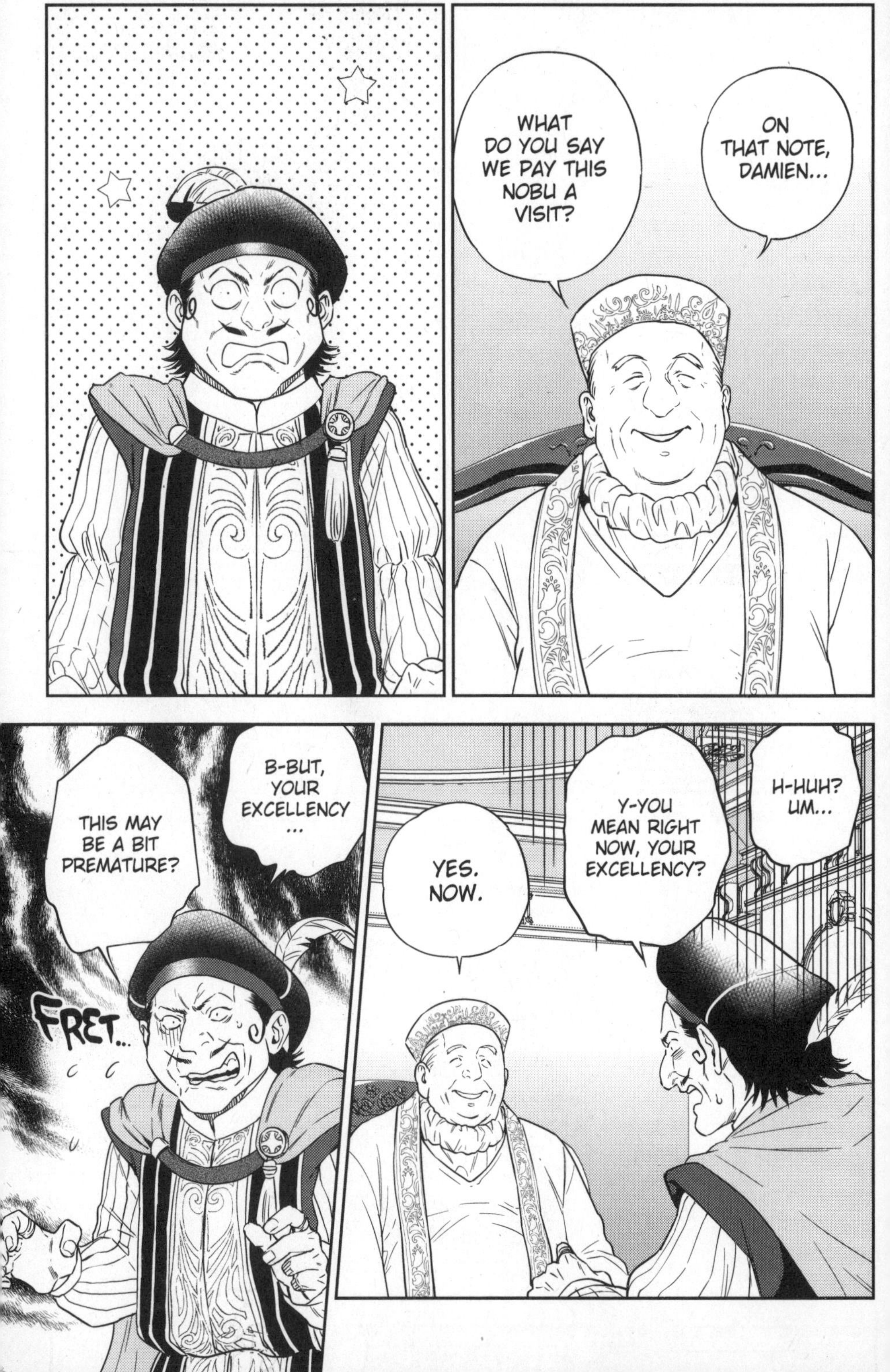
ON THAT NOTE, DAMIEN...
WHAT DO YOU SAY WE PAY THIS NOBU A VISIT?
H-HUH? UM...
Y-YOU MEAN RIGHT NOW, YOUR EXCELLENCY?
YES. NOW.
B-BUT, YOUR EXCELLENCY ...
THIS MAY BE A BIT PREMATURE?
FRET...

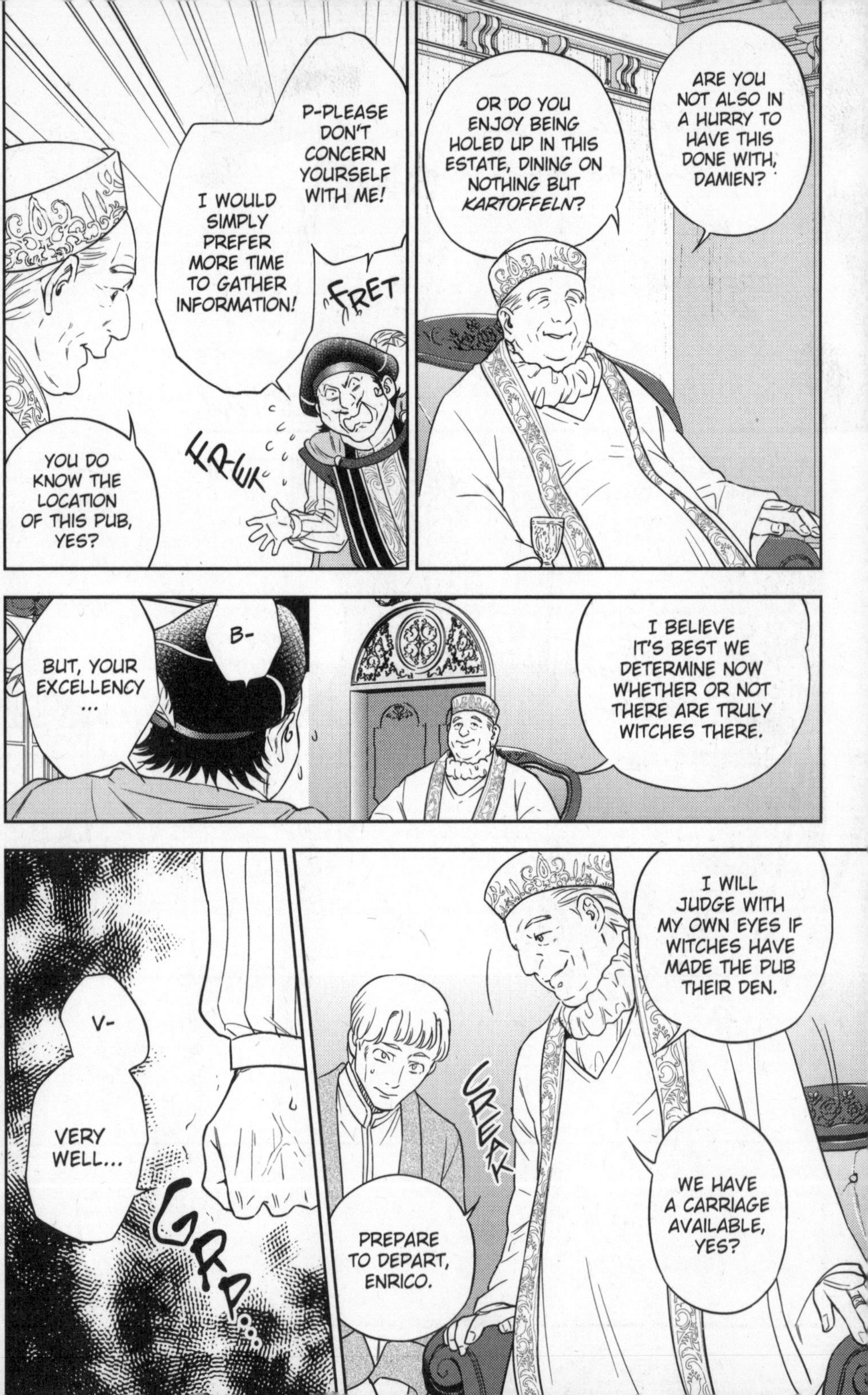
ARE YOU NOT ALSO IN A HURRY TO HAVE THIS DONE WITH, DAMIEN?
OR DO YOU ENJOY BEING HOLED UP IN THIS ESTATE, DINING ON NOTHING BUT *KARTOFFELN*?
P-PLEASE DON'T CONCERN YOURSELF WITH ME!
FRET
I WOULD SIMPLY PREFER MORE TIME TO GATHER INFORMATION!
FRET
YOU DO KNOW THE LOCATION OF THIS PUB, YES?
I BELIEVE IT'S BEST WE DETERMINE NOW WHETHER OR NOT THERE ARE TRULY WITCHES THERE.
B-
BUT, YOUR EXCELLENCY ...
I WILL JUDGE WITH MY OWN EYES IF WITCHES HAVE MADE THE PUB THEIR DEN.
CREAK
WE HAVE A CARRIAGE AVAILABLE, YES?
PREPARE TO DEPART, ENRICO.
V-
VERY WELL...
GRR...

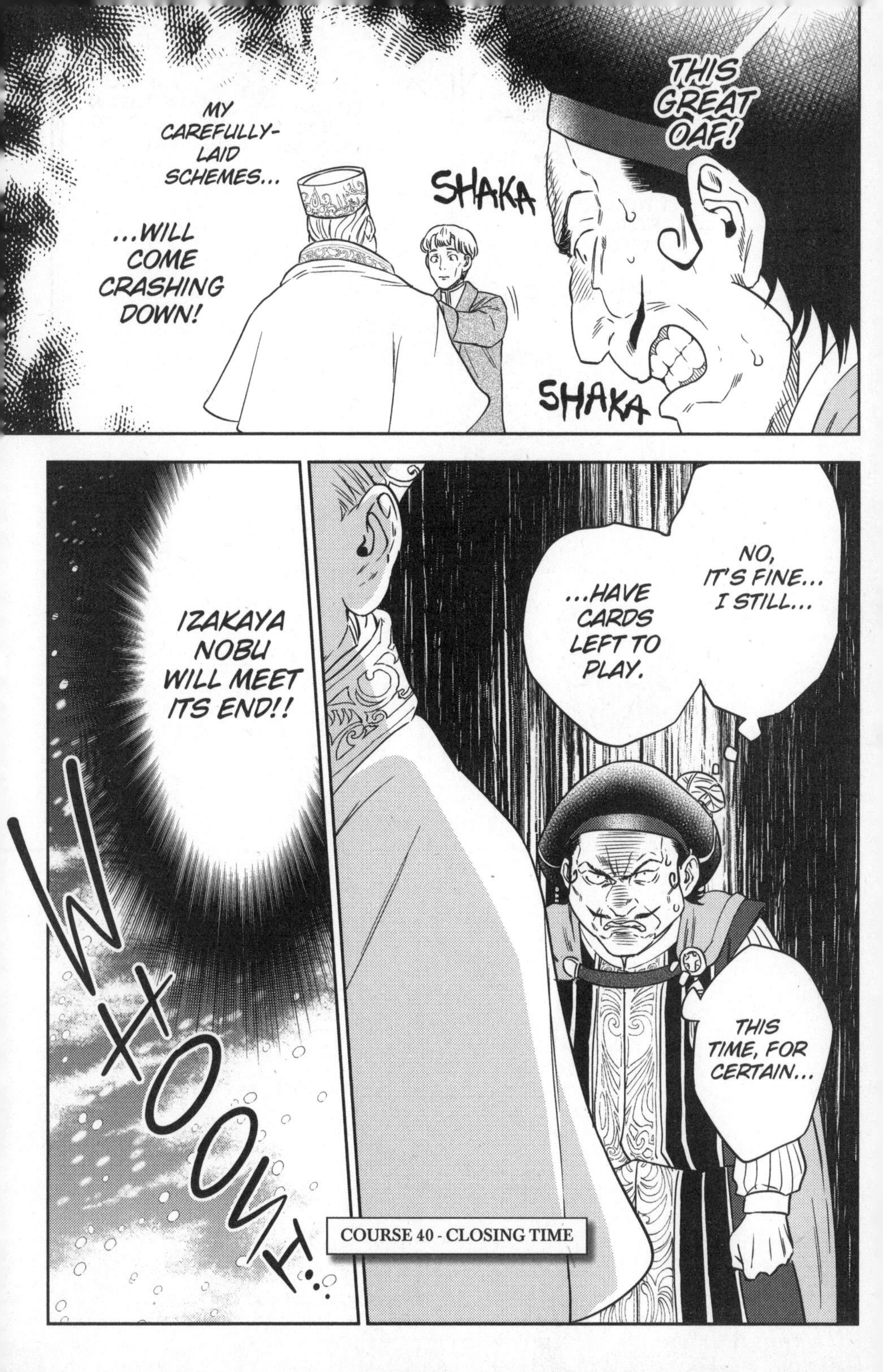
THIS GREAT OAF!
SHAKA
SHAKA
MY CAREFULLY-LAID SCHEMES...
...WILL COME CRASHING DOWN!
NO, IT'S FINE... I STILL...
...HAVE CARDS LEFT TO PLAY.
THIS TIME, FOR CERTAIN...
IZAKAYA NOBU WILL MEET ITS END!!
WHOOM!
COURSE 40 - CLOSING TIME

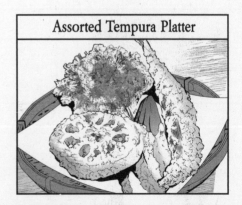
Assorted Tempura Platter

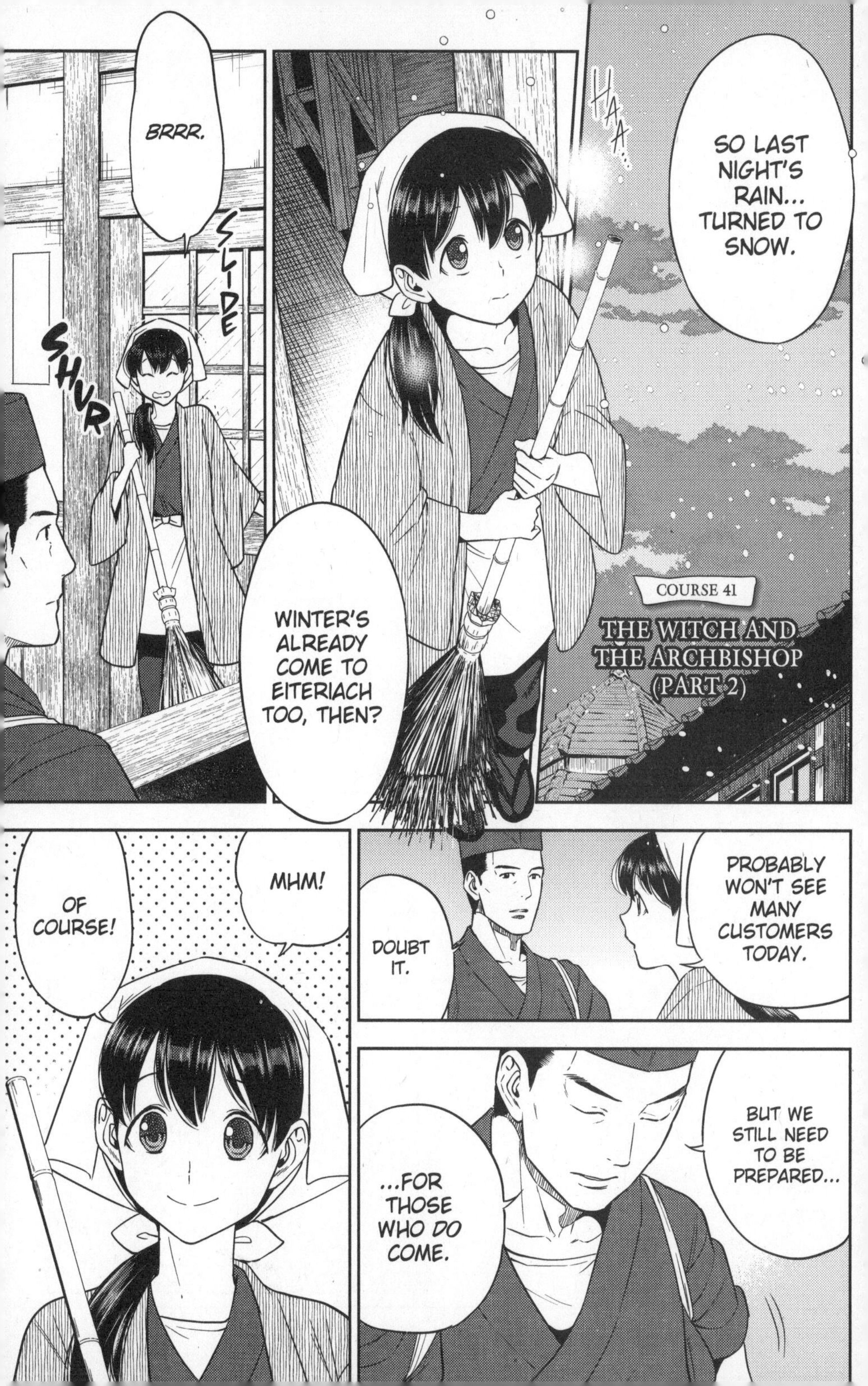
HAAA...
SO LAST NIGHT'S RAIN... TURNED TO SNOW.
COURSE 41
THE WITCH AND THE ARCHBISHOP (PART 2)
WINTER'S ALREADY COME TO EITERIACH TOO, THEN?
BRRR.
SLIDE
SHUR
PROBABLY WON'T SEE MANY CUSTOMERS TODAY.
DOUBT IT.
BUT WE STILL NEED TO BE PREPARED...
...FOR THOSE WHO DO COME.
MHM!
OF COURSE!

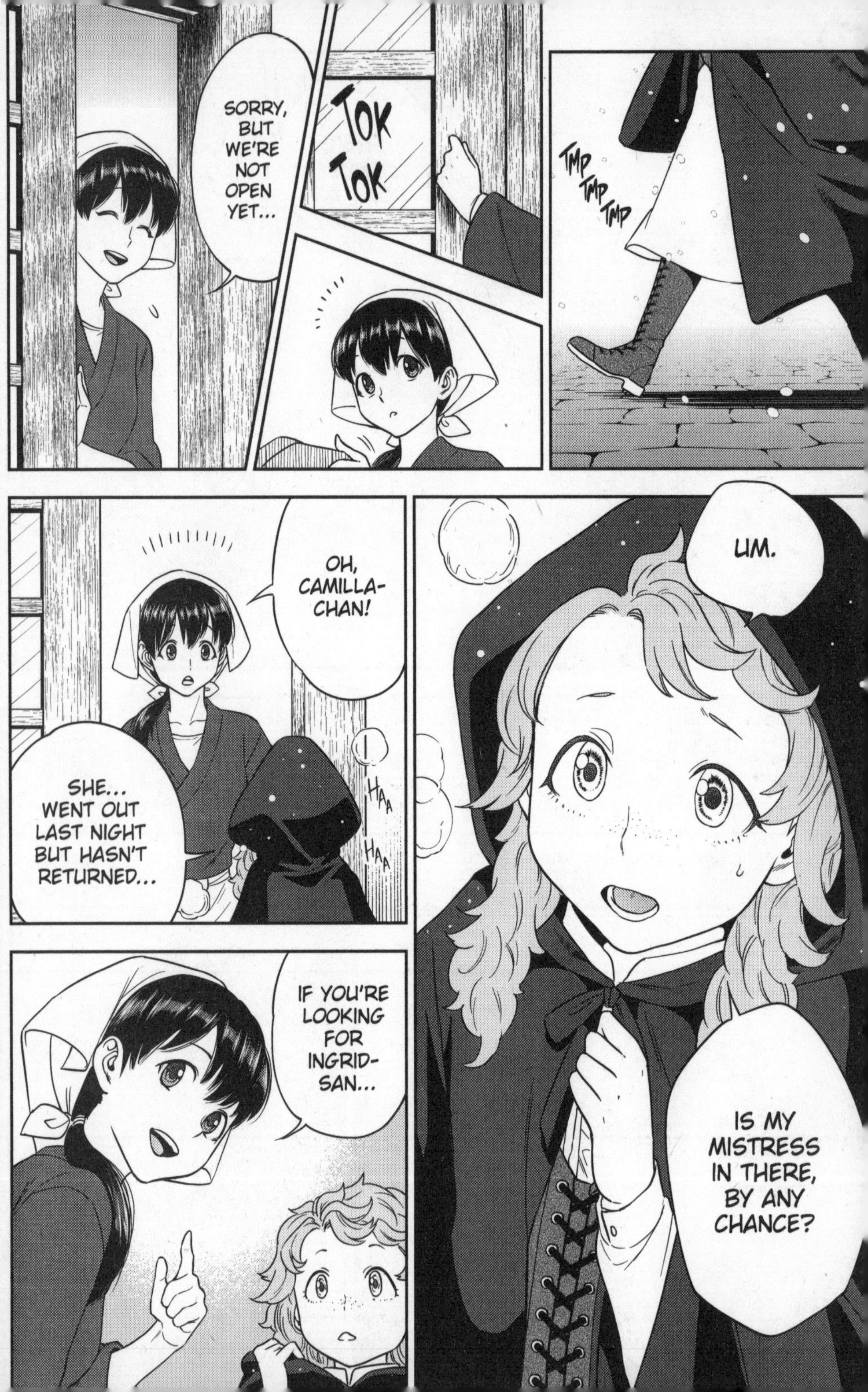
TMP TMP TMP
TOK TOK
SORRY, BUT WE'RE NOT OPEN YET...
UM.
IS MY MISTRESS IN THERE, BY ANY CHANCE?
OH, CAMILLA-CHAN!
HAA HAA
SHE... WENT OUT LAST NIGHT BUT HASN'T RETURNED...
IF YOU'RE LOOKING FOR INGRID-SAN...

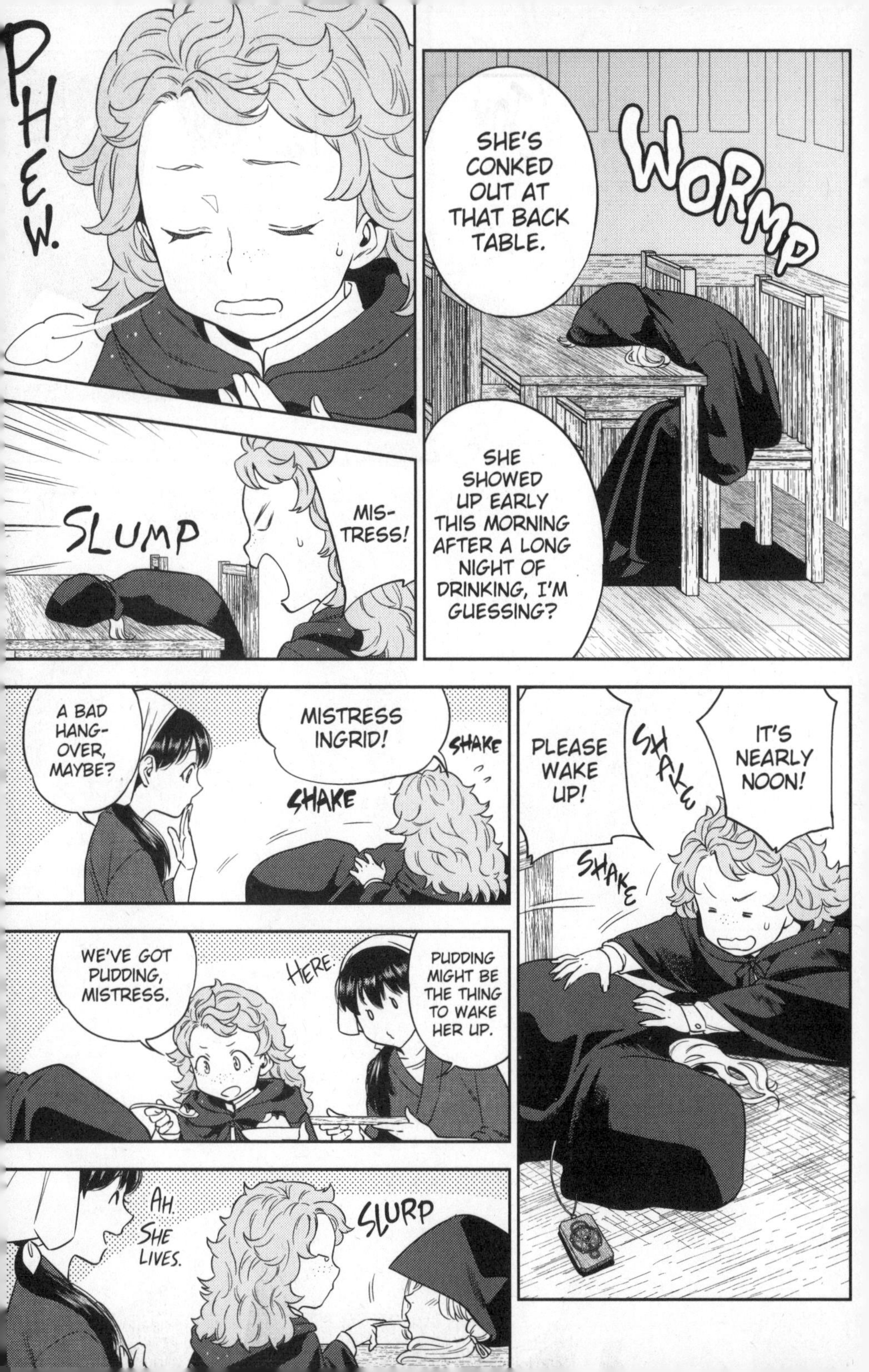
SHE'S CONKED OUT AT THAT BACK TABLE.
WORMP
SHE SHOWED UP EARLY THIS MORNING AFTER A LONG NIGHT OF DRINKING, I'M GUESSING?
PHEW.
MIS-TRESS!
SLUMP
IT'S NEARLY NOON!
SHAKE
PLEASE WAKE UP!
SHAKE
SHAKE
MISTRESS INGRID!
SHAKE
A BAD HANG-OVER, MAYBE?
PUDDING MIGHT BE THE THING TO WAKE HER UP.
HERE.
WE'VE GOT PUDDING, MISTRESS.
SLURP
AH. SHE LIVES.

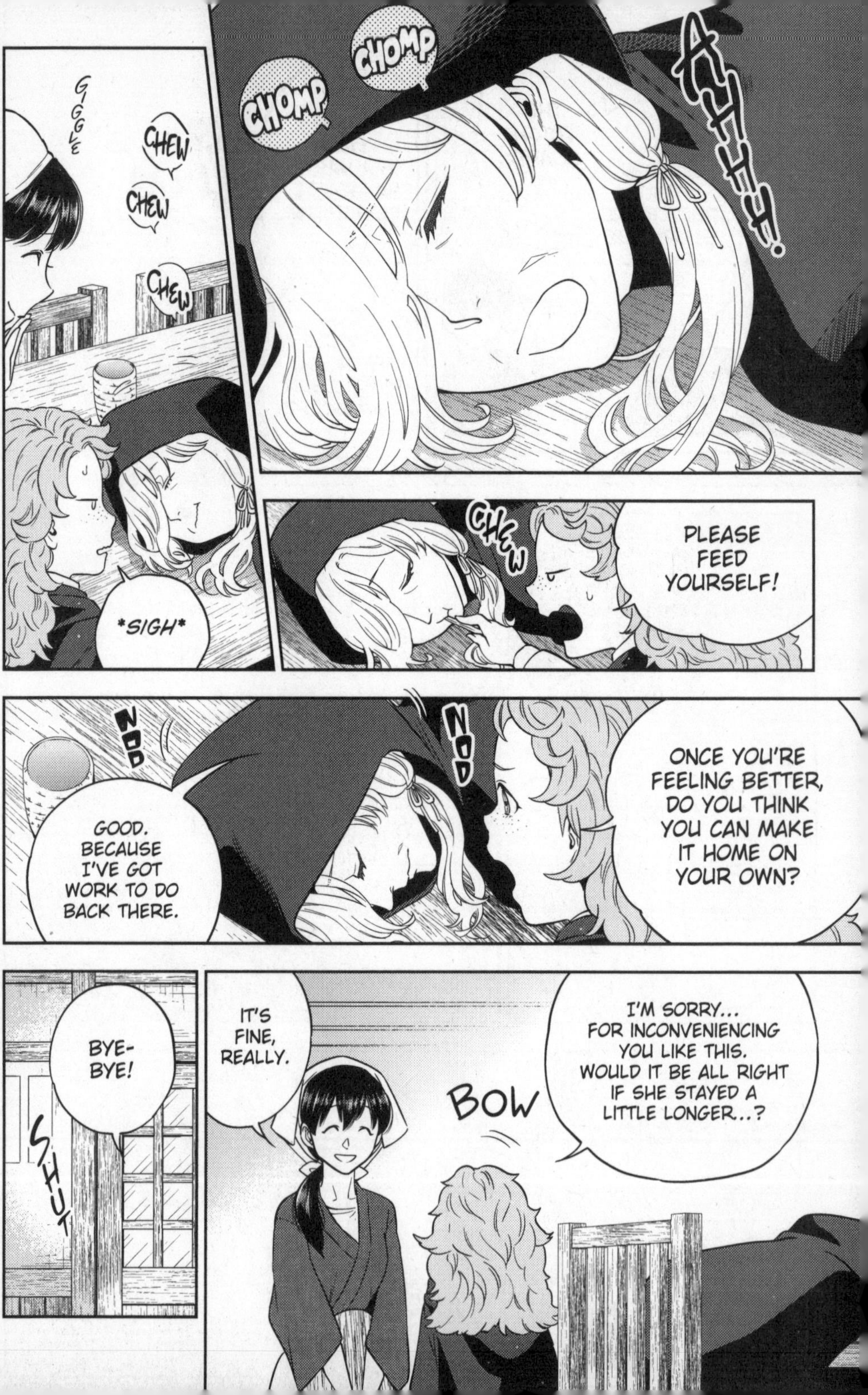
AHHHH!
CHOMP
CHOMP
CHEW
PLEASE FEED YOURSELF!
GIGGLE
CHEW
CHEW
CHEW
SIGH
ONCE YOU'RE FEELING BETTER, DO YOU THINK YOU CAN MAKE IT HOME ON YOUR OWN?
NOD
NOD
GOOD. BECAUSE I'VE GOT WORK TO DO BACK THERE.
I'M SORRY... FOR INCONVENIENCING YOU LIKE THIS. WOULD IT BE ALL RIGHT IF SHE STAYED A LITTLE LONGER...?
BOW
IT'S FINE, REALLY.
BYE-BYE!
SHUT

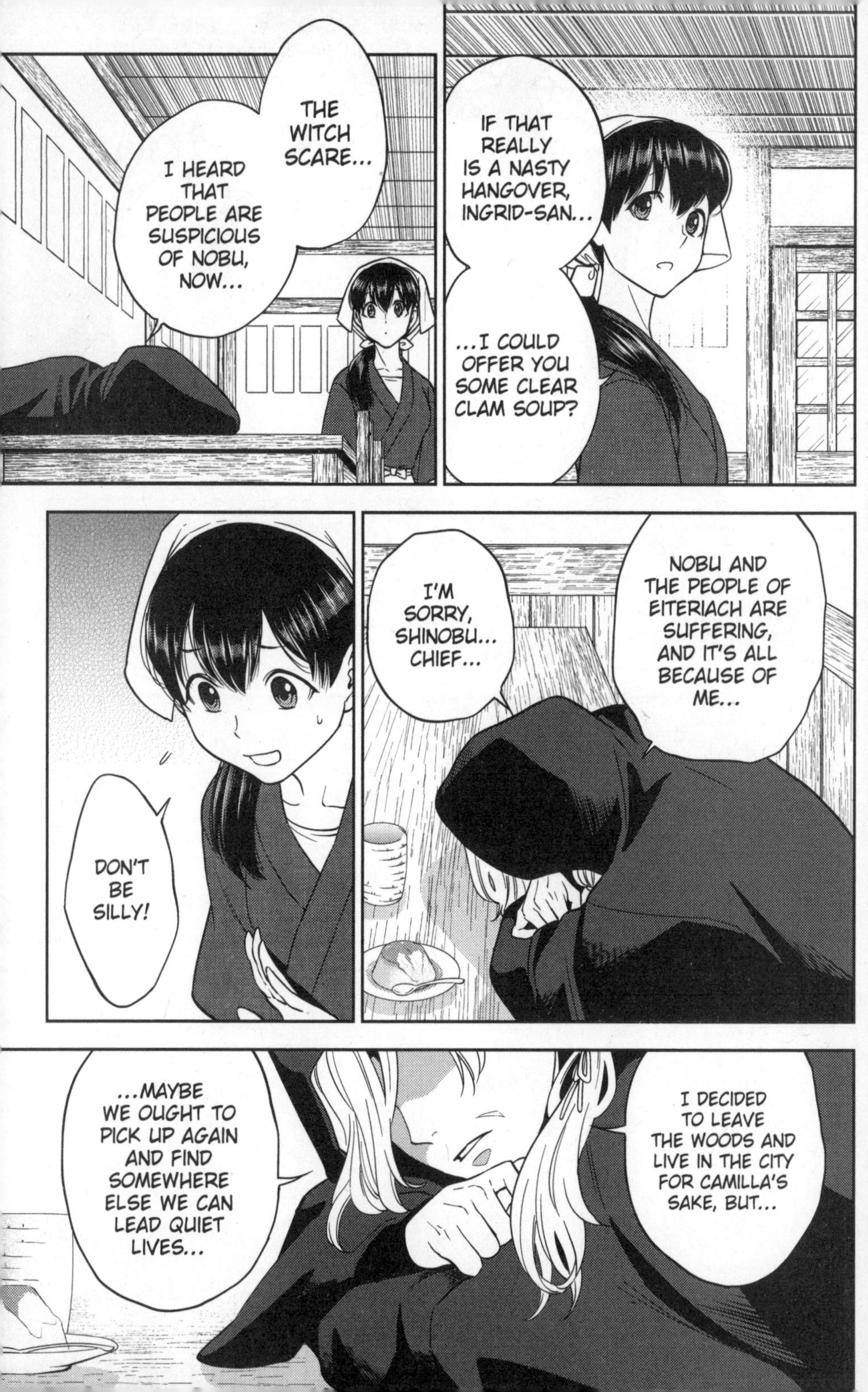
IF THAT REALLY IS A NASTY HANGOVER, INGRID-SAN...
...I COULD OFFER YOU SOME CLEAR CLAM SOUP?
THE WITCH SCARE...
I HEARD THAT PEOPLE ARE SUSPICIOUS OF NOBU, NOW...
NOBU AND THE PEOPLE OF EITERIACH ARE SUFFERING, AND IT'S ALL BECAUSE OF ME...
I'M SORRY, SHINOBU... CHIEF...
DON'T BE SILLY!
I DECIDED TO LEAVE THE WOODS AND LIVE IN THE CITY FOR CAMILLA'S SAKE, BUT...
...MAYBE WE OUGHT TO PICK UP AGAIN AND FIND SOMEWHERE ELSE WE CAN LEAD QUIET LIVES...

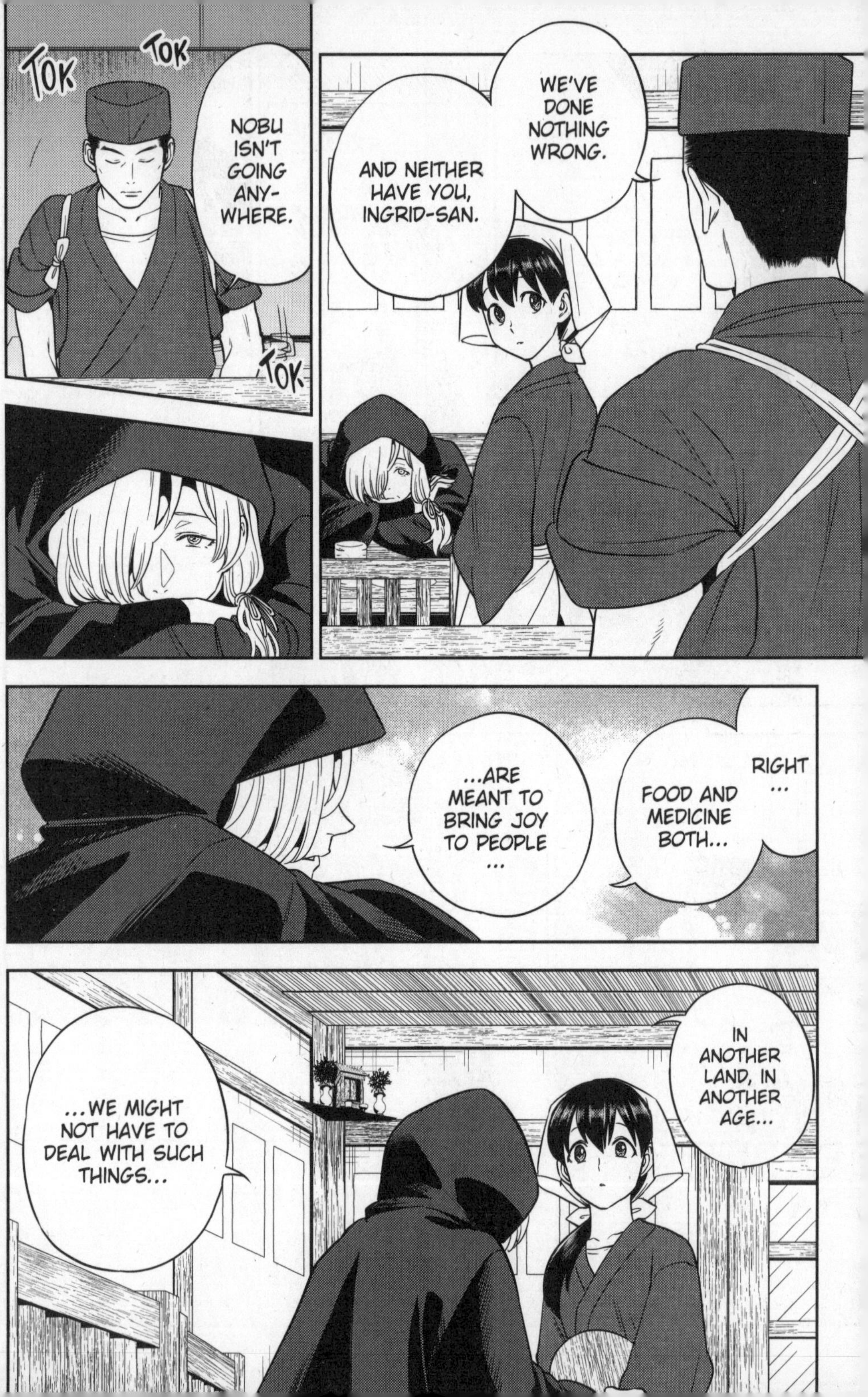
WE'VE DONE NOTHING WRONG.
AND NEITHER HAVE YOU, INGRID-SAN.
TOK TOK
NOBU ISN'T GOING ANY-WHERE.
TOK
RIGHT...
FOOD AND MEDICINE BOTH...
...ARE MEANT TO BRING JOY TO PEOPLE...
IN ANOTHER LAND, IN ANOTHER AGE...
...WE MIGHT NOT HAVE TO DEAL WITH SUCH THINGS...

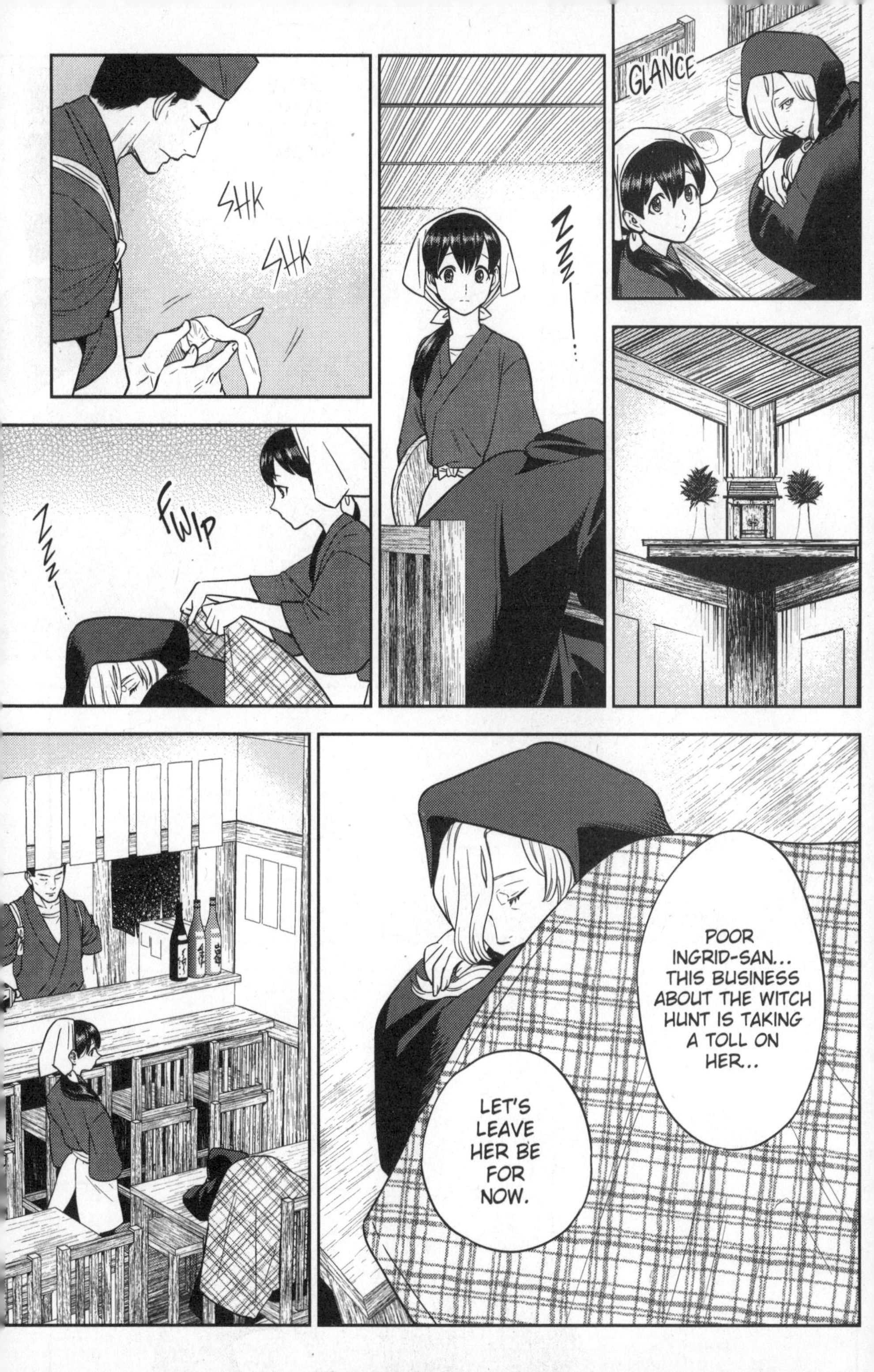
GLANCE
ZZZ—...
SHK
SHK
FWIP
ZZZ—...
POOR INGRID-SAN... THIS BUSINESS ABOUT THE WITCH HUNT IS TAKING A TOLL ON HER..
LET'S LEAVE HER BE FOR NOW.

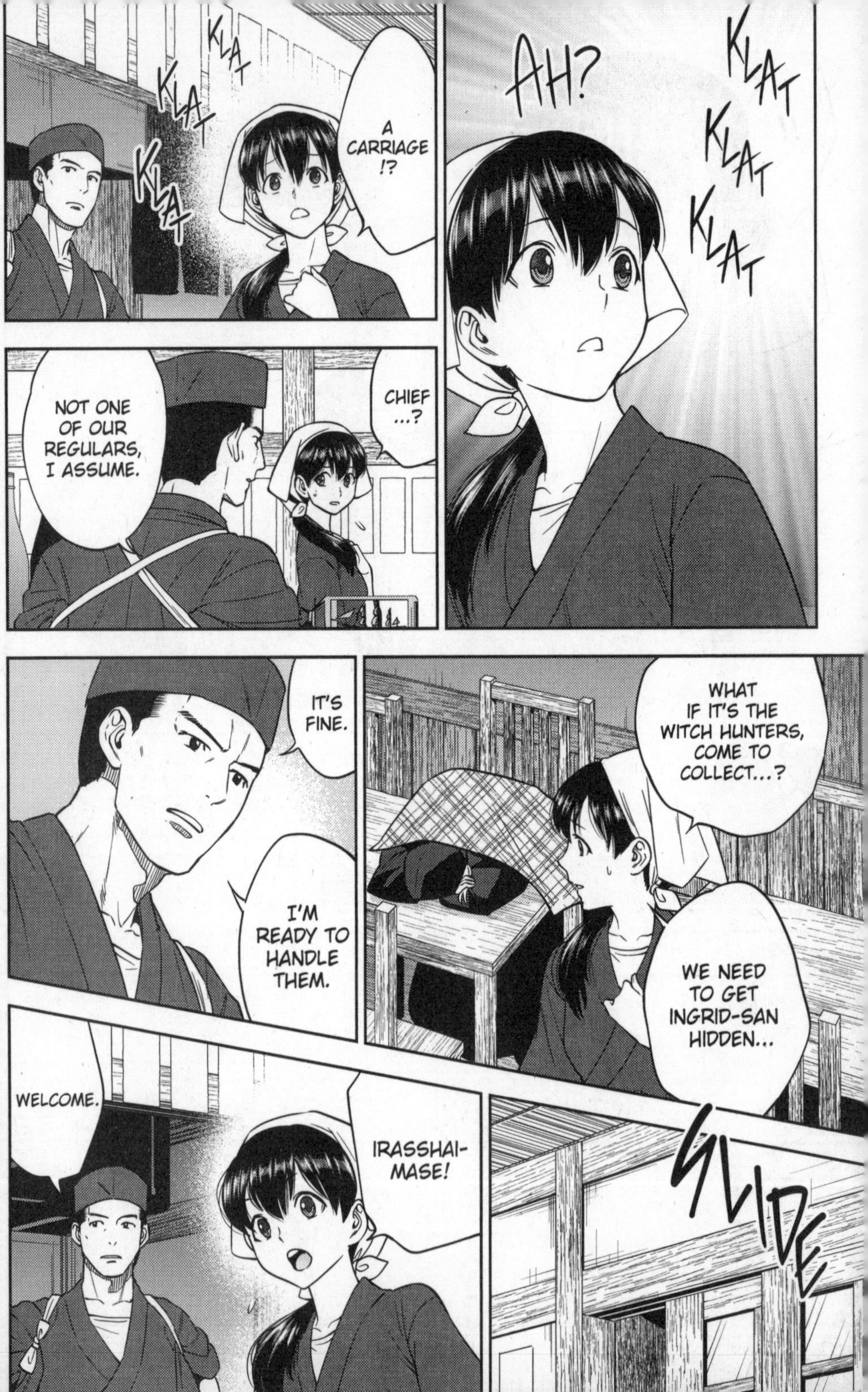
AH?
KLAT
KLAT
KLAT
KLAT
KLAT
KLAT
A CARRIAGE !?
CHIEF ...?
NOT ONE OF OUR REGULARS, I ASSUME.
WHAT IF IT'S THE WITCH HUNTERS, COME TO COLLECT...?
WE NEED TO GET INGRID-SAN HIDDEN...
IT'S FINE.
I'M READY TO HANDLE THEM.
SLIDE
IRASSHAI-MASE!
WELCOME.

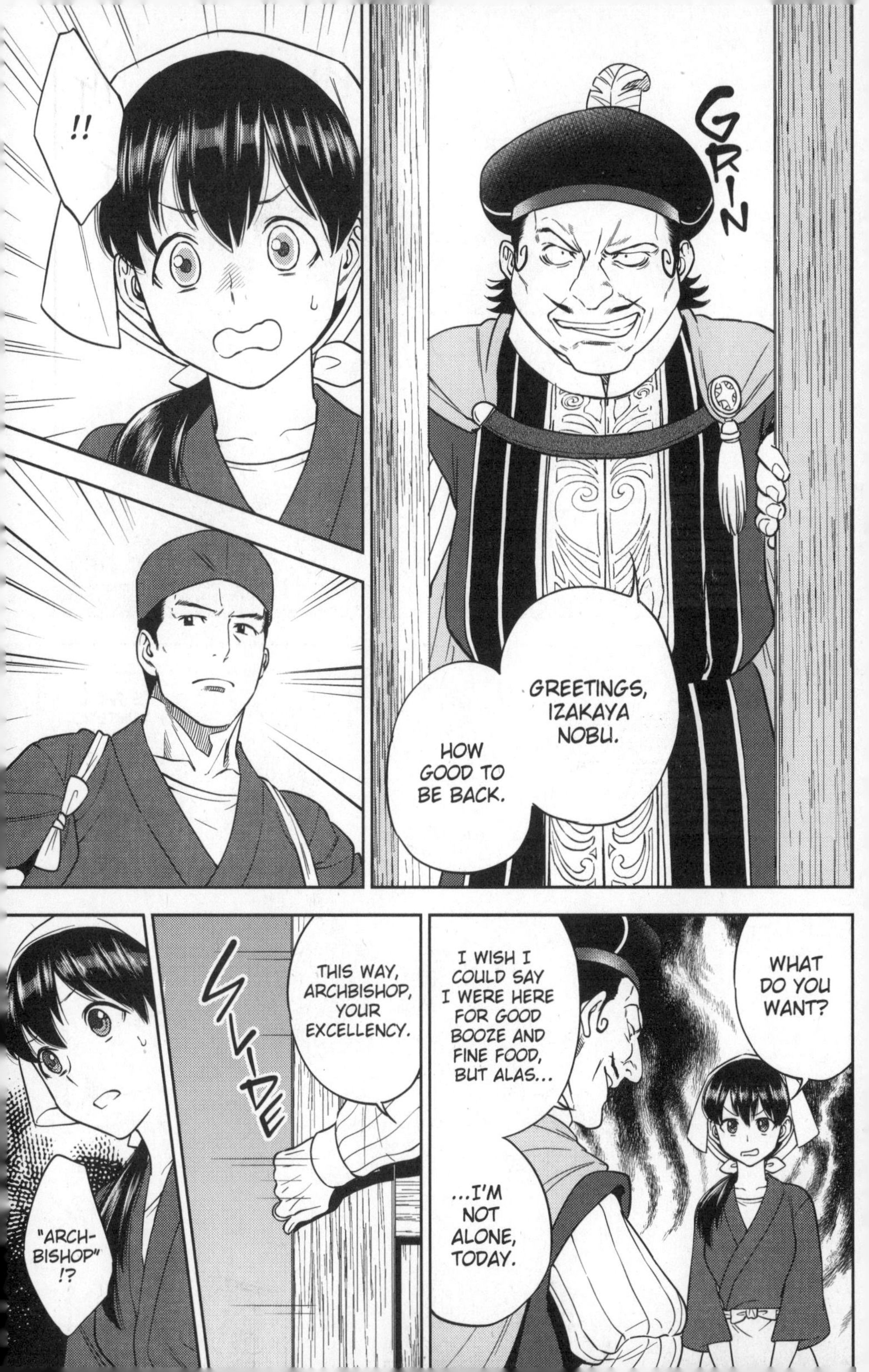
GRIN
GREETINGS, IZAKAYA NOBU.
HOW GOOD TO BE BACK.
!!
WHAT DO YOU WANT?
I WISH I COULD SAY I WERE HERE FOR GOOD BOOZE AND FINE FOOD, BUT ALAS...
...I'M NOT ALONE, TODAY.
THIS WAY, ARCHBISHOP, YOUR EXCELLENCY.
SLIDE
"ARCH-BISHOP" !?

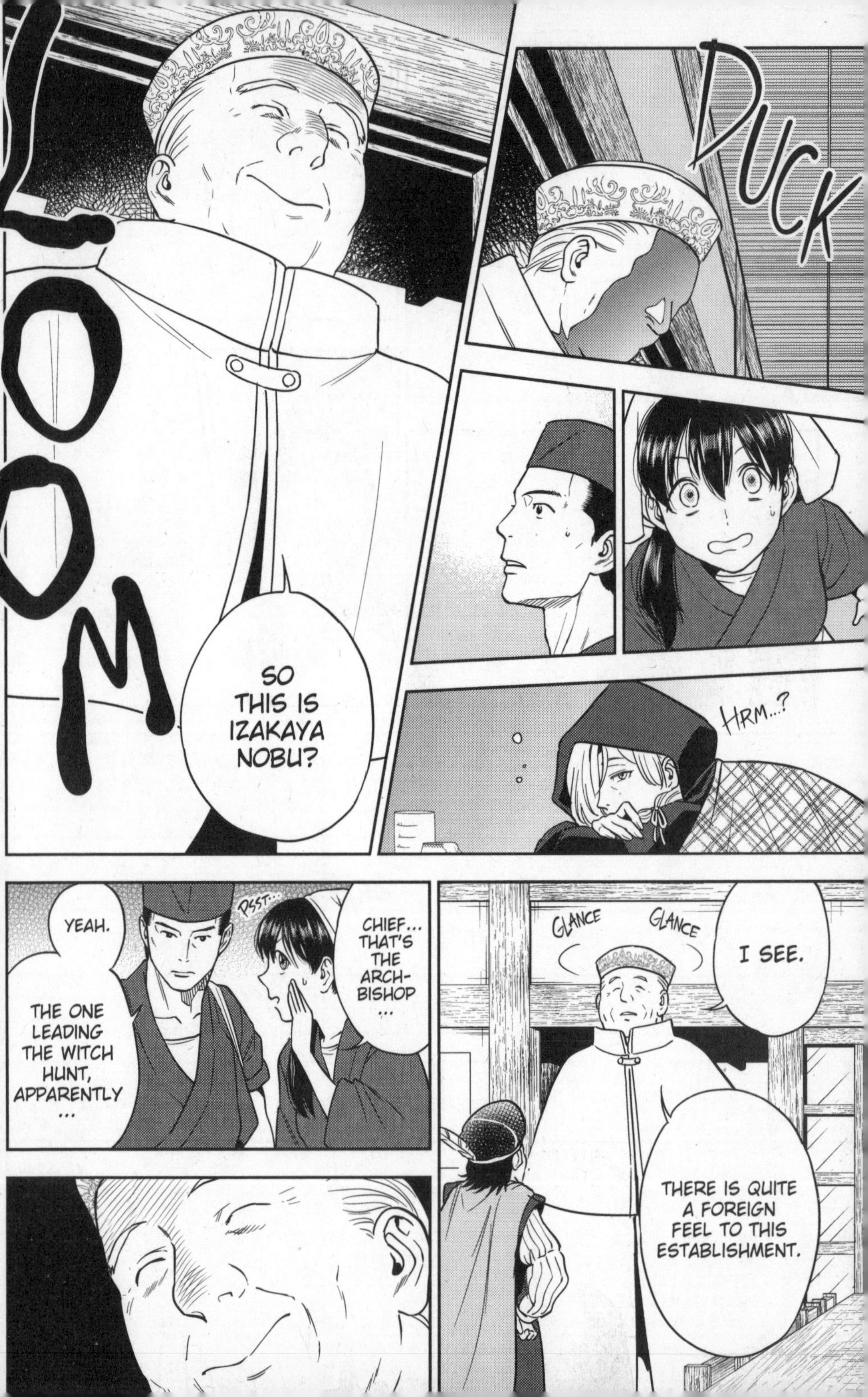
DUCK
HRM...?
LOOM
SO THIS IS IZAKAYA NOBU?
GLANCE GLANCE
I SEE.
THERE IS QUITE A FOREIGN FEEL TO THIS ESTABLISHMENT.
PSST...
CHIEF... THAT'S THE ARCHBISHOP...
YEAH.
THE ONE LEADING THE WITCH HUNT, APPARENTLY...

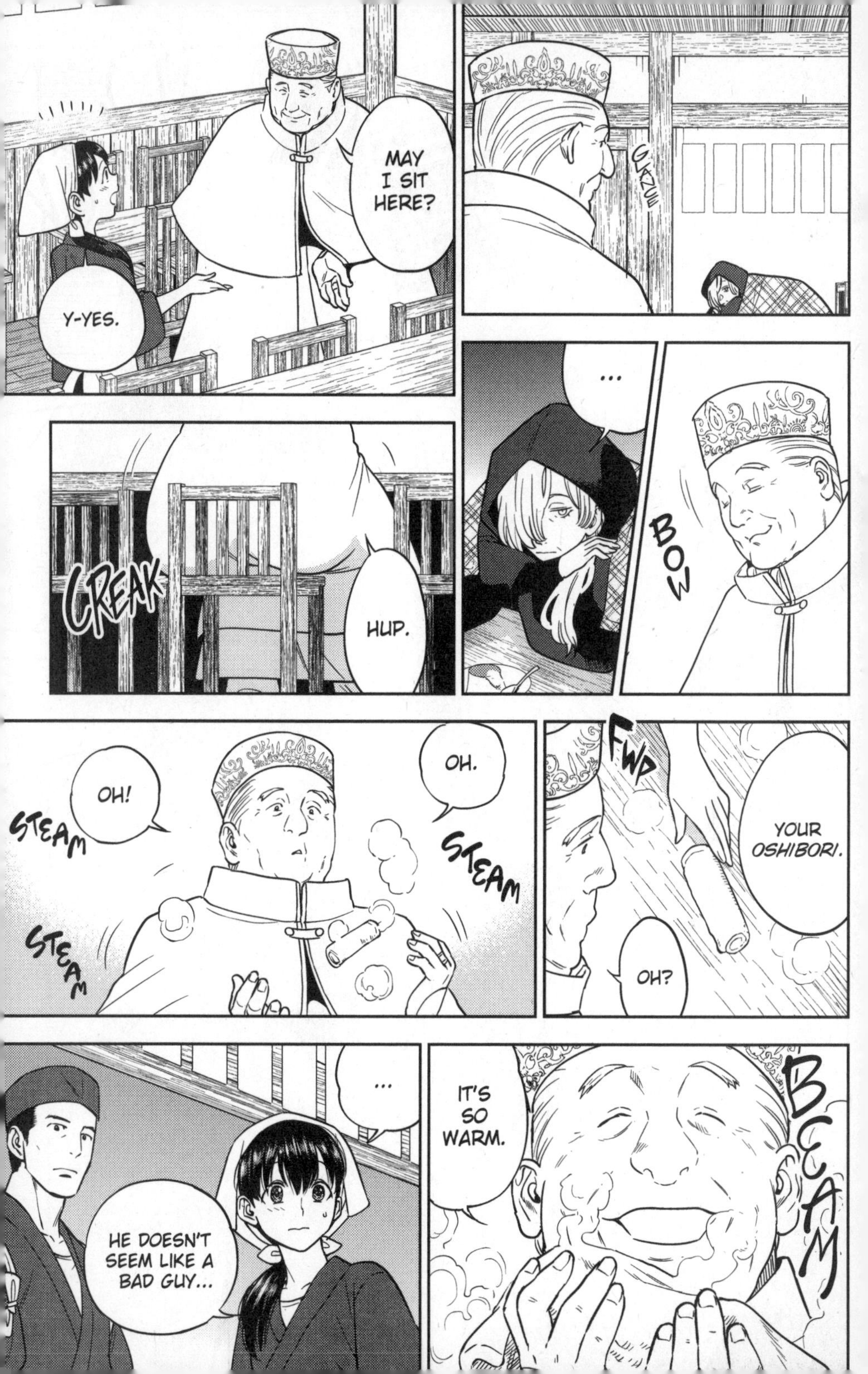
GLANCE
MAY I SIT HERE?
Y-YES.
BOW
...
HUP.
CREAK
FWP
YOUR OSHIBORI.
OH?
OH.
STEAM
OH!
STEAM
STEAM
BEAM
IT'S SO WARM.
...
HE DOESN'T SEEM LIKE A BAD GUY...

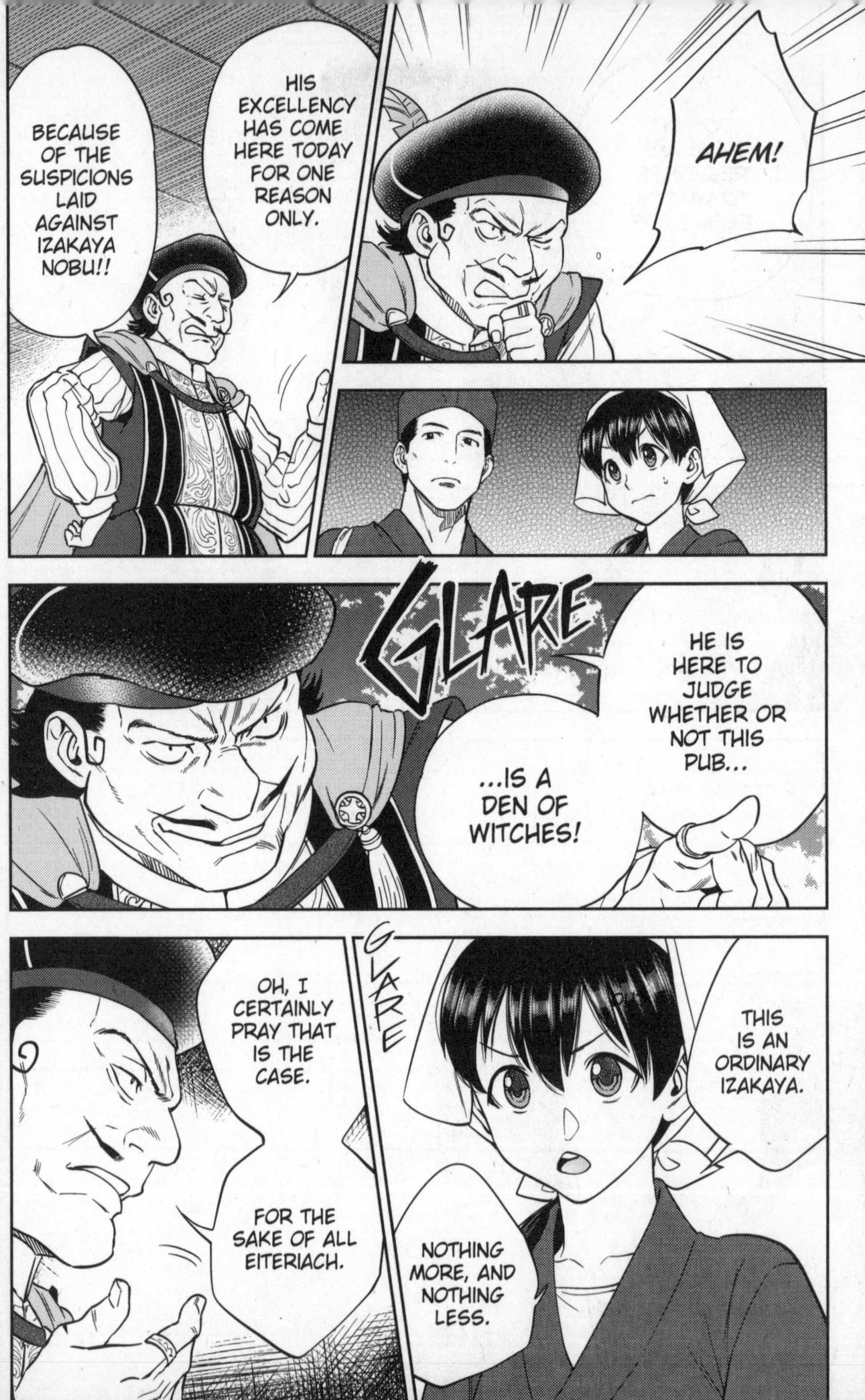
AHEM!
HIS EXCELLENCY HAS COME HERE TODAY FOR ONE REASON ONLY.
BECAUSE OF THE SUSPICIONS LAID AGAINST IZAKAYA NOBU!!
GLARE
HE IS HERE TO JUDGE WHETHER OR NOT THIS PUB...
...IS A DEN OF WITCHES!
THIS IS AN ORDINARY IZAKAYA.
NOTHING MORE, AND NOTHING LESS.
GLARE
OH, I CERTAINLY PRAY THAT IS THE CASE.
FOR THE SAKE OF ALL EITERIACH.

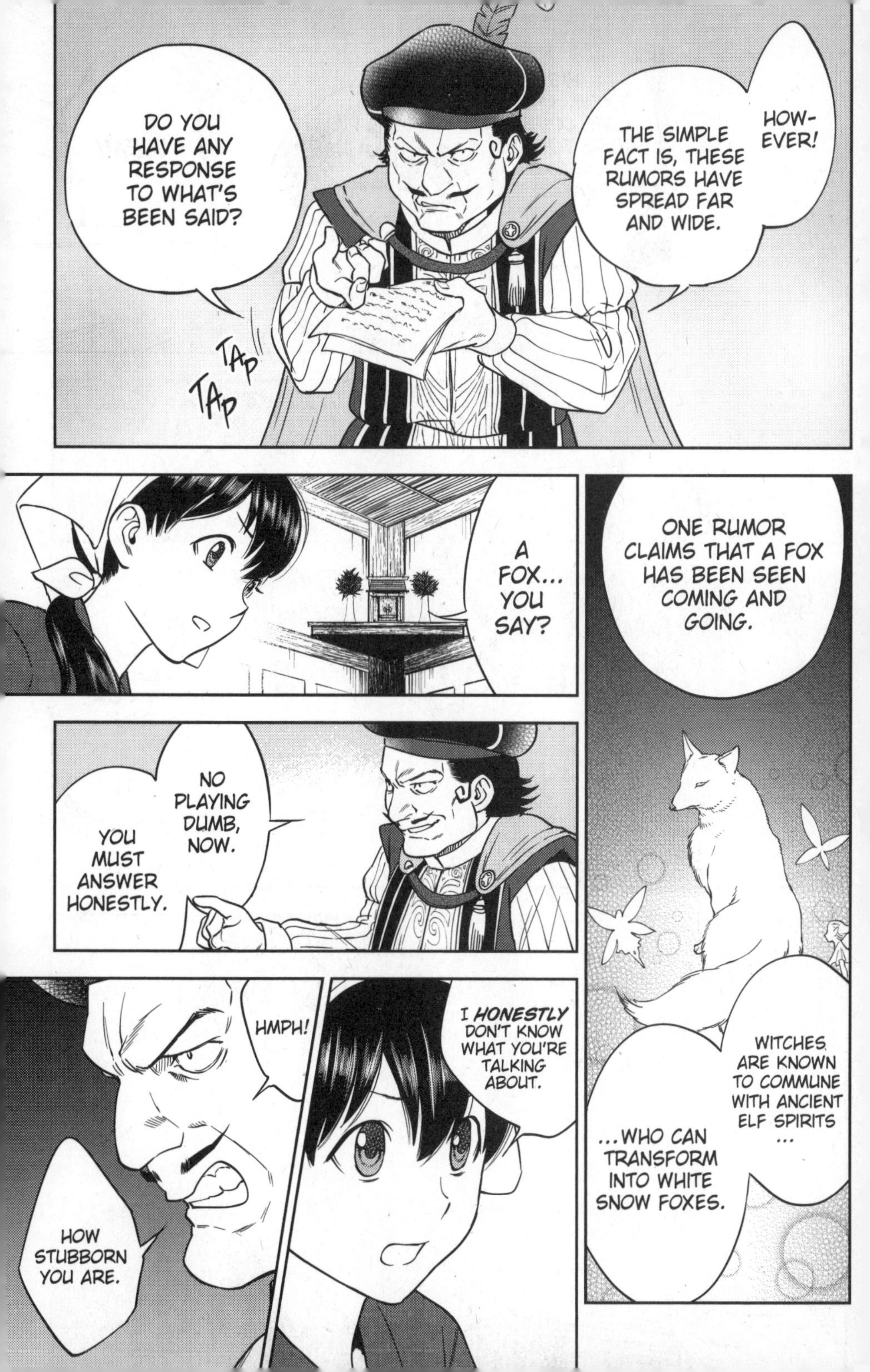
HOW-EVER!
THE SIMPLE FACT IS, THESE RUMORS HAVE SPREAD FAR AND WIDE.
DO YOU HAVE ANY RESPONSE TO WHAT'S BEEN SAID?
TAP TAP
ONE RUMOR CLAIMS THAT A FOX HAS BEEN SEEN COMING AND GOING.
WITCHES ARE KNOWN TO COMMUNE WITH ANCIENT ELF SPIRITS...
...WHO CAN TRANSFORM INTO WHITE SNOW FOXES.
A FOX... YOU SAY?
NO PLAYING DUMB, NOW.
YOU MUST ANSWER HONESTLY.
I *HONESTLY* DON'T KNOW WHAT YOU'RE TALKING ABOUT.
HMPH!
HOW STUBBORN YOU ARE.

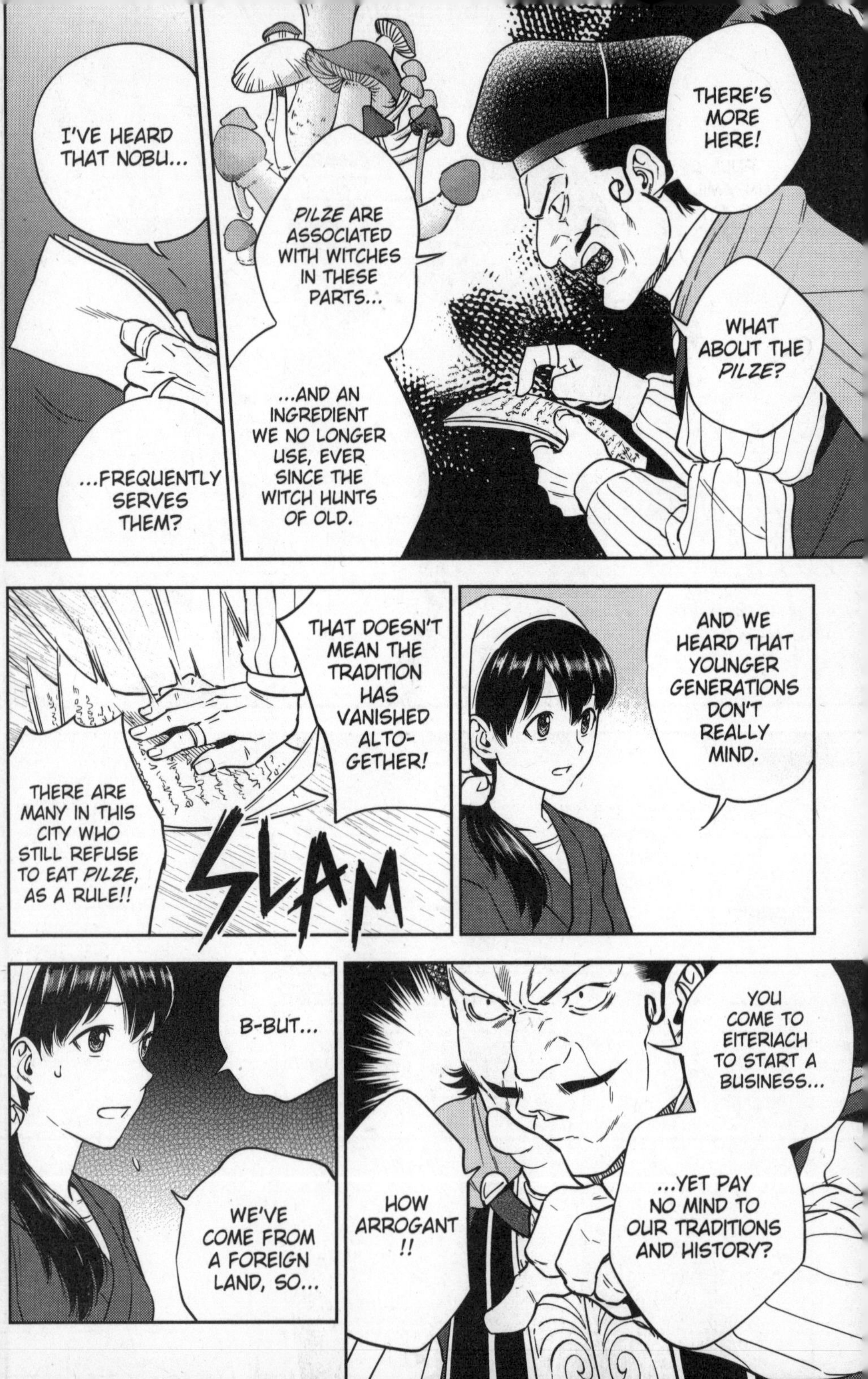
THERE'S MORE HERE!
WHAT ABOUT THE *PILZE*?
PILZE ARE ASSOCIATED WITH WITCHES IN THESE PARTS...
...AND AN INGREDIENT WE NO LONGER USE, EVER SINCE THE WITCH HUNTS OF OLD.
I'VE HEARD THAT NOBU...
...FREQUENTLY SERVES THEM?
AND WE HEARD THAT YOUNGER GENERATIONS DON'T REALLY MIND.
THAT DOESN'T MEAN THE TRADITION HAS VANISHED ALTO-GETHER!
SLAM
THERE ARE MANY IN THIS CITY WHO STILL REFUSE TO EAT *PILZE*, AS A RULE!!
YOU COME TO EITERIACH TO START A BUSINESS...
...YET PAY NO MIND TO OUR TRADITIONS AND HISTORY?
HOW ARROGANT !!
B-BUT...
WE'VE COME FROM A FOREIGN LAND, SO...

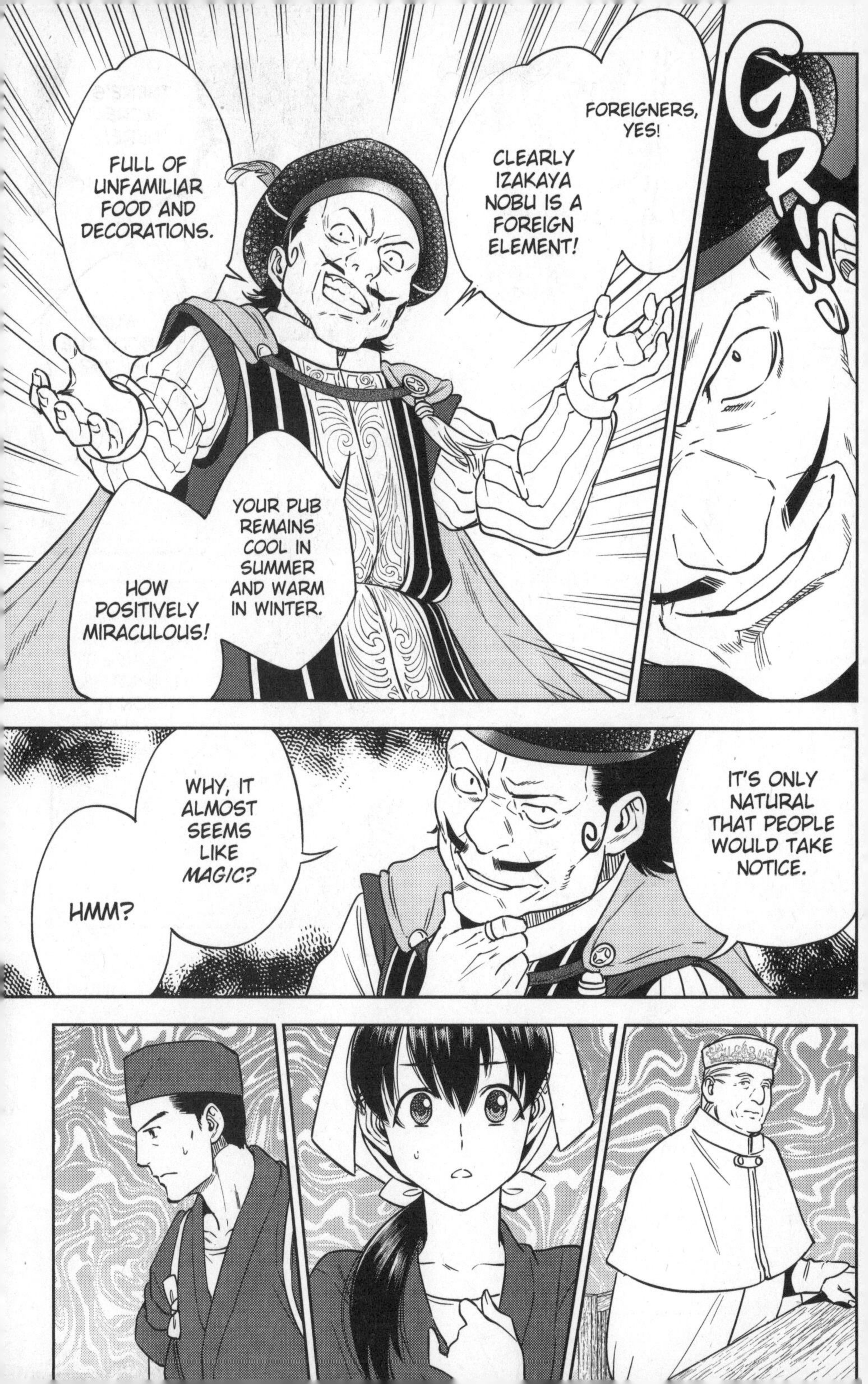
GRIN
FOREIGNERS, YES!
CLEARLY IZAKAYA NOBU IS A FOREIGN ELEMENT!
FULL OF UNFAMILIAR FOOD AND DECORATIONS.
YOUR PUB REMAINS COOL IN SUMMER AND WARM IN WINTER.
HOW POSITIVELY MIRACULOUS!
IT'S ONLY NATURAL THAT PEOPLE WOULD TAKE NOTICE.
WHY, IT ALMOST SEEMS LIKE *MAGIC*?
HMM?

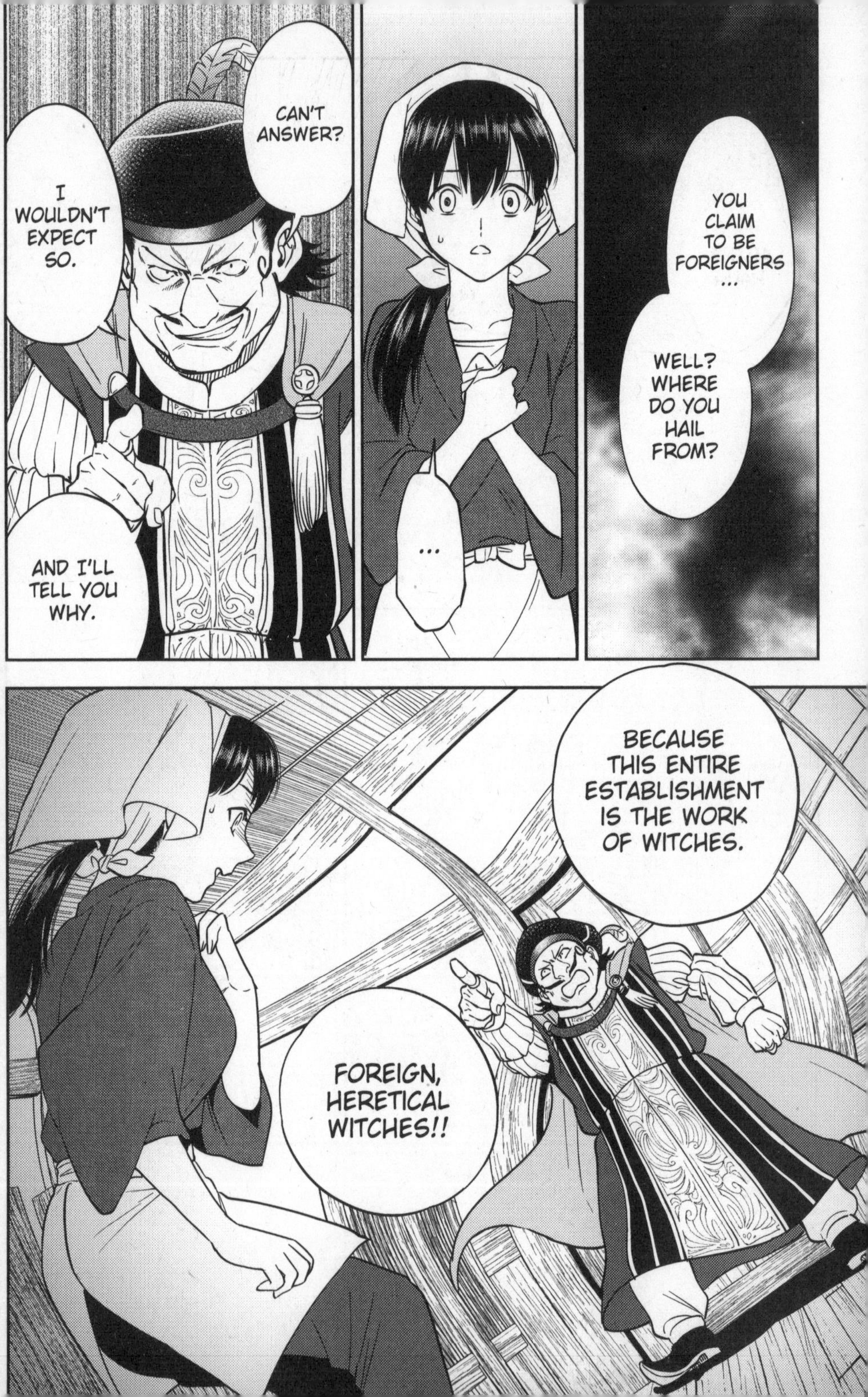
YOU CLAIM TO BE FOREIGNERS...
WELL? WHERE DO YOU HAIL FROM?
...
CAN'T ANSWER?
I WOULDN'T EXPECT SO.
AND I'LL TELL YOU WHY.
BECAUSE THIS ENTIRE ESTABLISHMENT IS THE WORK OF WITCHES.
FOREIGN, HERETICAL WITCHES!!

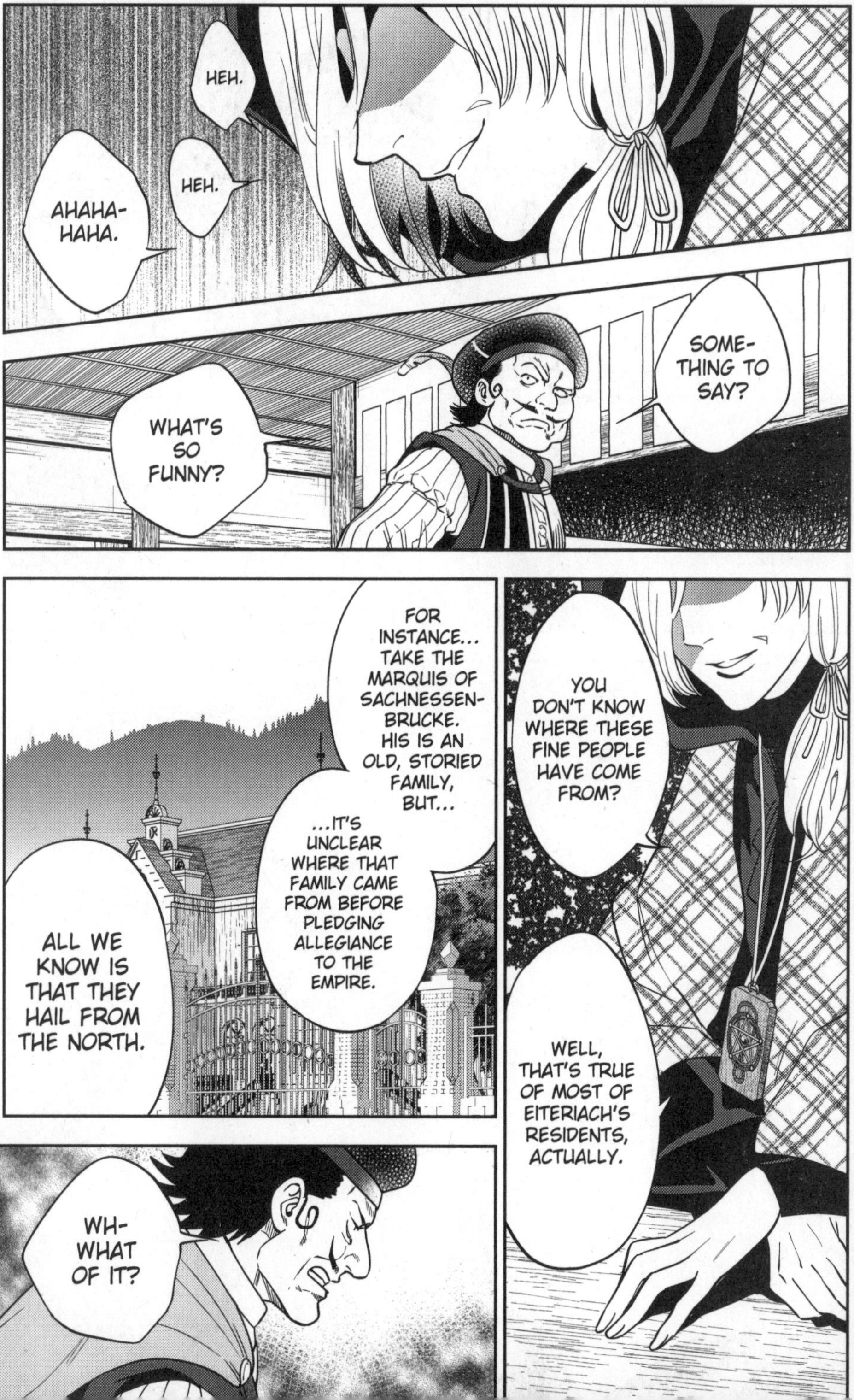
HEH.
HEH.
AHAHA-HAHA.
SOME-THING TO SAY?
WHAT'S SO FUNNY?
YOU DON'T KNOW WHERE THESE FINE PEOPLE HAVE COME FROM?
WELL, THAT'S TRUE OF MOST OF EITERIACH'S RESIDENTS, ACTUALLY.
FOR INSTANCE... TAKE THE MARQUIS OF SACHNESSEN-BRUCKE. HIS IS AN OLD, STORIED FAMILY, BUT...
...IT'S UNCLEAR WHERE THAT FAMILY CAME FROM BEFORE PLEDGING ALLEGIANCE TO THE EMPIRE.
ALL WE KNOW IS THAT THEY HAIL FROM THE NORTH.
WH-WHAT OF IT?

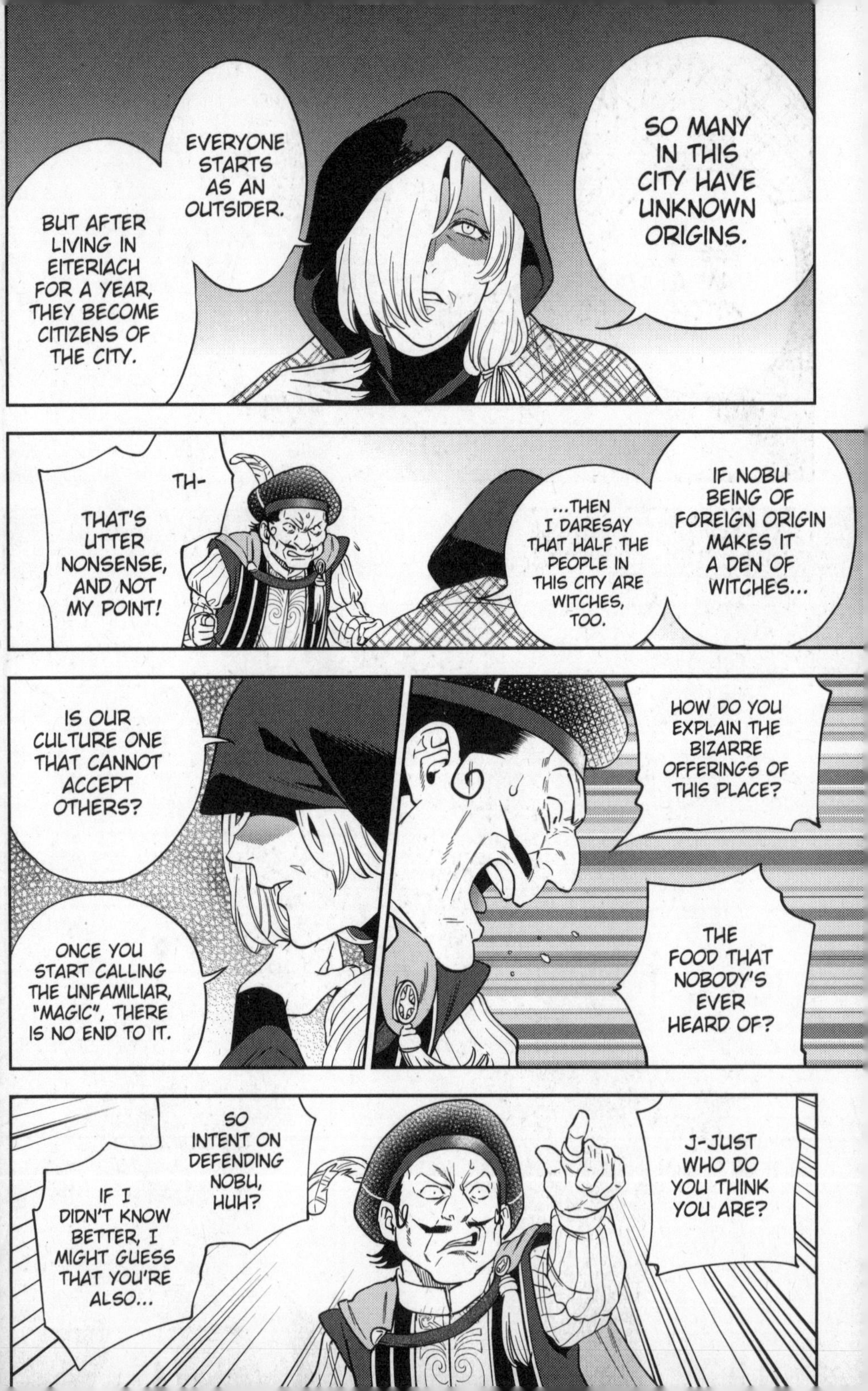
SO MANY IN THIS CITY HAVE UNKNOWN ORIGINS.
EVERYONE STARTS AS AN OUTSIDER.
BUT AFTER LIVING IN EITERIACH FOR A YEAR, THEY BECOME CITIZENS OF THE CITY.
IF NOBU BEING OF FOREIGN ORIGIN MAKES IT A DEN OF WITCHES...
...THEN I DARESAY THAT HALF THE PEOPLE IN THIS CITY ARE WITCHES, TOO.
TH-
THAT'S UTTER NONSENSE, AND NOT MY POINT!
HOW DO YOU EXPLAIN THE BIZARRE OFFERINGS OF THIS PLACE?
THE FOOD THAT NOBODY'S EVER HEARD OF?
IS OUR CULTURE ONE THAT CANNOT ACCEPT OTHERS?
ONCE YOU START CALLING THE UNFAMILIAR, "MAGIC", THERE IS NO END TO IT.
J-JUST WHO DO YOU THINK YOU ARE?
SO INTENT ON DEFENDING NOBU, HUH?
IF I DIDN'T KNOW BETTER, I MIGHT GUESS THAT YOU'RE ALSO...

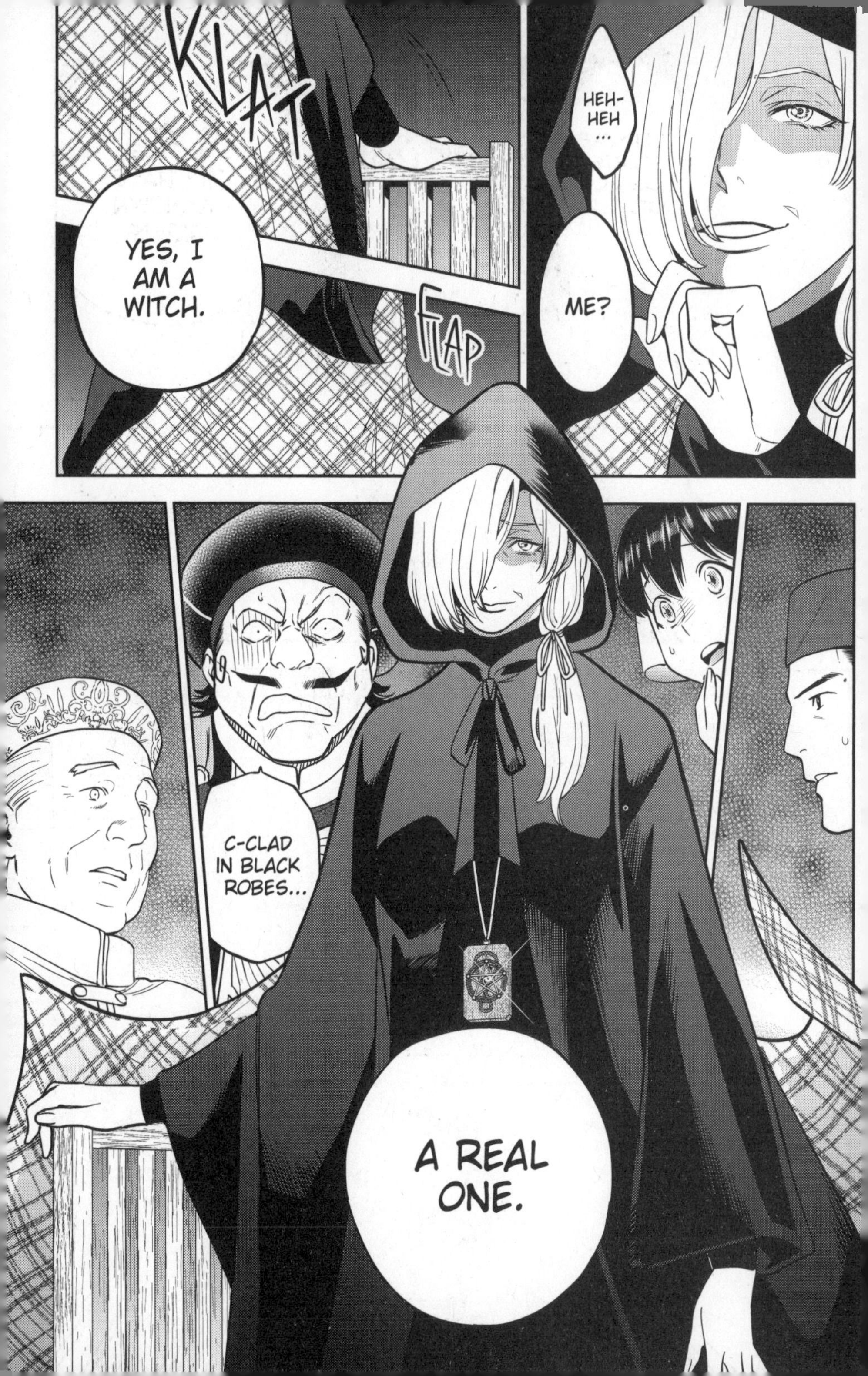
HEH-HEH ...
ME?
KLAT
YES, I AM A WITCH.
FLAP
C-CLAD IN BLACK ROBES...
A REAL ONE.

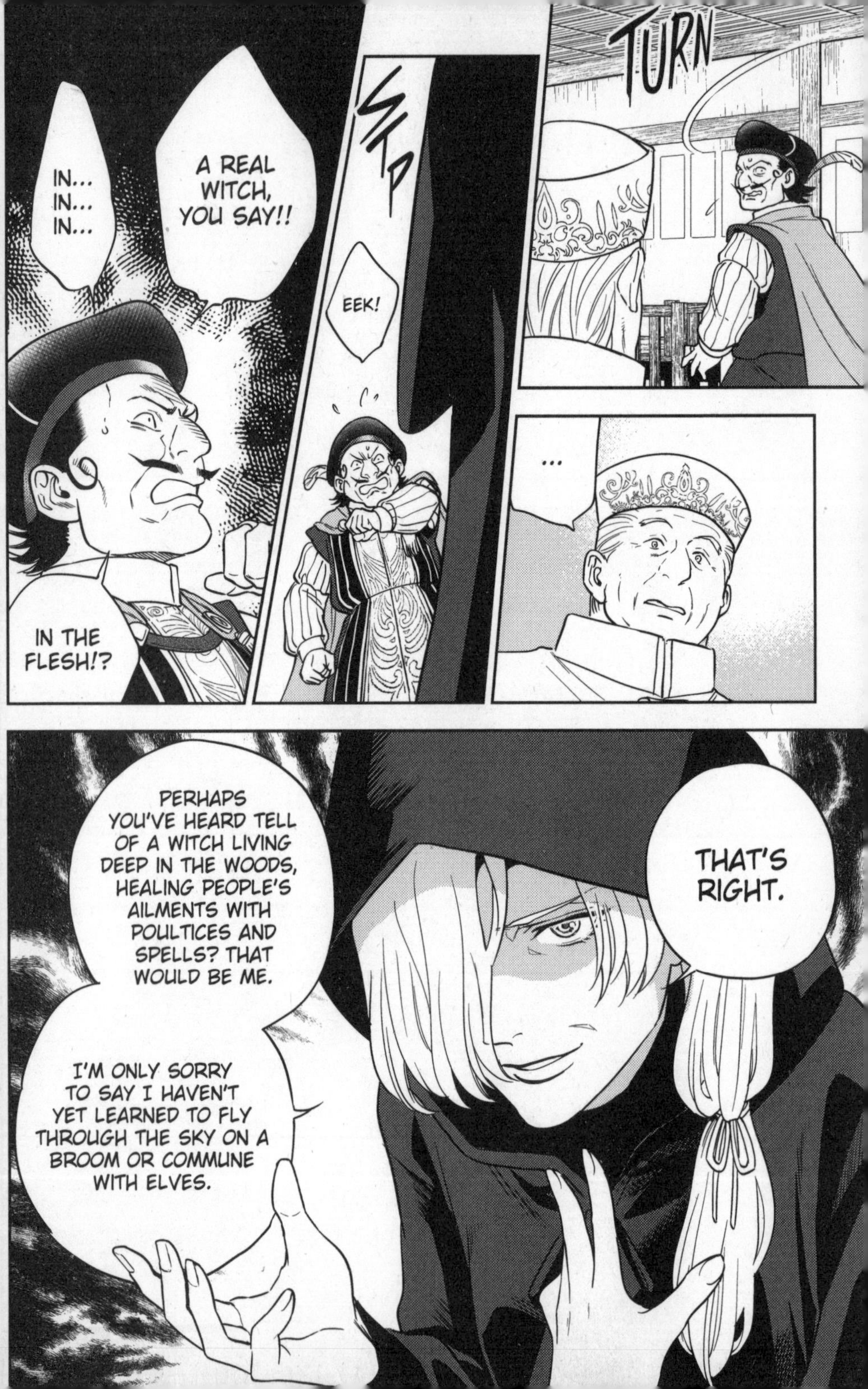
TURN
...
SKIP
EEK!
A REAL WITCH, YOU SAY!!
IN... IN... IN...
IN THE FLESH!?
THAT'S RIGHT.
PERHAPS YOU'VE HEARD TELL OF A WITCH LIVING DEEP IN THE WOODS, HEALING PEOPLE'S AILMENTS WITH POULTICES AND SPELLS? THAT WOULD BE ME.
I'M ONLY SORRY TO SAY I HAVEN'T YET LEARNED TO FLY THROUGH THE SKY ON A BROOM OR COMMUNE WITH ELVES.

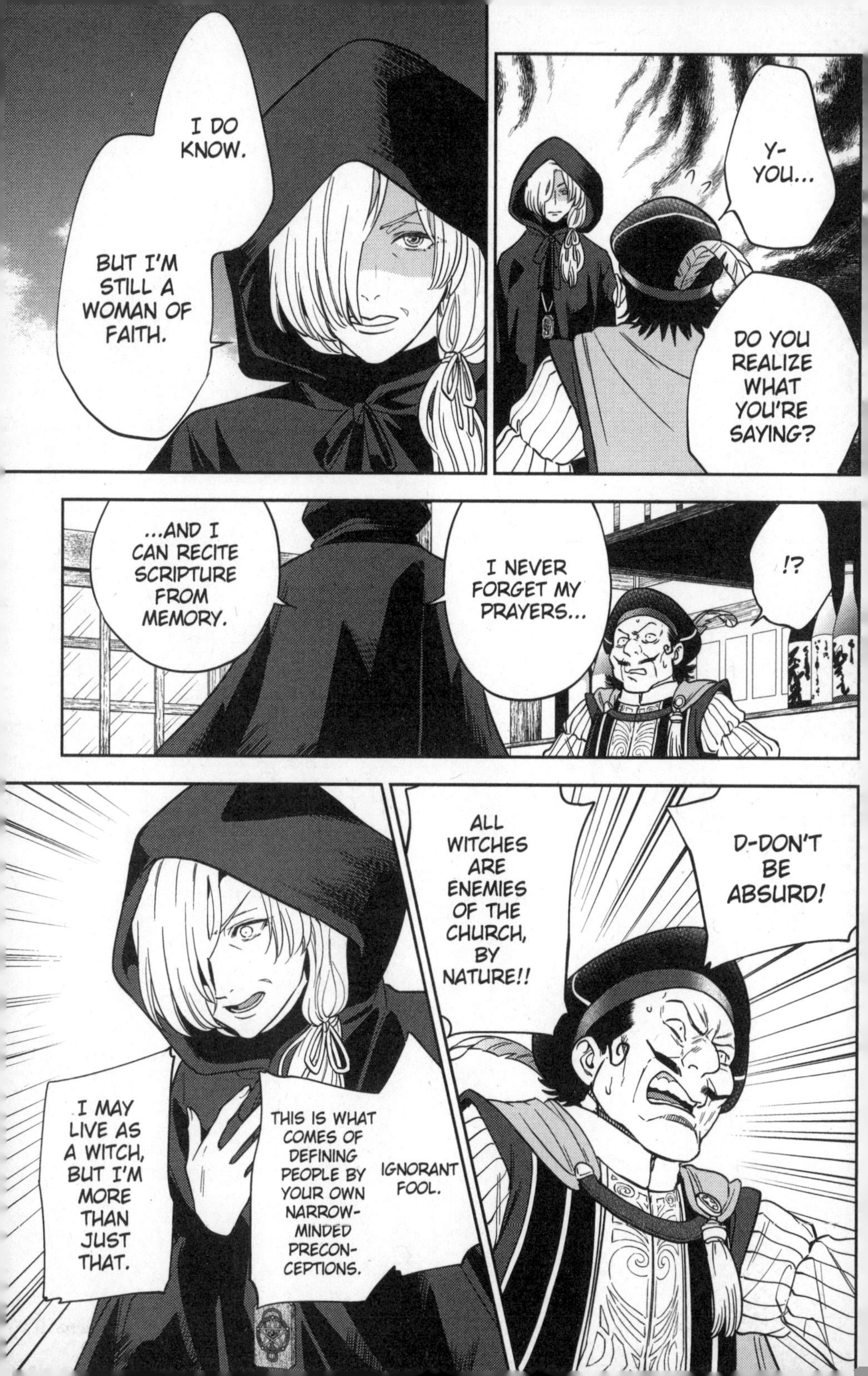
Y- YOU...
DO YOU REALIZE WHAT YOU'RE SAYING?
I DO KNOW.
BUT I'M STILL A WOMAN OF FAITH.
!?
I NEVER FORGET MY PRAYERS...
...AND I CAN RECITE SCRIPTURE FROM MEMORY.
D-DON'T BE ABSURD!
ALL WITCHES ARE ENEMIES OF THE CHURCH, BY NATURE!!
IGNORANT FOOL.
THIS IS WHAT COMES OF DEFINING PEOPLE BY YOUR OWN NARROW-MINDED PRECON-CEPTIONS.
I MAY LIVE AS A WITCH, BUT I'M MORE THAN JUST THAT.

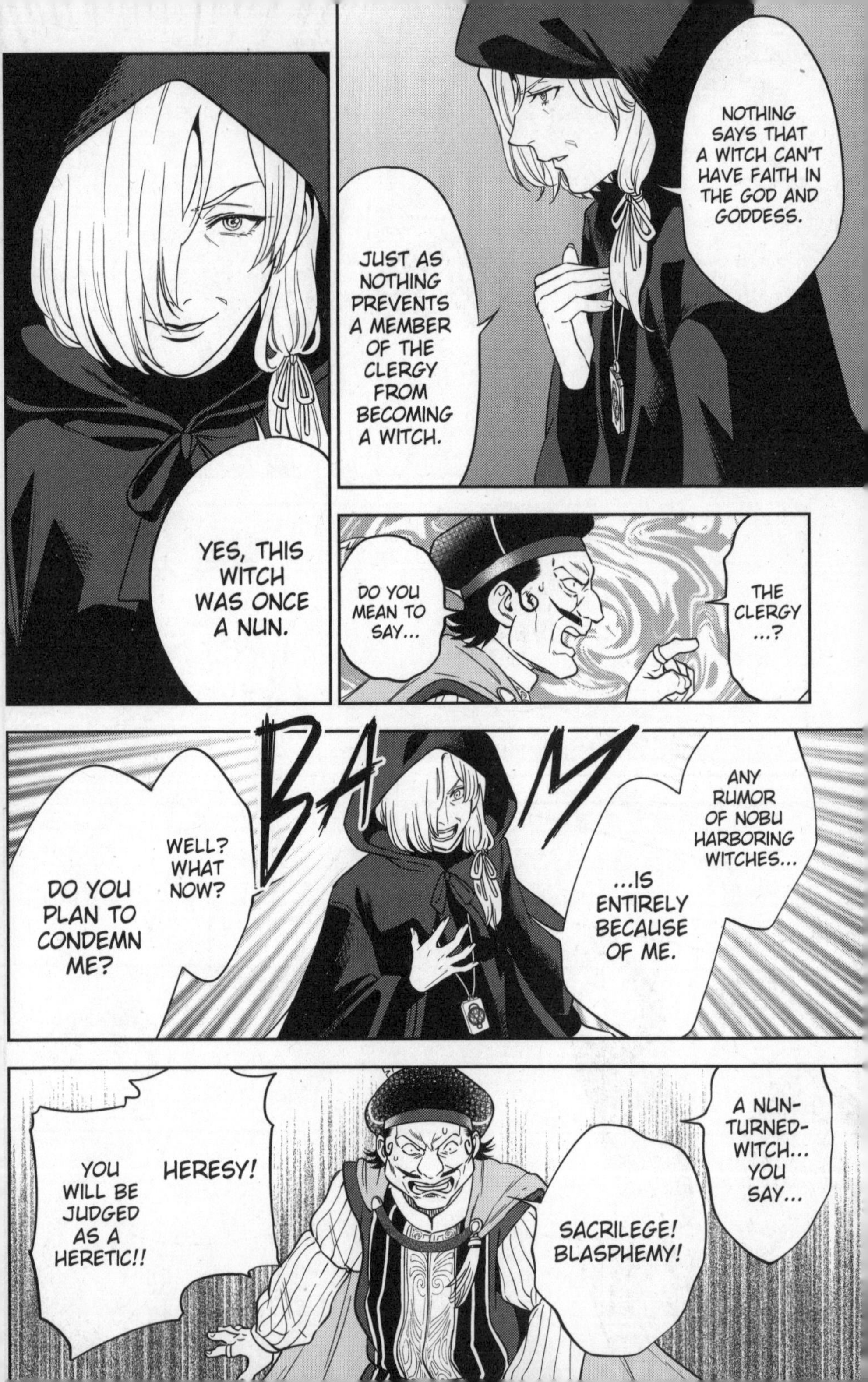
NOTHING SAYS THAT A WITCH CAN'T HAVE FAITH IN THE GOD AND GODDESS.
JUST AS NOTHING PREVENTS A MEMBER OF THE CLERGY FROM BECOMING A WITCH.
THE CLERGY ...?
DO YOU MEAN TO SAY...
YES, THIS WITCH WAS ONCE A NUN.
BAM
ANY RUMOR OF NOBU HARBORING WITCHES...
...IS ENTIRELY BECAUSE OF ME.
WELL? WHAT NOW?
DO YOU PLAN TO CONDEMN ME?
A NUN-TURNED-WITCH... YOU SAY...
SACRILEGE! BLASPHEMY!
HERESY!
YOU WILL BE JUDGED AS A HERETIC!!

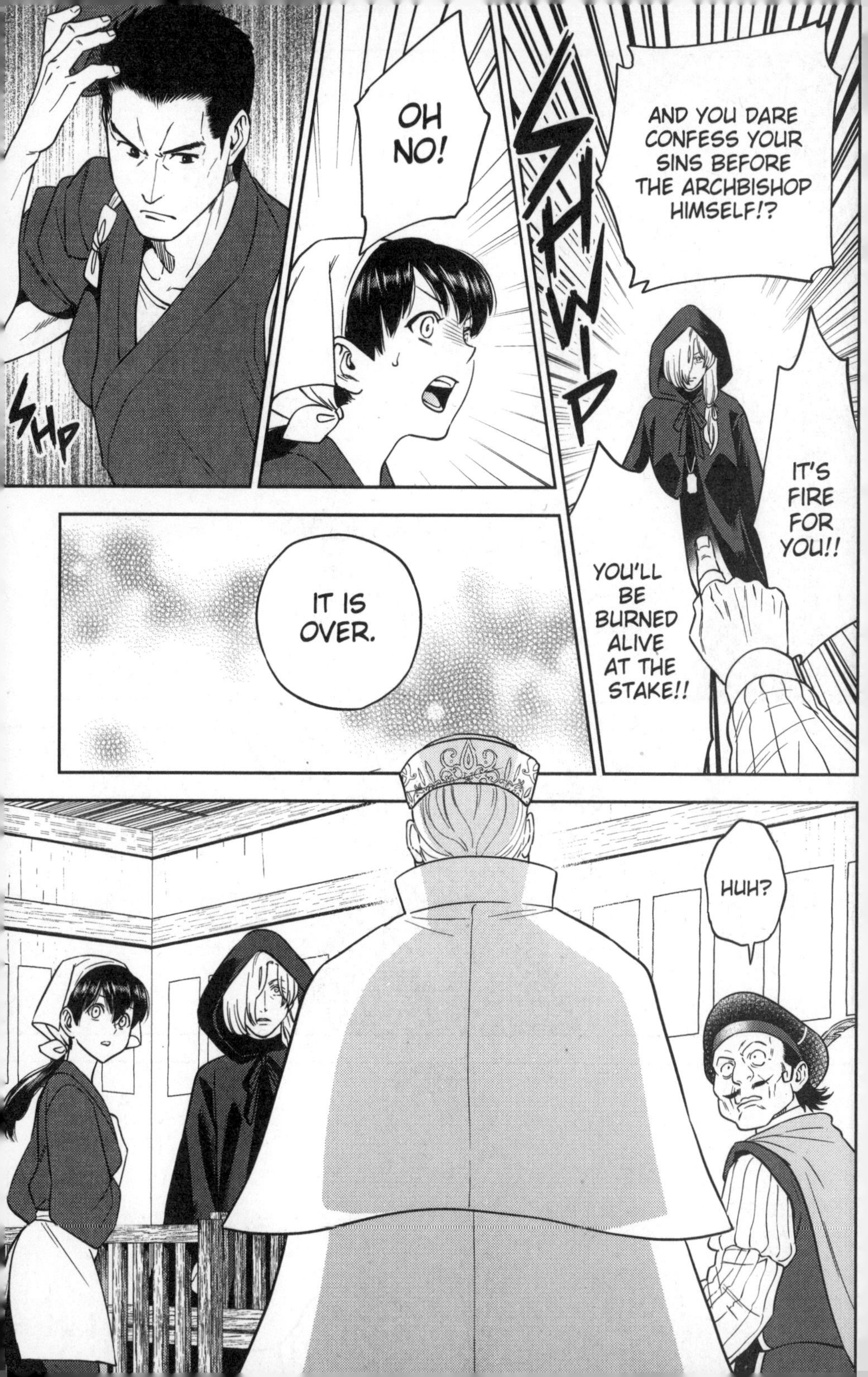
AND YOU DARE CONFESS YOUR SINS BEFORE THE ARCHBISHOP HIMSELF!?
SHWIP
IT'S FIRE FOR YOU!!
YOU'LL BE BURNED ALIVE AT THE STAKE!!
OH NO!
SHP
IT IS OVER.
HUH?

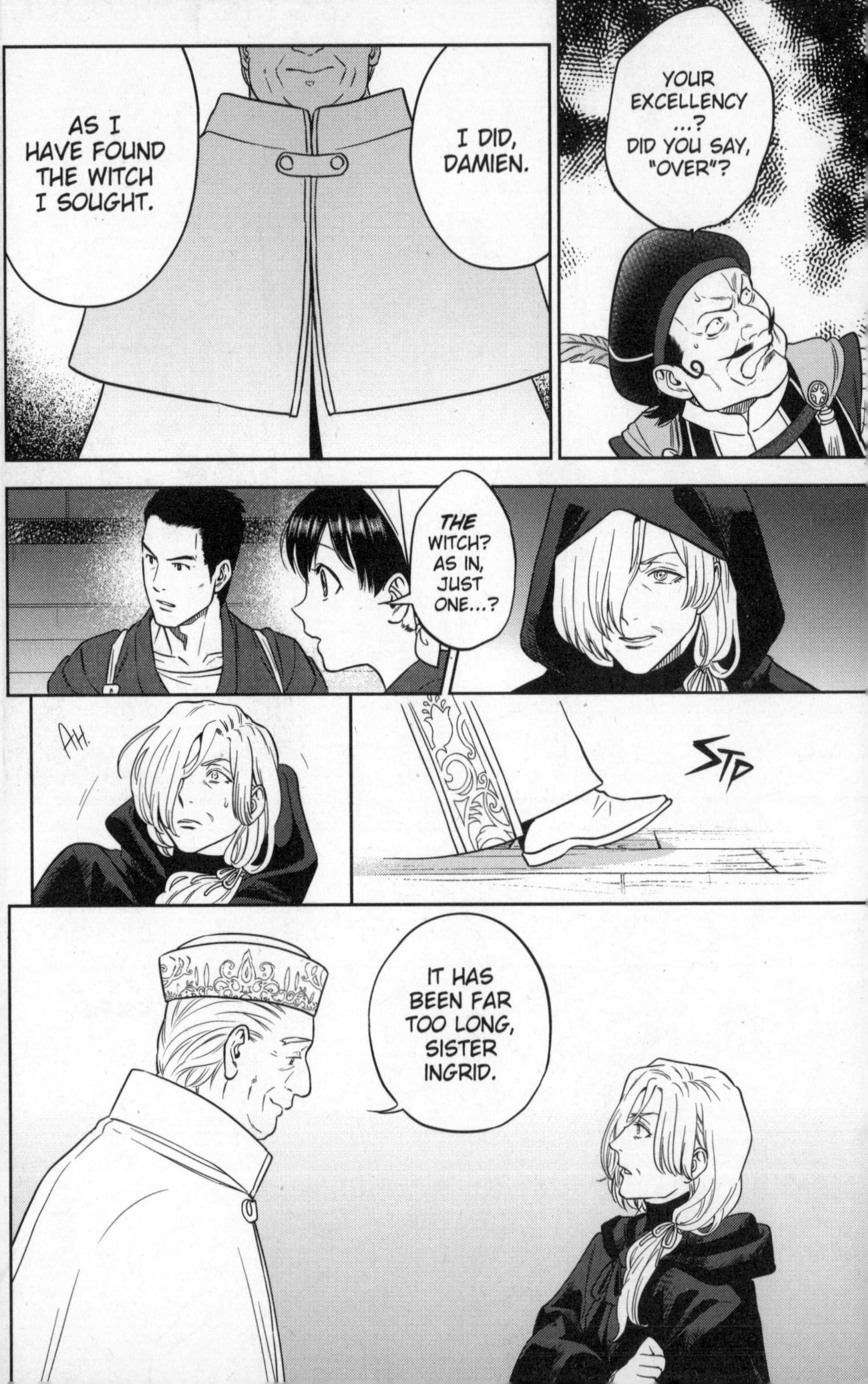
YOUR EXCELLENCY ...? DID YOU SAY, "OVER"?
I DID, DAMIEN.
AS I HAVE FOUND THE WITCH I SOUGHT.
THE WITCH? AS IN, JUST ONE...?
STP
AH.
IT HAS BEEN FAR TOO LONG, SISTER INGRID.

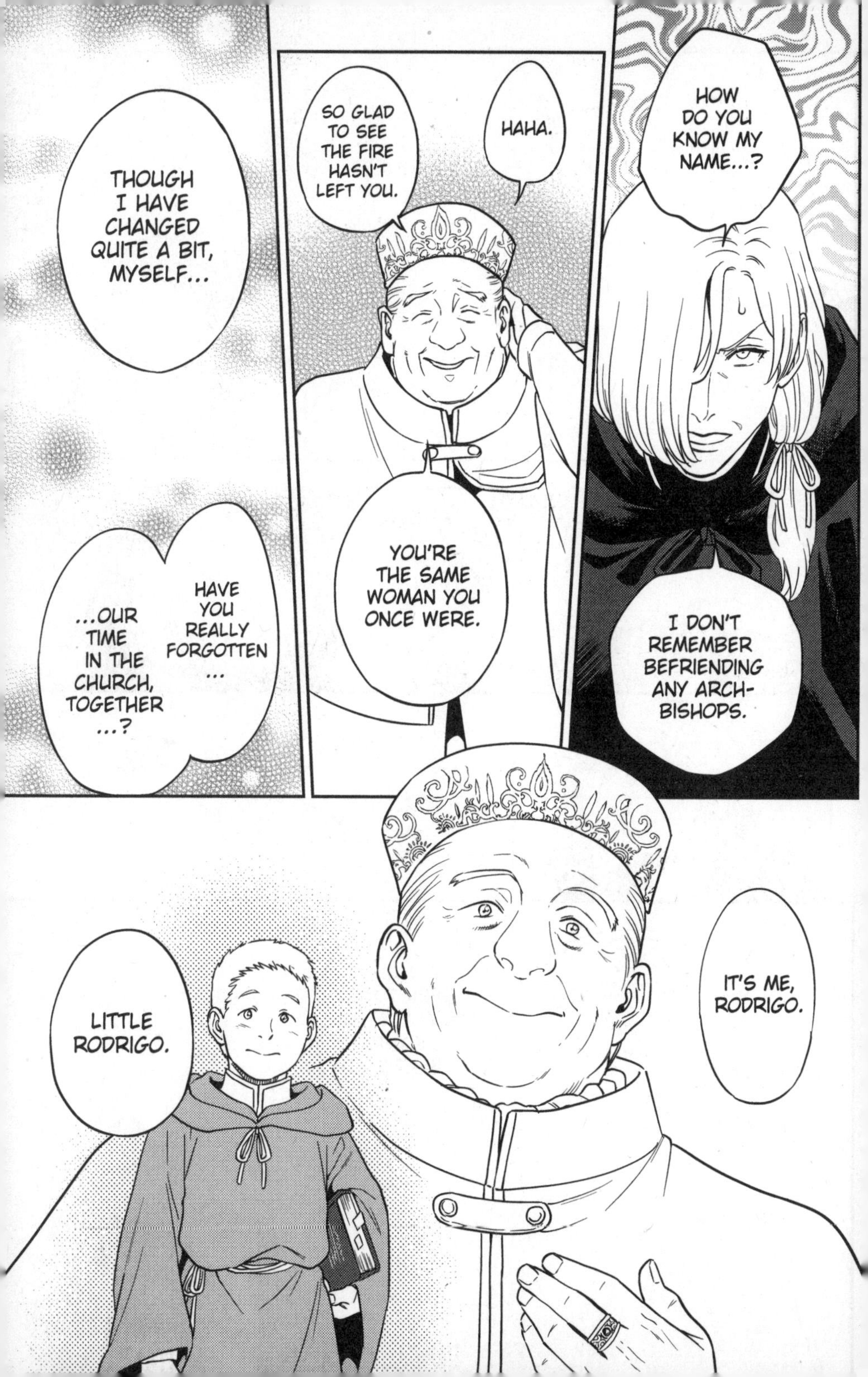
HOW DO YOU KNOW MY NAME...?
I DON'T REMEMBER BEFRIENDING ANY ARCH-BISHOPS.
HAHA.
SO GLAD TO SEE THE FIRE HASN'T LEFT YOU.
YOU'RE THE SAME WOMAN YOU ONCE WERE.
THOUGH I HAVE CHANGED QUITE A BIT, MYSELF...
HAVE YOU REALLY FORGOTTEN...
...OUR TIME IN THE CHURCH, TOGETHER...?
IT'S ME, RODRIGO.
LITTLE RODRIGO.

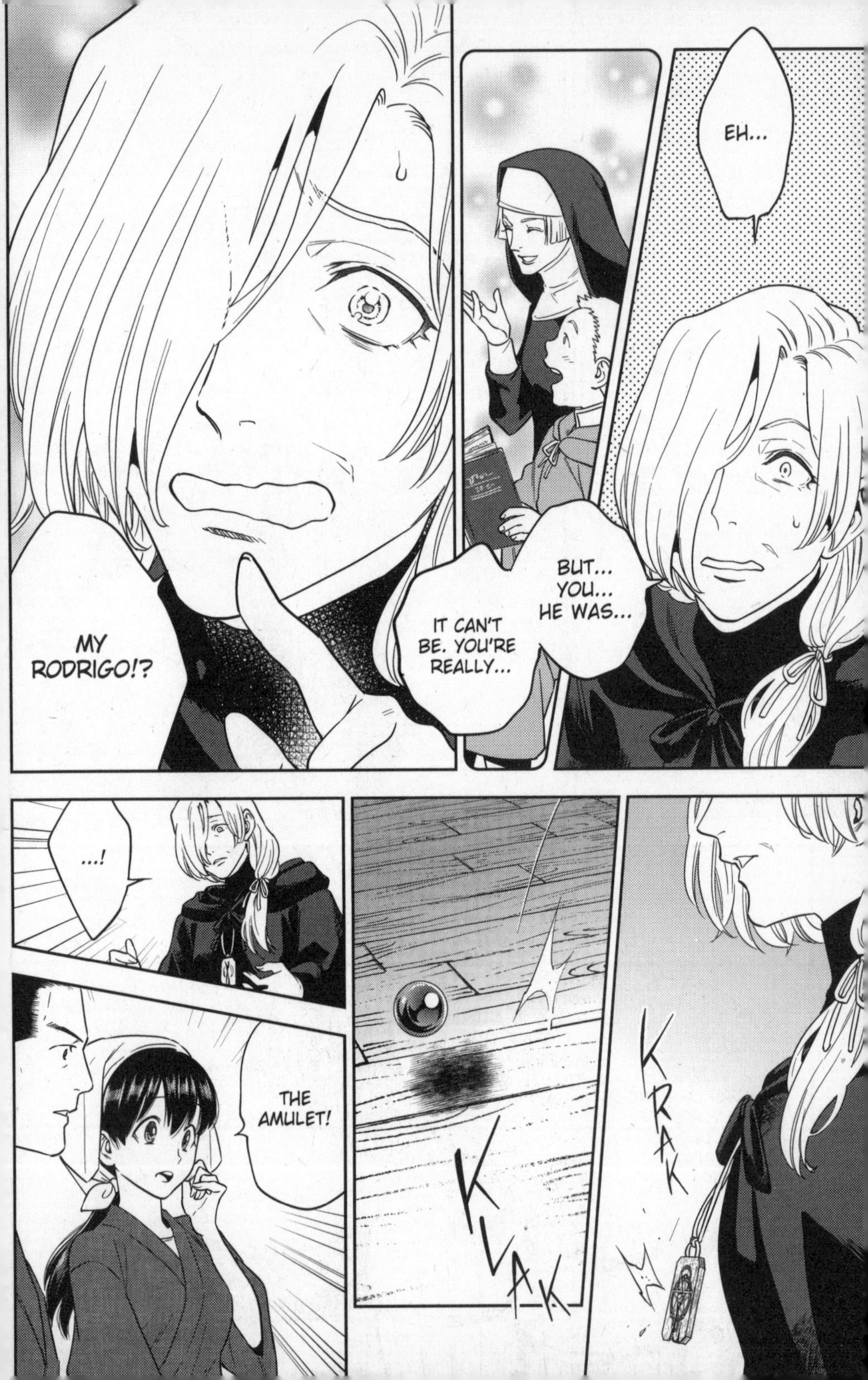
EH...
BUT... YOU... HE WAS...
IT CAN'T BE. YOU'RE REALLY...
MY RODRIGO!?
KRAK
KLAK
...!
THE AMULET!

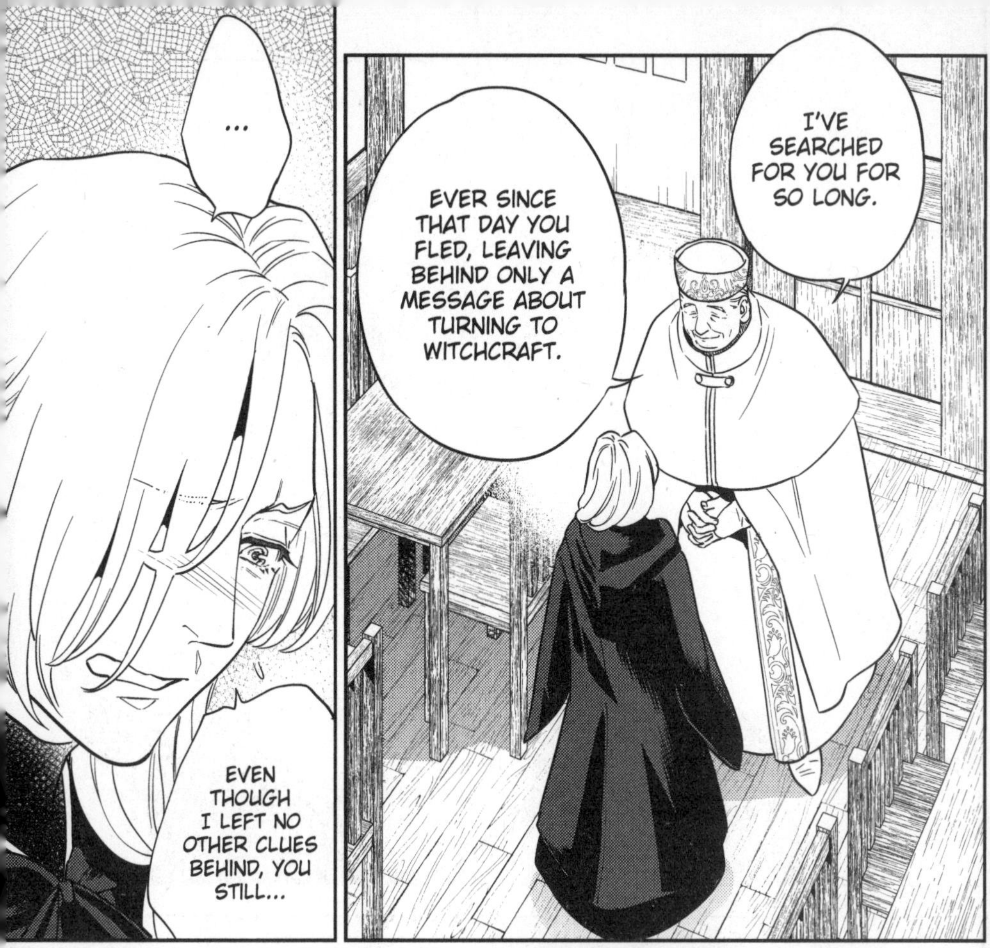
I'VE SEARCHED FOR YOU FOR SO LONG.
EVER SINCE THAT DAY YOU FLED, LEAVING BEHIND ONLY A MESSAGE ABOUT TURNING TO WITCHCRAFT.
...
EVEN THOUGH I LEFT NO OTHER CLUES BEHIND, YOU STILL...

*KÜRBISKUCHEN IS GERMAN FOR PUMPKIN PIE

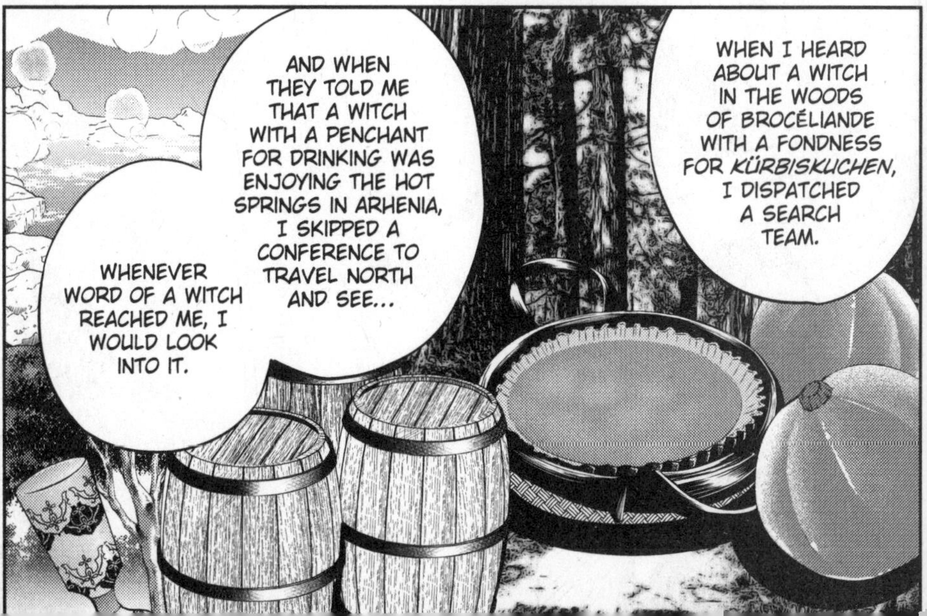
WHEN I HEARD ABOUT A WITCH IN THE WOODS OF BROCÉLIANDE WITH A FONDNESS FOR KÜRBISKUCHEN, I DISPATCHED A SEARCH TEAM.
AND WHEN THEY TOLD ME THAT A WITCH WITH A PENCHANT FOR DRINKING WAS ENJOYING THE HOT SPRINGS IN ARHENIA, I SKIPPED A CONFERENCE TO TRAVEL NORTH AND SEE...
WHENEVER WORD OF A WITCH REACHED ME, I WOULD LOOK INTO IT.

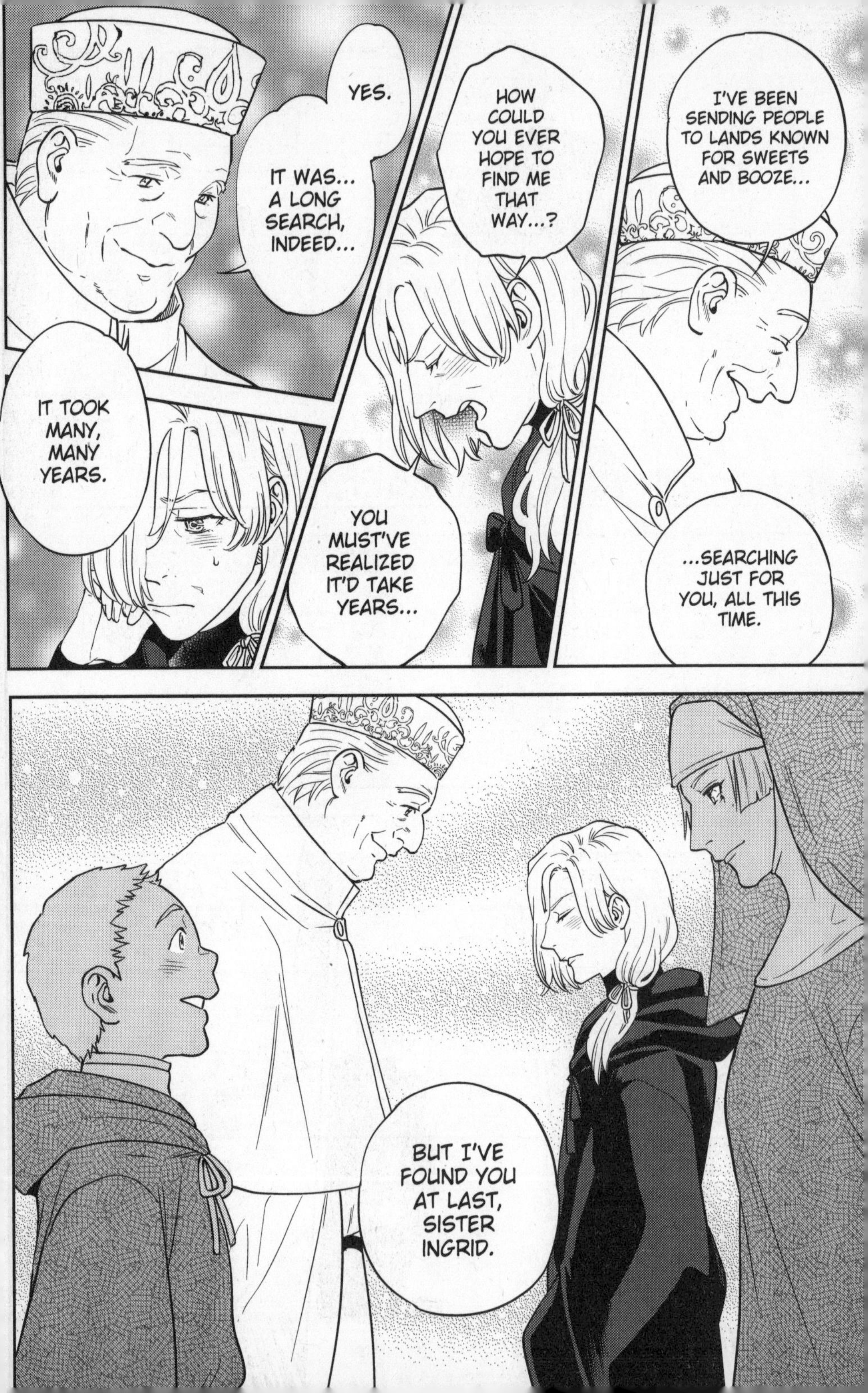
I'VE BEEN SENDING PEOPLE TO LANDS KNOWN FOR SWEETS AND BOOZE...
...SEARCHING JUST FOR YOU, ALL THIS TIME.
HOW COULD YOU EVER HOPE TO FIND ME THAT WAY...?
YOU MUST'VE REALIZED IT'D TAKE YEARS...
YES.
IT WAS... A LONG SEARCH, INDEED...
IT TOOK MANY, MANY YEARS.
BUT I'VE FOUND YOU AT LAST, SISTER INGRID.

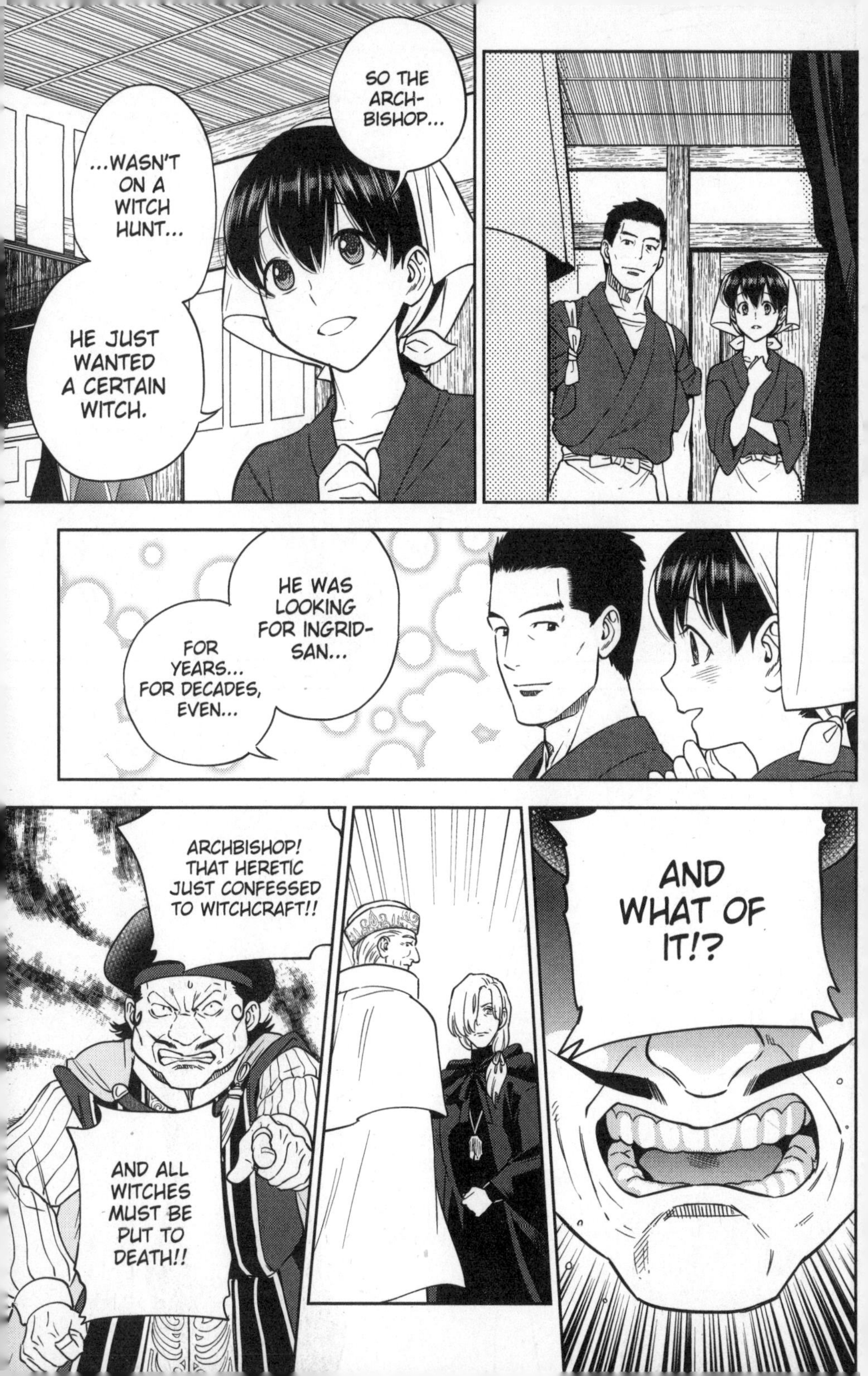
SO THE ARCH-BISHOP...
...WASN'T ON A WITCH HUNT...
HE JUST WANTED A CERTAIN WITCH.
HE WAS LOOKING FOR INGRID-SAN...
FOR YEARS... FOR DECADES, EVEN...
AND WHAT OF IT!?
ARCHBISHOP! THAT HERETIC JUST CONFESSED TO WITCHCRAFT!!
AND ALL WITCHES MUST BE PUT TO DEATH!!

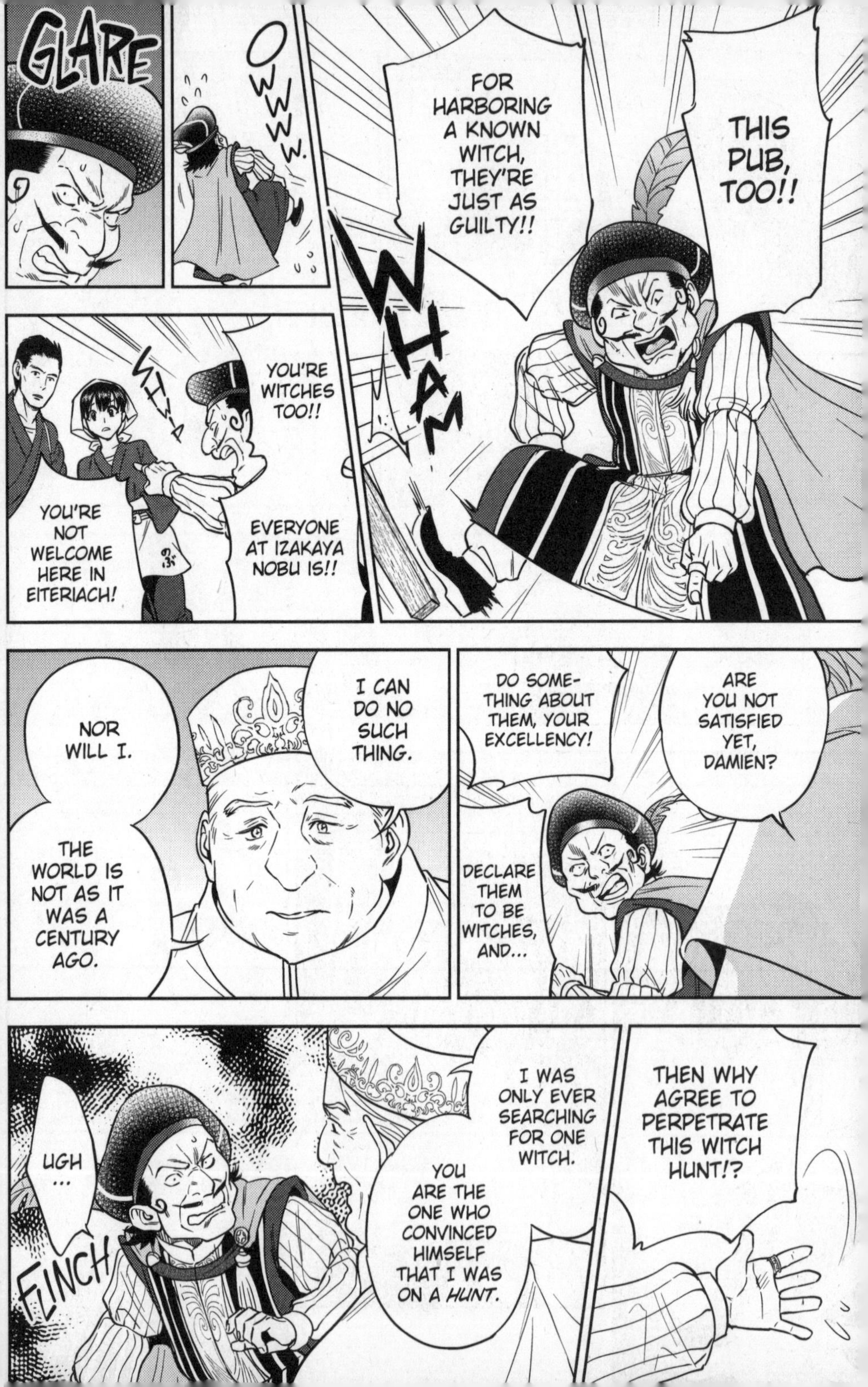
THIS PUB, TOO!!
FOR HARBORING A KNOWN WITCH, THEY'RE JUST AS GUILTY!!
WHAM
OWWWWW.
GLARE
YOU'RE WITCHES TOO!!
SHWA
EVERYONE AT IZAKAYA NOBU IS!!
YOU'RE NOT WELCOME HERE IN EITERIACH!
のぶ
ARE YOU NOT SATISFIED YET, DAMIEN?
DO SOME-THING ABOUT THEM, YOUR EXCELLENCY!
DECLARE THEM TO BE WITCHES, AND...
I CAN DO NO SUCH THING.
NOR WILL I.
THE WORLD IS NOT AS IT WAS A CENTURY AGO.
THEN WHY AGREE TO PERPETRATE THIS WITCH HUNT!?
I WAS ONLY EVER SEARCHING FOR ONE WITCH.
YOU ARE THE ONE WHO CONVINCED HIMSELF THAT I WAS ON A *HUNT*.
UGH...
FLINCH

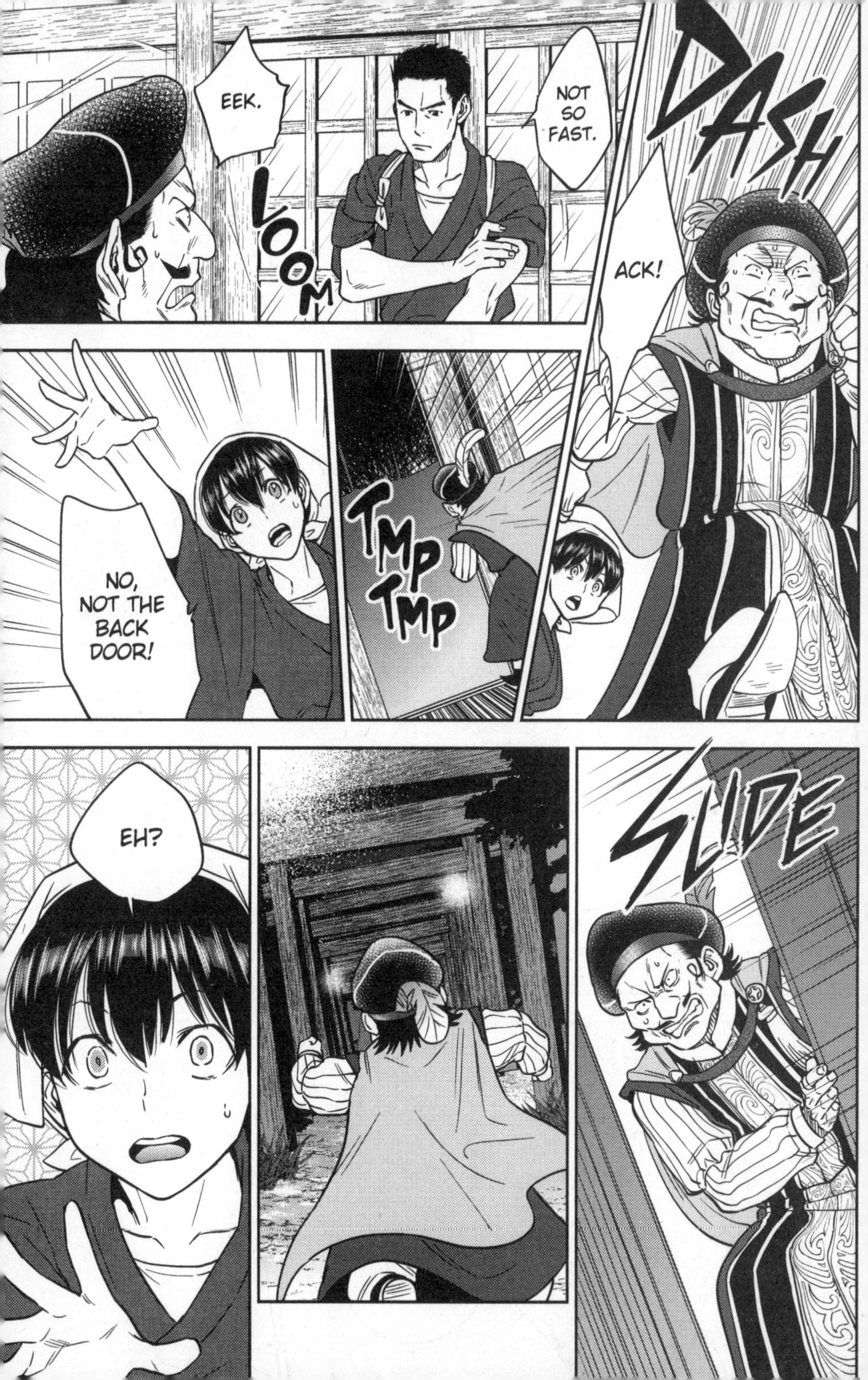
DASH
ACK!
NOT SO FAST.
EEK.
VOOM
TMP TMP
NO, NOT THE BACK DOOR!
SLIDE
EH?

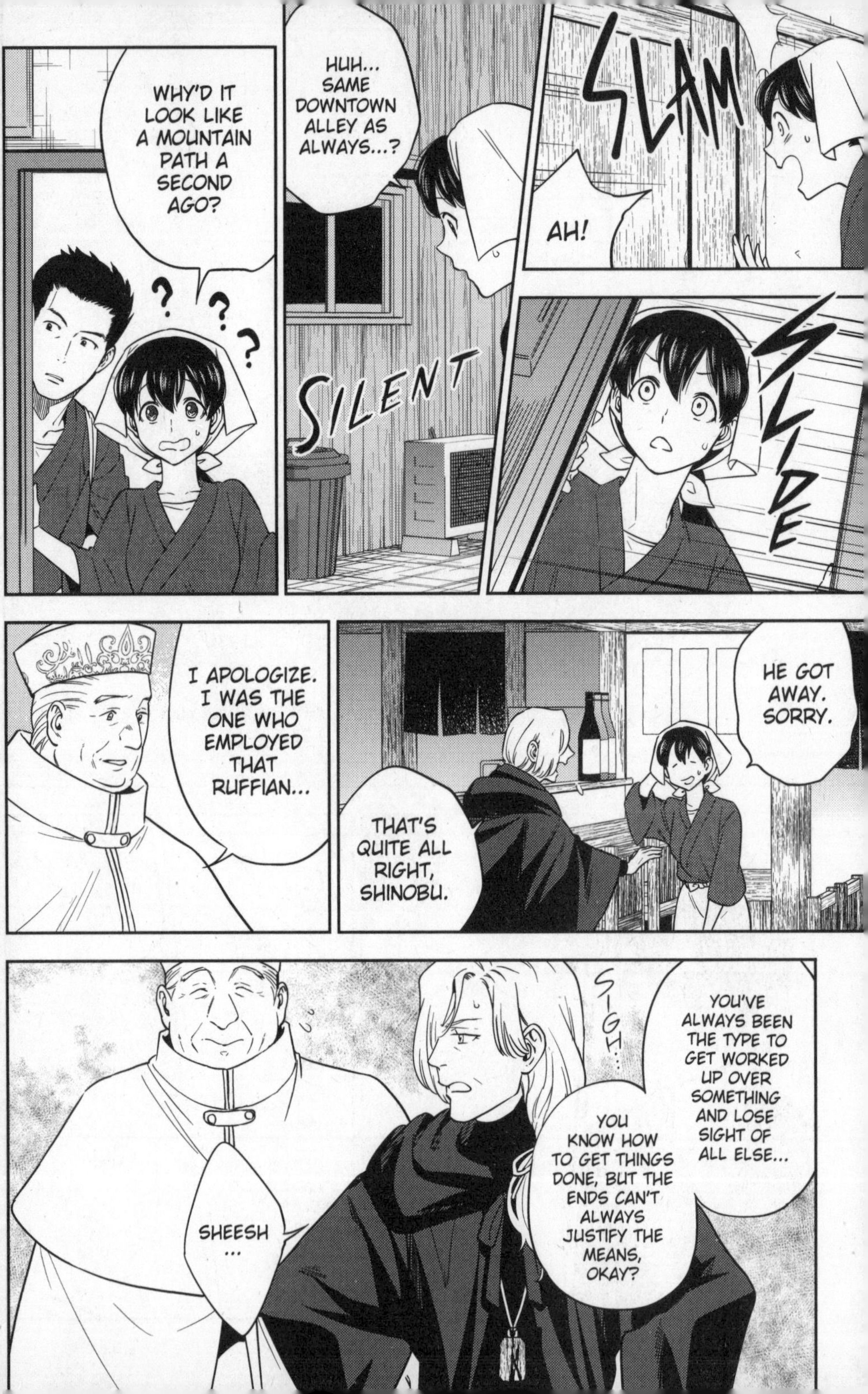
SLAM
AH!
SLIDE
HUH... SAME DOWNTOWN ALLEY AS ALWAYS...?
SILENT
WHY'D IT LOOK LIKE A MOUNTAIN PATH A SECOND AGO?
? ? ?
HE GOT AWAY. SORRY.
THAT'S QUITE ALL RIGHT, SHINOBU.
I APOLOGIZE. I WAS THE ONE WHO EMPLOYED THAT RUFFIAN...
SIGH...
YOU'VE ALWAYS BEEN THE TYPE TO GET WORKED UP OVER SOMETHING AND LOSE SIGHT OF ALL ELSE...
YOU KNOW HOW TO GET THINGS DONE, BUT THE ENDS CAN'T ALWAYS JUSTIFY THE MEANS, OKAY?
SHEESH...

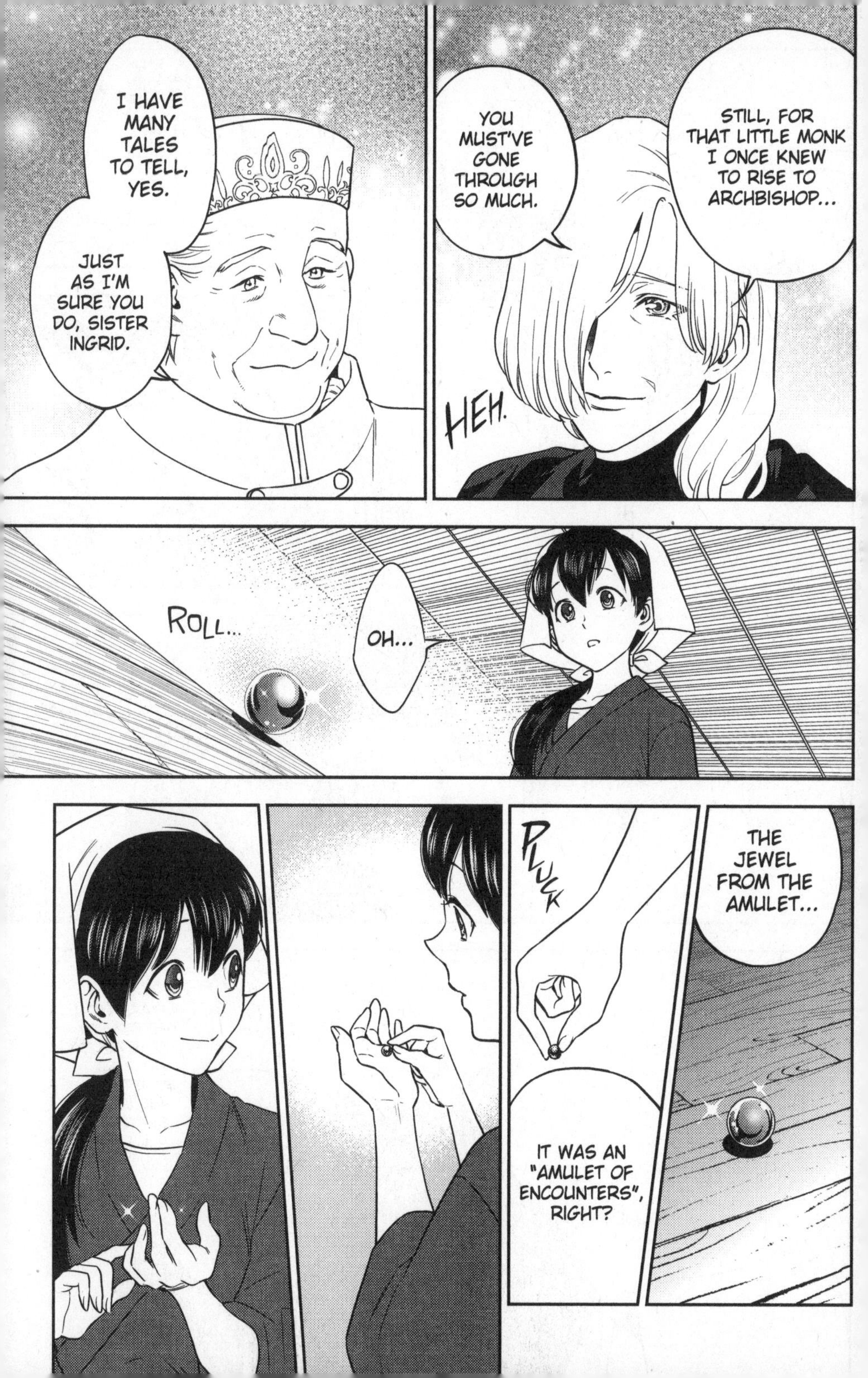
STILL, FOR THAT LITTLE MONK I ONCE KNEW TO RISE TO ARCHBISHOP...
YOU MUST'VE GONE THROUGH SO MUCH.
HEH.
I HAVE MANY TALES TO TELL, YES.
JUST AS I'M SURE YOU DO, SISTER INGRID.
OH...
ROLL...
THE JEWEL FROM THE AMULET...
PLUCK
IT WAS AN "AMULET OF ENCOUNTERS", RIGHT?

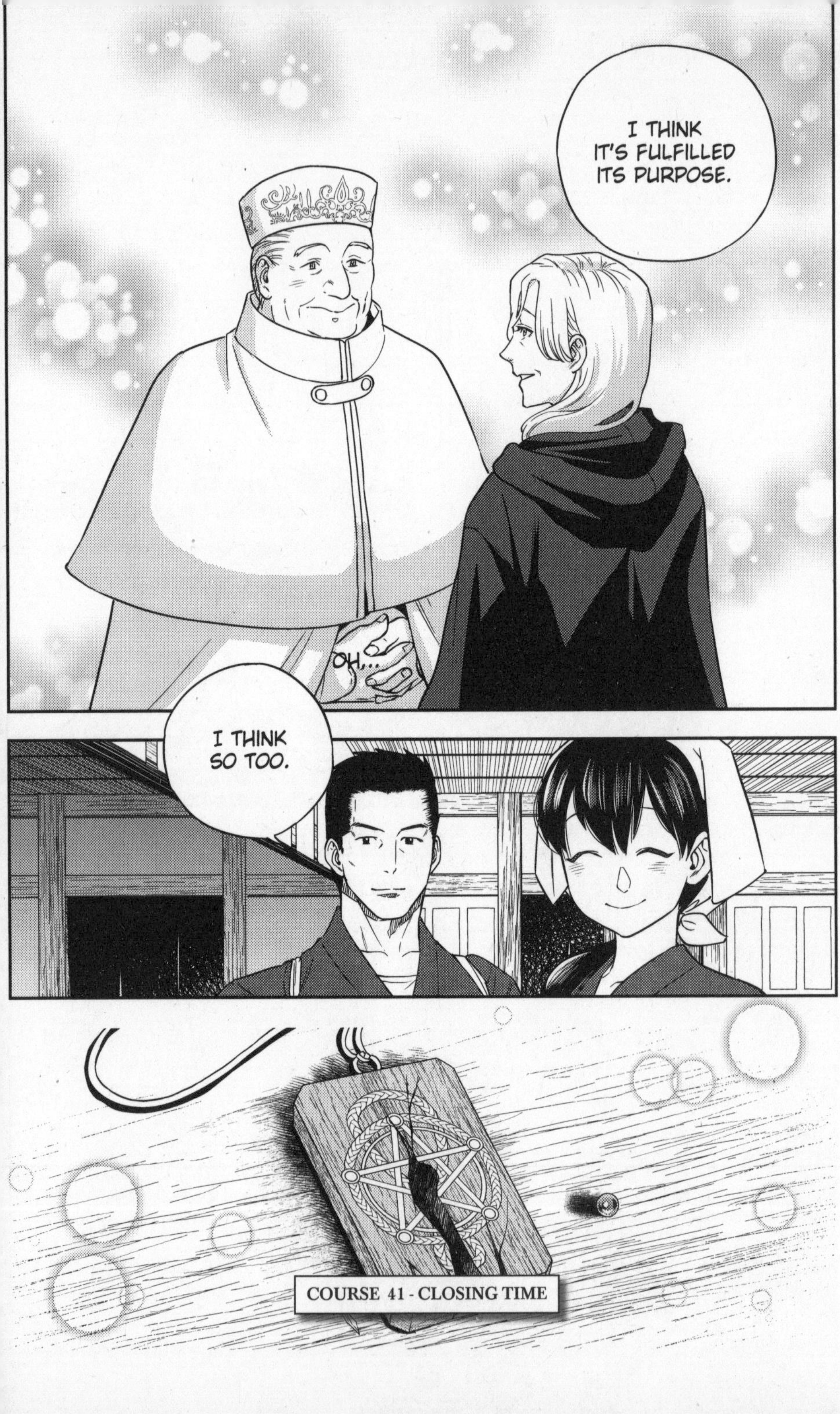
I THINK IT'S FULFILLED ITS PURPOSE.
OH...
I THINK SO TOO.
COURSE 41 - CLOSING TIME

OTHERWORLDLY IZAKAYA
NOBU

OTHERWORLDLY IZAKAYA

NOBU

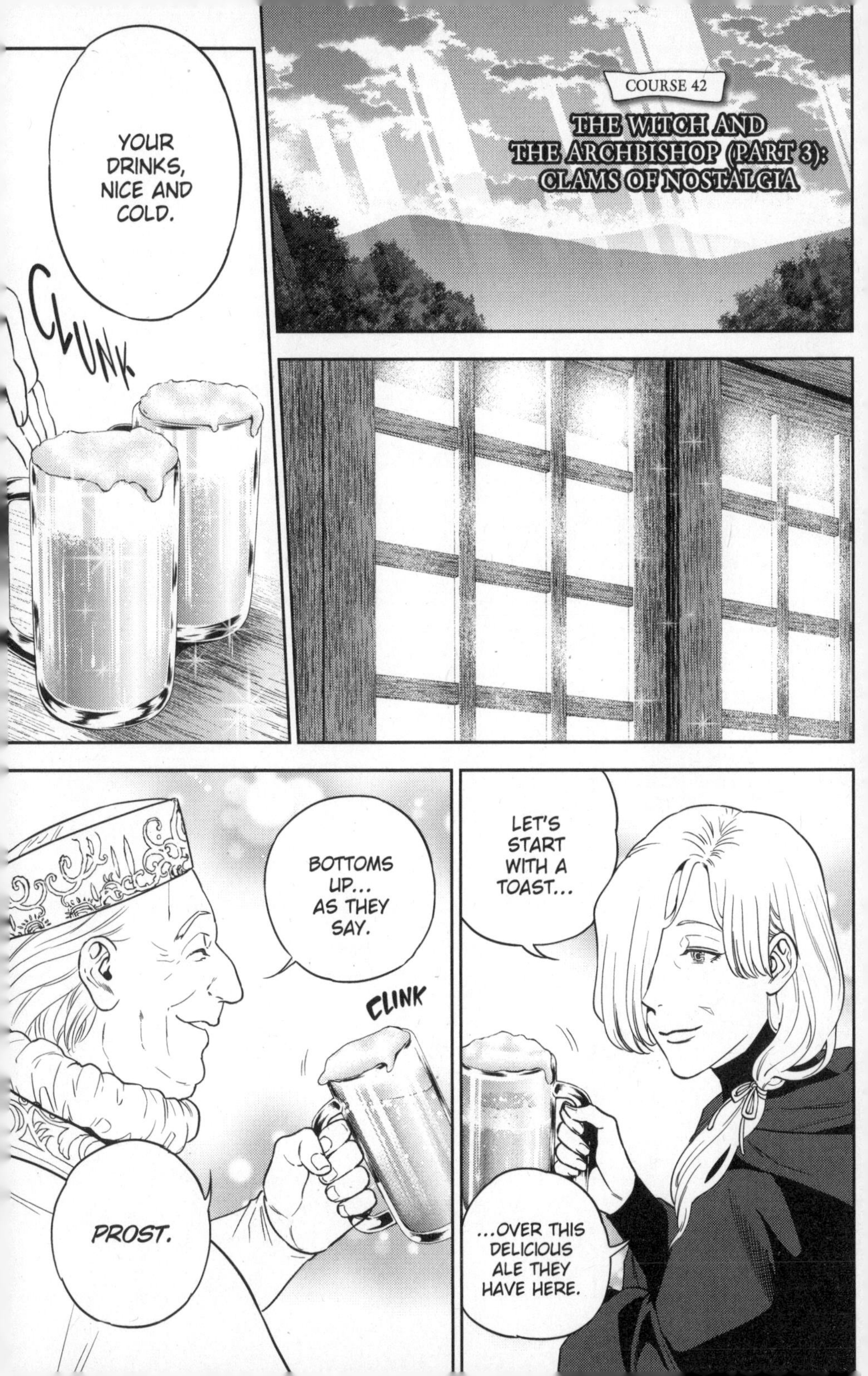
COURSE 42
THE WITCH AND THE ARCHBISHOP (PART 3): CLAMS OF NOSTALGIA
YOUR DRINKS, NICE AND COLD.
CLUNK
LET'S START WITH A TOAST...
...OVER THIS DELICIOUS ALE THEY HAVE HERE.
BOTTOMS UP... AS THEY SAY.
CLINK
PROST.

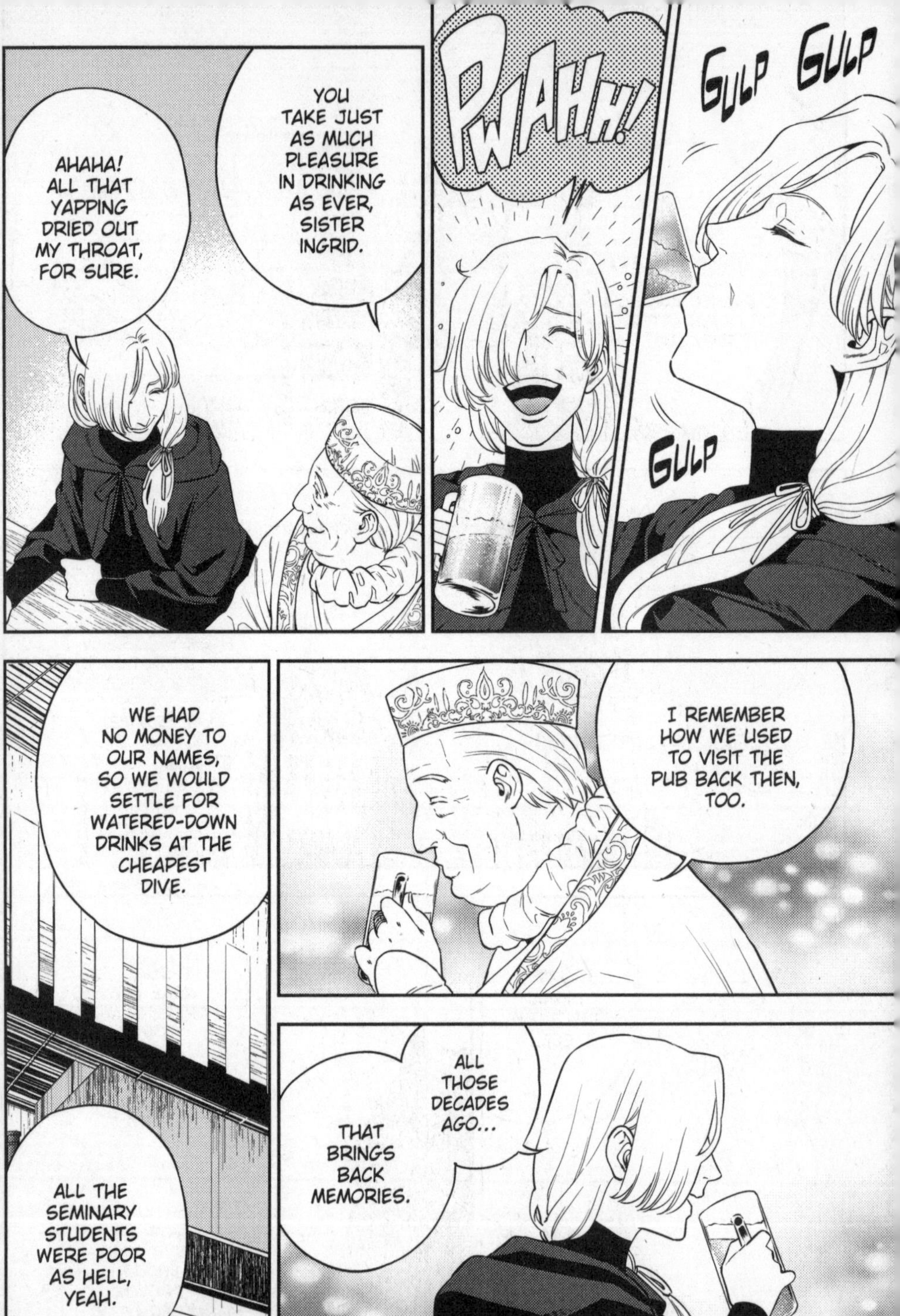
GULP GULP
GULP
PWAHH!
YOU TAKE JUST AS MUCH PLEASURE IN DRINKING AS EVER, SISTER INGRID.
AHAHA! ALL THAT YAPPING DRIED OUT MY THROAT, FOR SURE.
I REMEMBER HOW WE USED TO VISIT THE PUB BACK THEN, TOO.
ALL THOSE DECADES AGO...
THAT BRINGS BACK MEMORIES.
WE HAD NO MONEY TO OUR NAMES, SO WE WOULD SETTLE FOR WATERED-DOWN DRINKS AT THE CHEAPEST DIVE.
ALL THE SEMINARY STUDENTS WERE POOR AS HELL, YEAH.

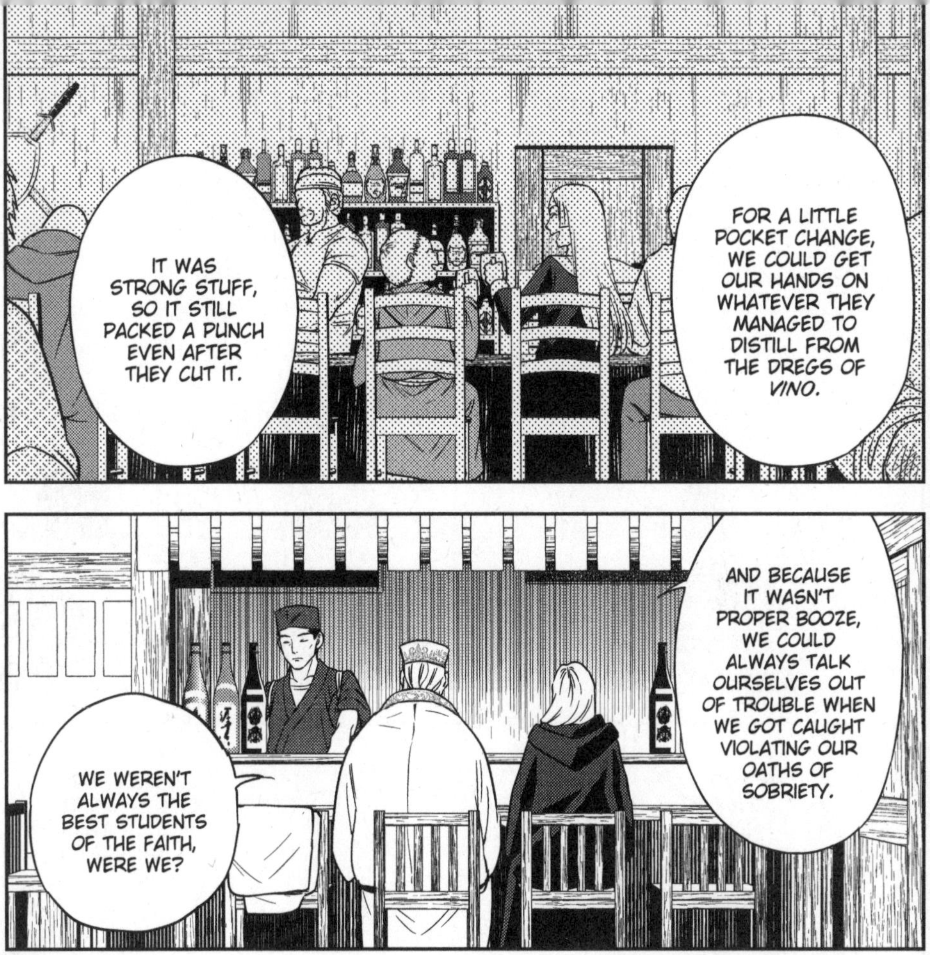
FOR A LITTLE POCKET CHANGE, WE COULD GET OUR HANDS ON WHATEVER THEY MANAGED TO DISTILL FROM THE DREGS OF *VINO*.
IT WAS STRONG STUFF, SO IT STILL PACKED A PUNCH EVEN AFTER THEY CUT IT.
AND BECAUSE IT WASN'T PROPER BOOZE, WE COULD ALWAYS TALK OURSELVES OUT OF TROUBLE WHEN WE GOT CAUGHT VIOLATING OUR OATHS OF SOBRIETY.
WE WEREN'T ALWAYS THE BEST STUDENTS OF THE FAITH, WERE WE?

*LATTE IS ITALIAN FOR MILK

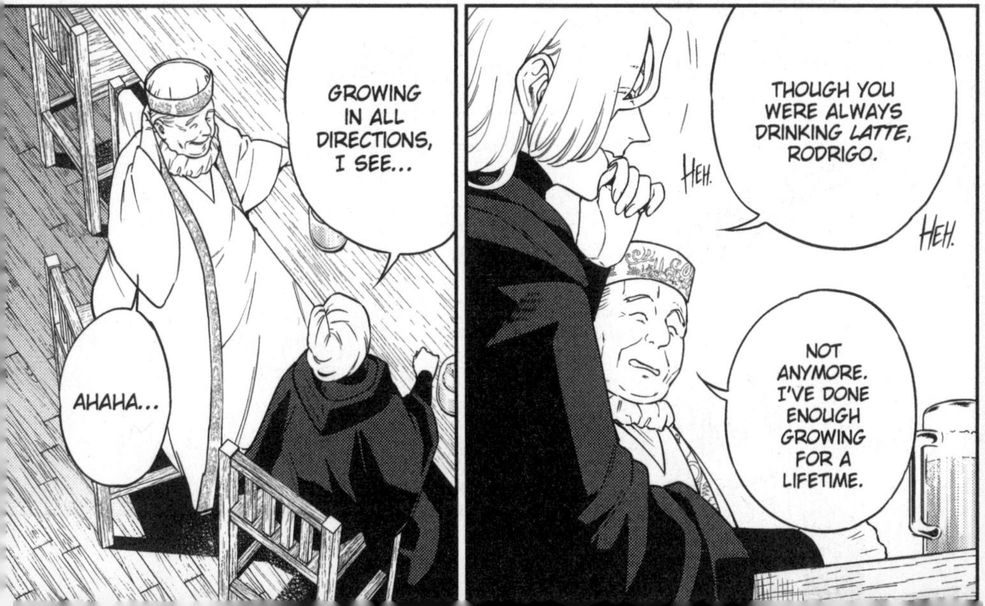
THOUGH YOU WERE ALWAYS DRINKING *LATTE*, RODRIGO.
HEH.
HEH.
NOT ANYMORE. I'VE DONE ENOUGH GROWING FOR A LIFETIME.
GROWING IN ALL DIRECTIONS, I SEE...
AHAHA...

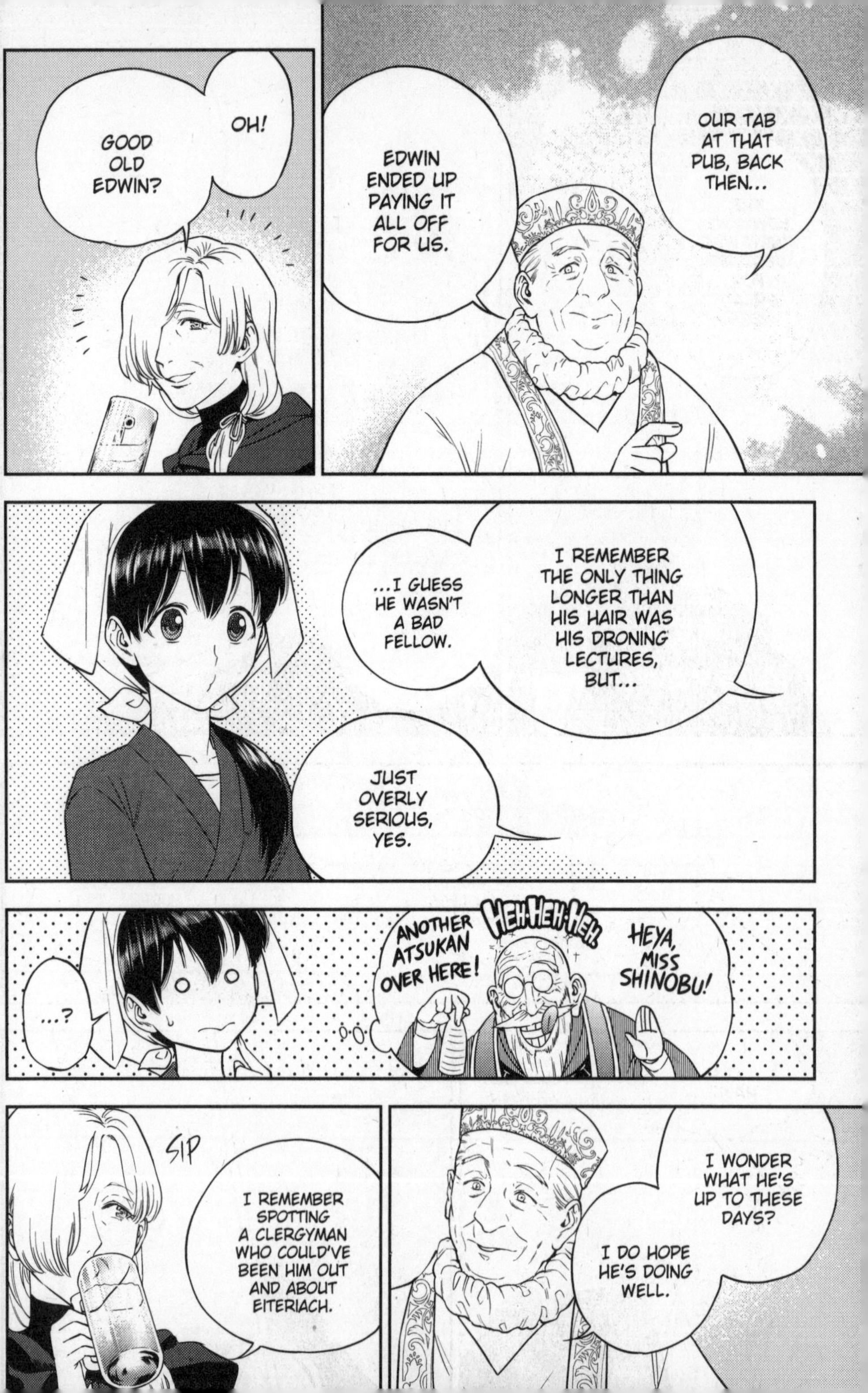
OUR TAB AT THAT PUB, BACK THEN...
EDWIN ENDED UP PAYING IT ALL OFF FOR US.
OH!
GOOD OLD EDWIN?
I REMEMBER THE ONLY THING LONGER THAN HIS HAIR WAS HIS DRONING LECTURES, BUT...
...I GUESS HE WASN'T A BAD FELLOW.
JUST OVERLY SERIOUS, YES.
HEYA, MISS SHINOBU!
HEH-HEH-HEH
ANOTHER ATSUKAN OVER HERE!
...?
I WONDER WHAT HE'S UP TO THESE DAYS?
I DO HOPE HE'S DOING WELL.
SIP
I REMEMBER SPOTTING A CLERGYMAN WHO COULD'VE BEEN HIM OUT AND ABOUT EITERIACH.

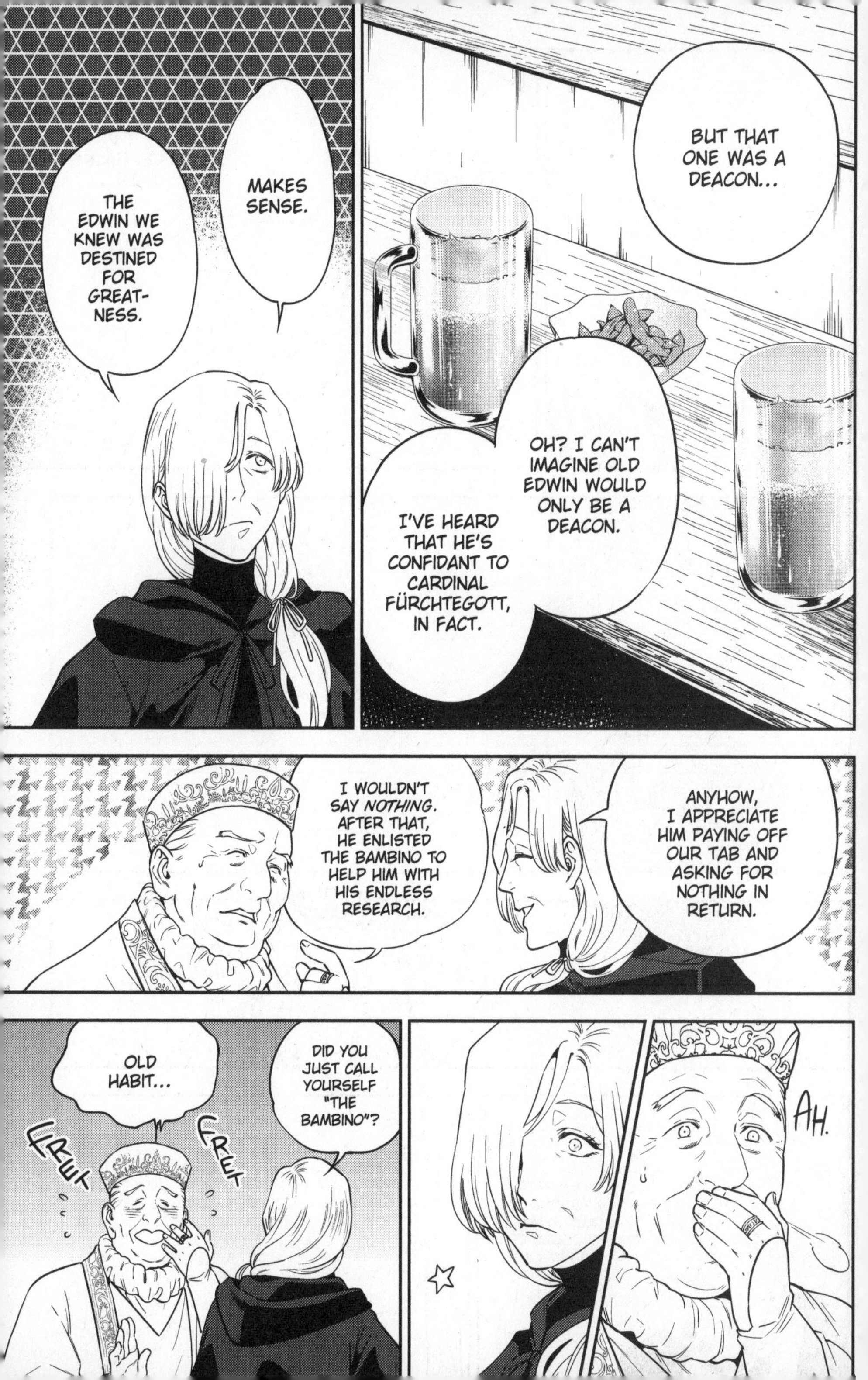
BUT THAT ONE WAS A DEACON...
OH? I CAN'T IMAGINE OLD EDWIN WOULD ONLY BE A DEACON.
I'VE HEARD THAT HE'S CONFIDANT TO CARDINAL FÜRCHTEGOTT, IN FACT.
MAKES SENSE.
THE EDWIN WE KNEW WAS DESTINED FOR GREAT-NESS.
ANYHOW, I APPRECIATE HIM PAYING OFF OUR TAB AND ASKING FOR NOTHING IN RETURN.
I WOULDN'T SAY *NOTHING*. AFTER THAT, HE ENLISTED THE BAMBINO TO HELP HIM WITH HIS ENDLESS RESEARCH.
AH.
DID YOU JUST CALL YOURSELF "THE BAMBINO"?
OLD HABIT...
FRET
FRET

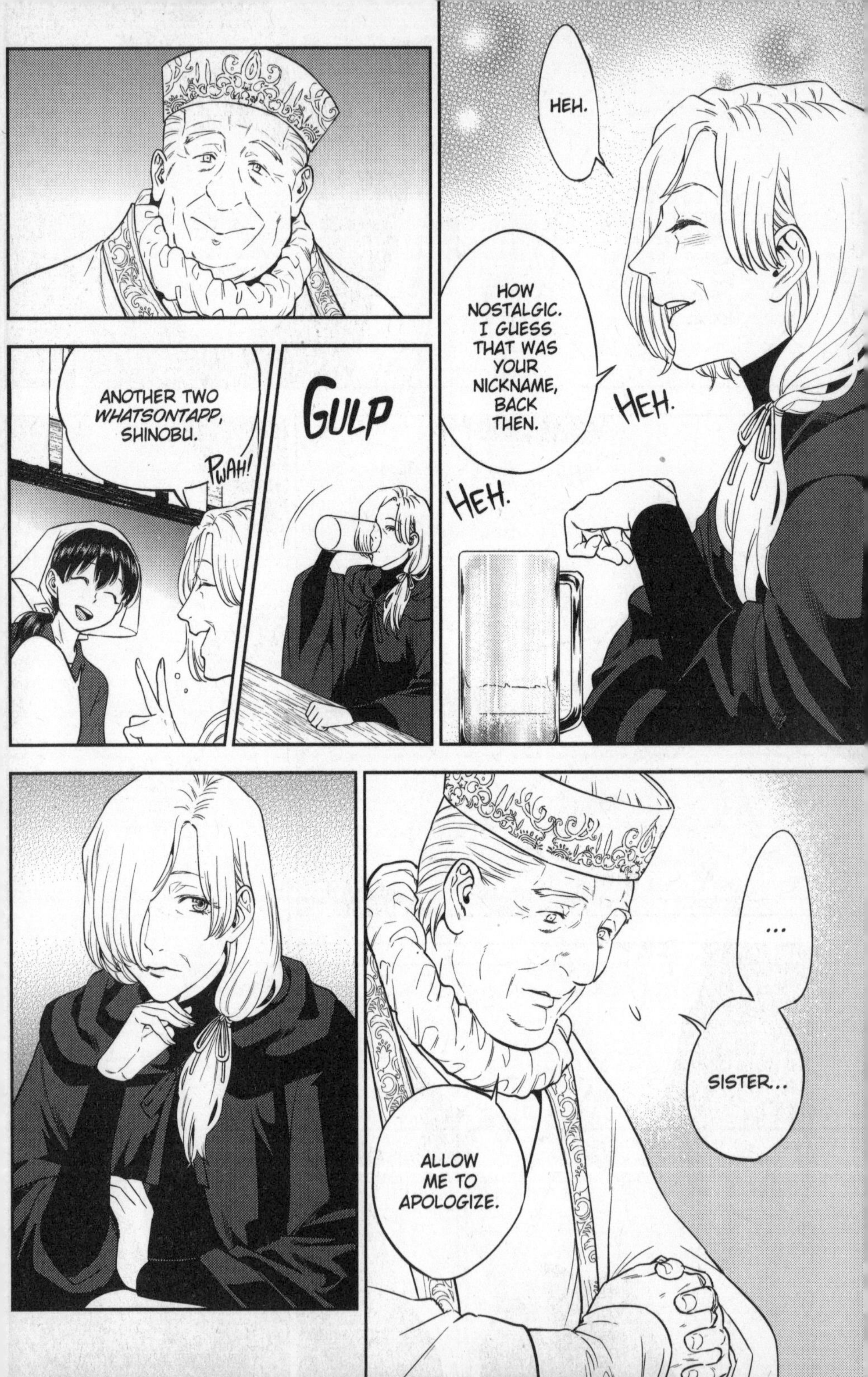
HEH.
HOW NOSTALGIC. I GUESS THAT WAS YOUR NICKNAME, BACK THEN.
HEH.
HEH.
GULP
ANOTHER TWO *WHATSONTAPP*, SHINOBU.
PWAH!
...
SISTER...
ALLOW ME TO APOLOGIZE.

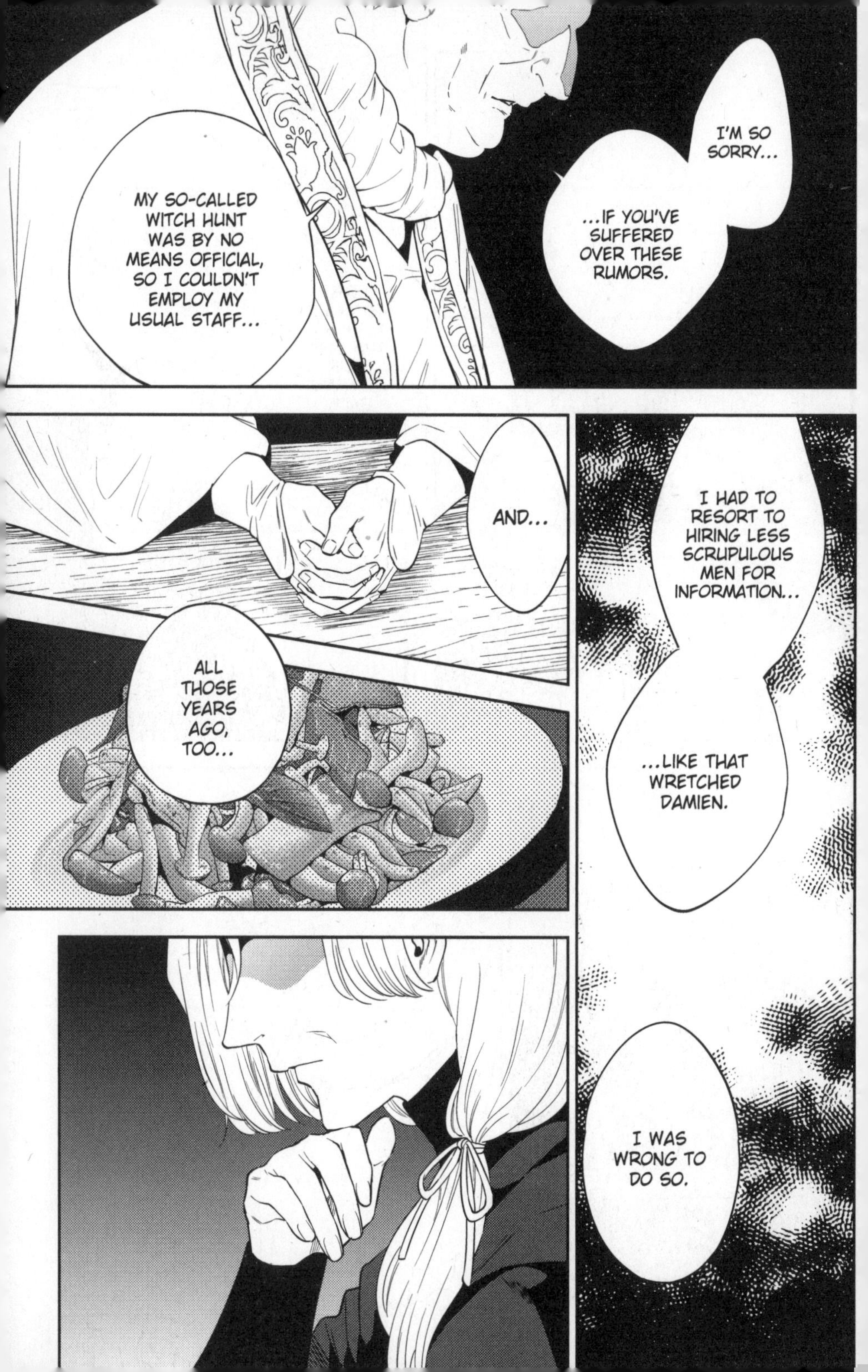
I'M SO SORRY...
...IF YOU'VE SUFFERED OVER THESE RUMORS.
MY SO-CALLED WITCH HUNT WAS BY NO MEANS OFFICIAL, SO I COULDN'T EMPLOY MY USUAL STAFF...
I HAD TO RESORT TO HIRING LESS SCRUPULOUS MEN FOR INFORMATION...
...LIKE THAT WRETCHED DAMIEN.
I WAS WRONG TO DO SO.
AND...
ALL THOSE YEARS AGO, TOO...

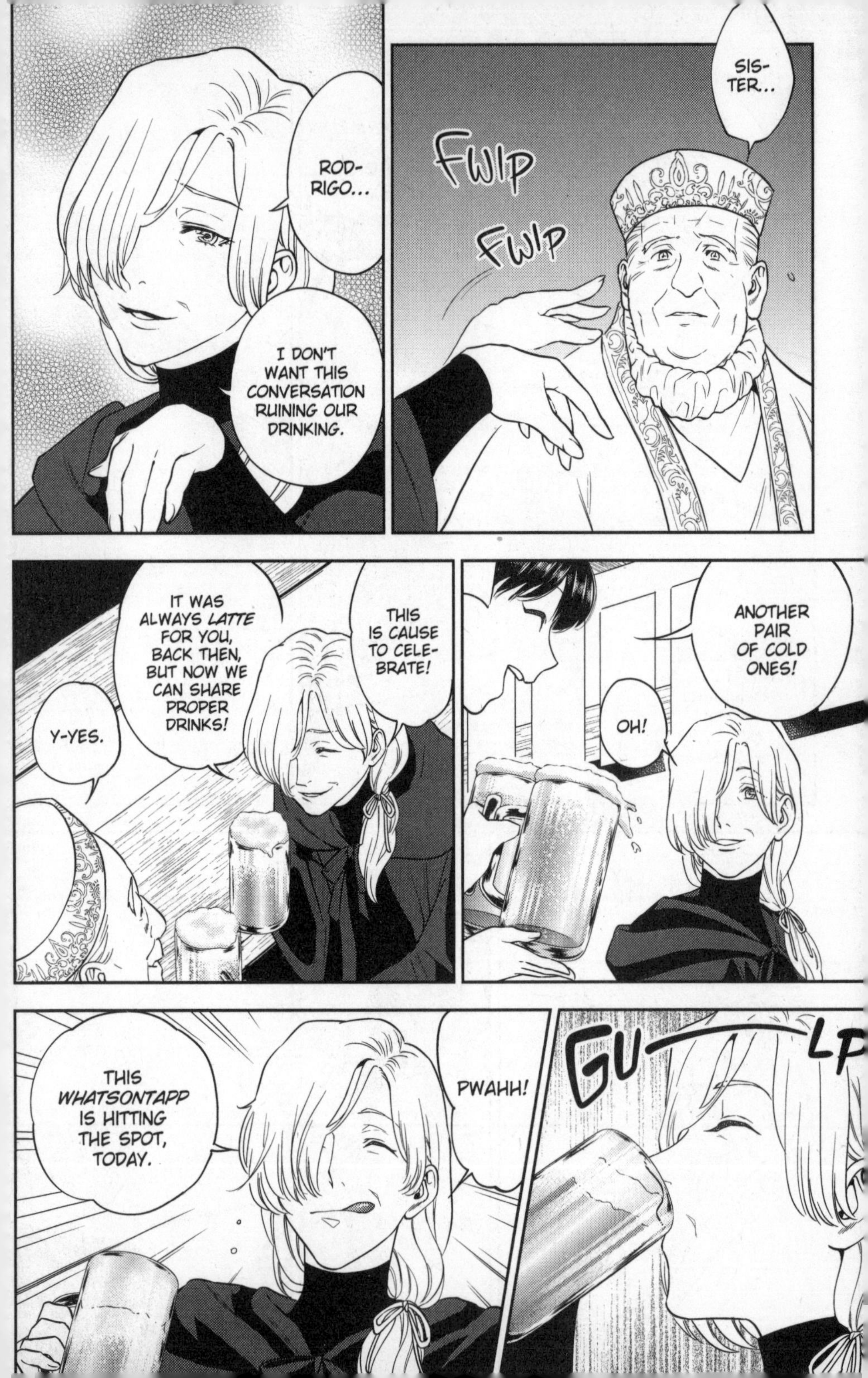
SISTER...
FWIP
FWIP
RODRIGO...
I DON'T WANT THIS CONVERSATION RUINING OUR DRINKING.
ANOTHER PAIR OF COLD ONES!
OH!
THIS IS CAUSE TO CELEBRATE!
IT WAS ALWAYS *LATTE* FOR YOU, BACK THEN, BUT NOW WE CAN SHARE PROPER DRINKS!
Y-YES.
GU—LP
PWAHH!
THIS *WHATSONTAPP* IS HITTING THE SPOT, TODAY.

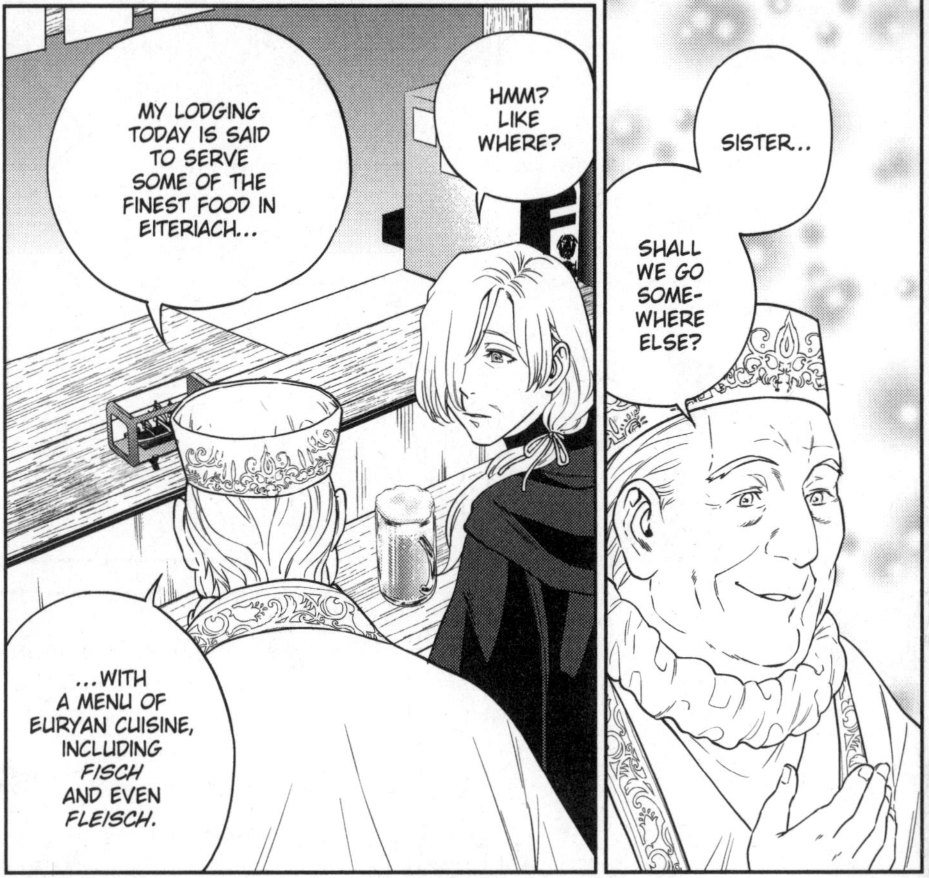
SISTER...
SHALL WE GO SOME-WHERE ELSE?
HMM? LIKE WHERE?
MY LODGING TODAY IS SAID TO SERVE SOME OF THE FINEST FOOD IN EITERIACH...
...WITH A MENU OF EURYAN CUISINE, INCLUDING *FISCH* AND EVEN *FLEISCH*.

*GERMAN FOR FISH AND MEAT, RESPECTIVELY

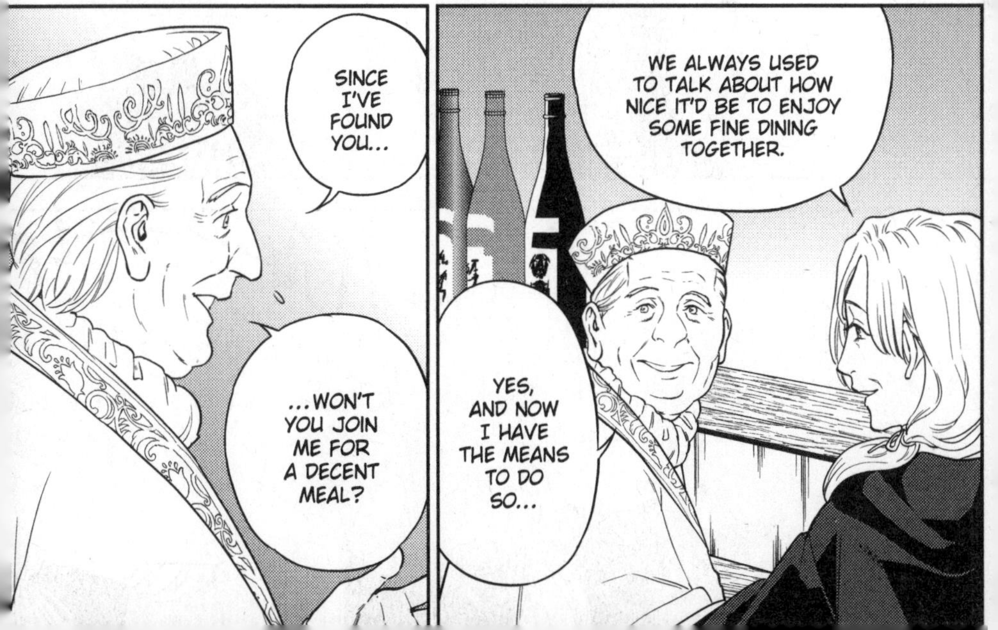
WE ALWAYS USED TO TALK ABOUT HOW NICE IT'D BE TO ENJOY SOME FINE DINING TOGETHER.
YES, AND NOW I HAVE THE MEANS TO DO SO...
SINCE I'VE FOUND YOU...
...WON'T YOU JOIN ME FOR A DECENT MEAL?

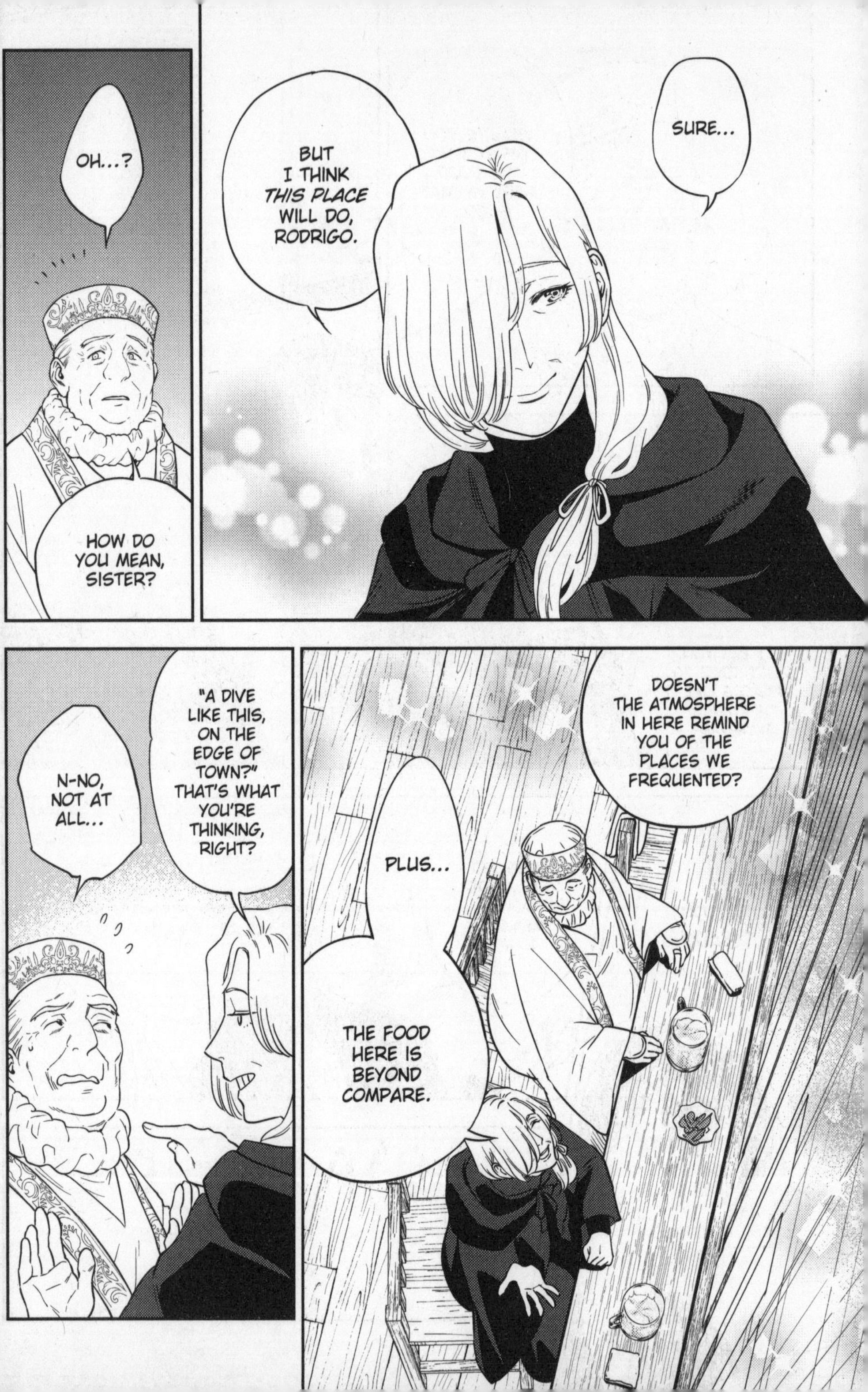
SURE...
BUT I THINK *THIS PLACE* WILL DO, RODRIGO.
OH...?
HOW DO YOU MEAN, SISTER?
DOESN'T THE ATMOSPHERE IN HERE REMIND YOU OF THE PLACES WE FREQUENTED?
PLUS...
THE FOOD HERE IS BEYOND COMPARE.
"A DIVE LIKE THIS, ON THE EDGE OF TOWN?" THAT'S WHAT YOU'RE THINKING, RIGHT?
N-NO, NOT AT ALL...

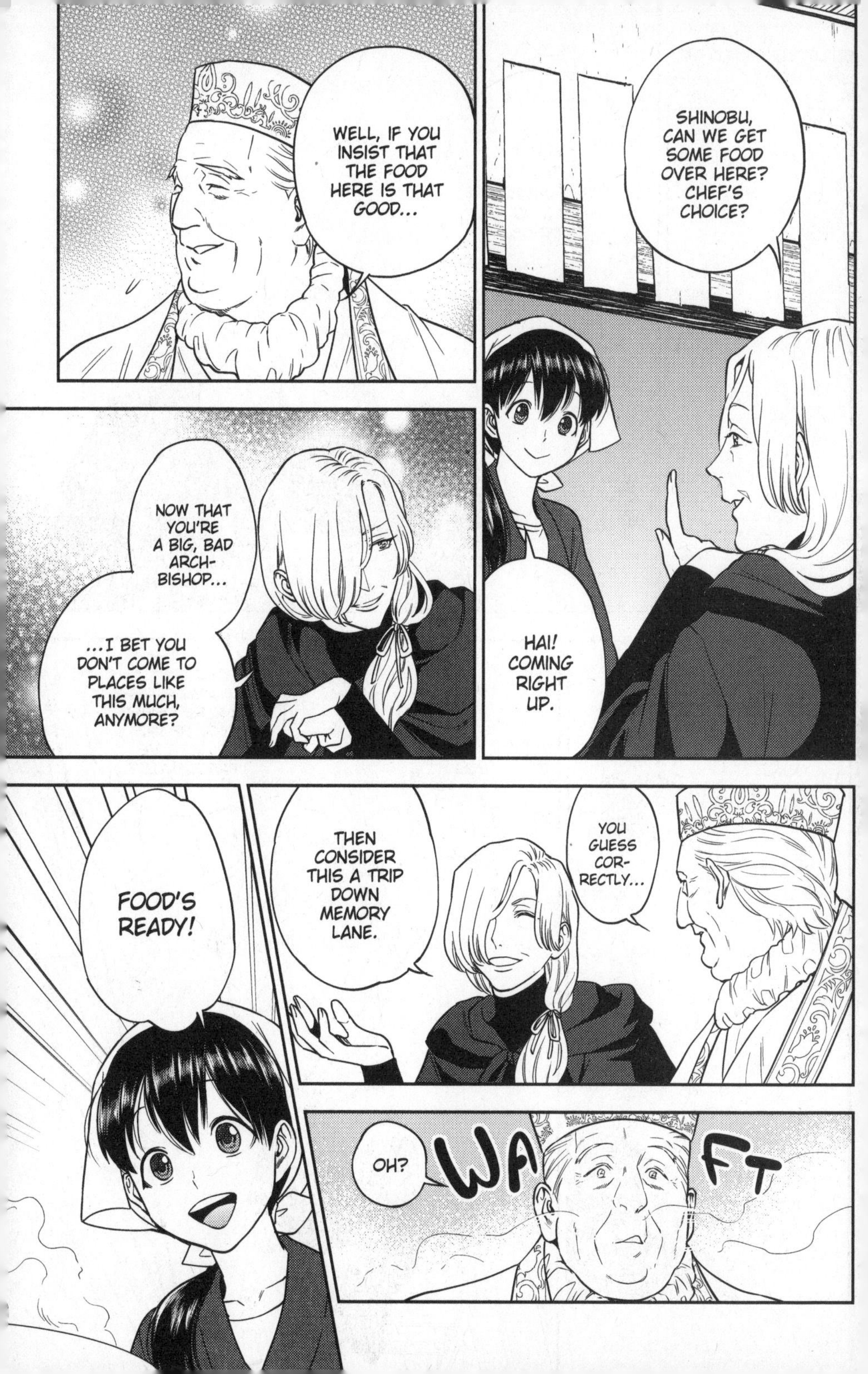
SHINOBU, CAN WE GET SOME FOOD OVER HERE? CHEF'S CHOICE?
HAI! COMING RIGHT UP.
WELL, IF YOU INSIST THAT THE FOOD HERE IS THAT GOOD...
NOW THAT YOU'RE A BIG, BAD ARCH-BISHOP...
...I BET YOU DON'T COME TO PLACES LIKE THIS MUCH, ANYMORE?
YOU GUESS COR-RECTLY...
THEN CONSIDER THIS A TRIP DOWN MEMORY LANE.
FOOD'S READY!
OH?
WAFT

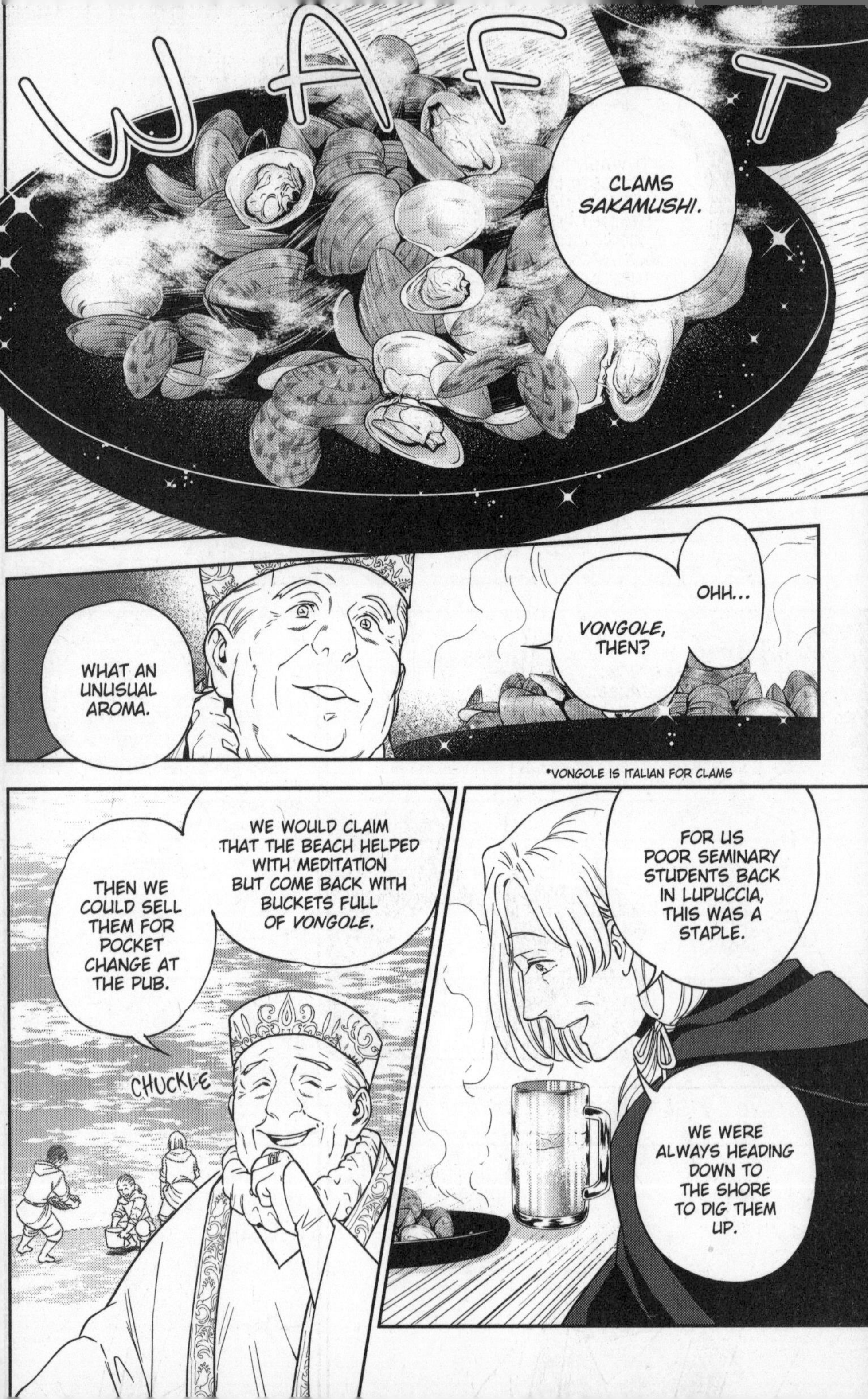
WAFT
CLAMS SAKAMUSHI.
OHH...
VONGOLE, THEN?
WHAT AN UNUSUAL AROMA.
FOR US POOR SEMINARY STUDENTS BACK IN LUPUCCIA, THIS WAS A STAPLE.
WE WERE ALWAYS HEADING DOWN TO THE SHORE TO DIG THEM UP.
WE WOULD CLAIM THAT THE BEACH HELPED WITH MEDITATION BUT COME BACK WITH BUCKETS FULL OF *VONGOLE*.
THEN WE COULD SELL THEM FOR POCKET CHANGE AT THE PUB.
CHUCKLE

*VONGOLE IS ITALIAN FOR CLAMS

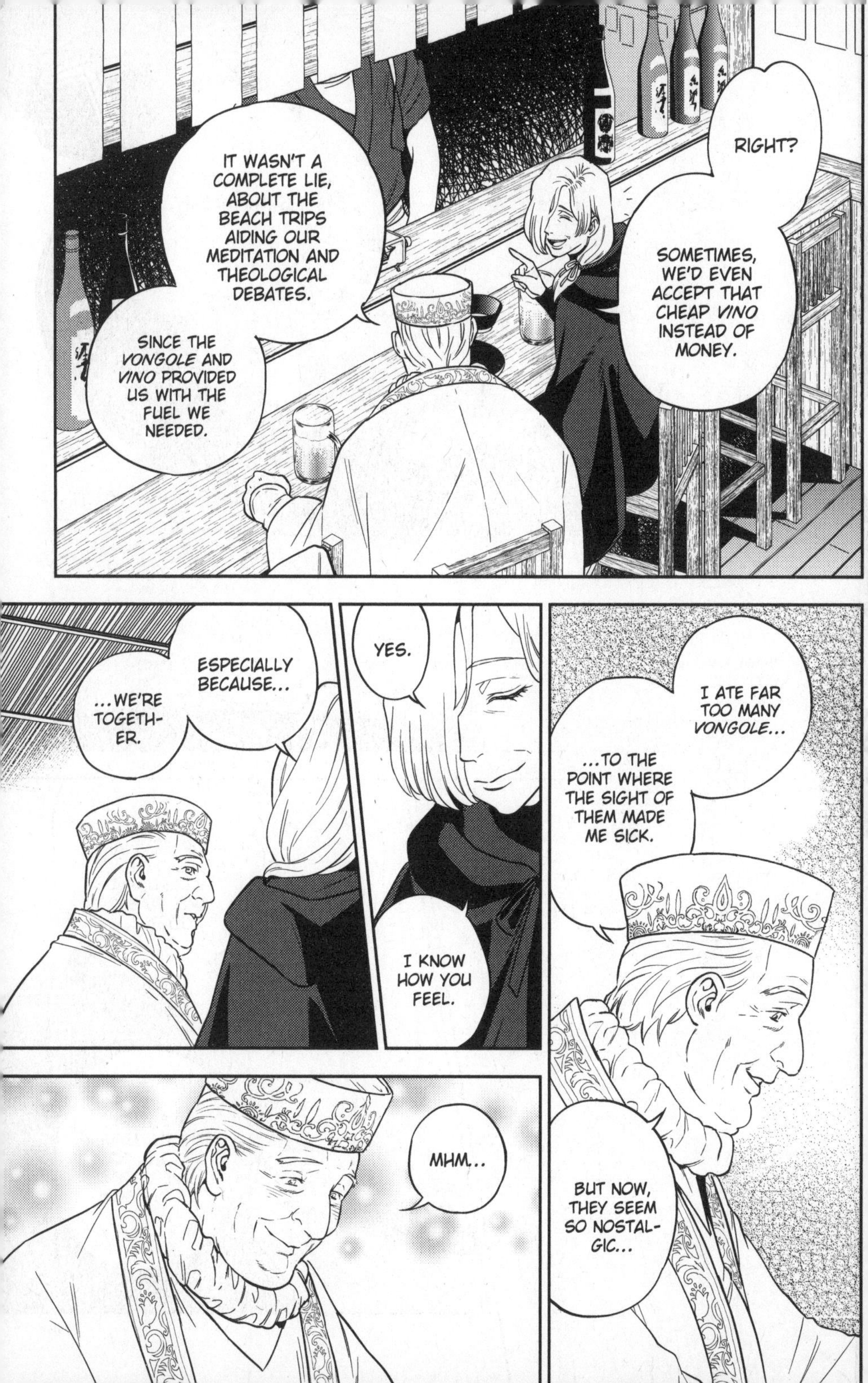
RIGHT?
SOMETIMES, WE'D EVEN ACCEPT THAT CHEAP *VINO* INSTEAD OF MONEY.
IT WASN'T A COMPLETE LIE, ABOUT THE BEACH TRIPS AIDING OUR MEDITATION AND THEOLOGICAL DEBATES.
SINCE THE *VONGOLE* AND *VINO* PROVIDED US WITH THE FUEL WE NEEDED.
I ATE FAR TOO MANY *VONGOLE*...
...TO THE POINT WHERE THE SIGHT OF THEM MADE ME SICK.
BUT NOW, THEY SEEM SO NOSTAL-GIC...
YES.
I KNOW HOW YOU FEEL.
ESPECIALLY BECAUSE...
...WE'RE TOGETH-ER.
MHM...

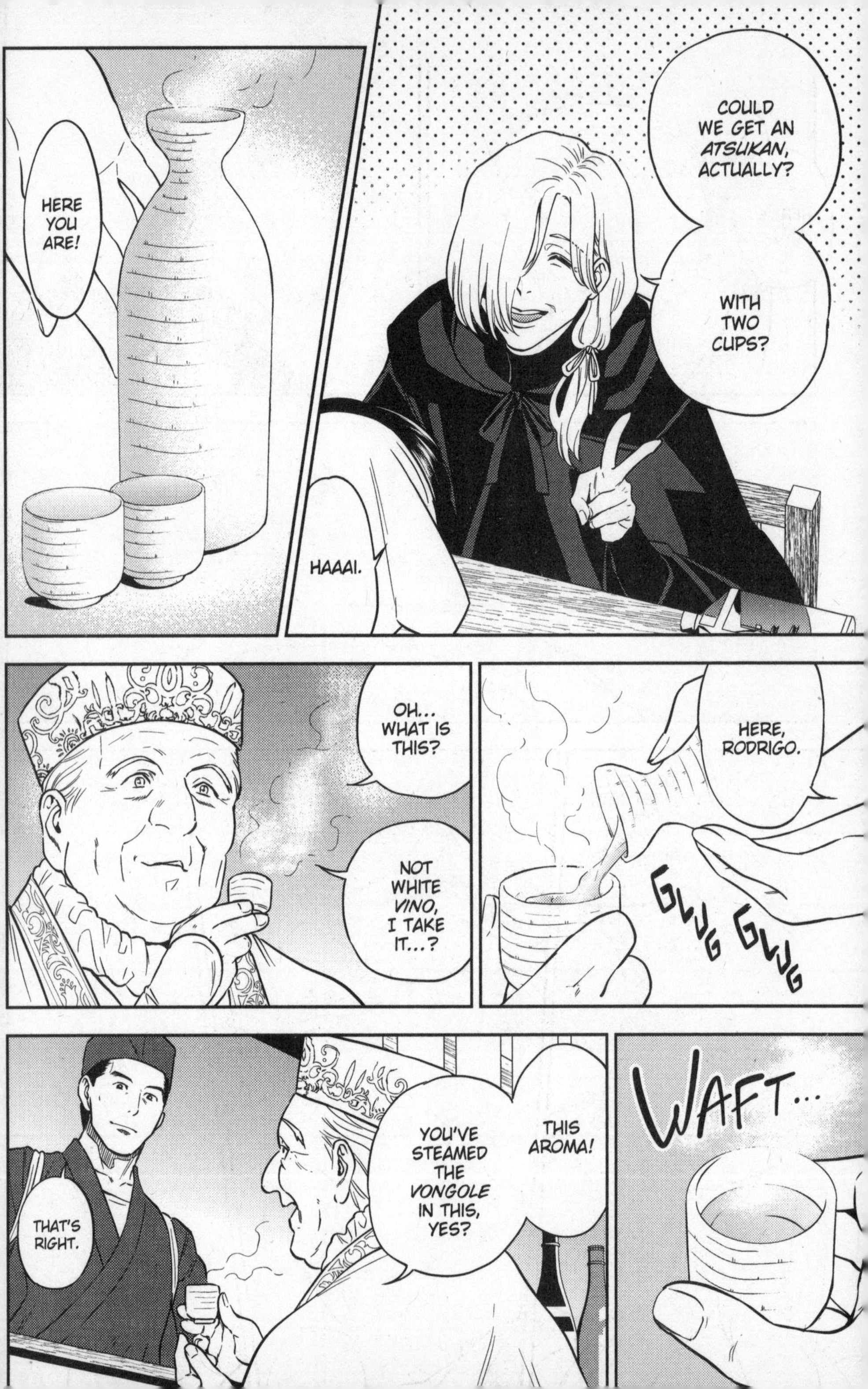
COULD WE GET AN *ATSUKAN*, ACTUALLY?
WITH TWO CUPS?
HAAAI.
HERE YOU ARE!
HERE, RODRIGO.
GLUG GLUG
OH... WHAT IS THIS?
NOT WHITE *VINO*, I TAKE IT...?
WAFT...
THIS AROMA!
YOU'VE STEAMED THE *VONGOLE* IN THIS, YES?
THAT'S RIGHT.

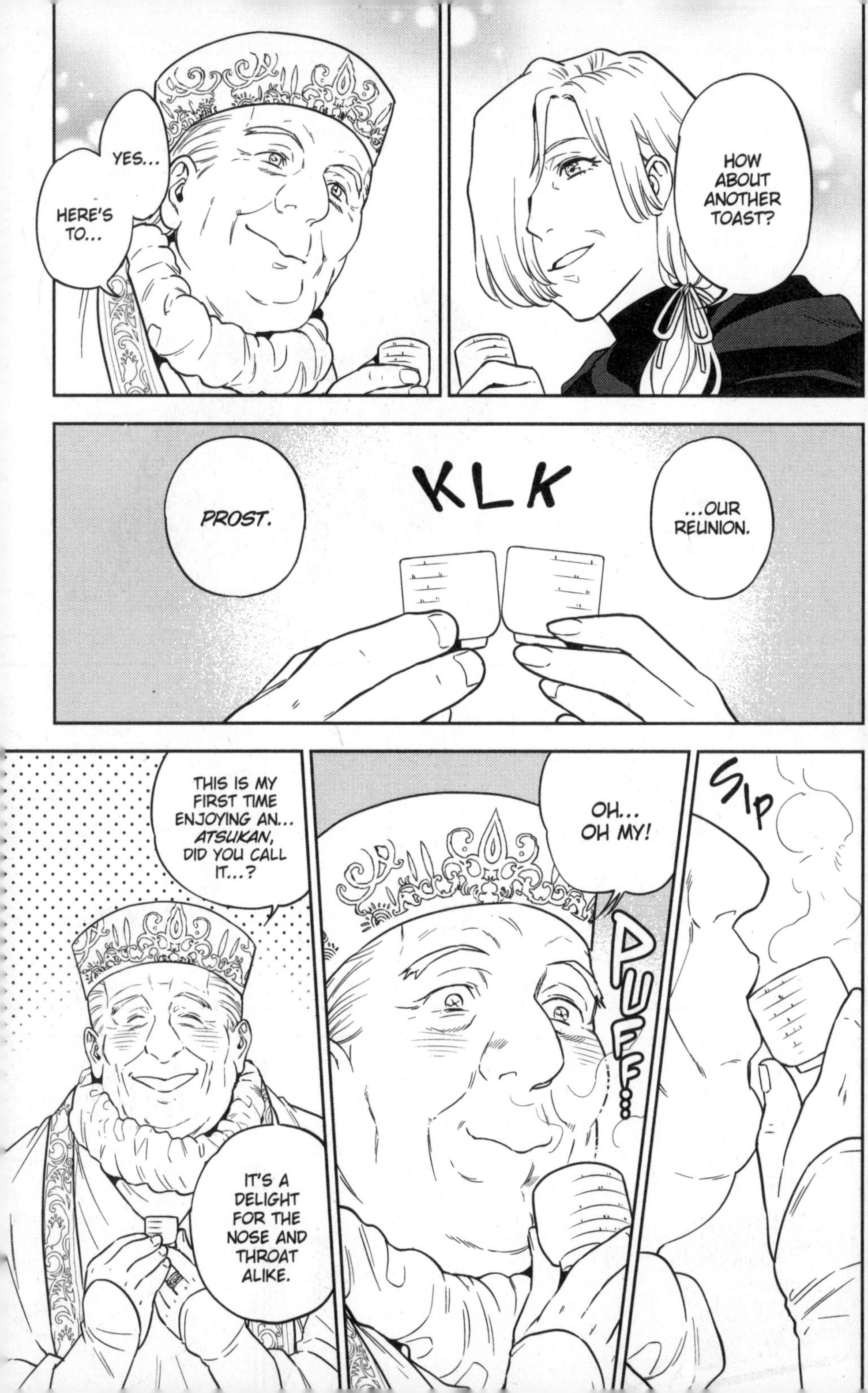
HOW ABOUT ANOTHER TOAST?
YES...
HERE'S TO...
...OUR REUNION.
KLK
PROST.
SIp
OH... OH MY!
PUFF...
THIS IS MY FIRST TIME ENJOYING AN... ATSUKAN, DID YOU CALL IT...?
IT'S A DELIGHT FOR THE NOSE AND THROAT ALIKE.

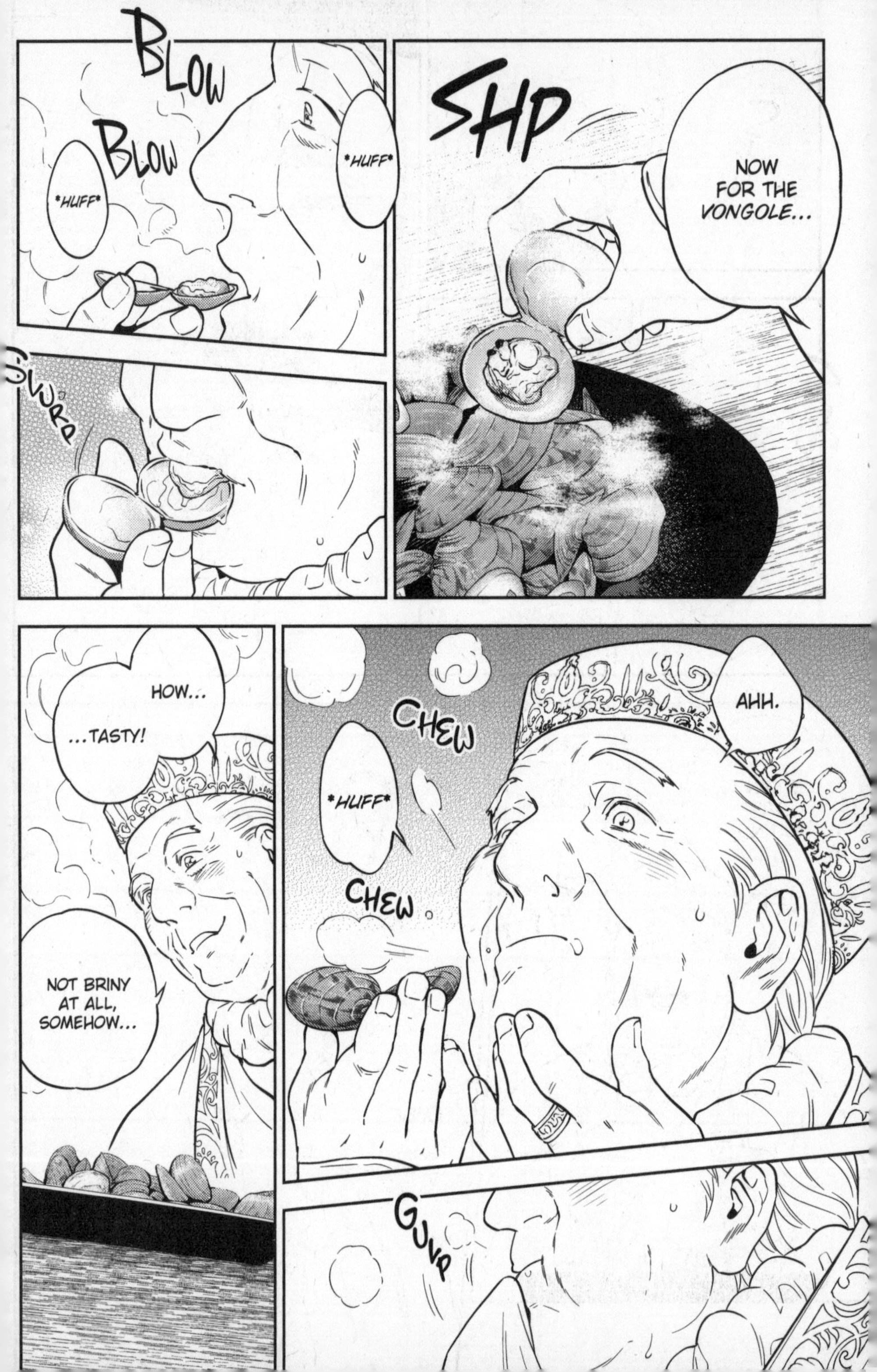
SHP
NOW FOR THE VONGOLE...
HUFF
BLOW
BLOW
HUFF
GLURP
AHH.
CHEW
HUFF
CHEW
GULP
HOW...
...TASTY!
NOT BRINY AT ALL, SOMEHOW...

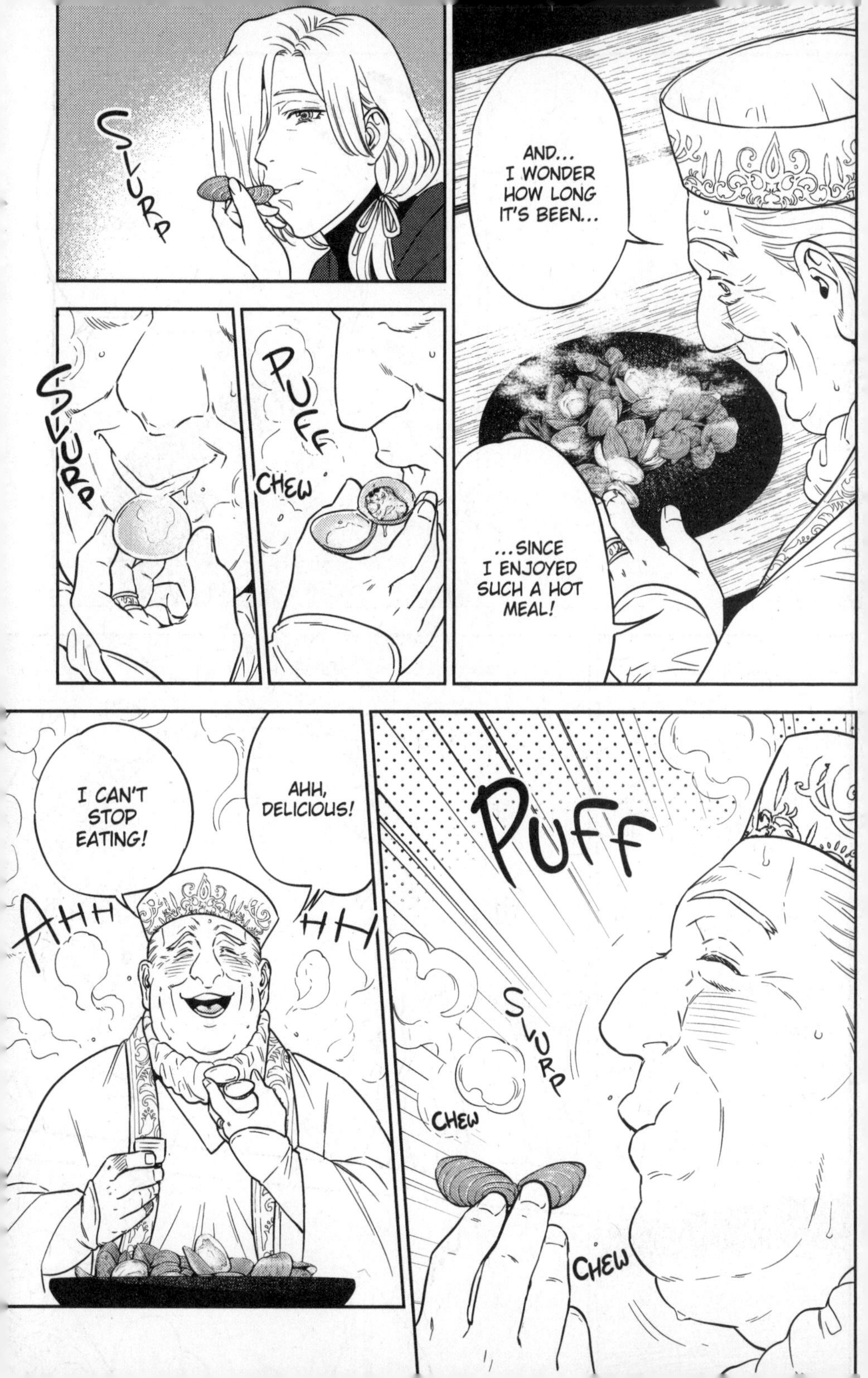
AND... I WONDER HOW LONG IT'S BEEN...
...SINCE I ENJOYED SUCH A HOT MEAL!
SLURP
PUFF
CHEW
SLURP
PUFF
SLURP
CHEW
CHEW
AHH, DELICIOUS!
HH
I CAN'T STOP EATING!
AHH

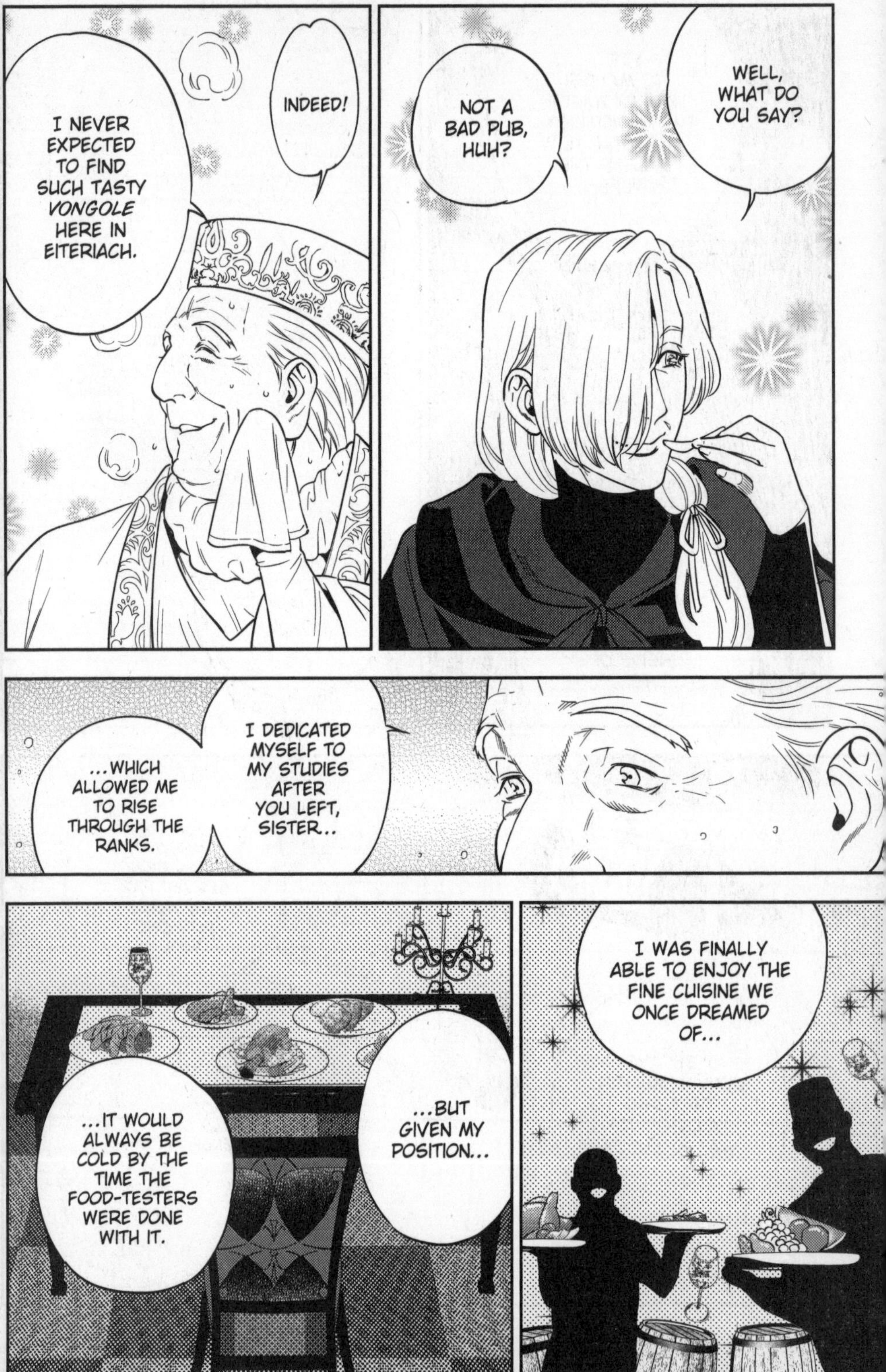
WELL, WHAT DO YOU SAY?
NOT A BAD PUB, HUH?
INDEED!
I NEVER EXPECTED TO FIND SUCH TASTY *VONGOLE* HERE IN EITERIACH.
I DEDICATED MYSELF TO MY STUDIES AFTER YOU LEFT, SISTER...
...WHICH ALLOWED ME TO RISE THROUGH THE RANKS.
I WAS FINALLY ABLE TO ENJOY THE FINE CUISINE WE ONCE DREAMED OF...
...BUT GIVEN MY POSITION...
...IT WOULD ALWAYS BE COLD BY THE TIME THE FOOD-TESTERS WERE DONE WITH IT.

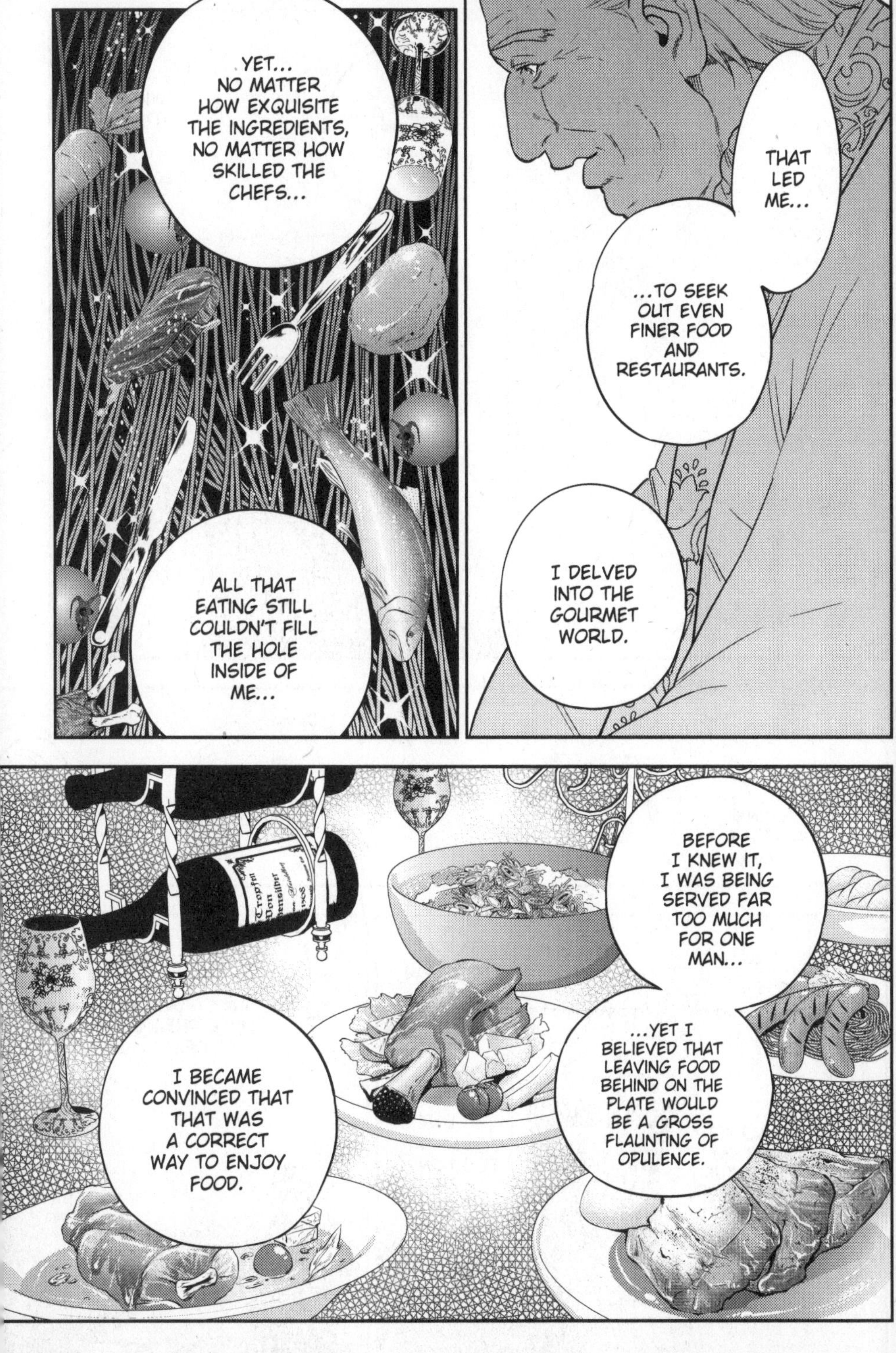

THAT LED ME...
...TO SEEK OUT EVEN FINER FOOD AND RESTAURANTS.
I DELVED INTO THE GOURMET WORLD.
YET... NO MATTER HOW EXQUISITE THE INGREDIENTS, NO MATTER HOW SKILLED THE CHEFS...
ALL THAT EATING STILL COULDN'T FILL THE HOLE INSIDE OF ME...
BEFORE I KNEW IT, I WAS BEING SERVED FAR TOO MUCH FOR ONE MAN...
...YET I BELIEVED THAT LEAVING FOOD BEHIND ON THE PLATE WOULD BE A GROSS FLAUNTING OF OPULENCE.
I BECAME CONVINCED THAT THAT WAS A CORRECT WAY TO ENJOY FOOD.

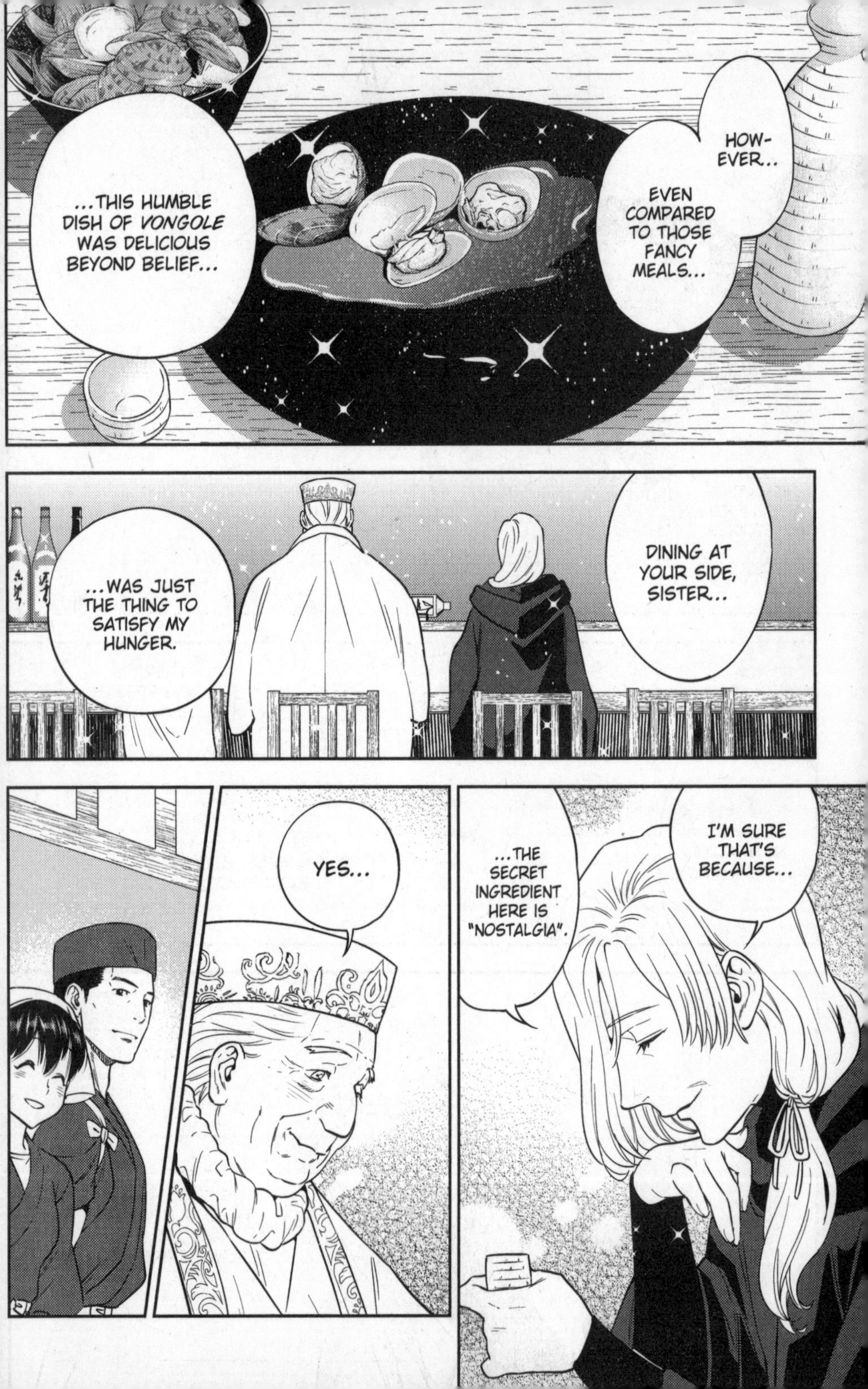
HOW-EVER...
EVEN COMPARED TO THOSE FANCY MEALS...
...THIS HUMBLE DISH OF *VONGOLE* WAS DELICIOUS BEYOND BELIEF...
DINING AT YOUR SIDE, SISTER...
...WAS JUST THE THING TO SATISFY MY HUNGER.
I'M SURE THAT'S BECAUSE...
...THE SECRET INGREDIENT HERE IS "NOSTALGIA".
YES...

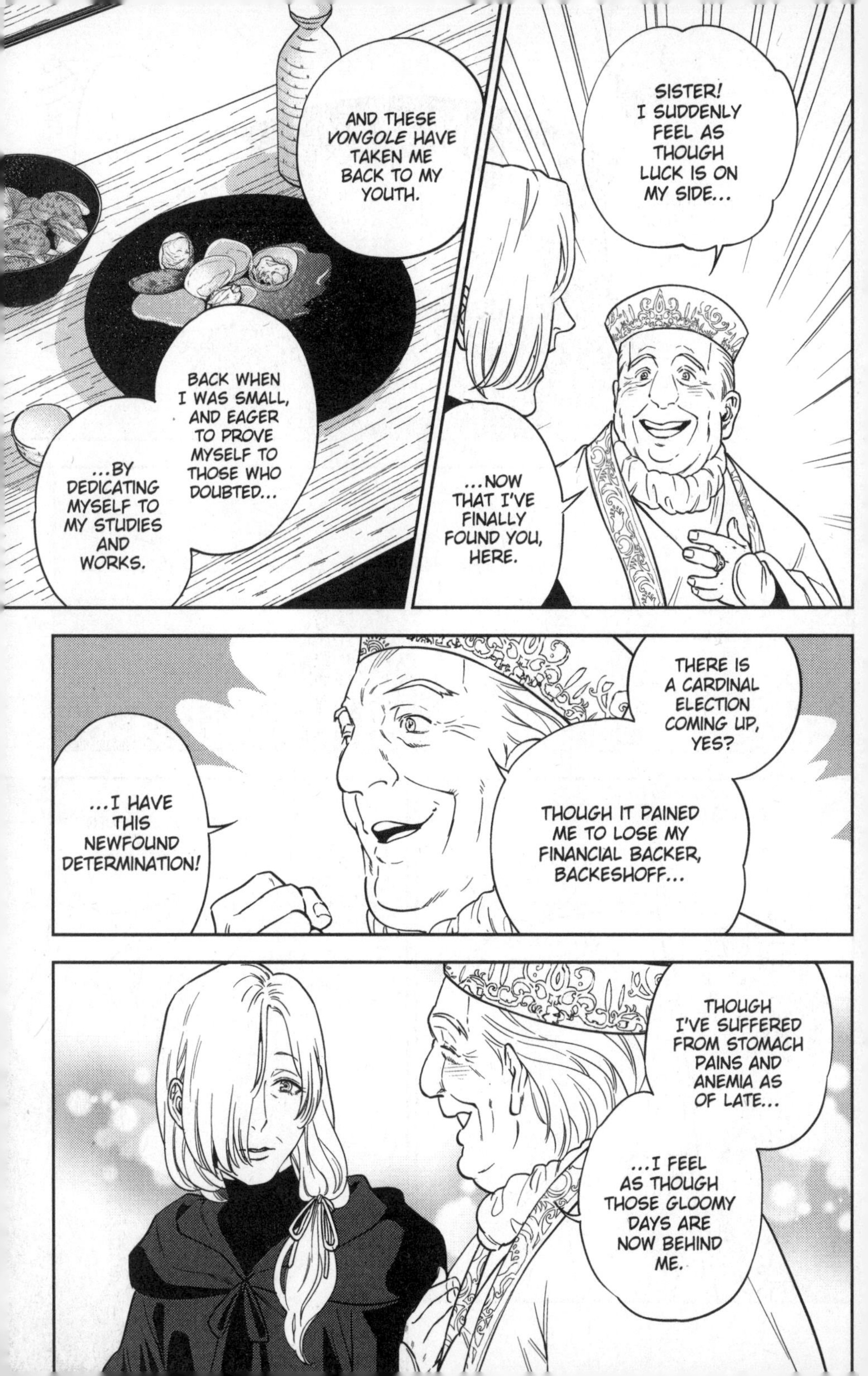
SISTER! I SUDDENLY FEEL AS THOUGH LUCK IS ON MY SIDE...
...NOW THAT I'VE FINALLY FOUND YOU, HERE.
AND THESE *VONGOLE* HAVE TAKEN ME BACK TO MY YOUTH.
BACK WHEN I WAS SMALL, AND EAGER TO PROVE MYSELF TO THOSE WHO DOUBTED...
...BY DEDICATING MYSELF TO MY STUDIES AND WORKS.
THERE IS A CARDINAL ELECTION COMING UP, YES?
THOUGH IT PAINED ME TO LOSE MY FINANCIAL BACKER, BACKESHOFF...
...I HAVE THIS NEWFOUND DETERMINATION!
THOUGH I'VE SUFFERED FROM STOMACH PAINS AND ANEMIA AS OF LATE...
...I FEEL AS THOUGH THOSE GLOOMY DAYS ARE NOW BEHIND ME.

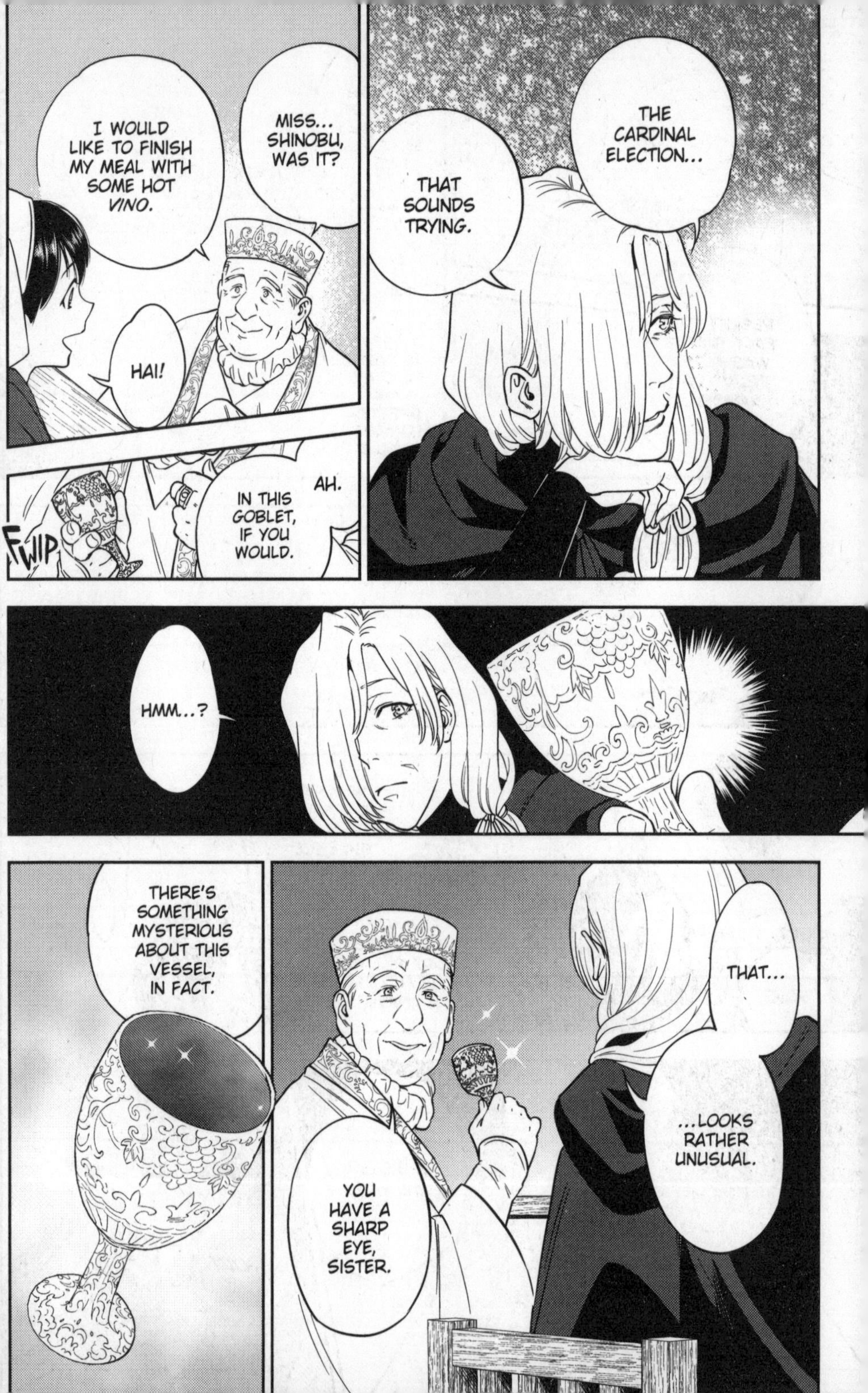
THE CARDINAL ELECTION...
THAT SOUNDS TRYING.
MISS... SHINOBU, WAS IT?
I WOULD LIKE TO FINISH MY MEAL WITH SOME HOT *VINO*.
HAI!
AH.
IN THIS GOBLET, IF YOU WOULD.
FWIP
HMM...?
THAT...
...LOOKS RATHER UNUSUAL.
YOU HAVE A SHARP EYE, SISTER.
THERE'S SOMETHING MYSTERIOUS ABOUT THIS VESSEL, IN FACT.

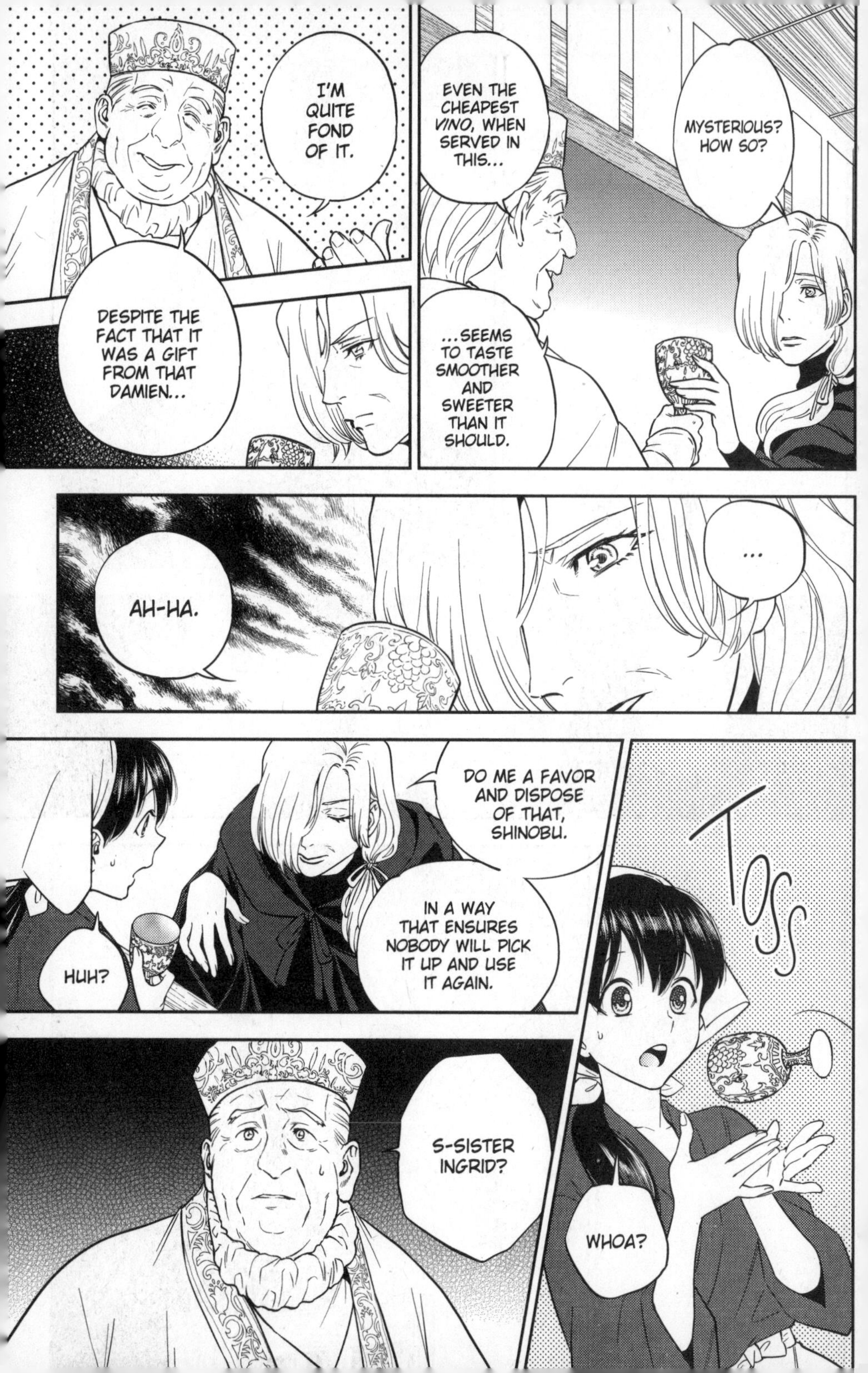
MYSTERIOUS? HOW SO?
EVEN THE CHEAPEST *VINO*, WHEN SERVED IN THIS...
...SEEMS TO TASTE SMOOTHER AND SWEETER THAN IT SHOULD.
I'M QUITE FOND OF IT.
DESPITE THE FACT THAT IT WAS A GIFT FROM THAT DAMIEN...
...
AH-HA.
TOSS
...
WHOA?
DO ME A FAVOR AND DISPOSE OF THAT, SHINOBU.
IN A WAY THAT ENSURES NOBODY WILL PICK IT UP AND USE IT AGAIN.
HUH?
S-SISTER INGRID?

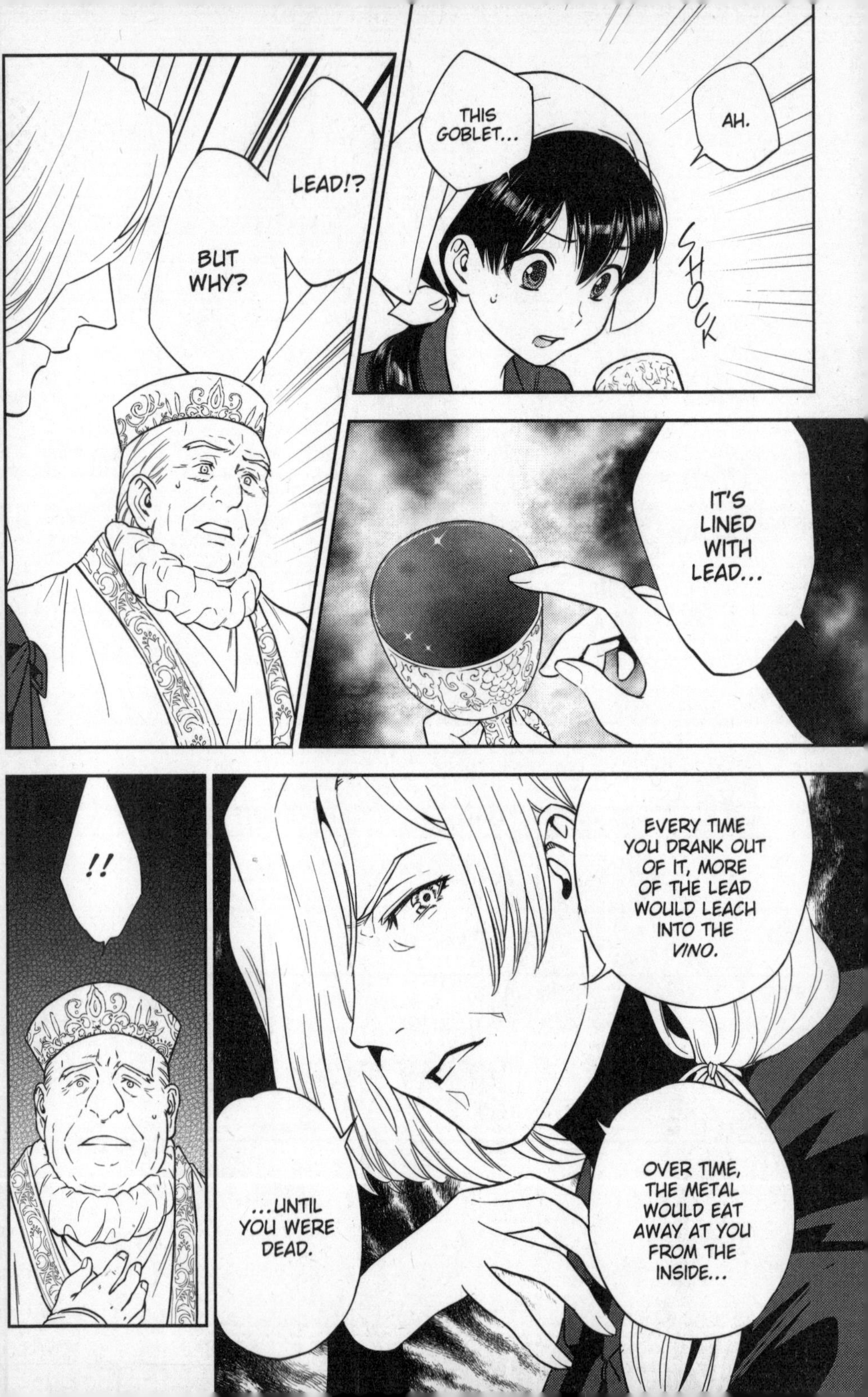
AH.
SHOCK
THIS GOBLET...
IT'S LINED WITH LEAD...
LEAD!?
BUT WHY?
EVERY TIME YOU DRANK OUT OF IT, MORE OF THE LEAD WOULD LEACH INTO THE *VINO*.
OVER TIME, THE METAL WOULD EAT AWAY AT YOU FROM THE INSIDE...
...UNTIL YOU WERE DEAD.
!!

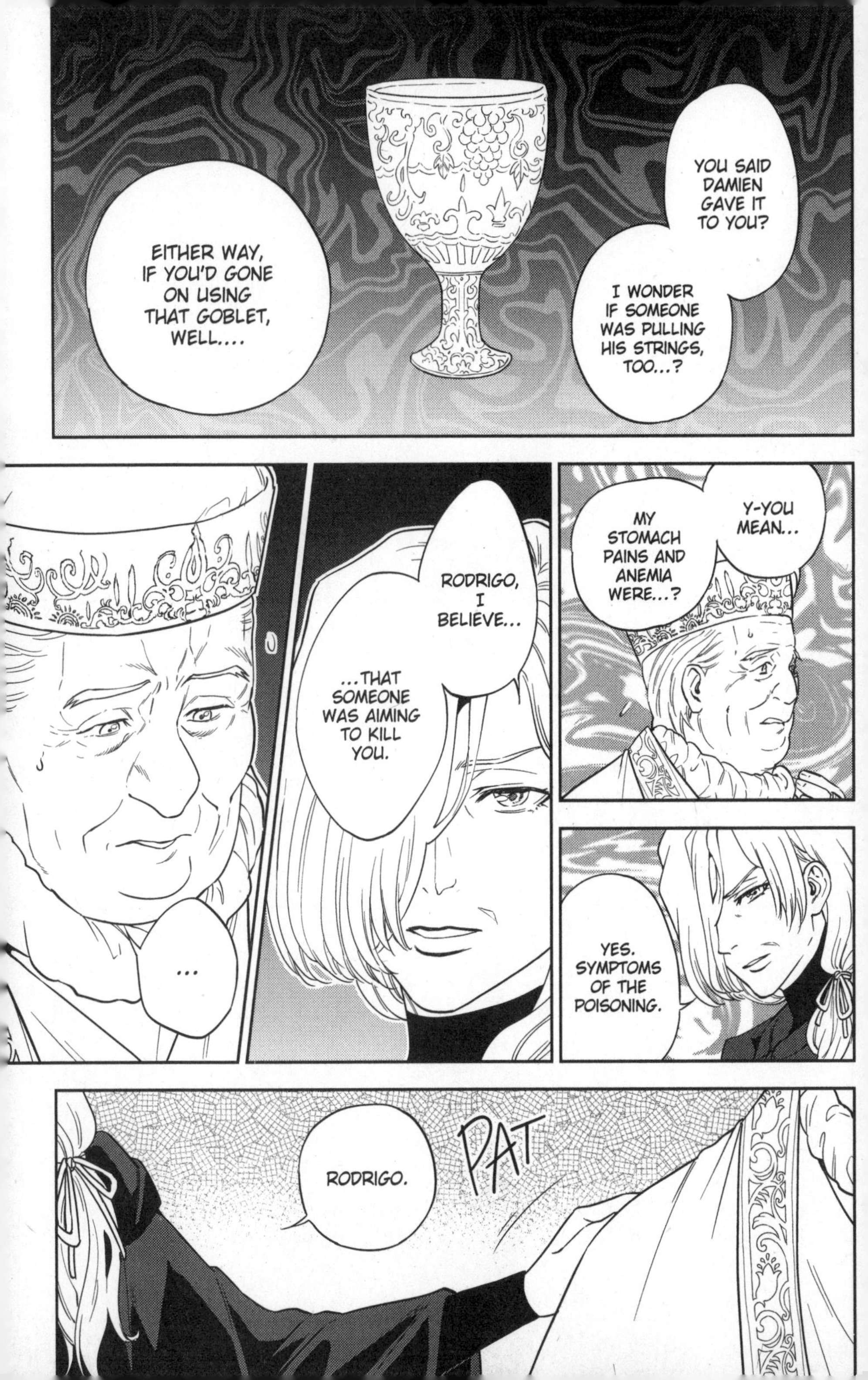
YOU SAID DAMIEN GAVE IT TO YOU?
I WONDER IF SOMEONE WAS PULLING HIS STRINGS, TOO...?
EITHER WAY, IF YOU'D GONE ON USING THAT GOBLET, WELL....
Y-YOU MEAN...
MY STOMACH PAINS AND ANEMIA WERE...?
YES. SYMPTOMS OF THE POISONING.
RODRIGO, I BELIEVE...
...THAT SOMEONE WAS AIMING TO KILL YOU.
...
PAT
RODRIGO.

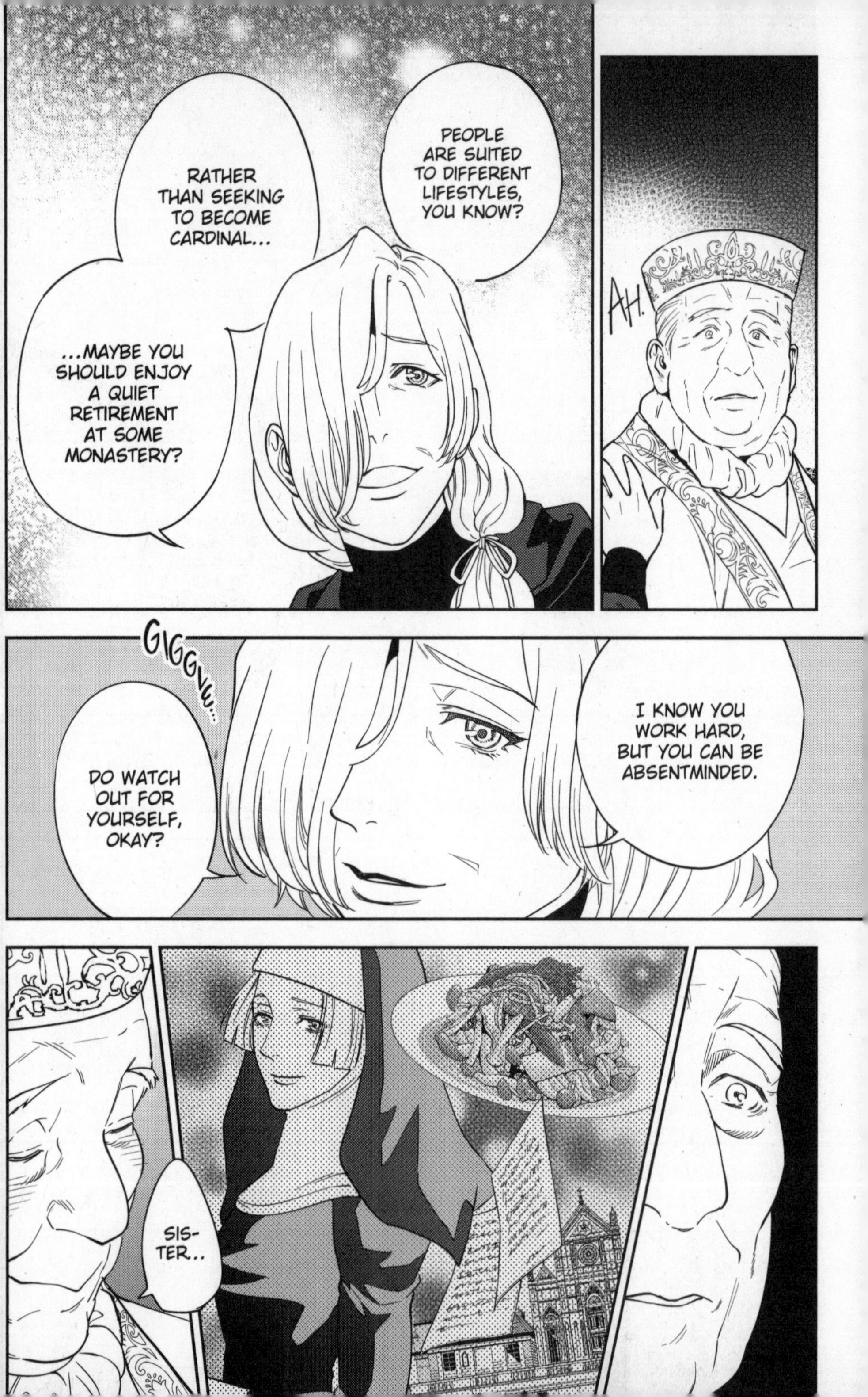
AH!
PEOPLE ARE SUITED TO DIFFERENT LIFESTYLES, YOU KNOW?
RATHER THAN SEEKING TO BECOME CARDINAL...
...MAYBE YOU SHOULD ENJOY A QUIET RETIREMENT AT SOME MONASTERY?
I KNOW YOU WORK HARD, BUT YOU CAN BE ABSENTMINDED.
GIGGLE...
DO WATCH OUT FOR YOURSELF, OKAY?
SIS- TER..

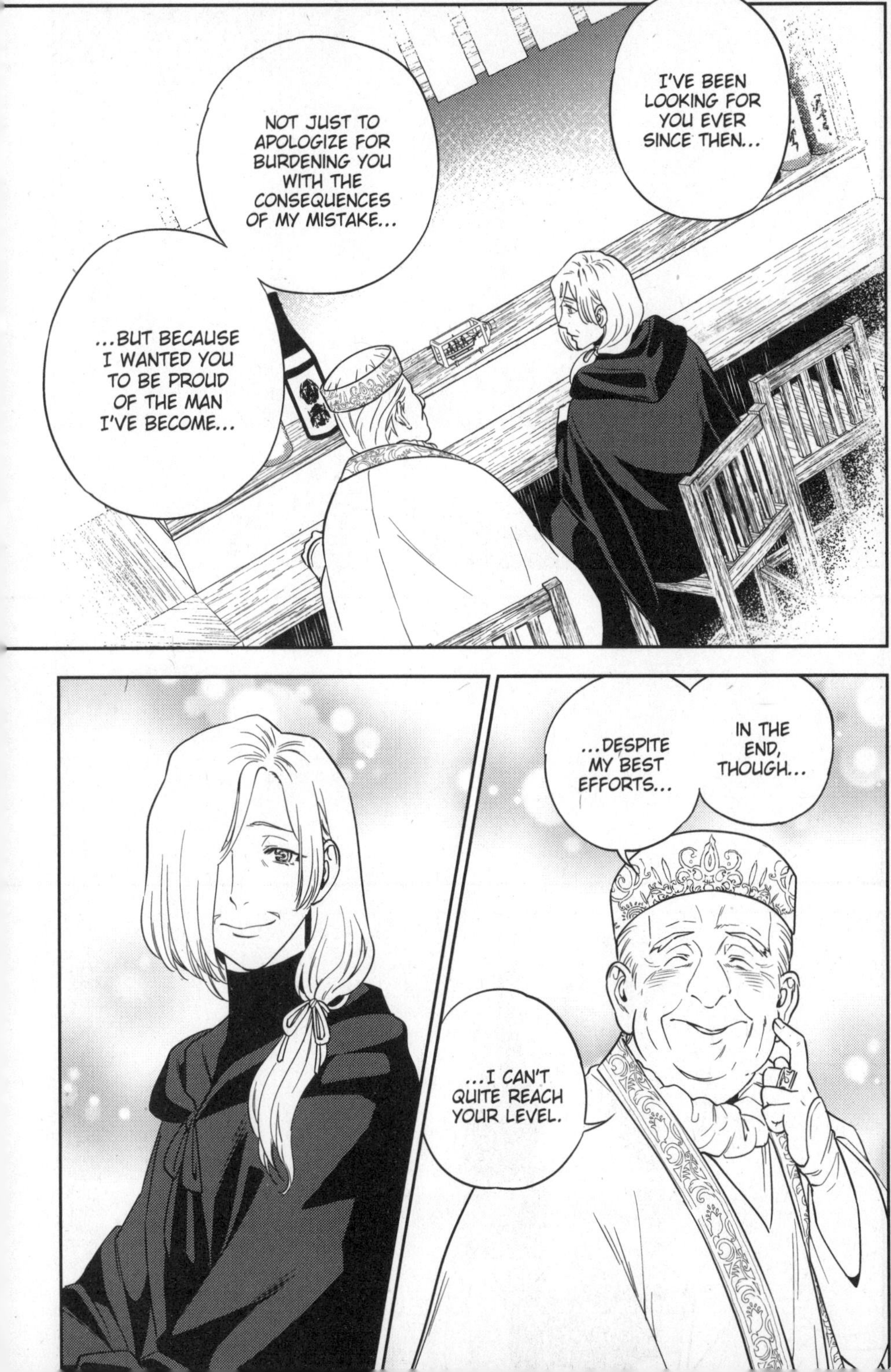
I'VE BEEN LOOKING FOR YOU EVER SINCE THEN...
NOT JUST TO APOLOGIZE FOR BURDENING YOU WITH THE CONSEQUENCES OF MY MISTAKE...
...BUT BECAUSE I WANTED YOU TO BE PROUD OF THE MAN I'VE BECOME...
IN THE END, THOUGH...
...DESPITE MY BEST EFFORTS...
...I CAN'T QUITE REACH YOUR LEVEL.

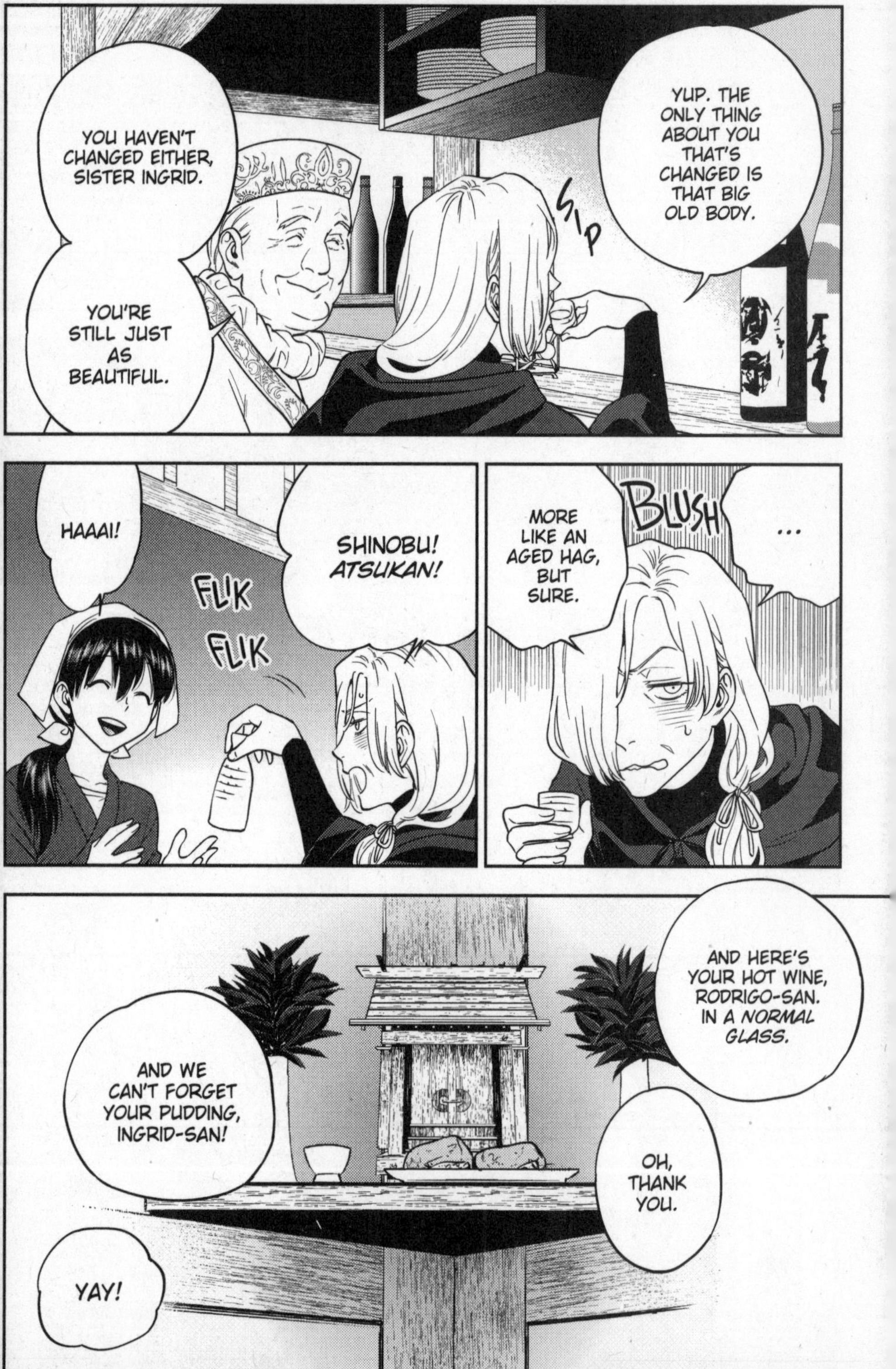
YUP. THE ONLY THING ABOUT YOU THAT'S CHANGED IS THAT BIG OLD BODY.
SIP
YOU HAVEN'T CHANGED EITHER, SISTER INGRID.
YOU'RE STILL JUST AS BEAUTIFUL.
...
BLUSH
MORE LIKE AN AGED HAG, BUT SURE.
SHINOBU! *ATSUKAN!*
FLIK
FLIK
HAAAI!
AND HERE'S YOUR HOT WINE, RODRIGO-SAN. IN A *NORMAL GLASS.*
OH, THANK YOU.
AND WE CAN'T FORGET YOUR PUDDING, INGRID-SAN!
YAY!

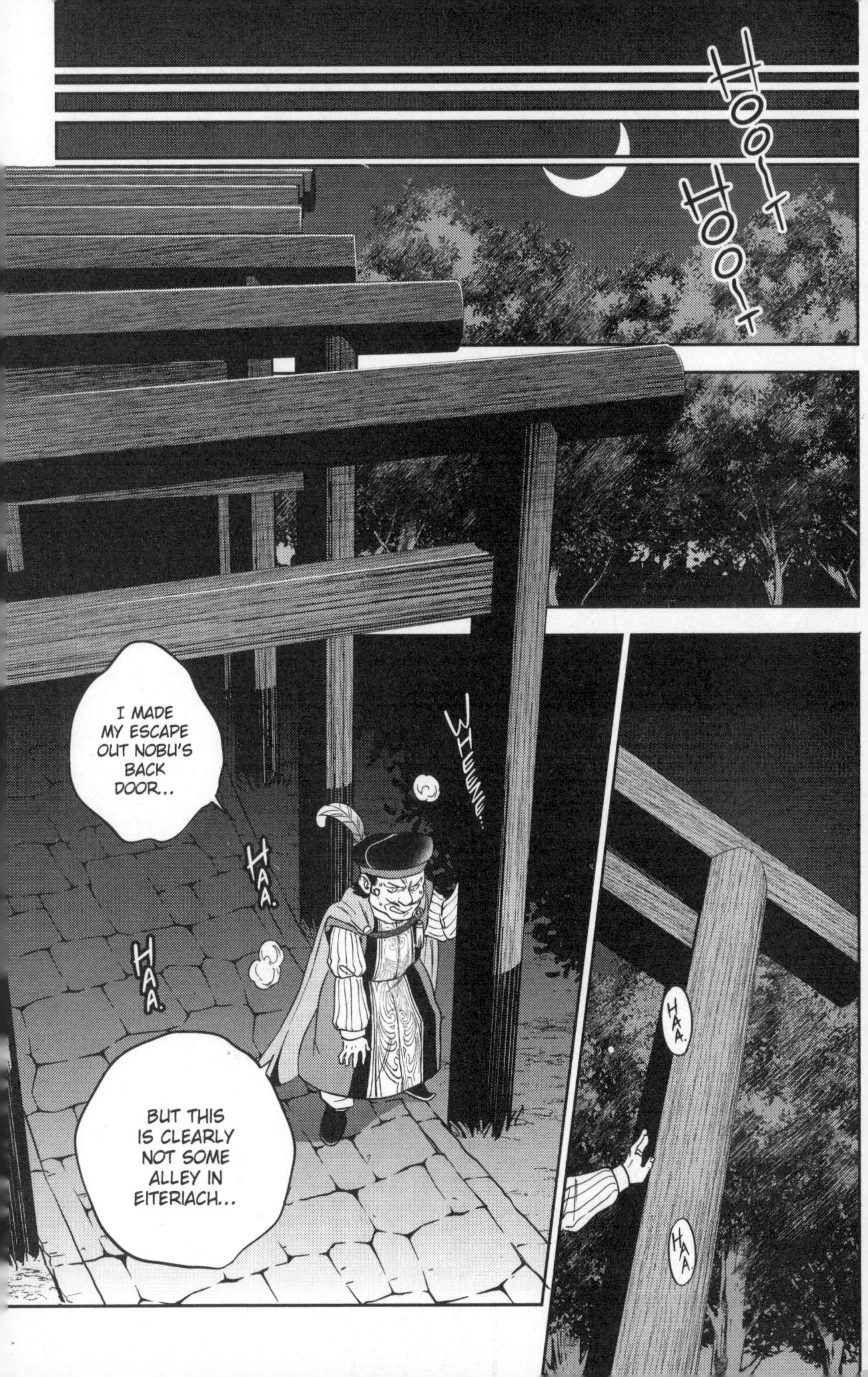
HOO-HOOT
HOO-HOOT
HAA.
HAA.
WHEEW...
I MADE MY ESCAPE OUT NOBU'S BACK DOOR...
HAA.
HAA.
BUT THIS IS CLEARLY NOT SOME ALLEY IN EITERIACH...

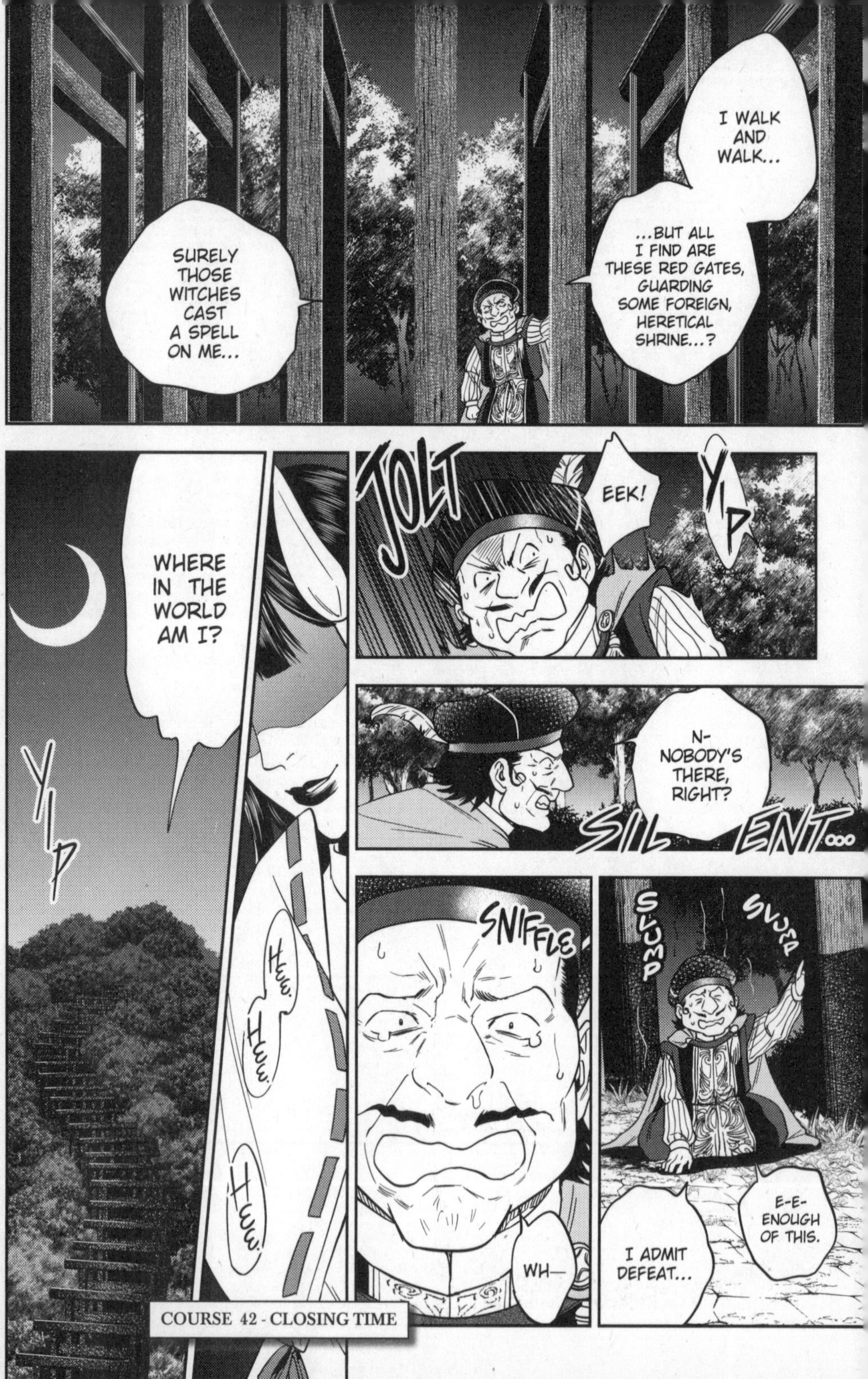
I WALK AND WALK...
...BUT ALL I FIND ARE THESE RED GATES, GUARDING SOME FOREIGN, HERETICAL SHRINE...?
SURELY THOSE WITCHES CAST A SPELL ON ME...
YIP
EEK!
JOLT
N-NOBODY'S THERE, RIGHT?
SILENT...
SLUMP
SLUMP
E-E-ENOUGH OF THIS.
I ADMIT DEFEAT...
SNIFFLE
WH—
WHERE IN THE WORLD AM I?
YIP
Heee.
Heee.
Heee.
COURSE 42 - CLOSING TIME

Clams Sakamushi

OTHERWORLDLY IZAKAYA

NOBU

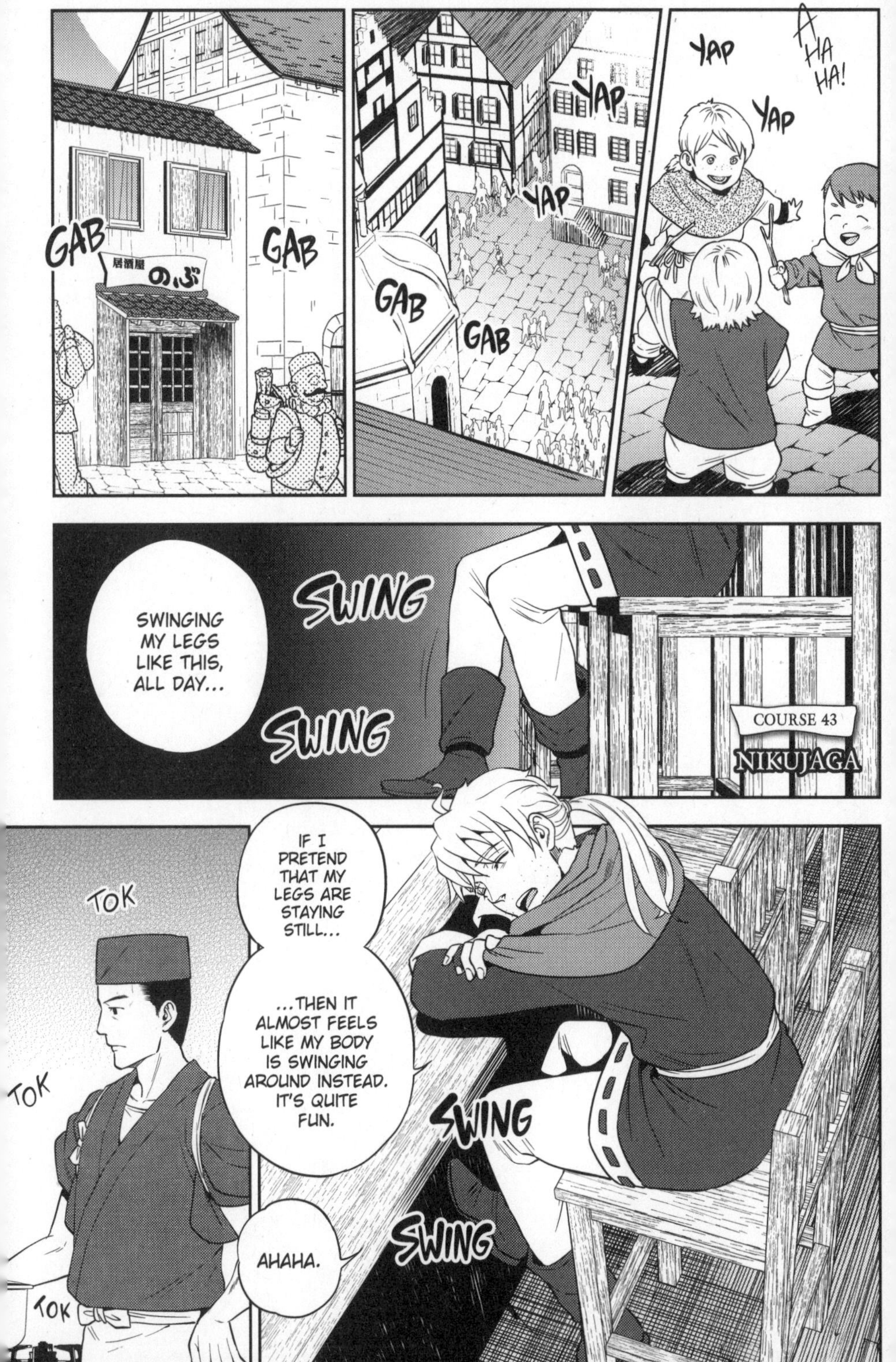
A HA HA!
YAP
YAP
YAP
YAP
GAB
GAB
居酒屋 のぶ
GAB
GAB
COURSE 43
NIKUJAGA
SWING
SWINGING MY LEGS LIKE THIS, ALL DAY...
SWING
IF I PRETEND THAT MY LEGS ARE STAYING STILL...
...THEN IT ALMOST FEELS LIKE MY BODY IS SWINGING AROUND INSTEAD. IT'S QUITE FUN.
SWING
SWING
AHAHA.
TOK
TOK
TOK

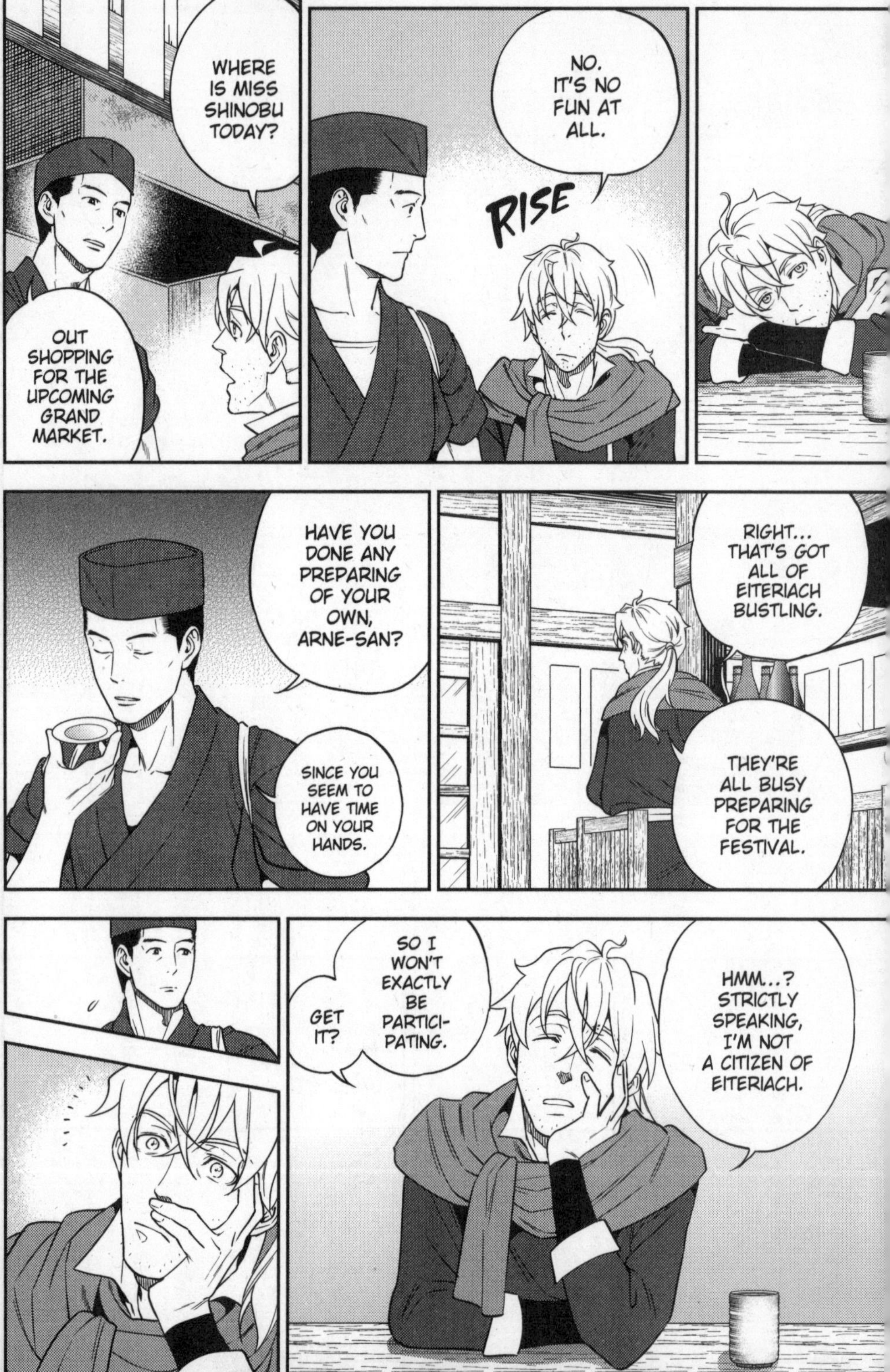
NO. IT'S NO FUN AT ALL.
RISE
WHERE IS MISS SHINOBU TODAY?
OUT SHOPPING FOR THE UPCOMING GRAND MARKET.
RIGHT... THAT'S GOT ALL OF EITERIACH BUSTLING.
THEY'RE ALL BUSY PREPARING FOR THE FESTIVAL.
HAVE YOU DONE ANY PREPARING OF YOUR OWN, ARNE-SAN?
SINCE YOU SEEM TO HAVE TIME ON YOUR HANDS.
HMM...? STRICTLY SPEAKING, I'M NOT A CITIZEN OF EITERIACH.
SO I WON'T EXACTLY BE PARTICI-PATING.
GET IT?

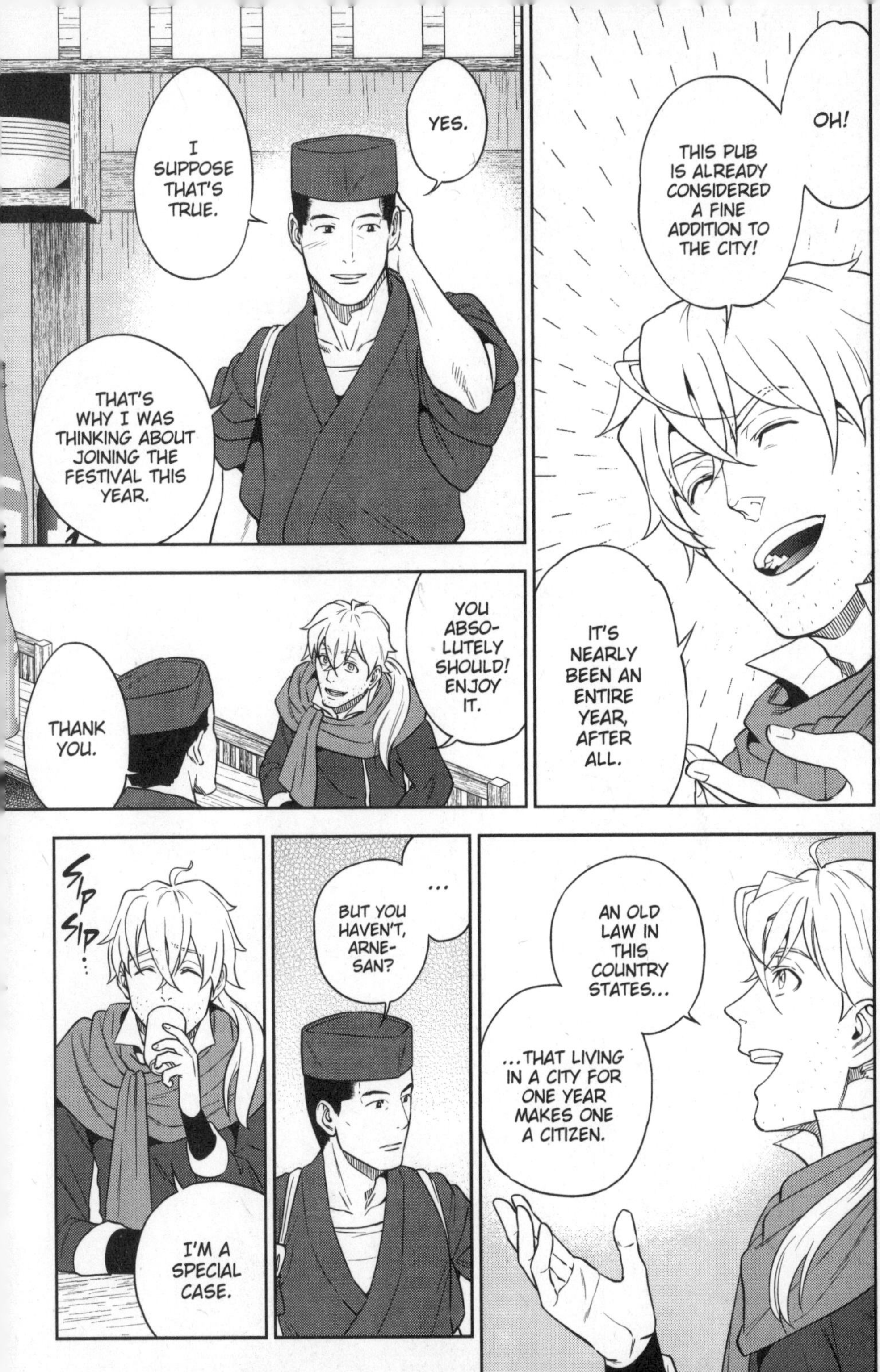
OH!
THIS PUB IS ALREADY CONSIDERED A FINE ADDITION TO THE CITY!
IT'S NEARLY BEEN AN ENTIRE YEAR, AFTER ALL.
YES.
I SUPPOSE THAT'S TRUE.
THAT'S WHY I WAS THINKING ABOUT JOINING THE FESTIVAL THIS YEAR.
YOU ABSOLUTELY SHOULD! ENJOY IT.
THANK YOU.
AN OLD LAW IN THIS COUNTRY STATES...
...THAT LIVING IN A CITY FOR ONE YEAR MAKES ONE A CITIZEN.
...
BUT YOU HAVEN'T, ARNE-SAN?
SIP SIP...
I'M A SPECIAL CASE.

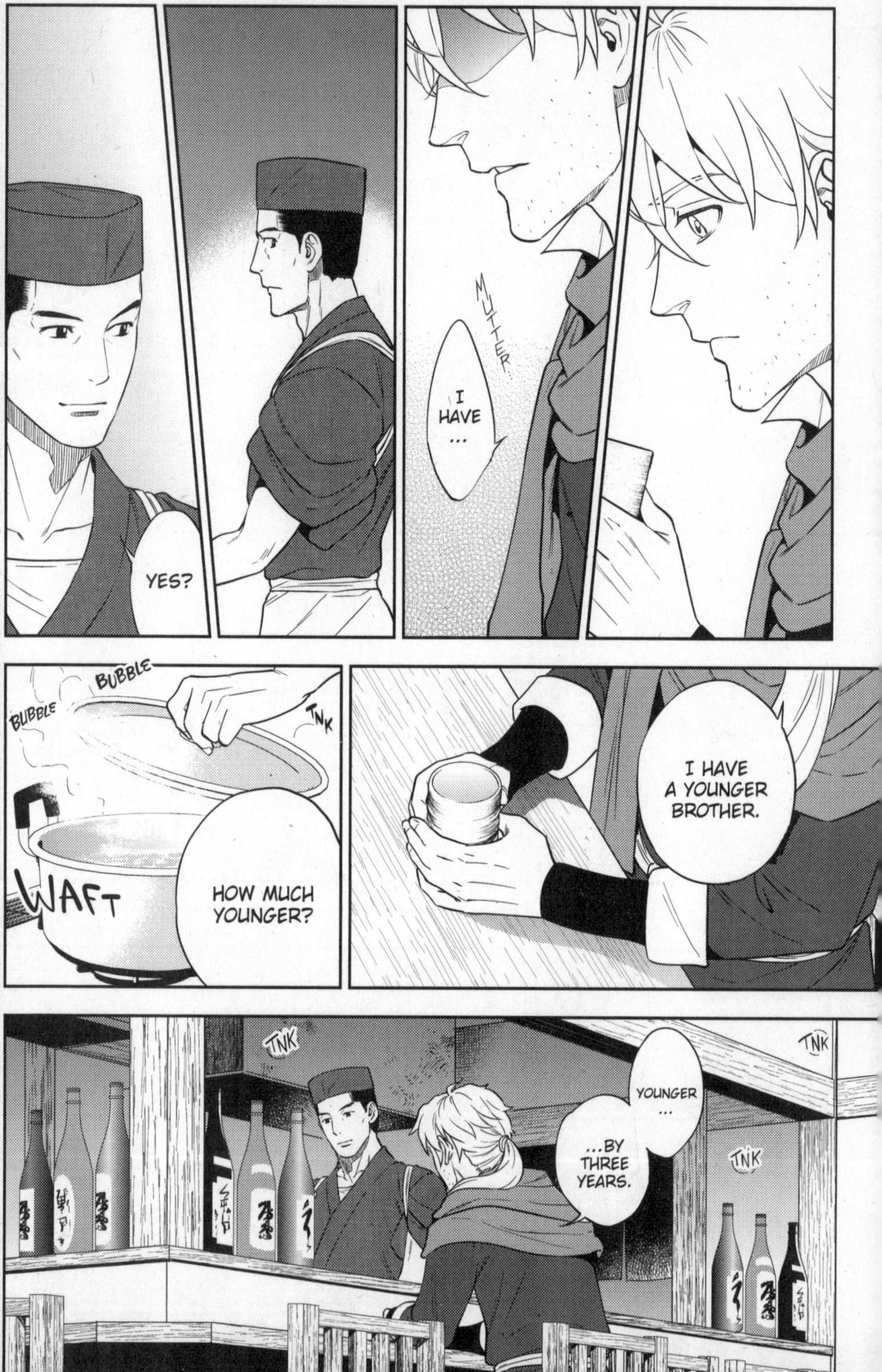
MUTTER
I HAVE ...
YES?
I HAVE A YOUNGER BROTHER.
TNK
BUBBLE
BUBBLE
WAFT
HOW MUCH YOUNGER?
TNK
TNK
YOUNGER ...
...BY THREE YEARS.
TNK

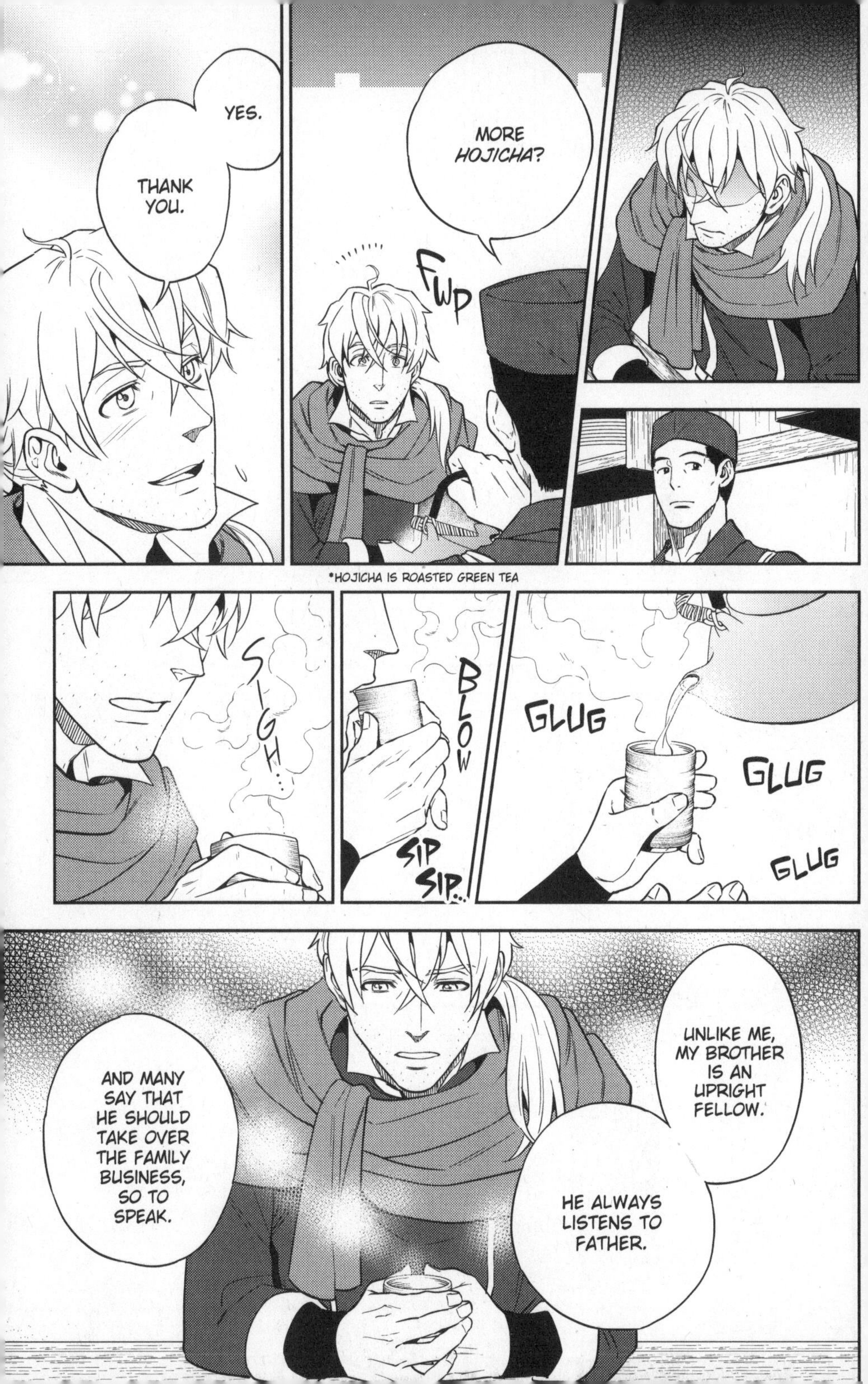
MORE HOJICHA?
FWP
YES.
THANK YOU.
*HOJICHA IS ROASTED GREEN TEA
GLUG
GLUG
GLUG
BLOW
SIP SIP...
SIGH...
UNLIKE ME, MY BROTHER IS AN UPRIGHT FELLOW.
HE ALWAYS LISTENS TO FATHER.
AND MANY SAY THAT HE SHOULD TAKE OVER THE FAMILY BUSINESS, SO TO SPEAK.

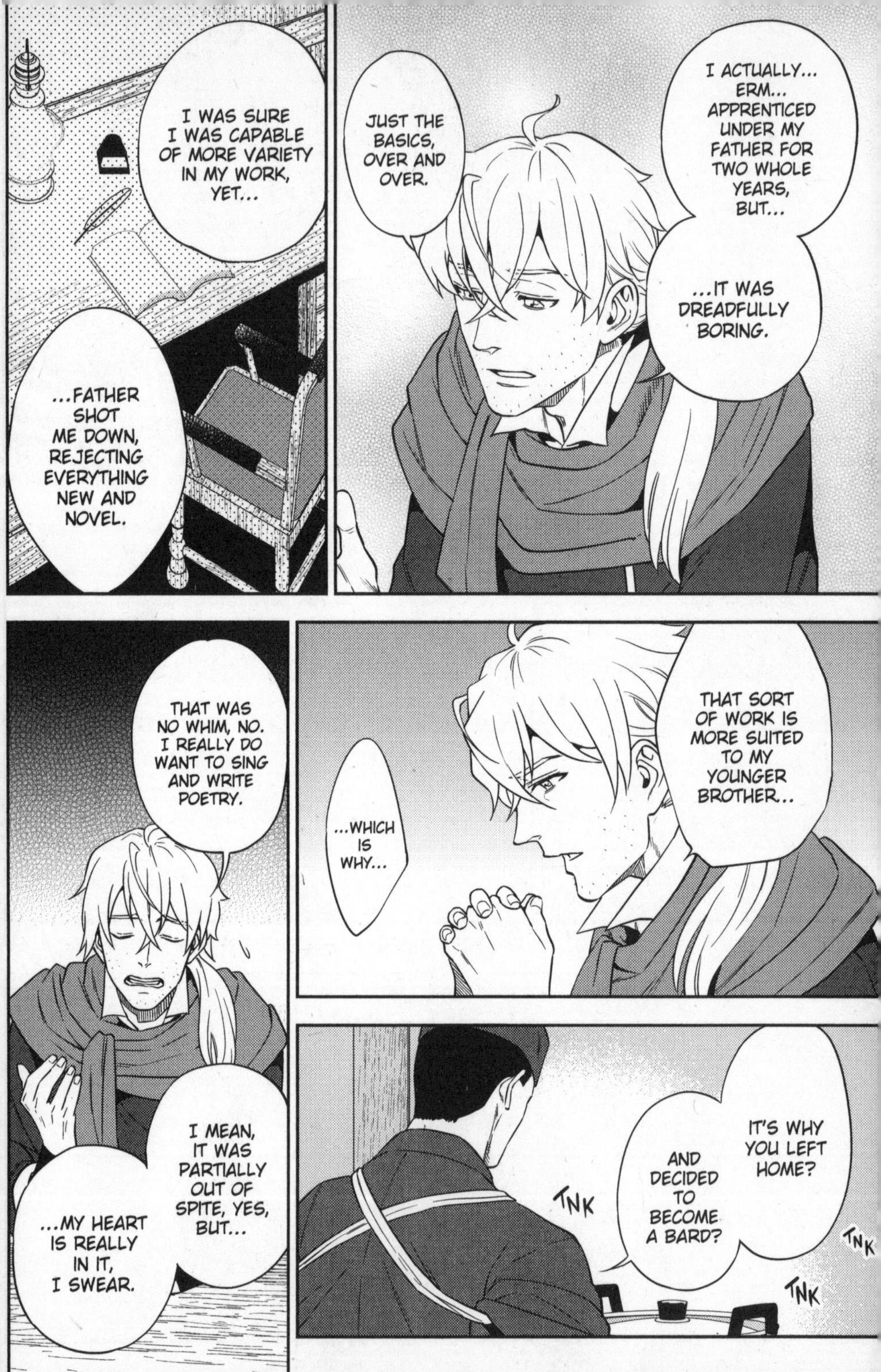
I ACTUALLY... ERM... APPRENTICED UNDER MY FATHER FOR TWO WHOLE YEARS, BUT...
...IT WAS DREADFULLY BORING.
JUST THE BASICS, OVER AND OVER.
I WAS SURE I WAS CAPABLE OF MORE VARIETY IN MY WORK, YET...
...FATHER SHOT ME DOWN, REJECTING EVERYTHING NEW AND NOVEL.
THAT SORT OF WORK IS MORE SUITED TO MY YOUNGER BROTHER...
...WHICH IS WHY...
IT'S WHY YOU LEFT HOME?
AND DECIDED TO BECOME A BARD?
TNK
TNK
TNK
THAT WAS NO WHIM, NO. I REALLY DO WANT TO SING AND WRITE POETRY.
I MEAN, IT WAS PARTIALLY OUT OF SPITE, YES, BUT...
...MY HEART IS REALLY IN IT, I SWEAR.

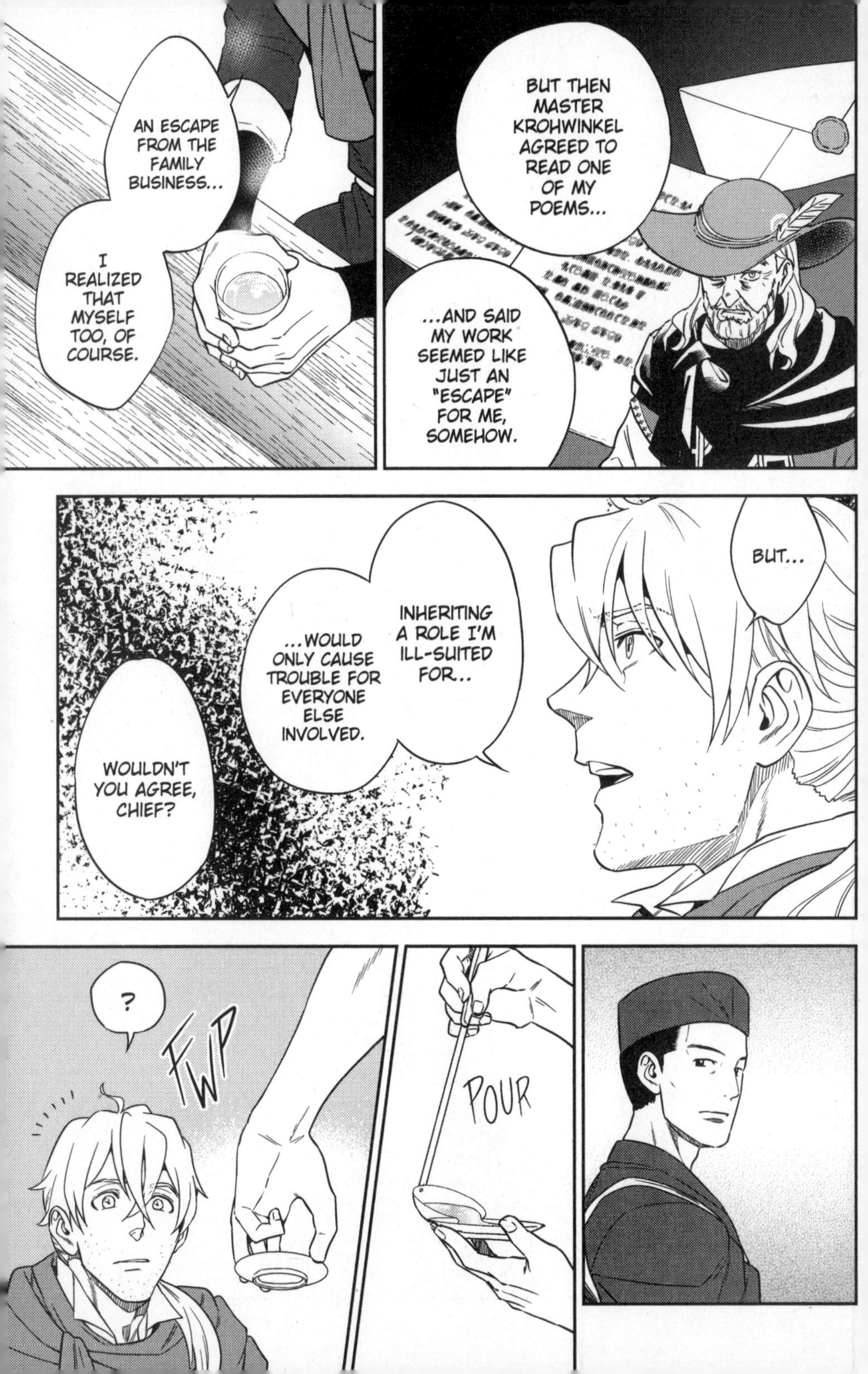
BUT THEN MASTER KROHWINKEL AGREED TO READ ONE OF MY POEMS...
...AND SAID MY WORK SEEMED LIKE JUST AN "ESCAPE" FOR ME, SOMEHOW.
AN ESCAPE FROM THE FAMILY BUSINESS...
I REALIZED THAT MYSELF TOO, OF COURSE.
BUT...
INHERITING A ROLE I'M ILL-SUITED FOR...
...WOULD ONLY CAUSE TROUBLE FOR EVERYONE ELSE INVOLVED.
WOULDN'T YOU AGREE, CHIEF?
POUR
?
FWP

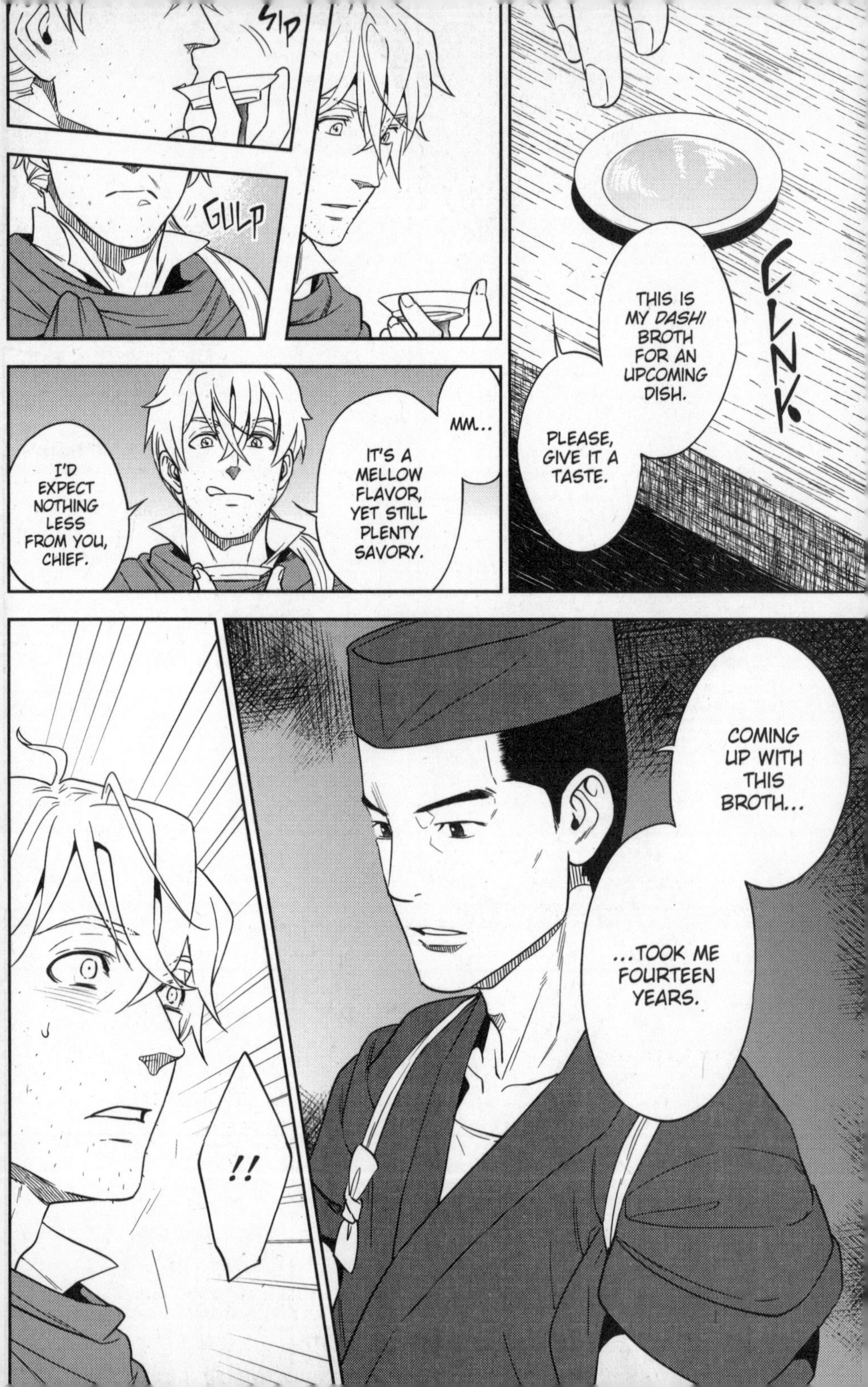
CLINK
THIS IS MY DASHI BROTH FOR AN UPCOMING DISH.
PLEASE, GIVE IT A TASTE.
SIP
GULP
MM...
IT'S A MELLOW FLAVOR, YET STILL PLENTY SAVORY.
I'D EXPECT NOTHING LESS FROM YOU, CHIEF.
COMING UP WITH THIS BROTH...
...TOOK ME FOURTEEN YEARS.
!!

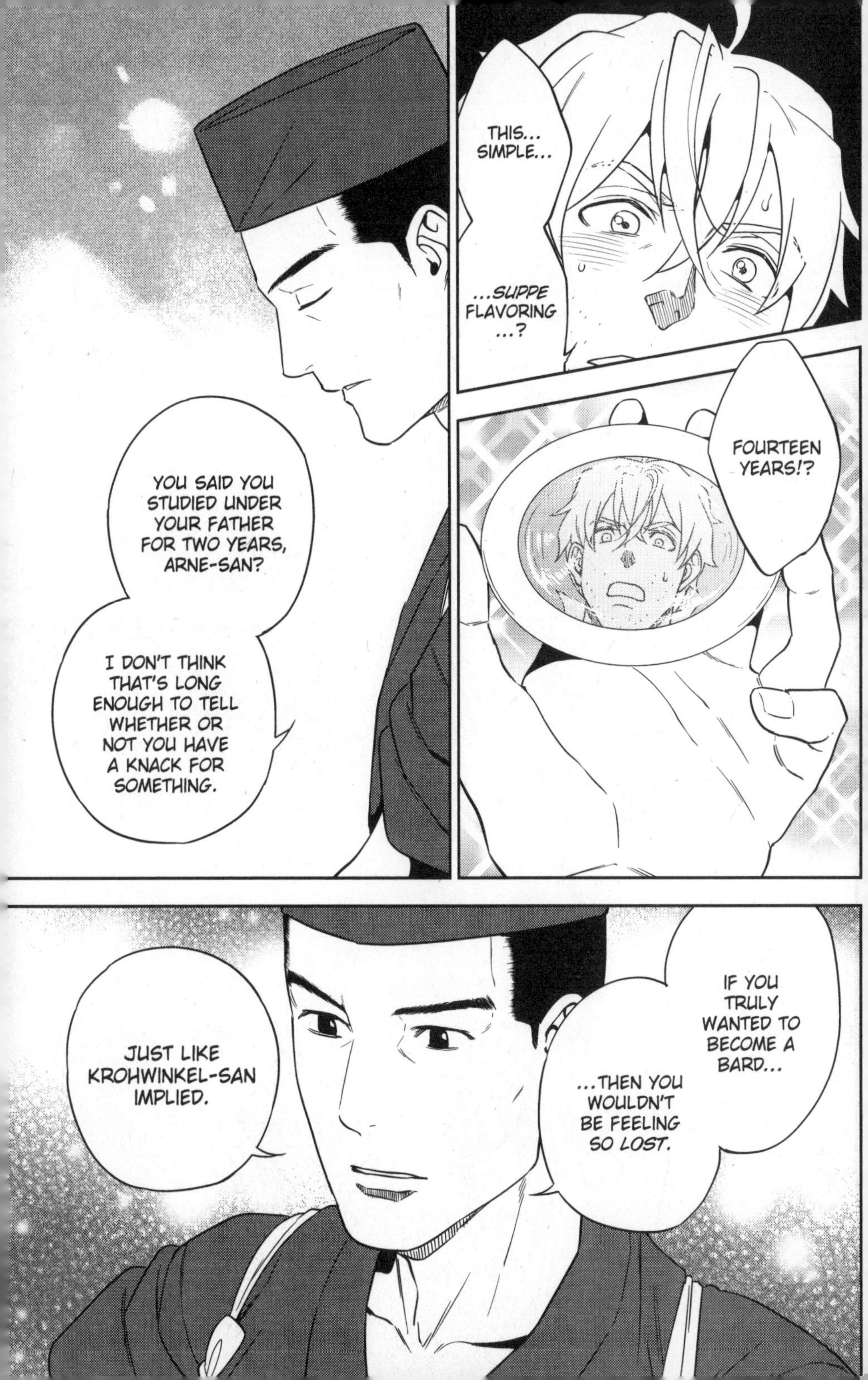
THIS... SIMPLE...
...SUPPE FLAVORING ...?
FOURTEEN YEARS!?
YOU SAID YOU STUDIED UNDER YOUR FATHER FOR TWO YEARS, ARNE-SAN?
I DON'T THINK THAT'S LONG ENOUGH TO TELL WHETHER OR NOT YOU HAVE A KNACK FOR SOMETHING.
IF YOU TRULY WANTED TO BECOME A BARD...
...THEN YOU WOULDN'T BE FEELING SO LOST.
JUST LIKE KROHWINKEL-SAN IMPLIED.

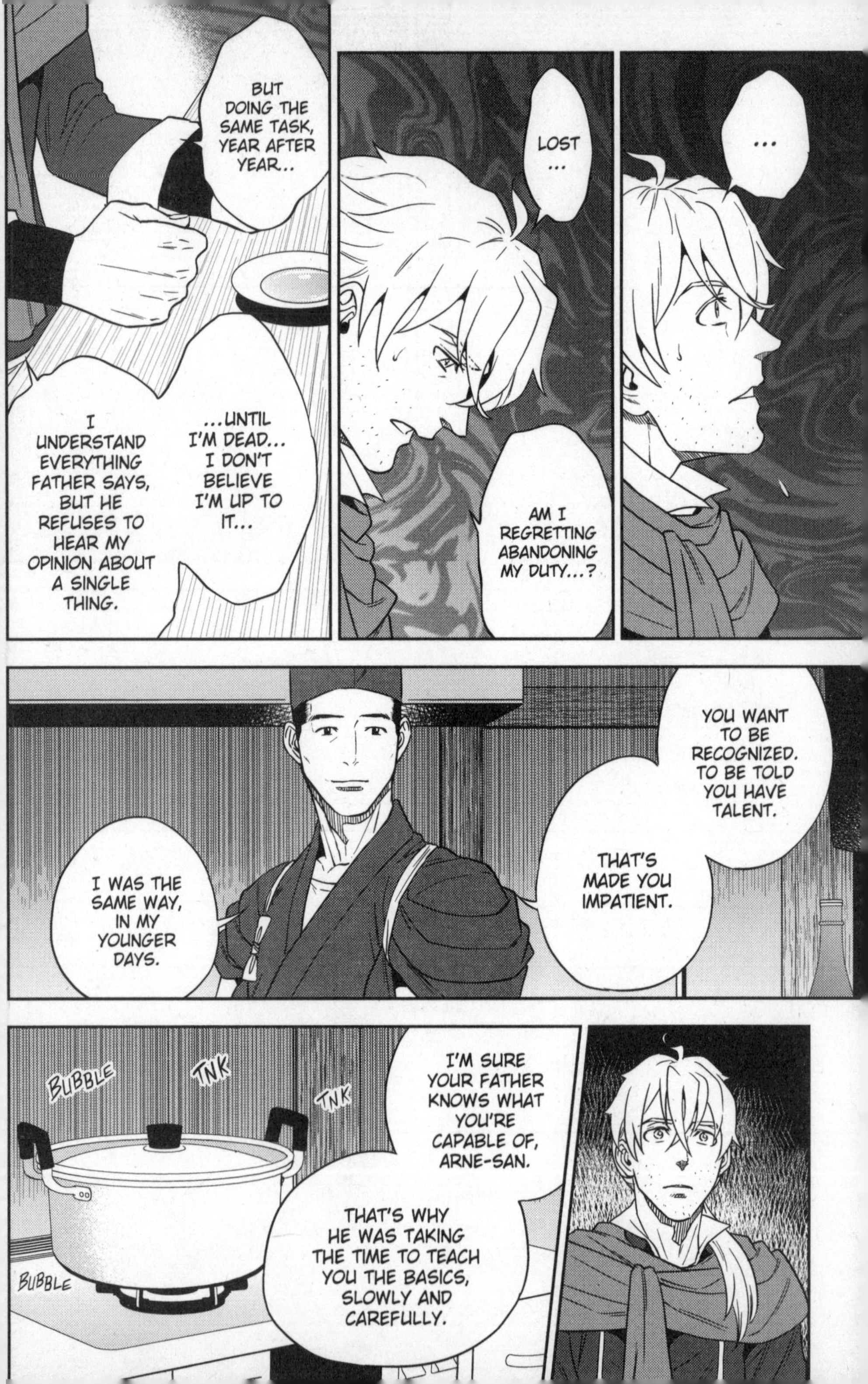
...
LOST ...
AM I REGRETTING ABANDONING MY DUTY...?
BUT DOING THE SAME TASK, YEAR AFTER YEAR...
...UNTIL I'M DEAD... I DON'T BELIEVE I'M UP TO IT...
I UNDERSTAND EVERYTHING FATHER SAYS, BUT HE REFUSES TO HEAR MY OPINION ABOUT A SINGLE THING.
YOU WANT TO BE RECOGNIZED. TO BE TOLD YOU HAVE TALENT.
THAT'S MADE YOU IMPATIENT.
I WAS THE SAME WAY, IN MY YOUNGER DAYS.
I'M SURE YOUR FATHER KNOWS WHAT YOU'RE CAPABLE OF, ARNE-SAN.
TNK
TNK
BUBBLE
THAT'S WHY HE WAS TAKING THE TIME TO TEACH YOU THE BASICS, SLOWLY AND CAREFULLY.
BUBBLE

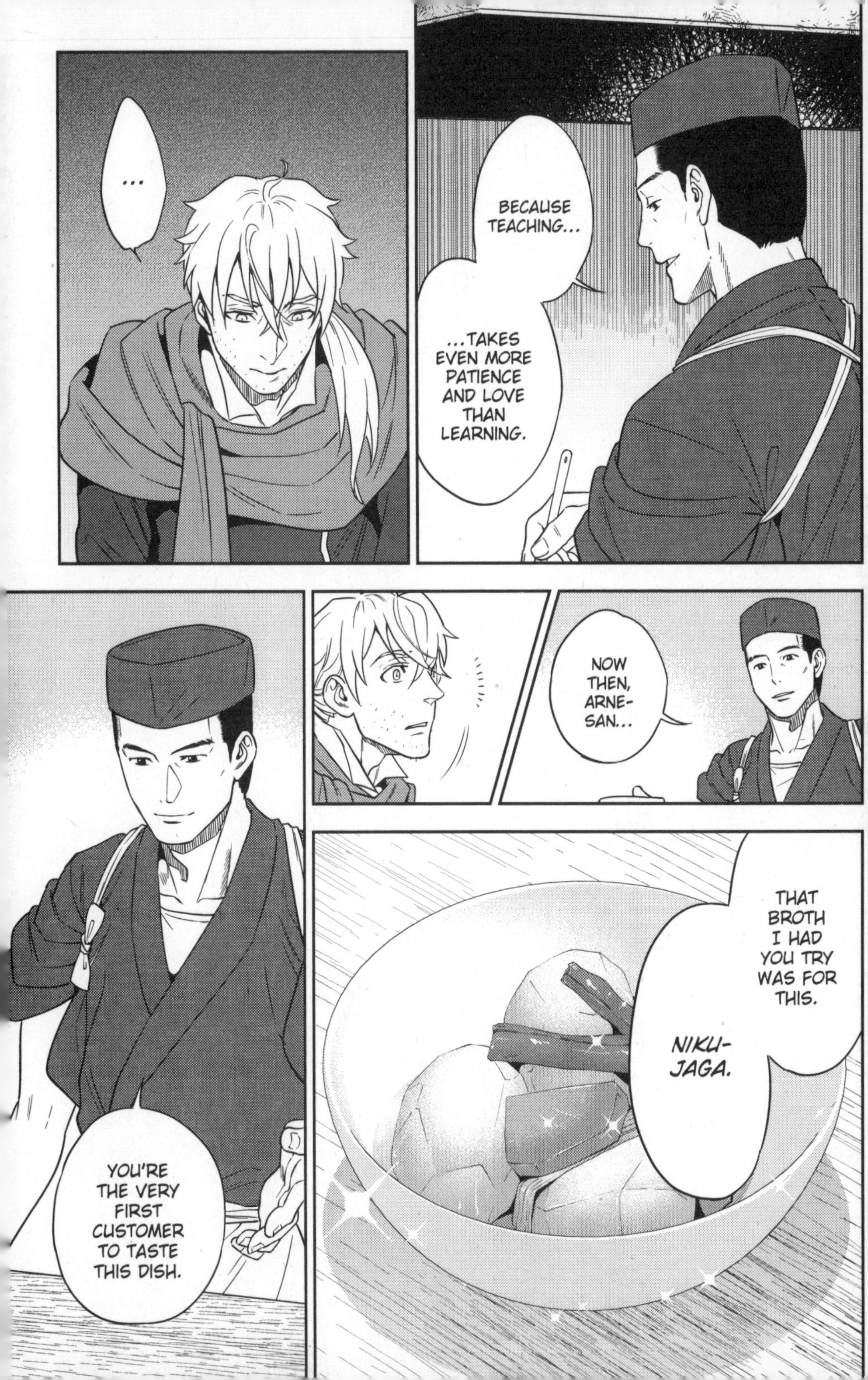
BECAUSE TEACHING...
...TAKES EVEN MORE PATIENCE AND LOVE THAN LEARNING.
...
NOW THEN, ARNE-SAN...
THAT BROTH I HAD YOU TRY WAS FOR THIS.
NIKU-JAGA.
YOU'RE THE VERY FIRST CUSTOMER TO TASTE THIS DISH.

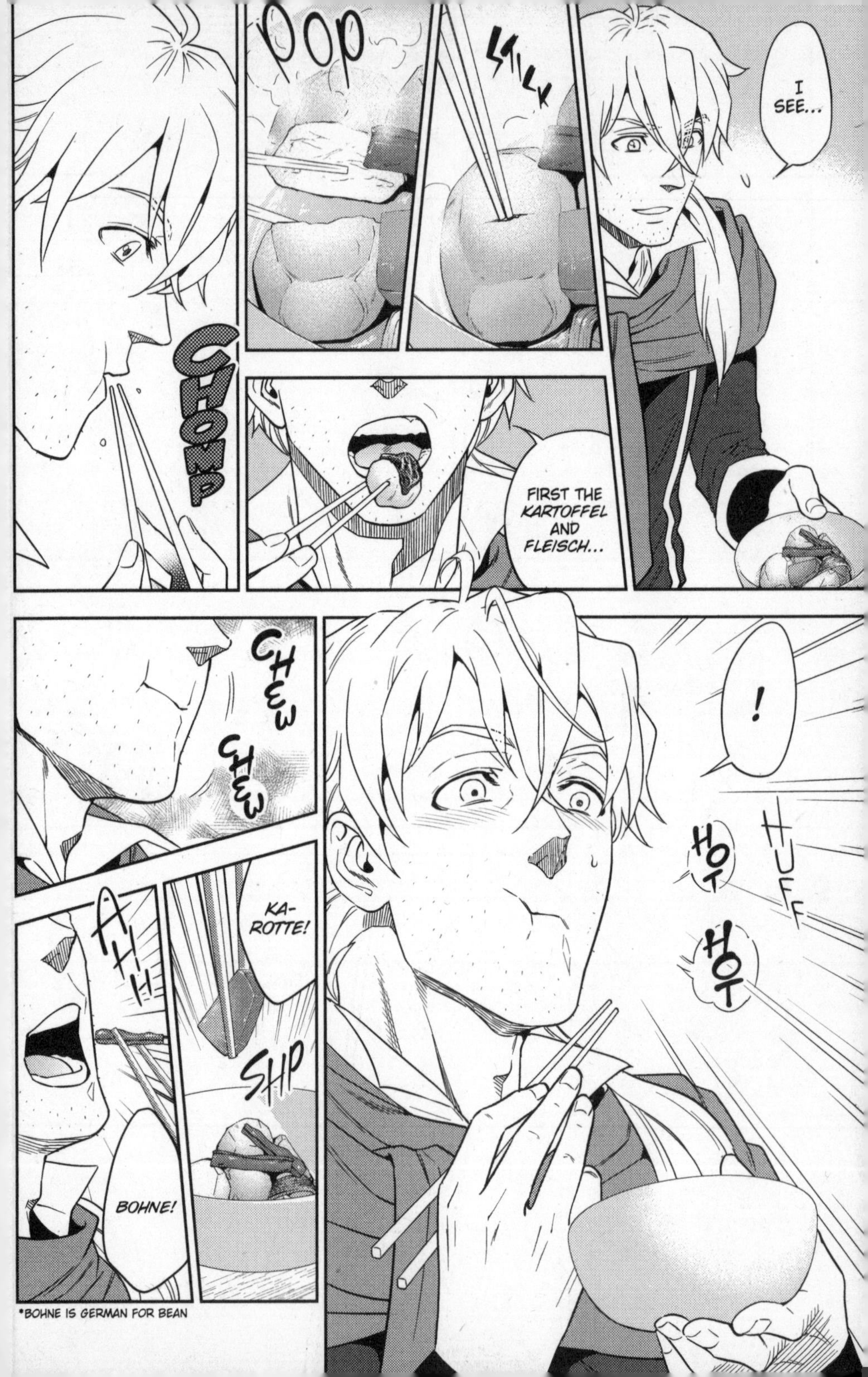
I SEE...
POP
FIRST THE KARTOFFEL AND FLEISCH...
CHOMP
!
HUFF
HOT
HOT
CHEW
CHEW
KA-ROTTE!
SHP
AHH
BOHNE!

*BOHNE IS GERMAN FOR BEAN

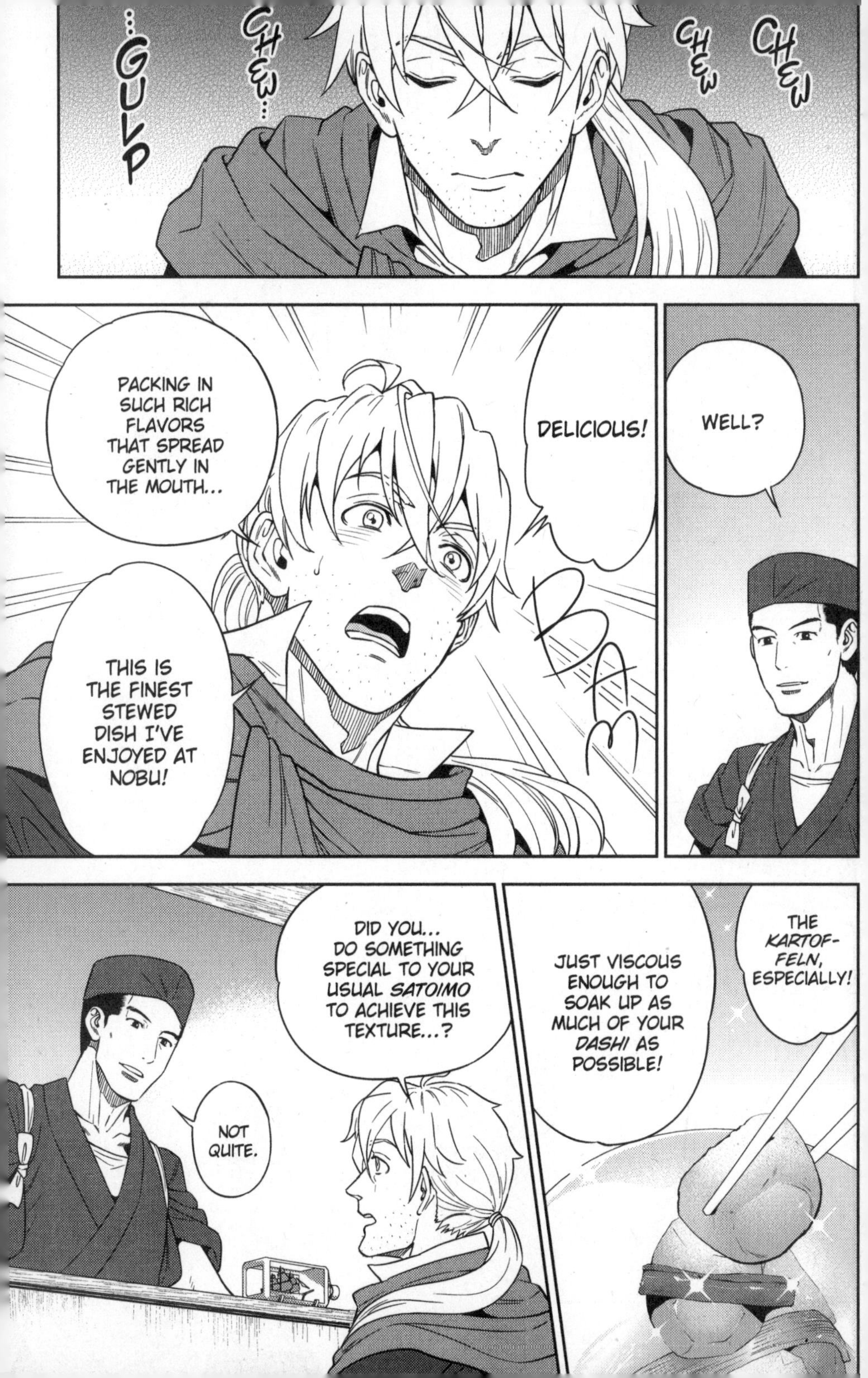
CHEW
CHEW
CHEW...
...GULP
WELL?
DELICIOUS!
BAM
PACKING IN SUCH RICH FLAVORS THAT SPREAD GENTLY IN THE MOUTH...
THIS IS THE FINEST STEWED DISH I'VE ENJOYED AT NOBU!
THE *KARTOFFELN*, ESPECIALLY!
JUST VISCOUS ENOUGH TO SOAK UP AS MUCH OF YOUR *DASHI* AS POSSIBLE!
DID YOU... DO SOMETHING SPECIAL TO YOUR USUAL *SATOIMO* TO ACHIEVE THIS TEXTURE...?
NOT QUITE.

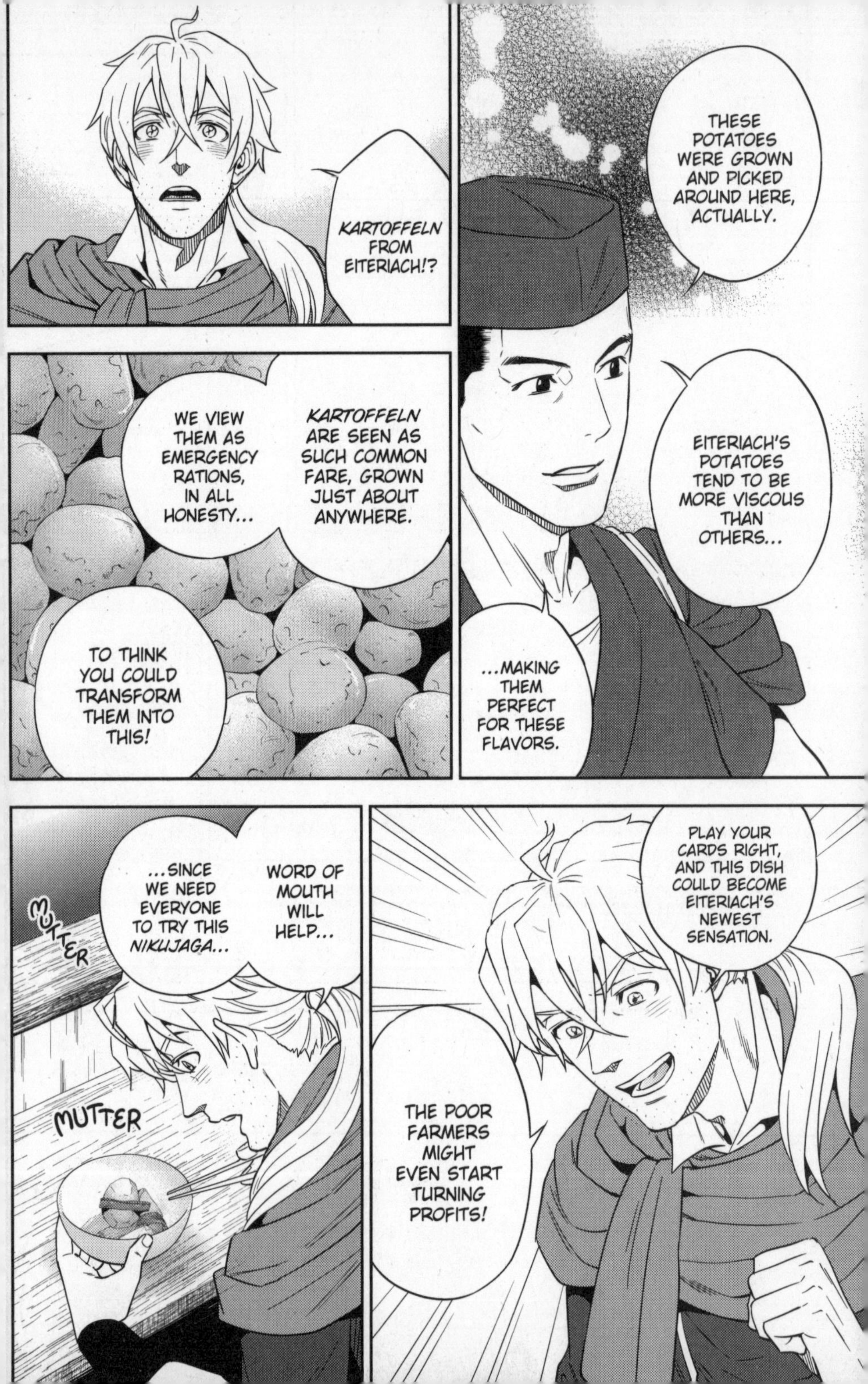
THESE POTATOES WERE GROWN AND PICKED AROUND HERE, ACTUALLY.
EITERIACH'S POTATOES TEND TO BE MORE VISCOUS THAN OTHERS...
...MAKING THEM PERFECT FOR THESE FLAVORS.
KARTOFFELN FROM EITERIACH!?
KARTOFFELN ARE SEEN AS SUCH COMMON FARE, GROWN JUST ABOUT ANYWHERE.
WE VIEW THEM AS EMERGENCY RATIONS, IN ALL HONESTY...
TO THINK YOU COULD TRANSFORM THEM INTO THIS!
PLAY YOUR CARDS RIGHT, AND THIS DISH COULD BECOME EITERIACH'S NEWEST SENSATION.
THE POOR FARMERS MIGHT EVEN START TURNING PROFITS!
WORD OF MOUTH WILL HELP...
...SINCE WE NEED EVERYONE TO TRY THIS *NIKUJAGA*...
MUTTER
MUTTER

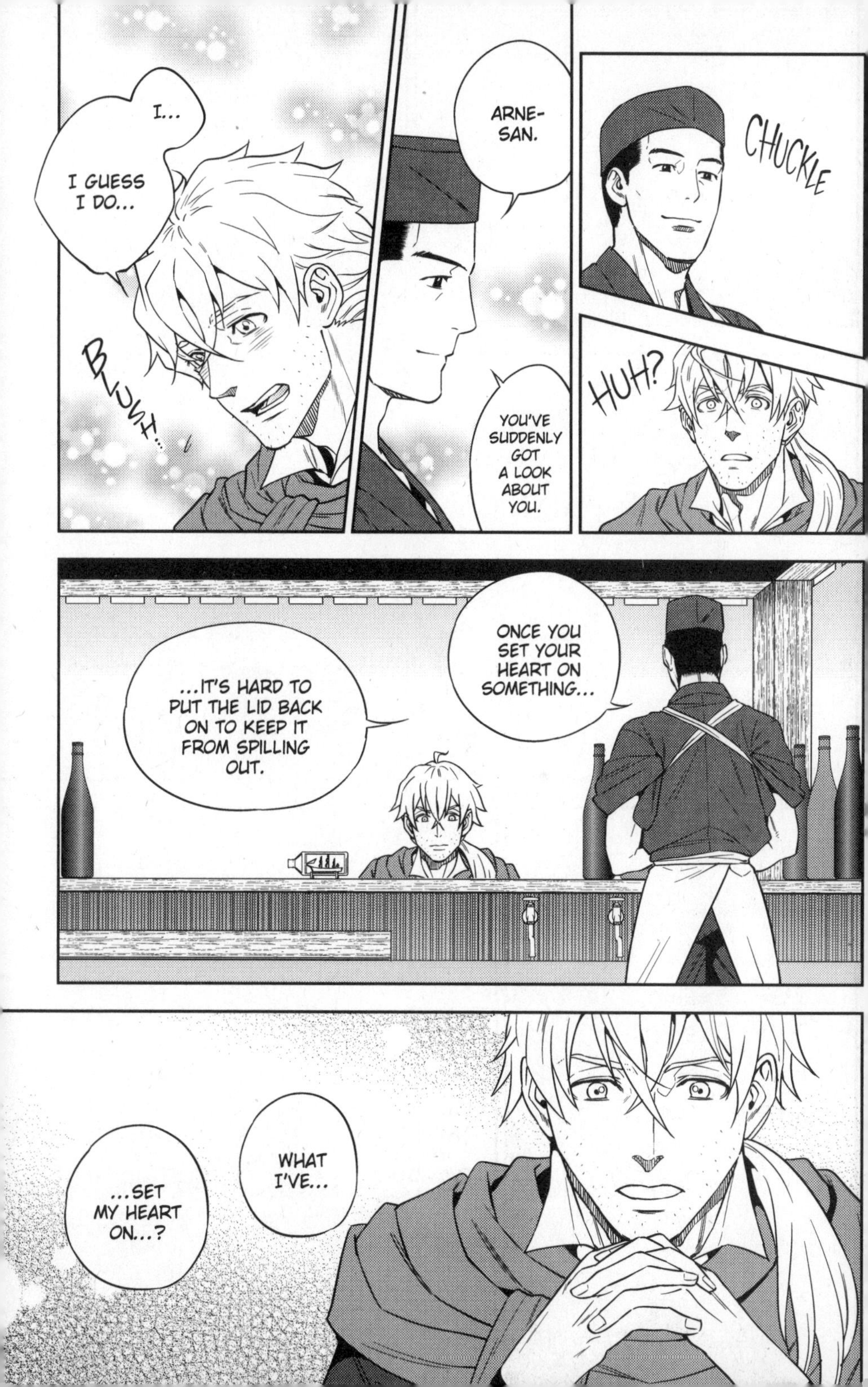
CHUCKLE
HUH?
ARNE-SAN.
YOU'VE SUDDENLY GOT A LOOK ABOUT YOU.
I...
I GUESS I DO...
BLUSH...
ONCE YOU SET YOUR HEART ON SOMETHING...
...IT'S HARD TO PUT THE LID BACK ON TO KEEP IT FROM SPILLING OUT.
WHAT I'VE...
...SET MY HEART ON...?

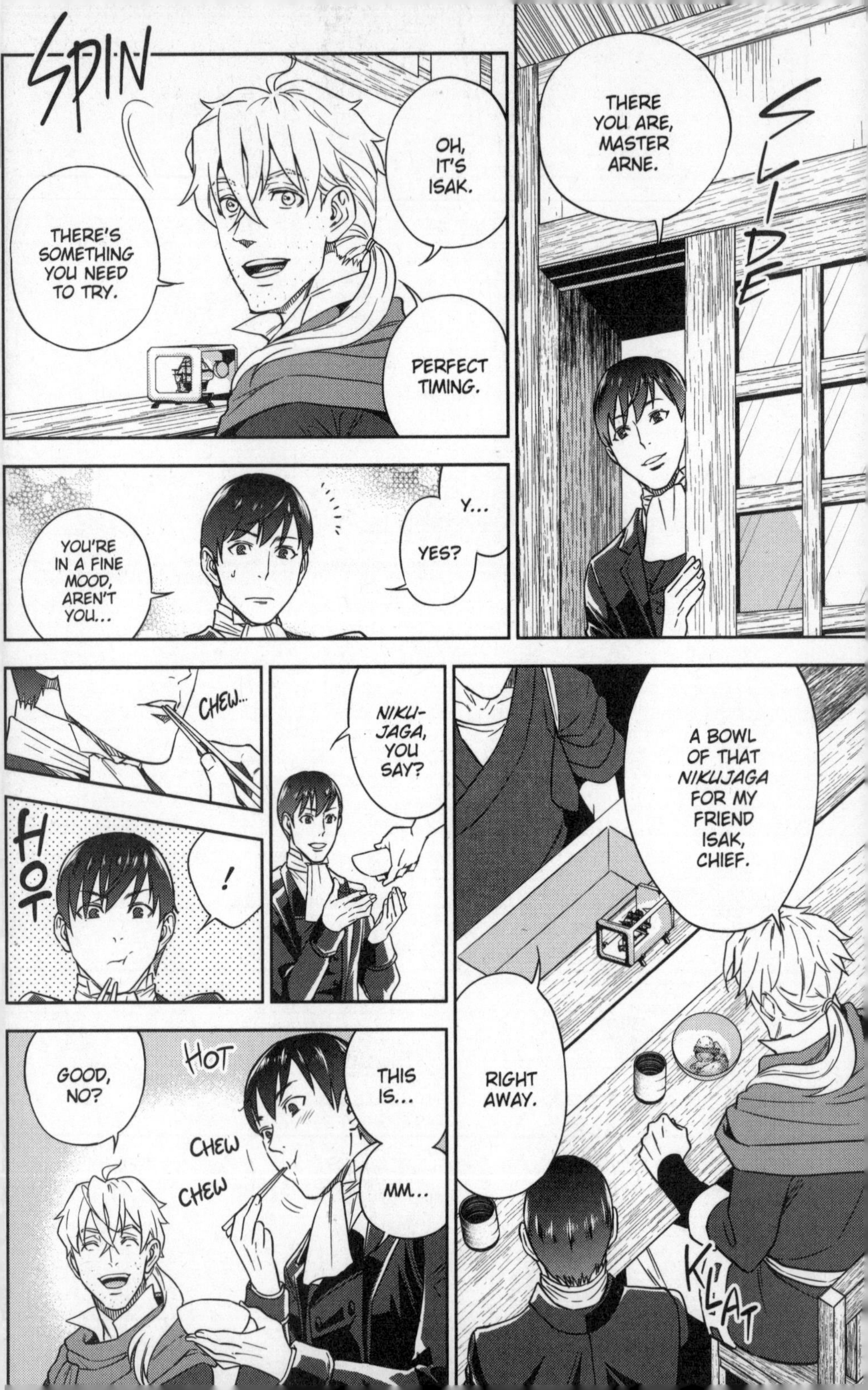
SLIDE
THERE YOU ARE, MASTER ARNE.
SPIN
OH, IT'S ISAK.
PERFECT TIMING.
THERE'S SOMETHING YOU NEED TO TRY.
Y... YES?
YOU'RE IN A FINE MOOD, AREN'T YOU...
A BOWL OF THAT NIKUJAGA FOR MY FRIEND ISAK, CHIEF.
RIGHT AWAY.
KLAT
NIKU-JAGA, YOU SAY?
CHEW...
HOT
!
THIS IS... MM...
HOT
CHEW
CHEW
GOOD, NO?

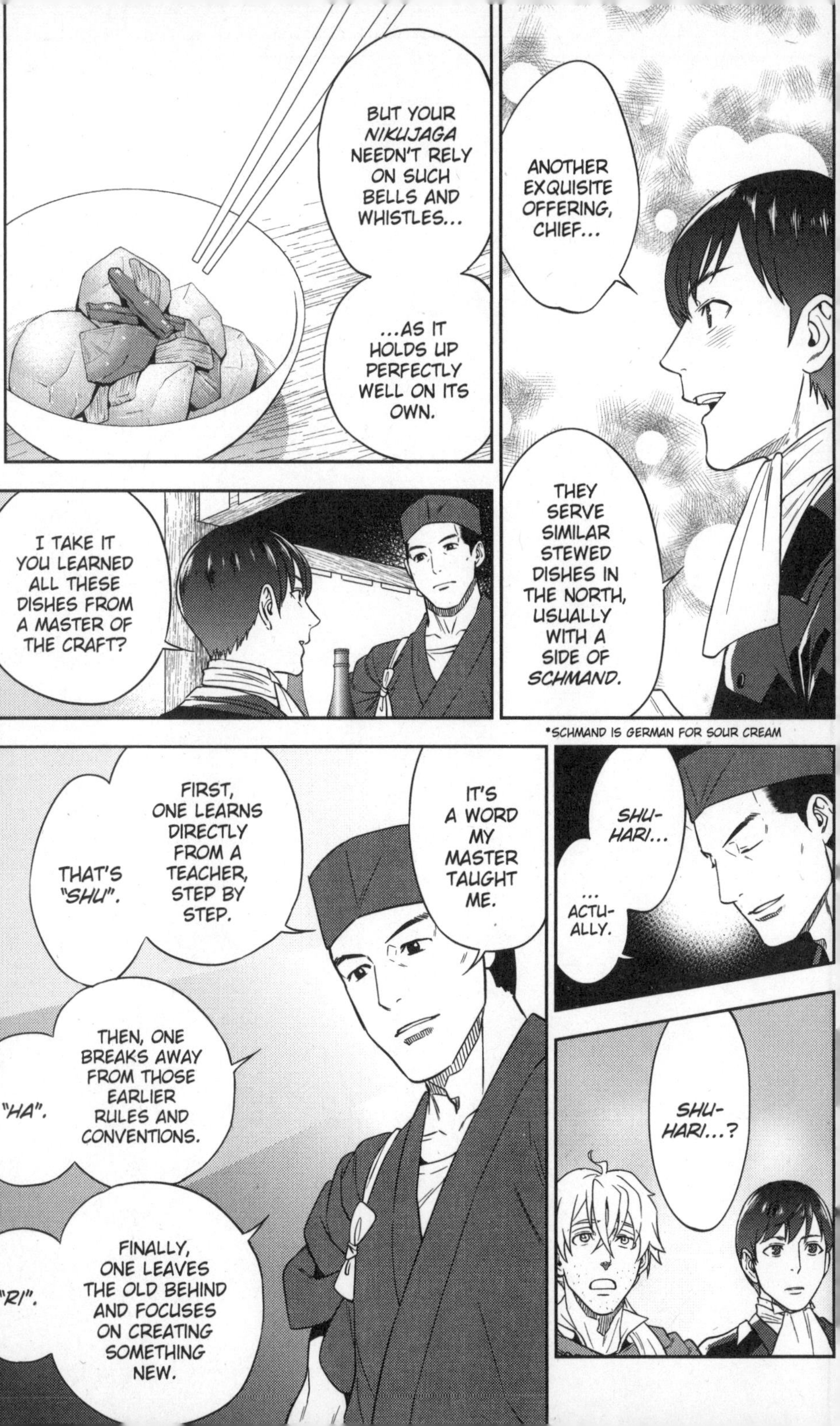
ANOTHER EXQUISITE OFFERING, CHIEF...
THEY SERVE SIMILAR STEWED DISHES IN THE NORTH, USUALLY WITH A SIDE OF *SCHMAND*.
BUT YOUR *NIKUJAGA* NEEDN'T RELY ON SUCH BELLS AND WHISTLES...
...AS IT HOLDS UP PERFECTLY WELL ON ITS OWN.
I TAKE IT YOU LEARNED ALL THESE DISHES FROM A MASTER OF THE CRAFT?
SHU-HARI...
...ACTUALLY.
SHU-HARI...?
IT'S A WORD MY MASTER TAUGHT ME.
FIRST, ONE LEARNS DIRECTLY FROM A TEACHER, STEP BY STEP.
THAT'S "*SHU*".
THEN, ONE BREAKS AWAY FROM THOSE EARLIER RULES AND CONVENTIONS.
"*HA*".
FINALLY, ONE LEAVES THE OLD BEHIND AND FOCUSES ON CREATING SOMETHING NEW.
"*RI*".

*SCHMAND IS GERMAN FOR SOUR CREAM

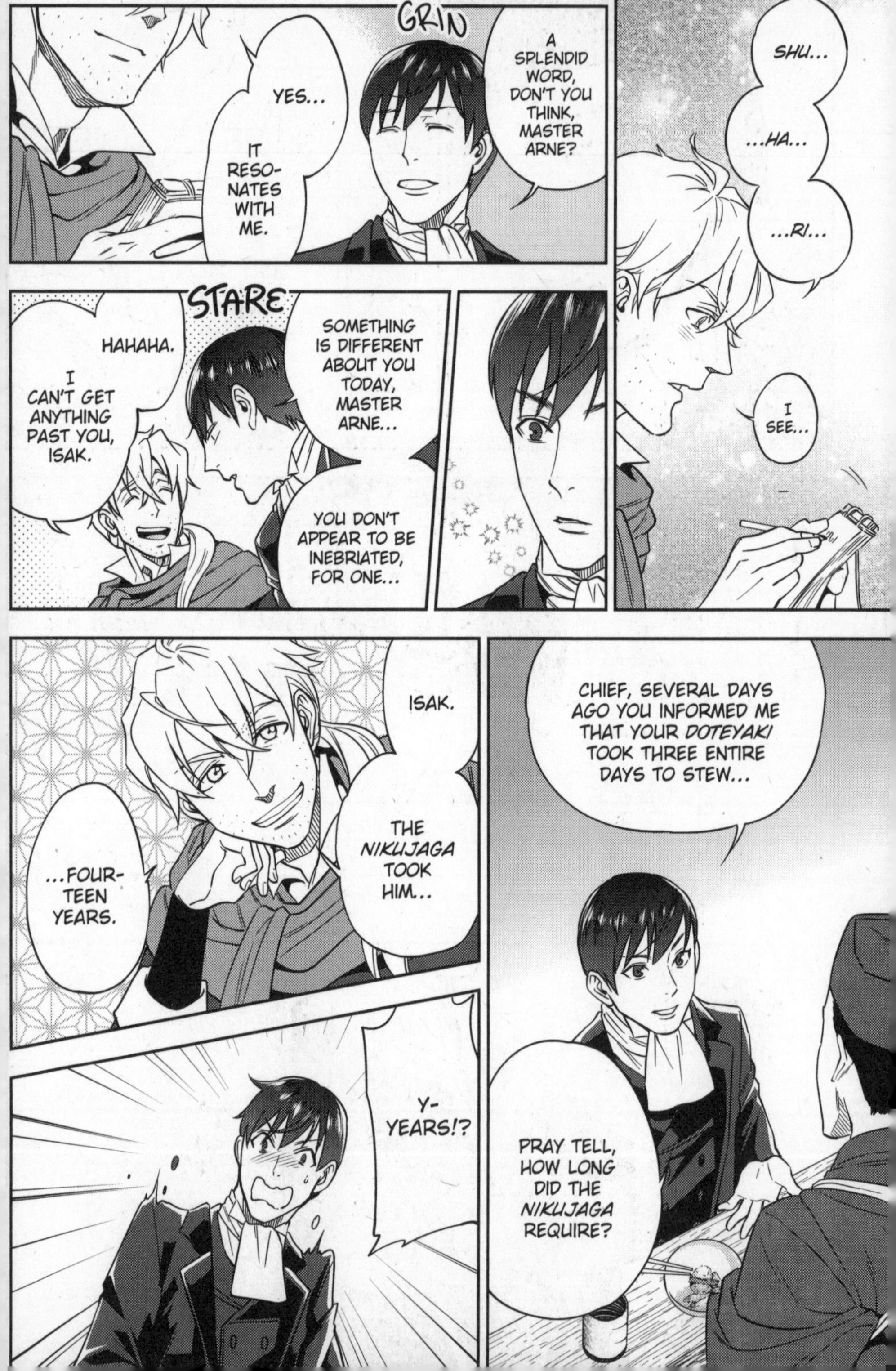
SHU...
...HA...
...RI...
I SEE...
GRIN
A SPLENDID WORD, DON'T YOU THINK, MASTER ARNE?
YES...
IT RESONATES WITH ME.
STARE
SOMETHING IS DIFFERENT ABOUT YOU TODAY, MASTER ARNE...
YOU DON'T APPEAR TO BE INEBRIATED, FOR ONE...
HAHAHA.
I CAN'T GET ANYTHING PAST YOU, ISAK.
CHIEF, SEVERAL DAYS AGO YOU INFORMED ME THAT YOUR *DOTEYAKI* TOOK THREE ENTIRE DAYS TO STEW...
PRAY TELL, HOW LONG DID THE *NIKUJAGA* REQUIRE?
ISAK.
THE *NIKUJAGA* TOOK HIM...
...FOURTEEN YEARS.
Y-YEARS!?

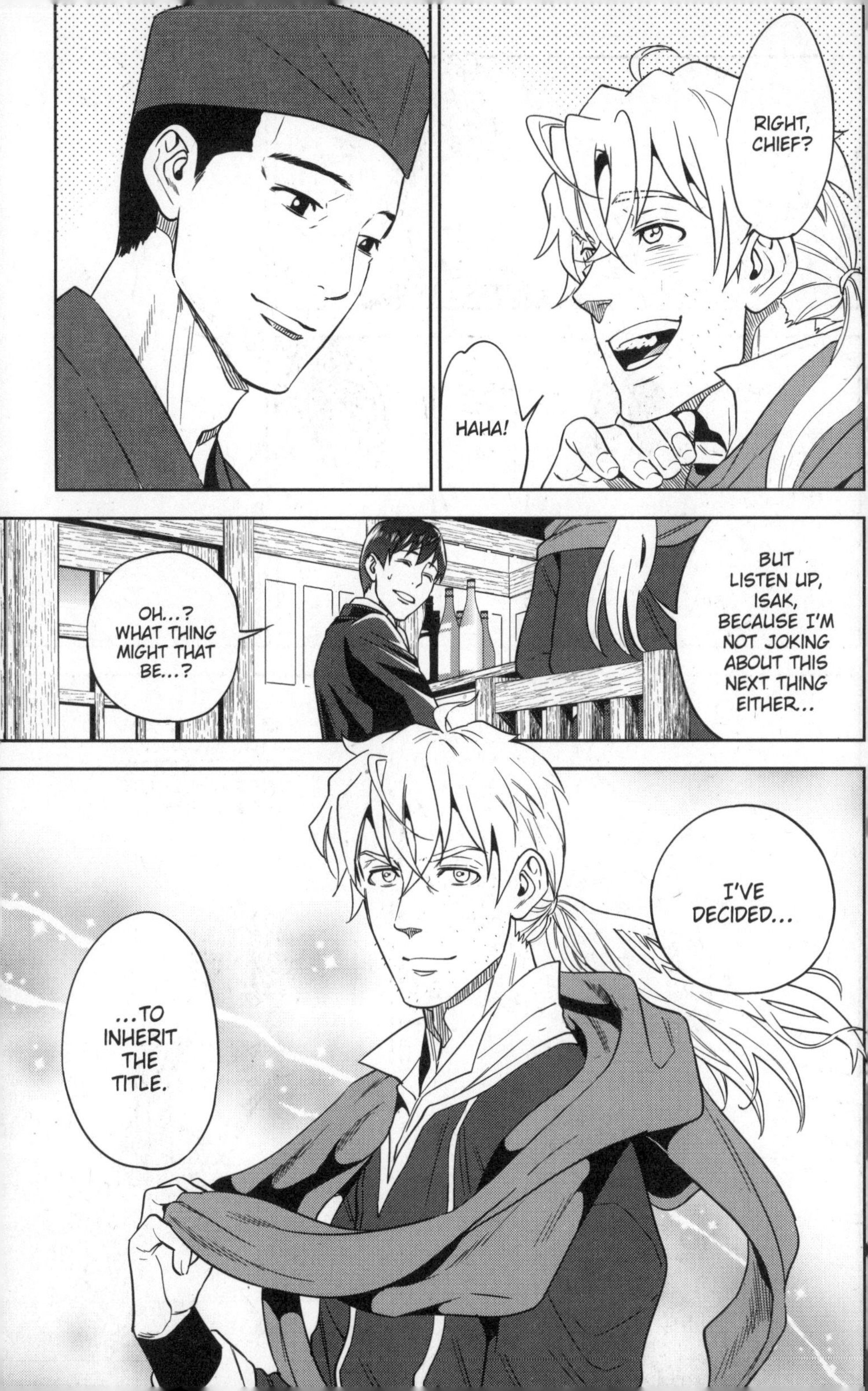
RIGHT, CHIEF?
HAHA!
BUT LISTEN UP, ISAK, BECAUSE I'M NOT JOKING ABOUT THIS NEXT THING EITHER...
OH...? WHAT THING MIGHT THAT BE...?
I'VE DECIDED...
...TO INHERIT THE TITLE.

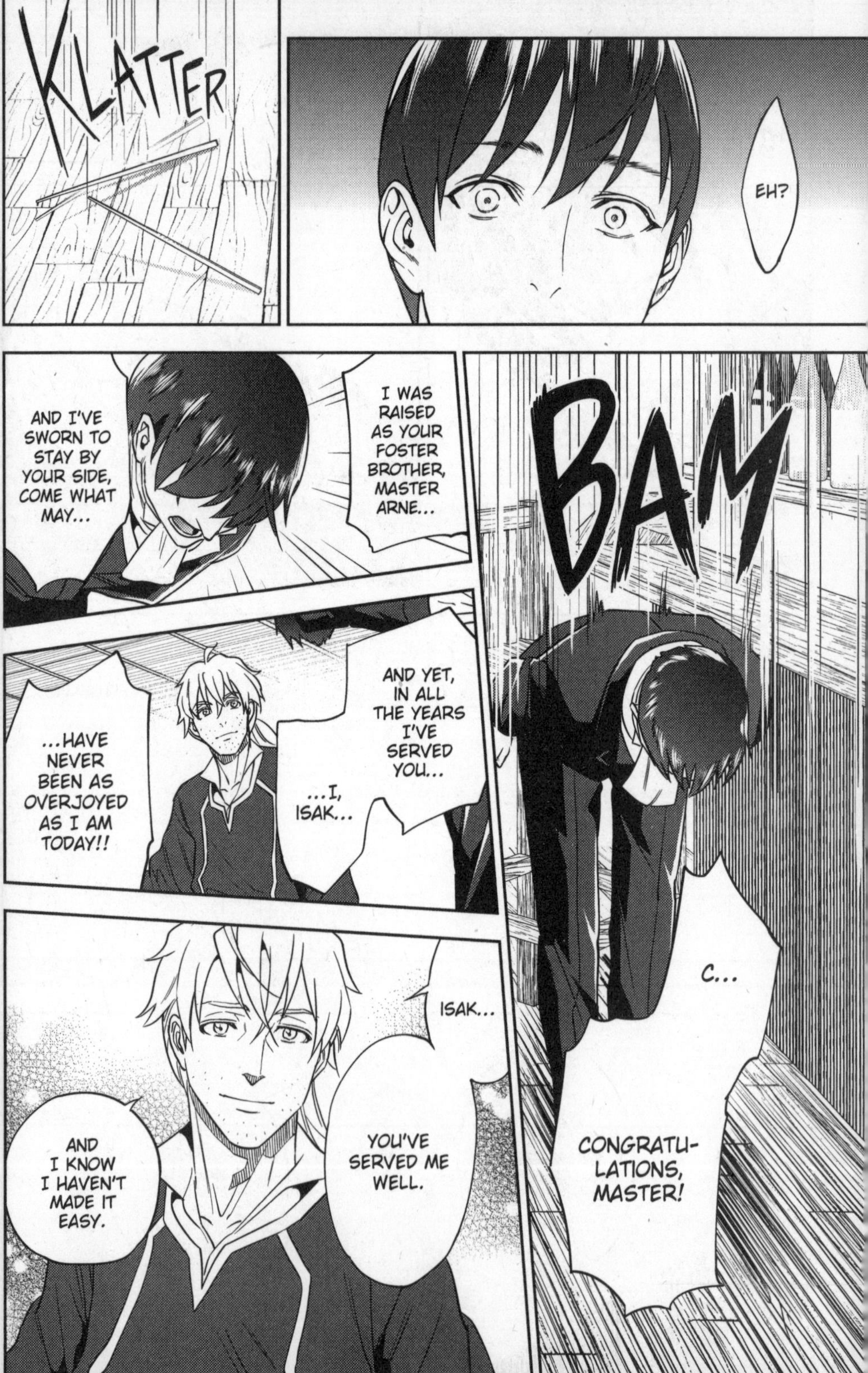
EH?
KLATTER
BAM
C...
CONGRATU-LATIONS, MASTER!
I WAS RAISED AS YOUR FOSTER BROTHER, MASTER ARNE...
AND I'VE SWORN TO STAY BY YOUR SIDE, COME WHAT MAY...
AND YET, IN ALL THE YEARS I'VE SERVED YOU...
...I, ISAK...
...HAVE NEVER BEEN AS OVERJOYED AS I AM TODAY!!
ISAK...
YOU'VE SERVED ME WELL.
AND I KNOW I HAVEN'T MADE IT EASY.

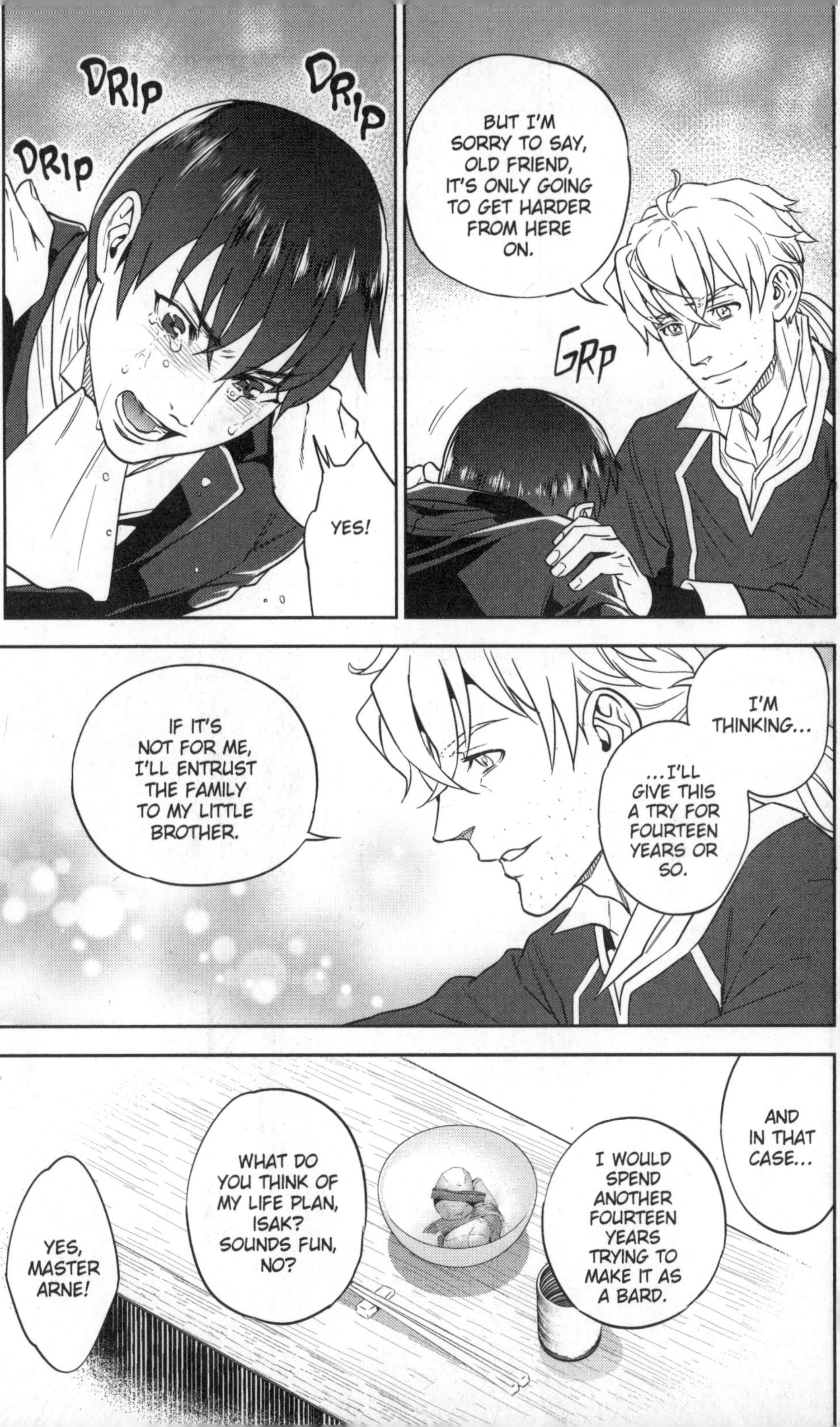
BUT I'M SORRY TO SAY, OLD FRIEND, IT'S ONLY GOING TO GET HARDER FROM HERE ON.
GRP
DRIP
DRIP
DRIP
YES!
I'M THINKING...
...I'LL GIVE THIS A TRY FOR FOURTEEN YEARS OR SO.
IF IT'S NOT FOR ME, I'LL ENTRUST THE FAMILY TO MY LITTLE BROTHER.
AND IN THAT CASE...
I WOULD SPEND ANOTHER FOURTEEN YEARS TRYING TO MAKE IT AS A BARD.
WHAT DO YOU THINK OF MY LIFE PLAN, ISAK? SOUNDS FUN, NO?
YES, MASTER ARNE!

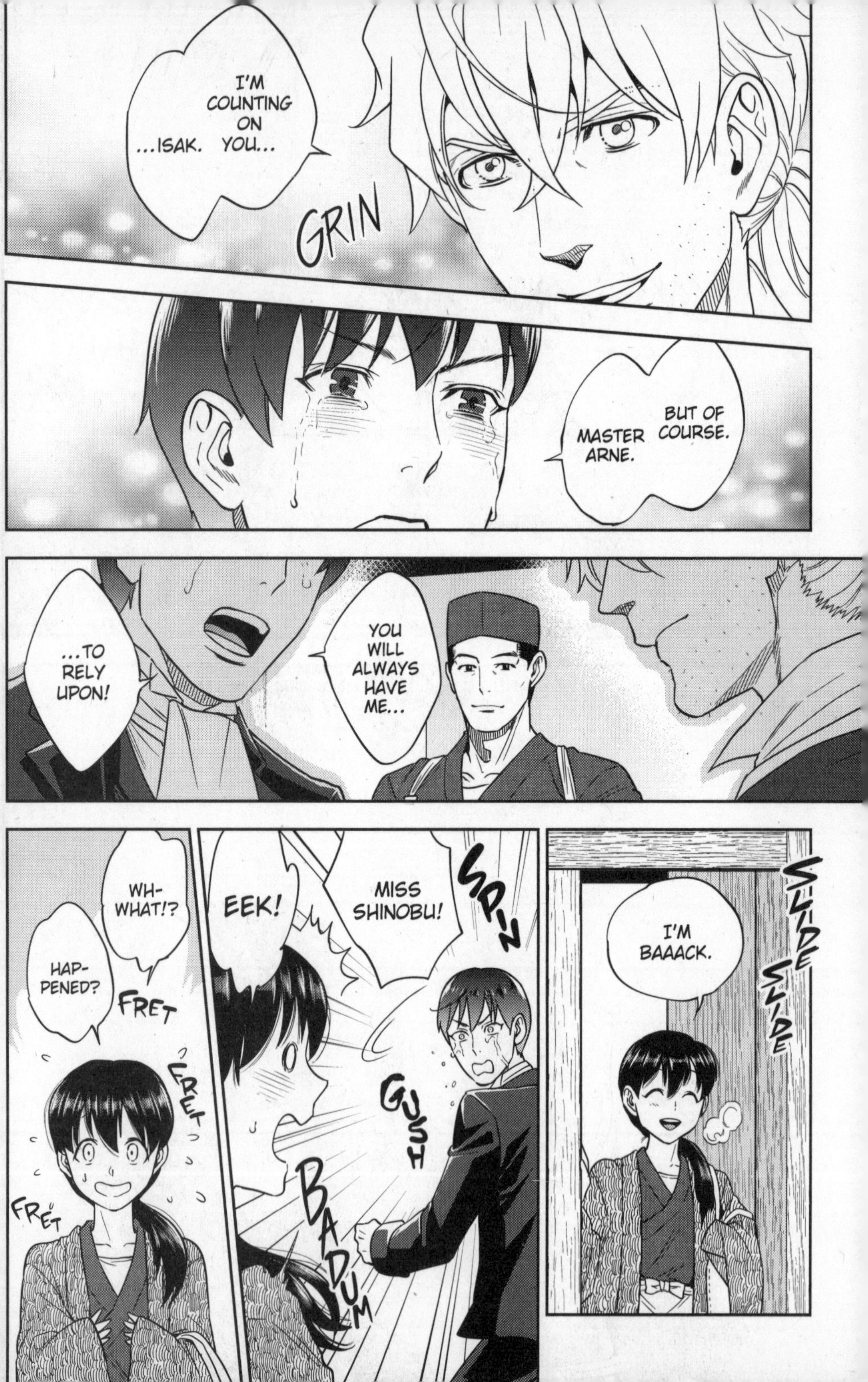
I'M COUNTING ON YOU...
...ISAK.
GRIN
BUT OF COURSE.
MASTER ARNE.
YOU WILL ALWAYS HAVE ME...
...TO RELY UPON!
SLIDE SLIDE
I'M BAAACK.
SPIN
MISS SHINOBU!
GUSH
BADUM
EEK!
WH-WHAT!?
HAP-PENED?
FRET
FRET
FRET

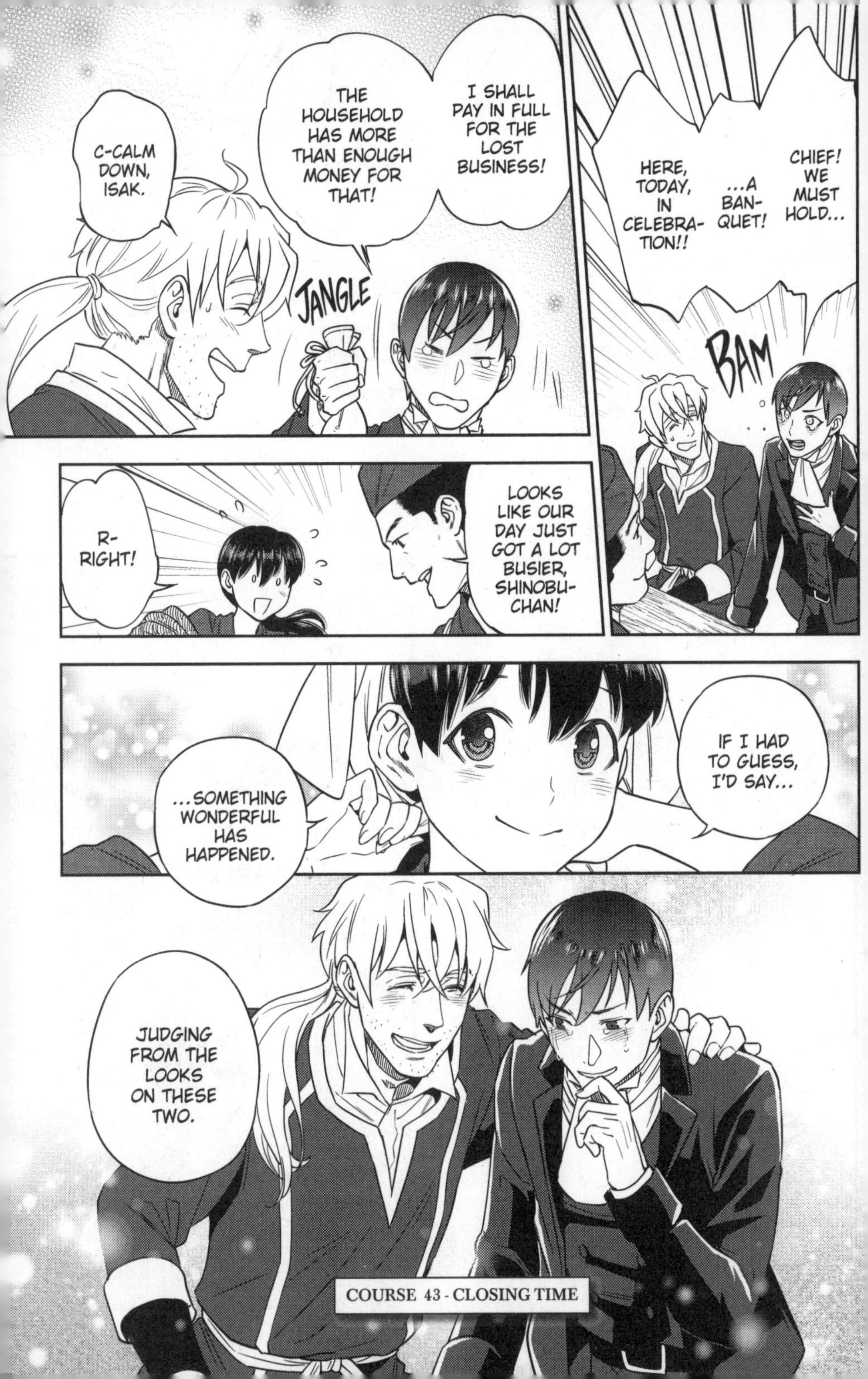
CHIEF! WE MUST HOLD...
...A BAN-QUET!
HERE, TODAY, IN CELEBRA-TION!!
BAM
I SHALL PAY IN FULL FOR THE LOST BUSINESS!
THE HOUSEHOLD HAS MORE THAN ENOUGH MONEY FOR THAT!
JANGLE
C-CALM DOWN, ISAK.
LOOKS LIKE OUR DAY JUST GOT A LOT BUSIER, SHINOBU-CHAN!
R-RIGHT!
IF I HAD TO GUESS, I'D SAY...
...SOMETHING WONDERFUL HAS HAPPENED.
JUDGING FROM THE LOOKS ON THESE TWO.
COURSE 43 - CLOSING TIME

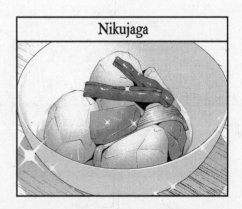
Nikujaga

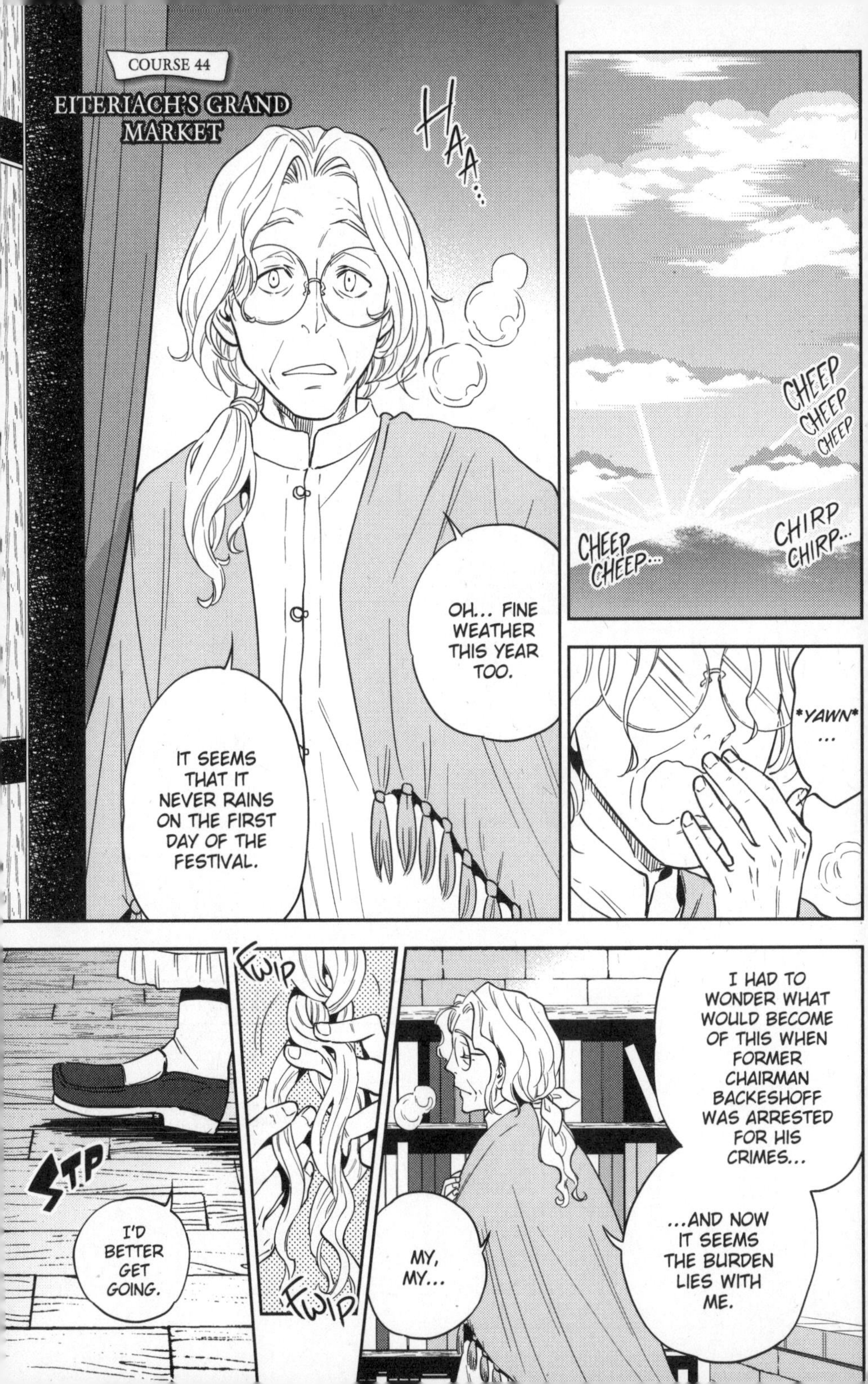
CHEEP CHEEP CHEEP
CHIRP CHIRP...
CHEEP CHEEP...
YAWN ...
COURSE 44
EITERIACH'S GRAND MARKET
HAAA...
OH... FINE WEATHER THIS YEAR TOO.
IT SEEMS THAT IT NEVER RAINS ON THE FIRST DAY OF THE FESTIVAL.
I HAD TO WONDER WHAT WOULD BECOME OF THIS WHEN FORMER CHAIRMAN BACKESHOFF WAS ARRESTED FOR HIS CRIMES...
...AND NOW IT SEEMS THE BURDEN LIES WITH ME.
MY, MY...
FWIP
FWIP
STP
I'D BETTER GET GOING.

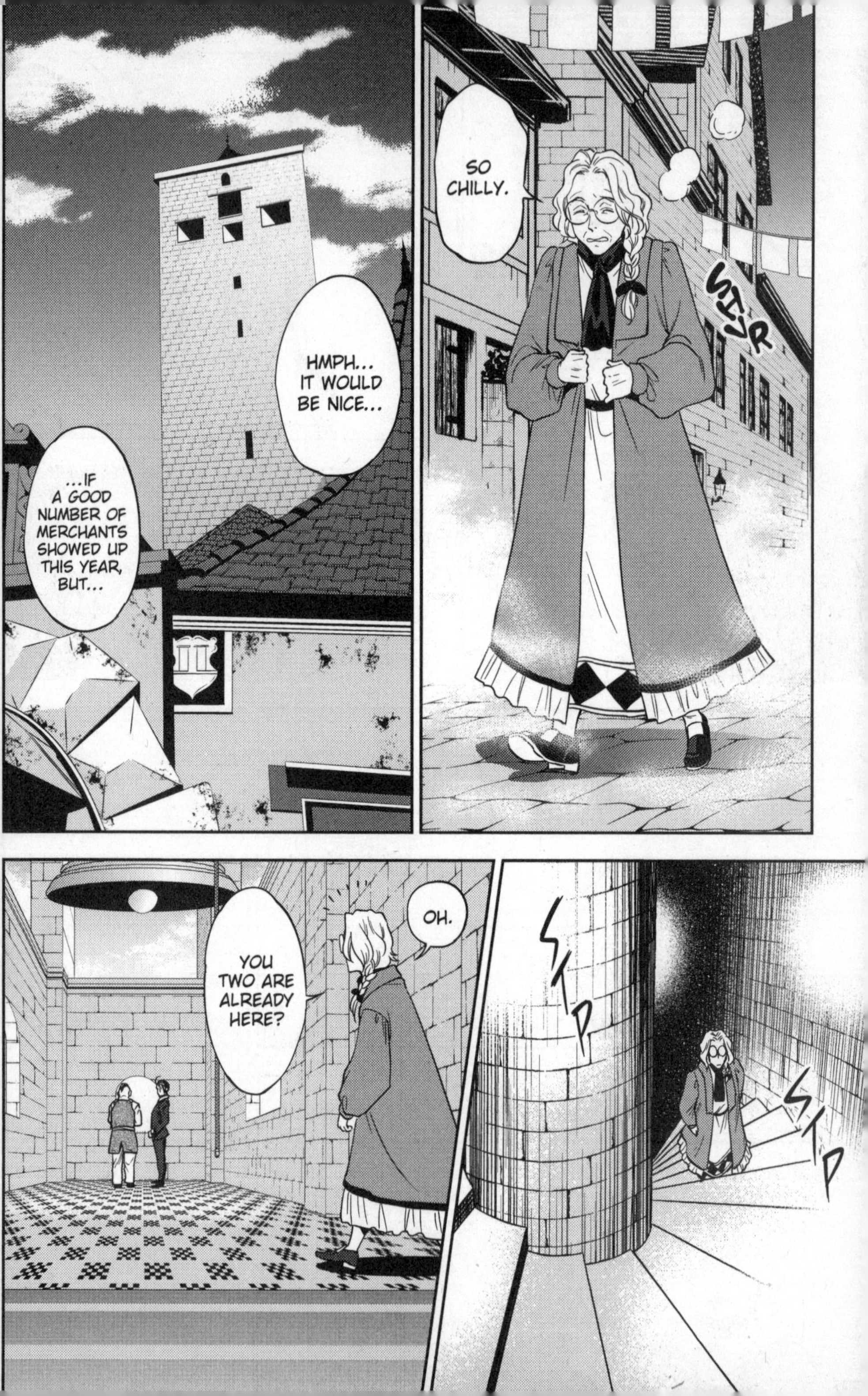
SO CHILLY.
SHIVR
HMPH... IT WOULD BE NICE...
...IF A GOOD NUMBER OF MERCHANTS SHOWED UP THIS YEAR, BUT...
STEP
STEP
OH.
YOU TWO ARE ALREADY HERE?

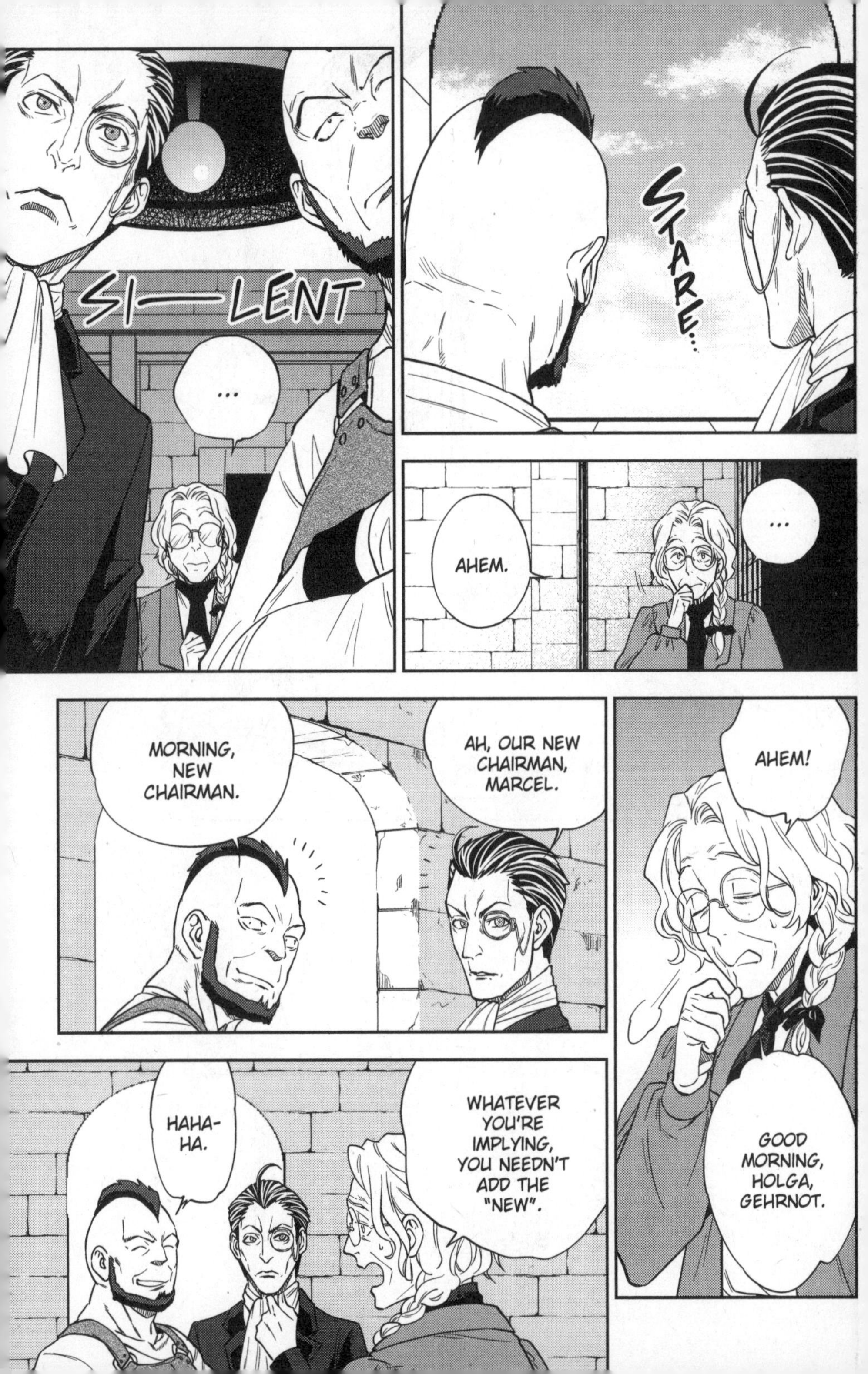
STARE...
...
AHEM.
SI—LENT
...
AHEM!
GOOD MORNING, HOLGA, GEHRNOT.
AH, OUR NEW CHAIRMAN, MARCEL.
MORNING, NEW CHAIRMAN.
WHATEVER YOU'RE IMPLYING, YOU NEEDN'T ADD THE "NEW".
HAHA-HA.

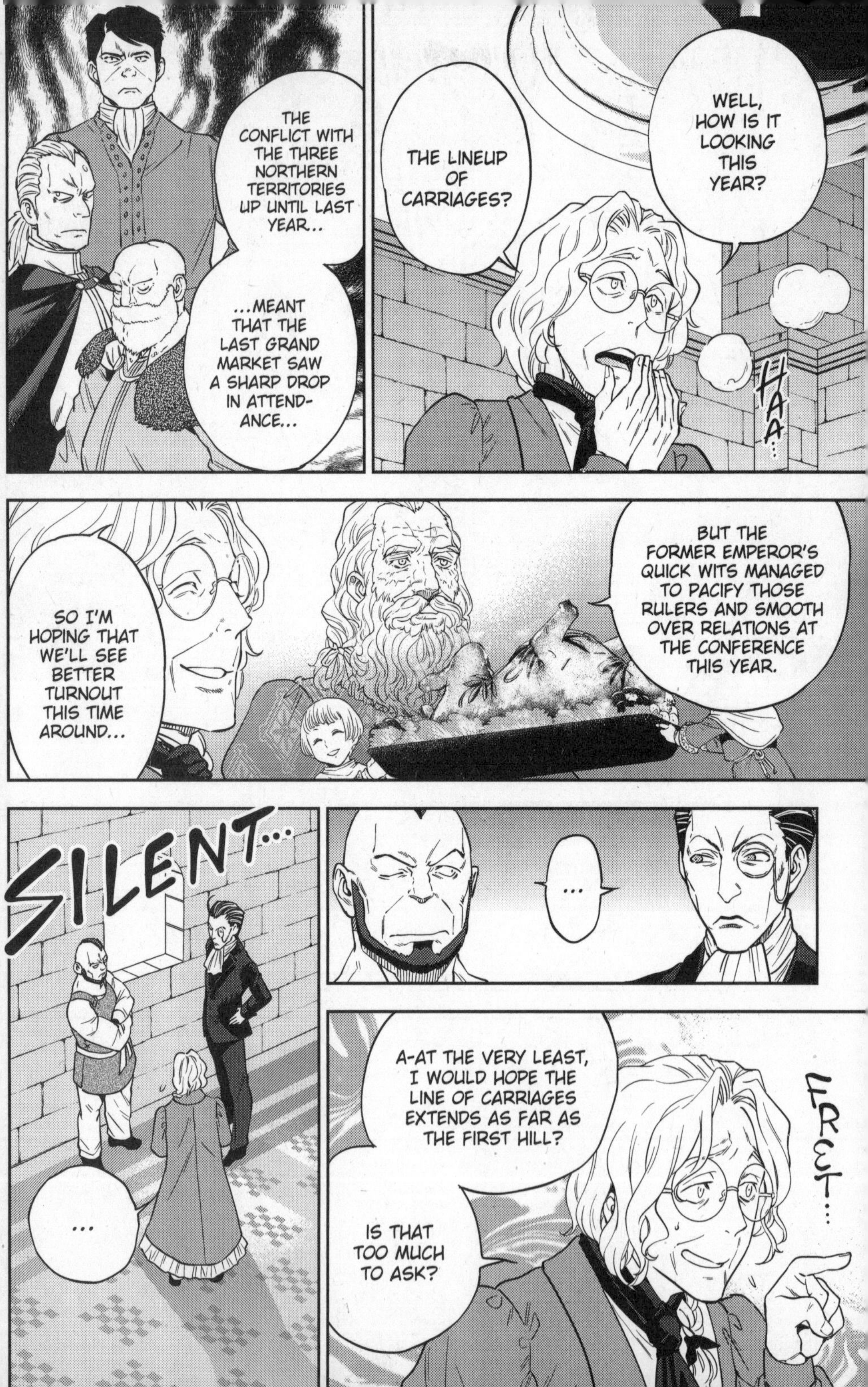
WELL, HOW IS IT LOOKING THIS YEAR?
THE LINEUP OF CARRIAGES?
HAA...
THE CONFLICT WITH THE THREE NORTHERN TERRITORIES UP UNTIL LAST YEAR...
...MEANT THAT THE LAST GRAND MARKET SAW A SHARP DROP IN ATTEND-ANCE...
BUT THE FORMER EMPEROR'S QUICK WITS MANAGED TO PACIFY THOSE RULERS AND SMOOTH OVER RELATIONS AT THE CONFERENCE THIS YEAR.
SO I'M HOPING THAT WE'LL SEE BETTER TURNOUT THIS TIME AROUND...
...
A-AT THE VERY LEAST, I WOULD HOPE THE LINE OF CARRIAGES EXTENDS AS FAR AS THE FIRST HILL?
IS THAT TOO MUCH TO ASK?
FRET...
SILENT...
...

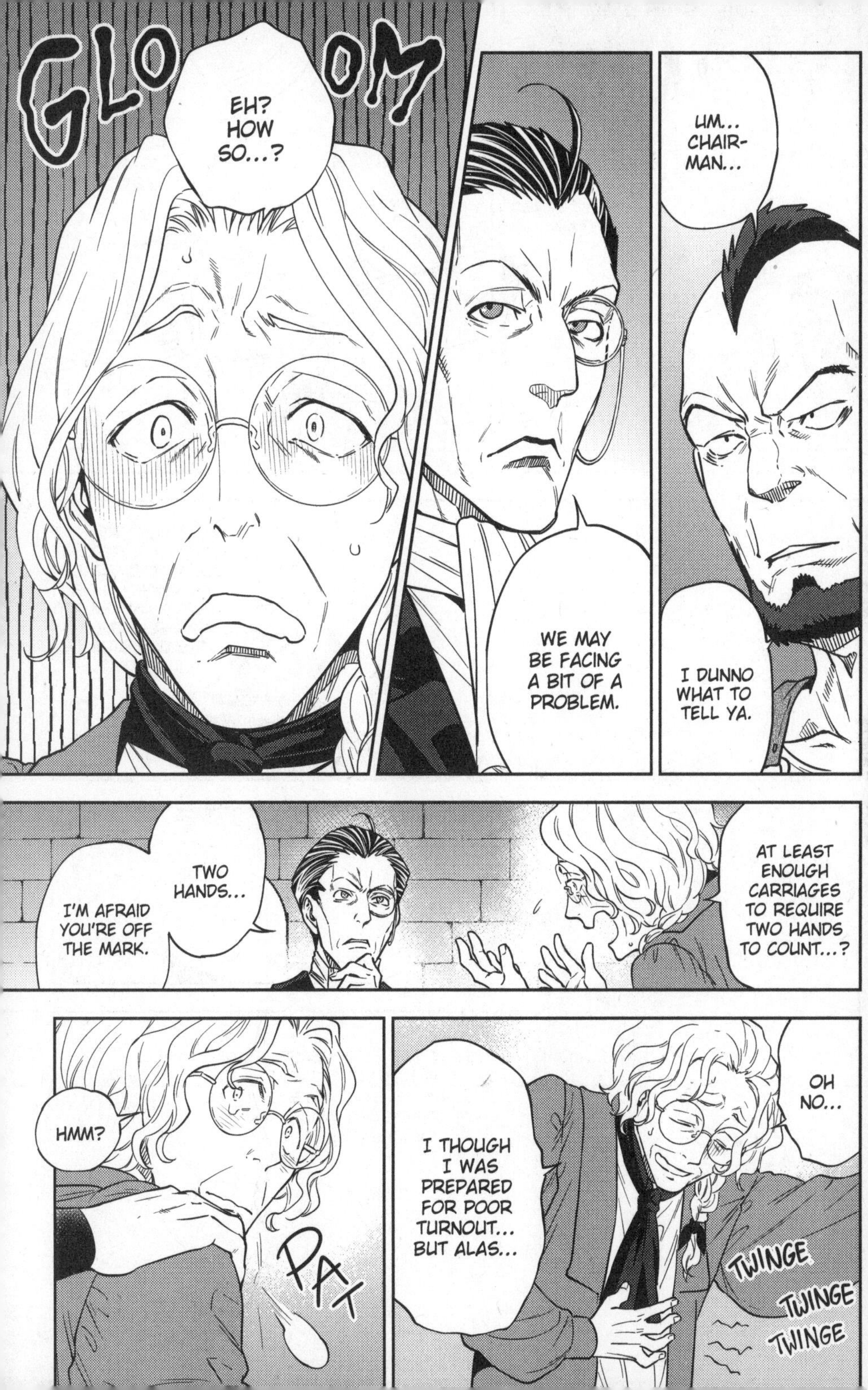
UM... CHAIR-MAN...
I DUNNO WHAT TO TELL YA.
WE MAY BE FACING A BIT OF A PROBLEM.
GLO OM
EH? HOW SO...?
AT LEAST ENOUGH CARRIAGES TO REQUIRE TWO HANDS TO COUNT...?
TWO HANDS...
I'M AFRAID YOU'RE OFF THE MARK.
OH NO...
I THOUGH I WAS PREPARED FOR POOR TURNOUT... BUT ALAS...
TWINGE
TWINGE
TWINGE
HMM?
PAT

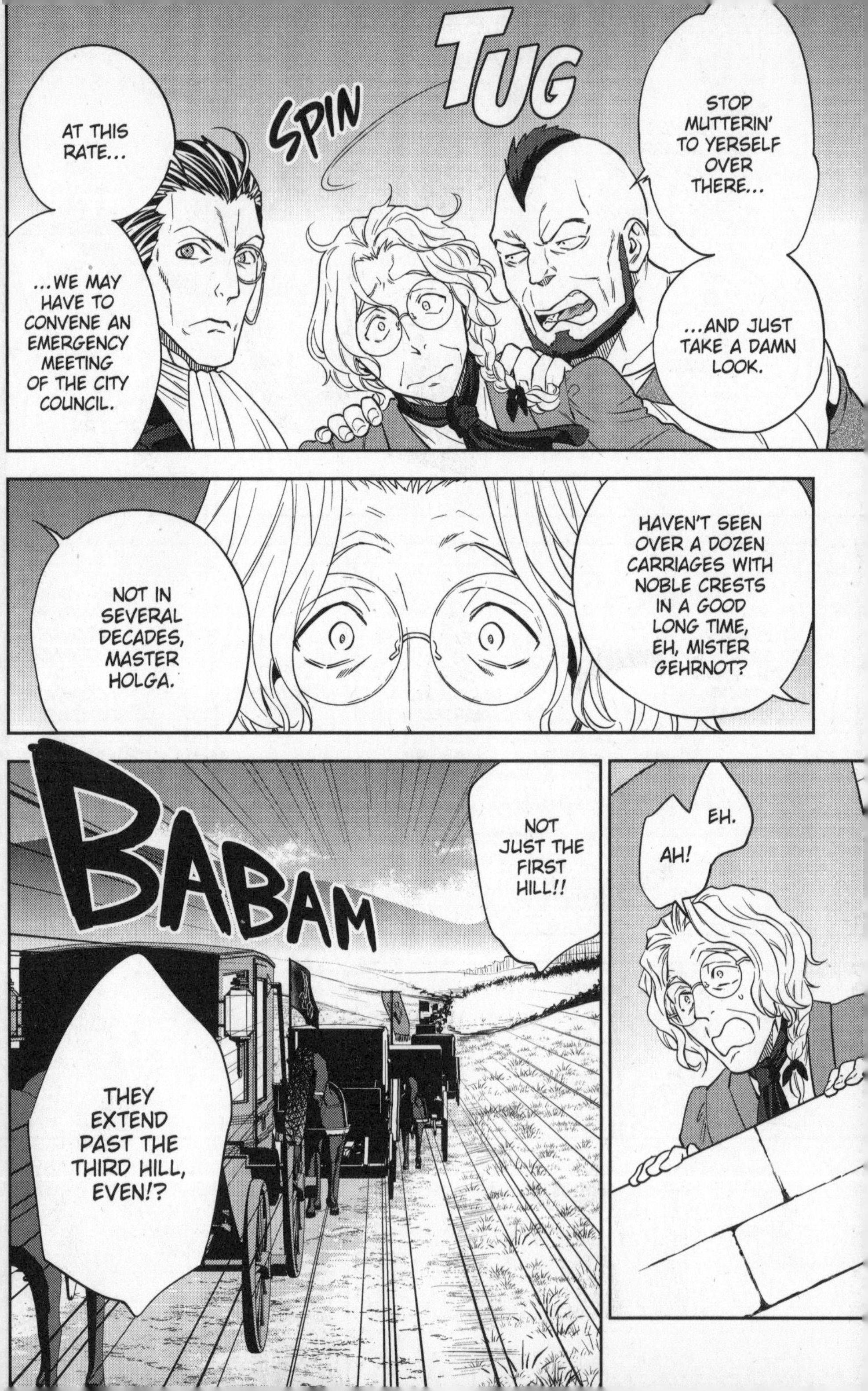
TUG
STOP MUTTERIN' TO YERSELF OVER THERE...
...AND JUST TAKE A DAMN LOOK.
SPIN
AT THIS RATE...
...WE MAY HAVE TO CONVENE AN EMERGENCY MEETING OF THE CITY COUNCIL.
HAVEN'T SEEN OVER A DOZEN CARRIAGES WITH NOBLE CRESTS IN A GOOD LONG TIME, EH, MISTER GEHRNOT?
NOT IN SEVERAL DECADES, MASTER HOLGA.
EH.
AH!
NOT JUST THE FIRST HILL!!
BABAM
THEY EXTEND PAST THE THIRD HILL, EVEN!?

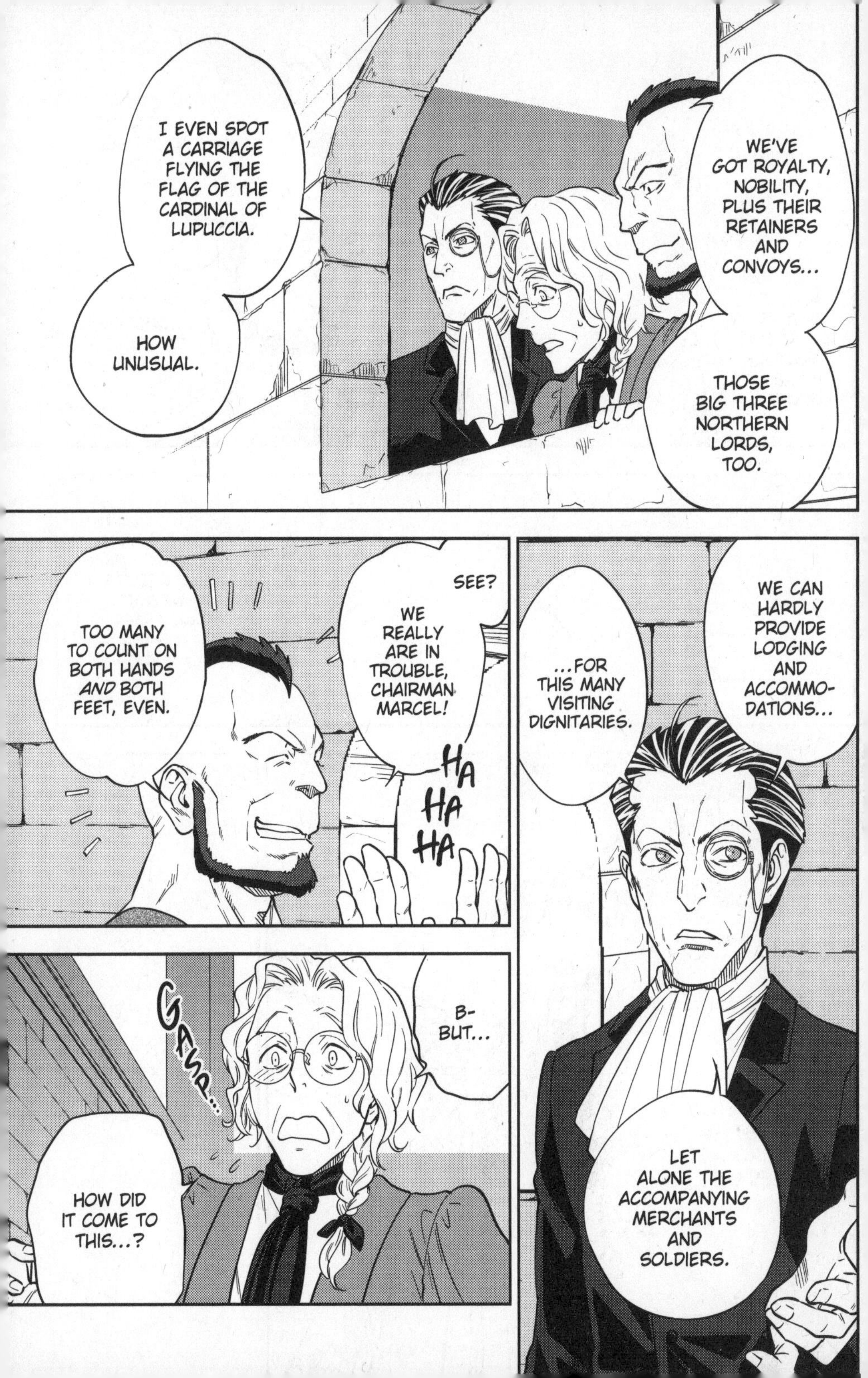
WE'VE GOT ROYALTY, NOBILITY, PLUS THEIR RETAINERS AND CONVOYS...
THOSE BIG THREE NORTHERN LORDS, TOO.
I EVEN SPOT A CARRIAGE FLYING THE FLAG OF THE CARDINAL OF LUPUCCIA.
HOW UNUSUAL.
WE CAN HARDLY PROVIDE LODGING AND ACCOMMO-DATIONS...
...FOR THIS MANY VISITING DIGNITARIES.
LET ALONE THE ACCOMPANYING MERCHANTS AND SOLDIERS.
SEE?
WE REALLY ARE IN TROUBLE, CHAIRMAN MARCEL!
HA HA HA
TOO MANY TO COUNT ON BOTH HANDS *AND* BOTH FEET, EVEN.
B-BUT...
GASP...
HOW DID IT COME TO THIS...?

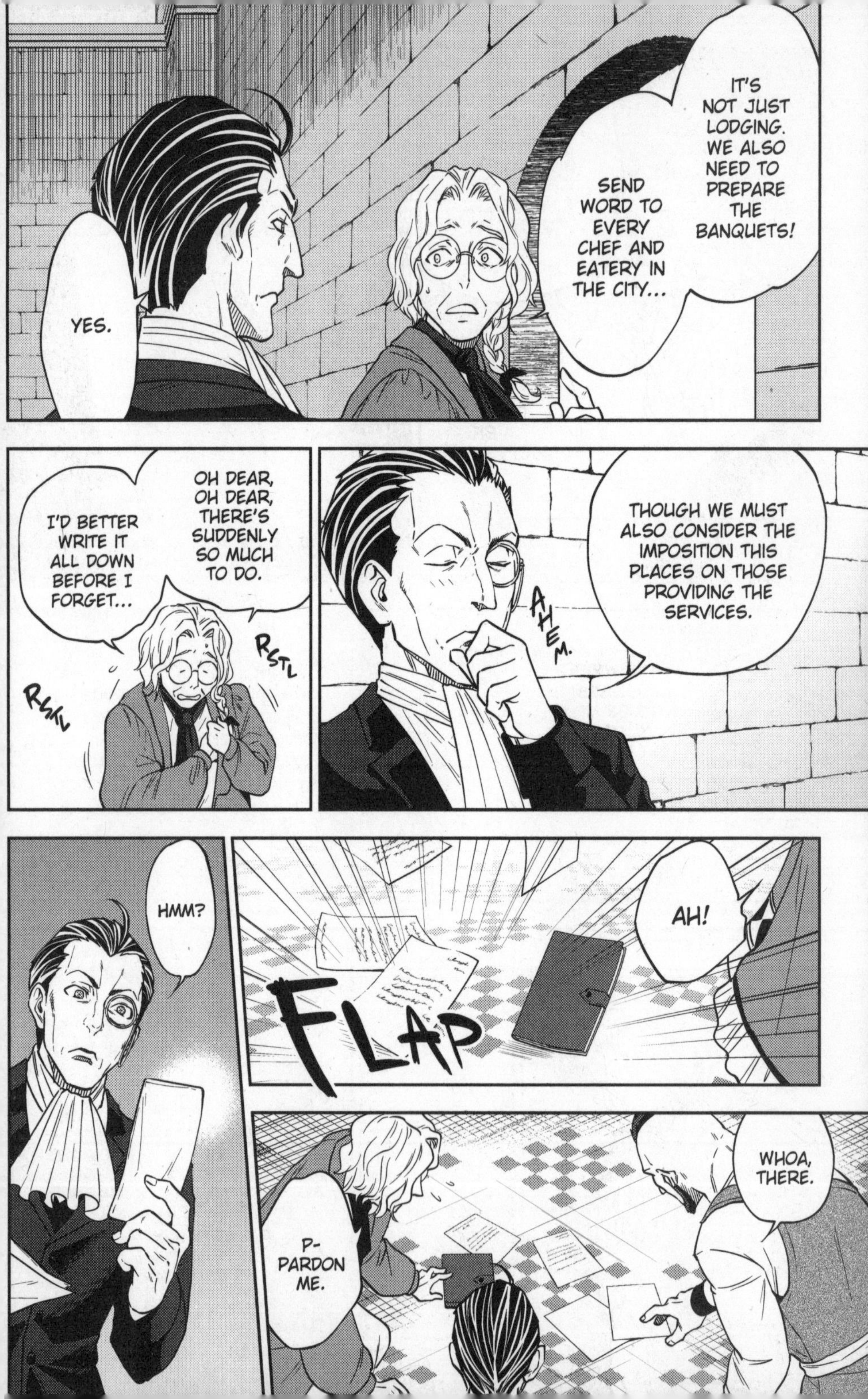
IT'S NOT JUST LODGING. WE ALSO NEED TO PREPARE THE BANQUETS!
SEND WORD TO EVERY CHEF AND EATERY IN THE CITY...
YES.
THOUGH WE MUST ALSO CONSIDER THE IMPOSITION THIS PLACES ON THOSE PROVIDING THE SERVICES.
AHEM.
OH DEAR, OH DEAR, THERE'S SUDDENLY SO MUCH TO DO.
I'D BETTER WRITE IT ALL DOWN BEFORE I FORGET...
RSTL
RSKL
AH!
FLAP
WHOA, THERE.
P-PARDON ME.
HMM?

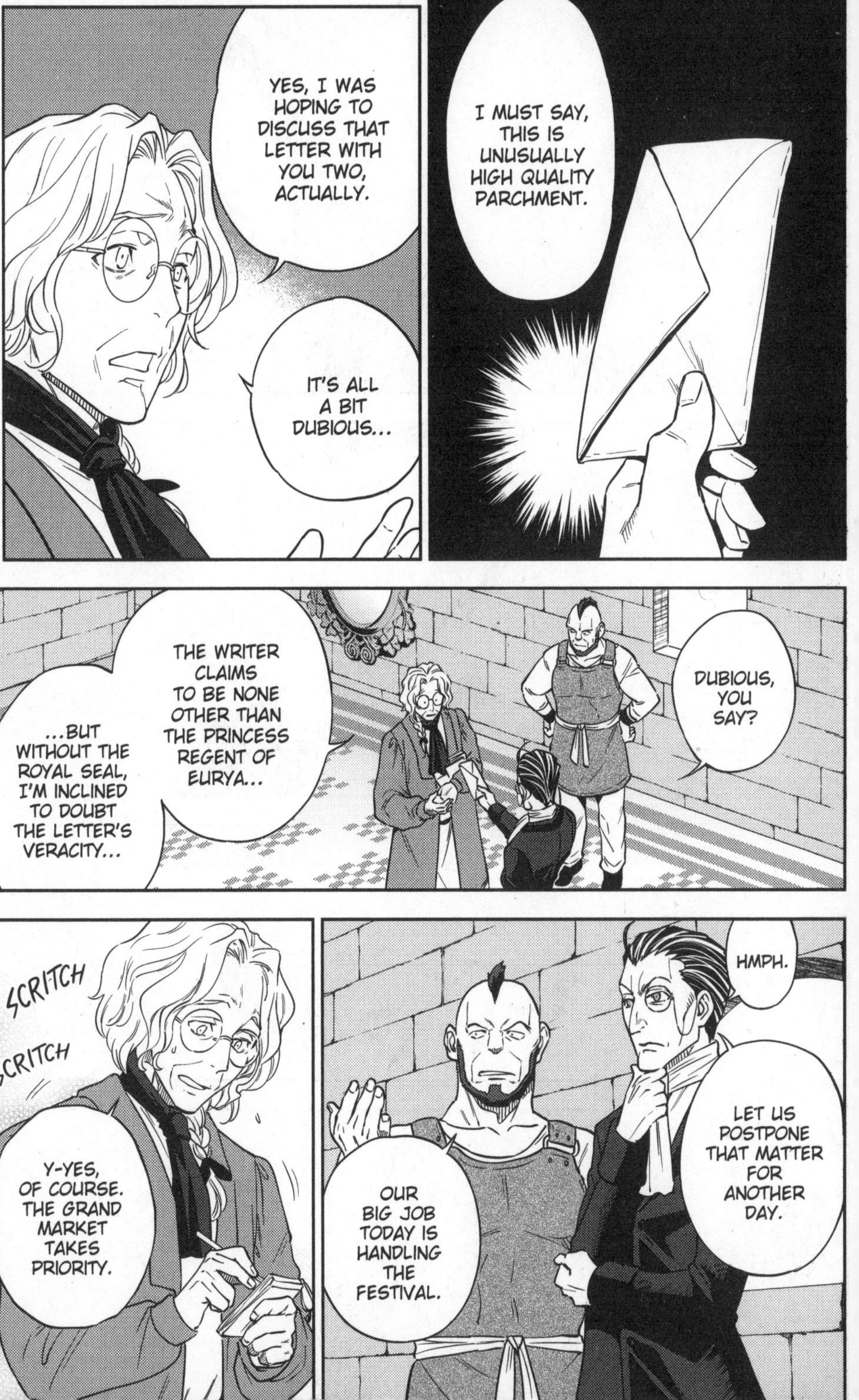
I MUST SAY, THIS IS UNUSUALLY HIGH QUALITY PARCHMENT.
YES, I WAS HOPING TO DISCUSS THAT LETTER WITH YOU TWO, ACTUALLY.
IT'S ALL A BIT DUBIOUS...
DUBIOUS, YOU SAY?
THE WRITER CLAIMS TO BE NONE OTHER THAN THE PRINCESS REGENT OF EURYA...
...BUT WITHOUT THE ROYAL SEAL, I'M INCLINED TO DOUBT THE LETTER'S VERACITY...
HMPH.
LET US POSTPONE THAT MATTER FOR ANOTHER DAY.
OUR BIG JOB TODAY IS HANDLING THE FESTIVAL.
SCRITCH
SCRITCH
Y-YES, OF COURSE. THE GRAND MARKET TAKES PRIORITY.

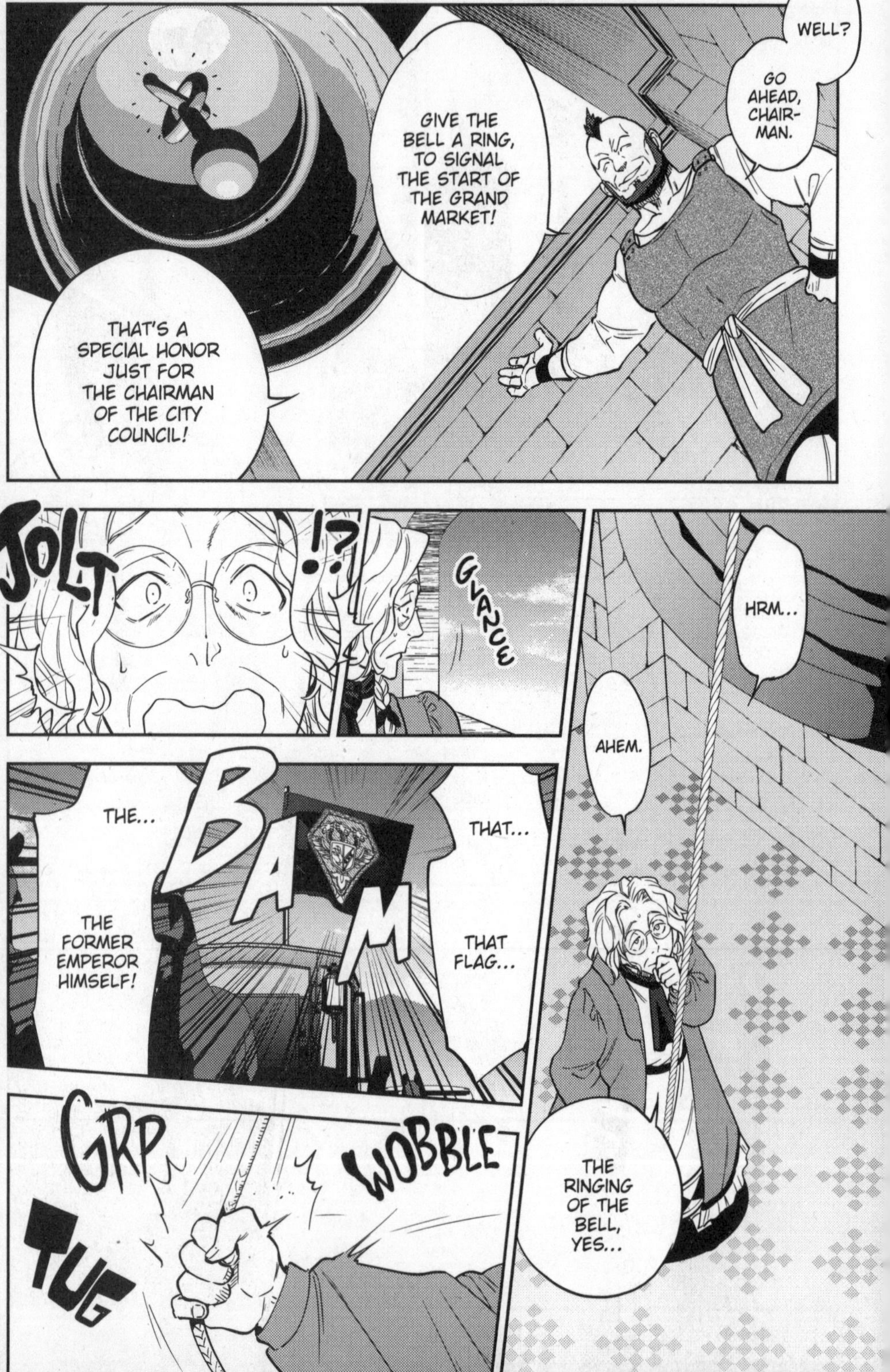
WELL?
GO AHEAD, CHAIR-MAN.
GIVE THE BELL A RING, TO SIGNAL THE START OF THE GRAND MARKET!
THAT'S A SPECIAL HONOR JUST FOR THE CHAIRMAN OF THE CITY COUNCIL!
HRM...
AHEM.
THE RINGING OF THE BELL, YES...
GLANCE
JOLT
!?
THAT...
THAT FLAG...
BAM
THE...
THE FORMER EMPEROR HIMSELF!
WOBBLE
GRP
TUG

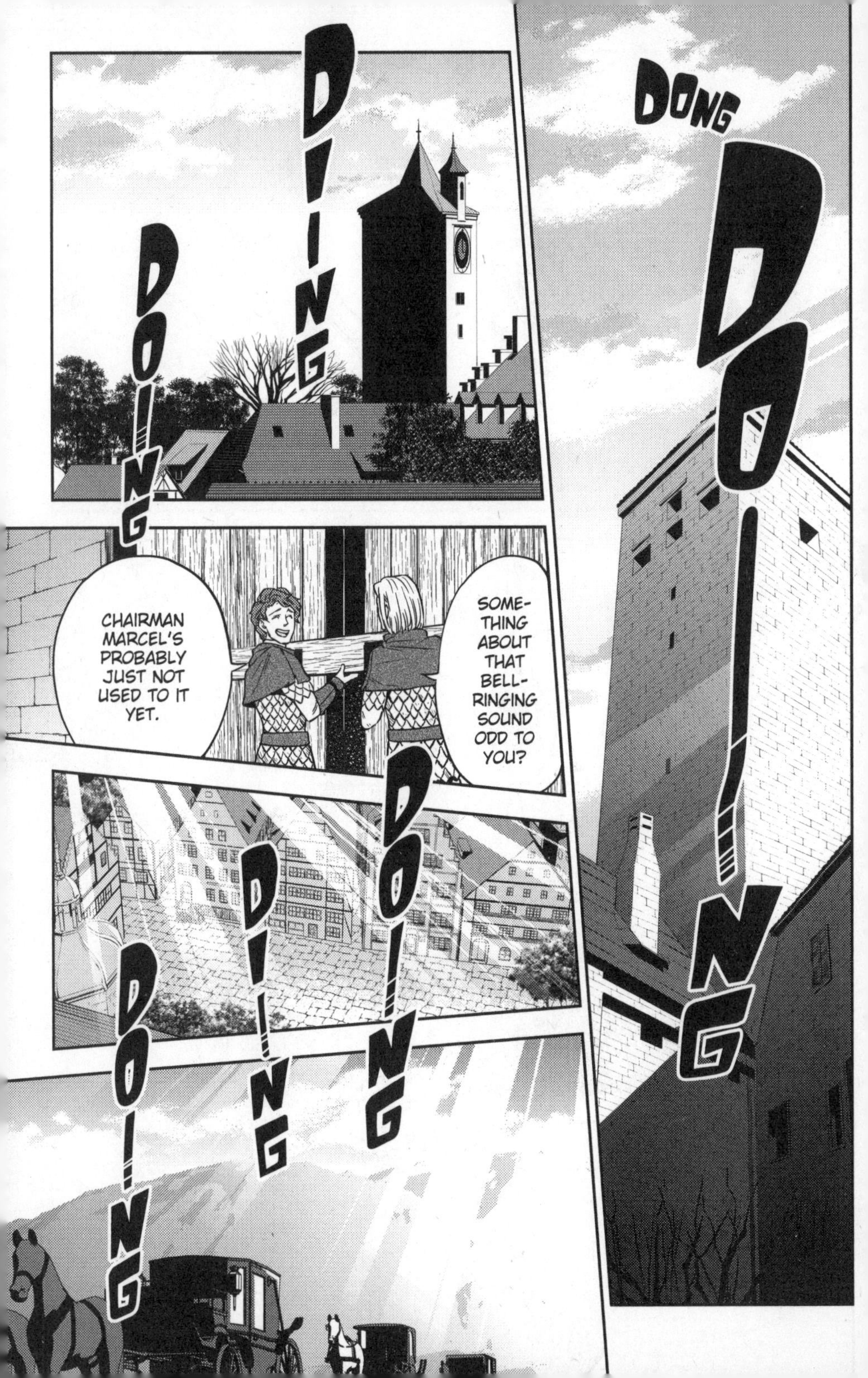
DONG
DOING
DING
DOING
SOME-THING ABOUT THAT BELL-RINGING SOUND ODD TO YOU?
CHAIRMAN MARCEL'S PROBABLY JUST NOT USED TO IT YET.
DOING
DING
DOING

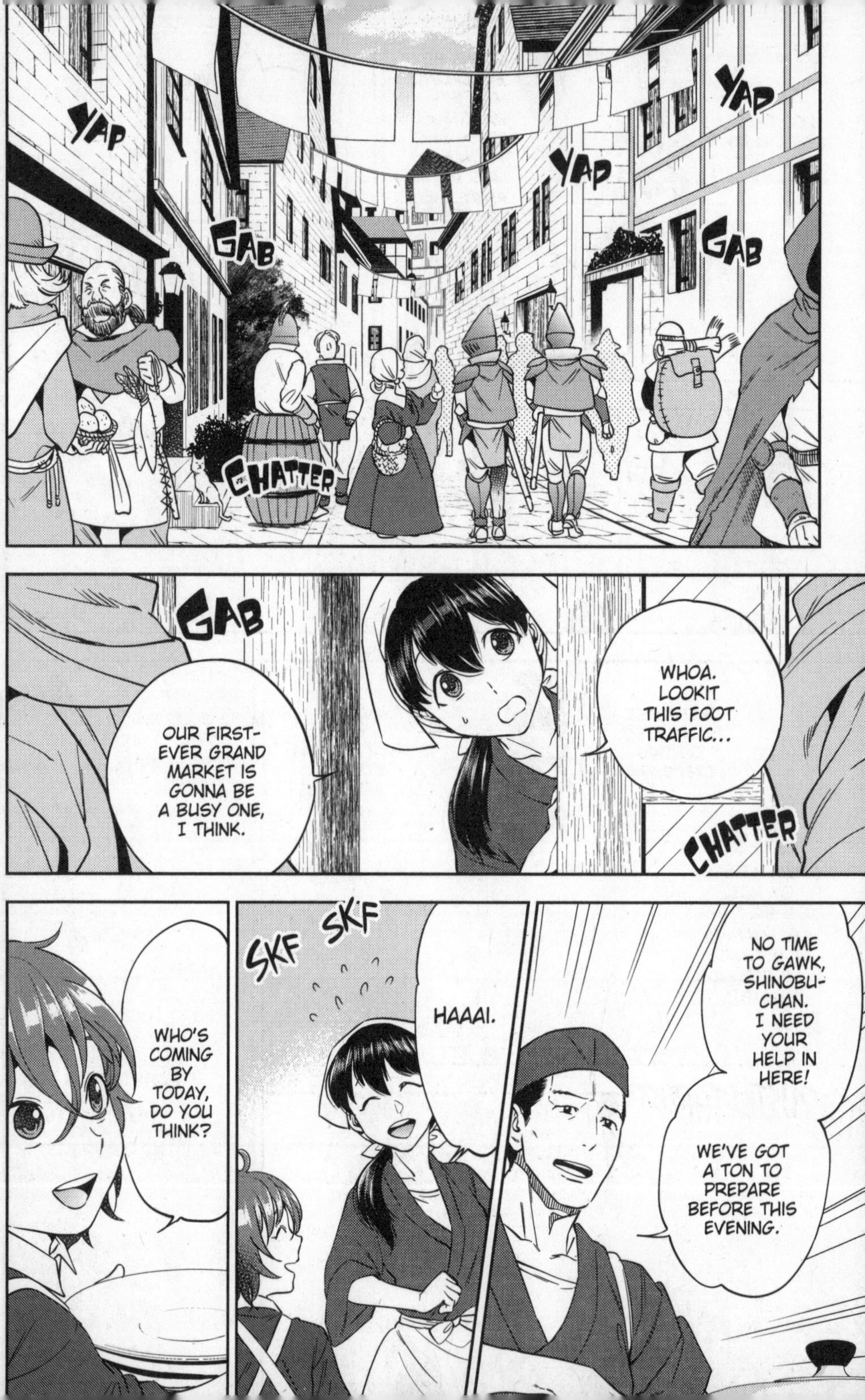
YAP
YAP
GAB
YAP
GAB
CHATTER
WHOA. LOOKIT THIS FOOT TRAFFIC...
CHATTER
GAB
OUR FIRST-EVER GRAND MARKET IS GONNA BE A BUSY ONE, I THINK.
NO TIME TO GAWK, SHINOBU-CHAN. I NEED YOUR HELP IN HERE!
WE'VE GOT A TON TO PREPARE BEFORE THIS EVENING.
HAAAI.
SKF SKF
WHO'S COMING BY TODAY, DO YOU THINK?

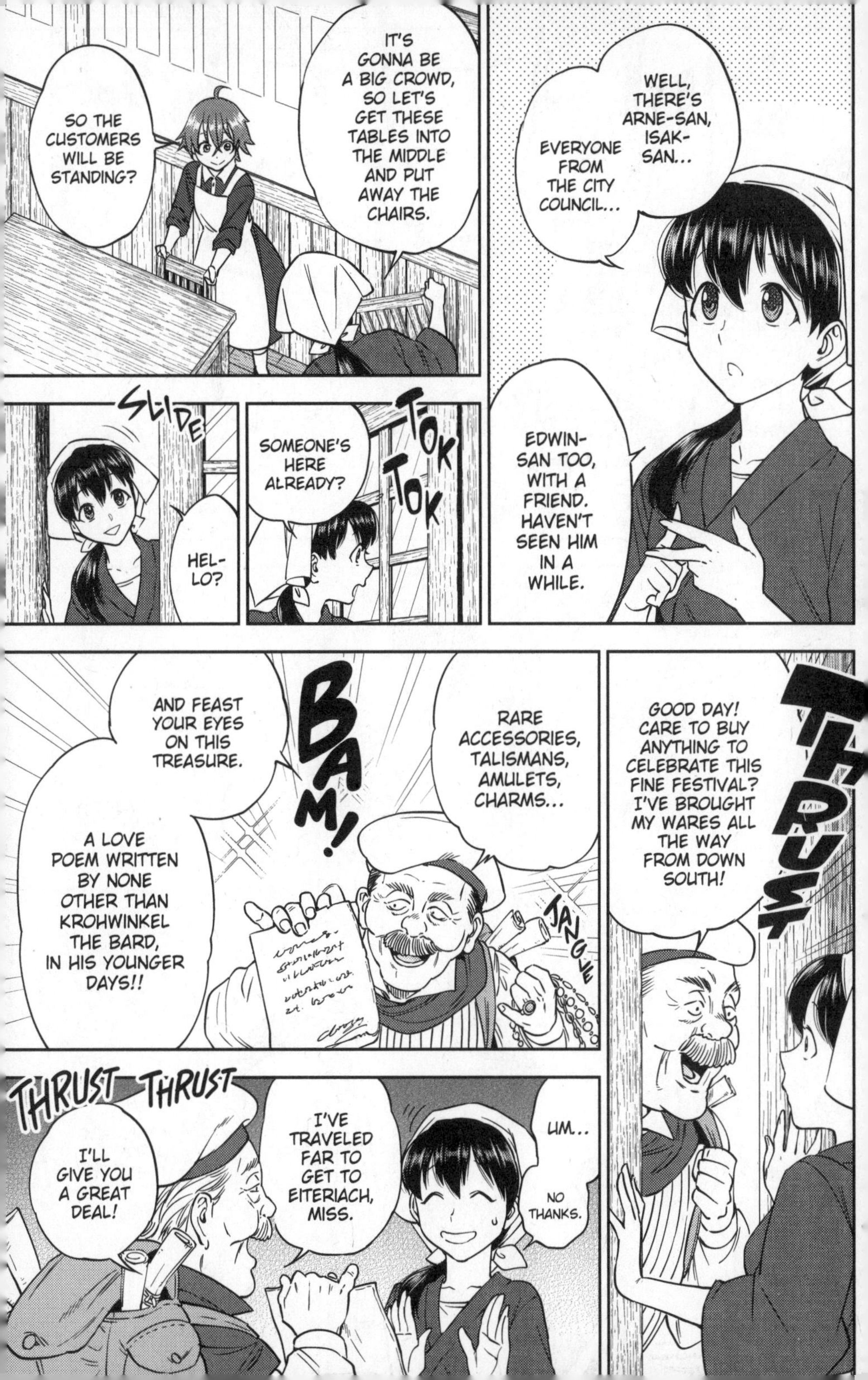

WELL, THERE'S ARNE-SAN, ISAK-SAN...
EVERYONE FROM THE CITY COUNCIL...
EDWIN-SAN TOO, WITH A FRIEND. HAVEN'T SEEN HIM IN A WHILE.
IT'S GONNA BE A BIG CROWD, SO LET'S GET THESE TABLES INTO THE MIDDLE AND PUT AWAY THE CHAIRS.
SO THE CUSTOMERS WILL BE STANDING?
TOK TOK
SOMEONE'S HERE ALREADY?
SLIDE
HEL-LO?
THRUST
GOOD DAY! CARE TO BUY ANYTHING TO CELEBRATE THIS FINE FESTIVAL? I'VE BROUGHT MY WARES ALL THE WAY FROM DOWN SOUTH!
RARE ACCESSORIES, TALISMANS, AMULETS, CHARMS...
BAM!
AND FEAST YOUR EYES ON THIS TREASURE.
A LOVE POEM WRITTEN BY NONE OTHER THAN KROHWINKEL THE BARD, IN HIS YOUNGER DAYS!!
JANGLE
UM...
NO THANKS.
I'VE TRAVELED FAR TO GET TO EITERIACH, MISS.
I'LL GIVE YOU A GREAT DEAL!
THRUST THRUST

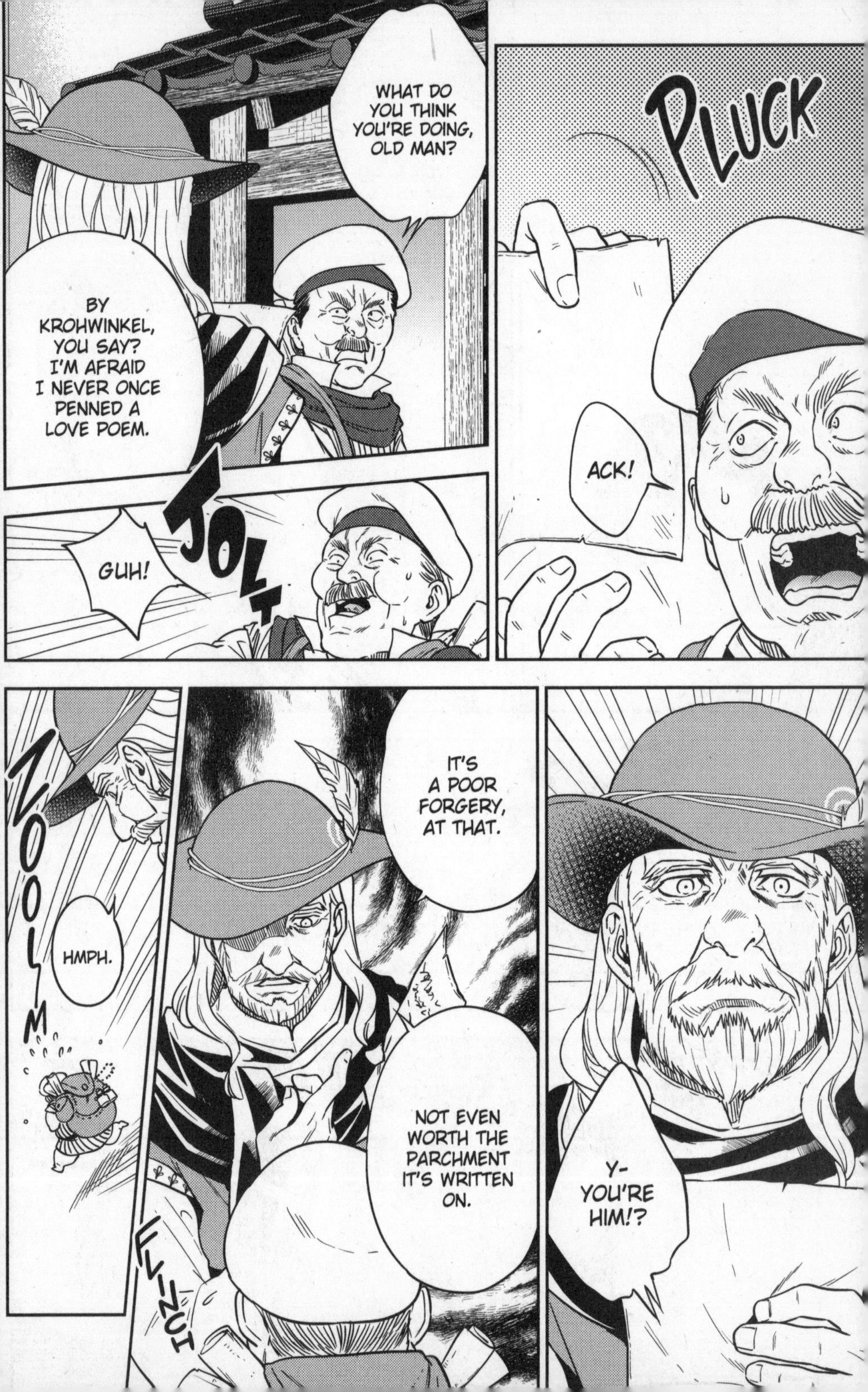
PLUCK
ACK!
WHAT DO YOU THINK YOU'RE DOING, OLD MAN?
BY KROHWINKEL, YOU SAY? I'M AFRAID I NEVER ONCE PENNED A LOVE POEM.
JOLT
GUH!
Y-YOU'RE HIM!?
IT'S A POOR FORGERY, AT THAT.
NOT EVEN WORTH THE PARCHMENT IT'S WRITTEN ON.
HMPH.

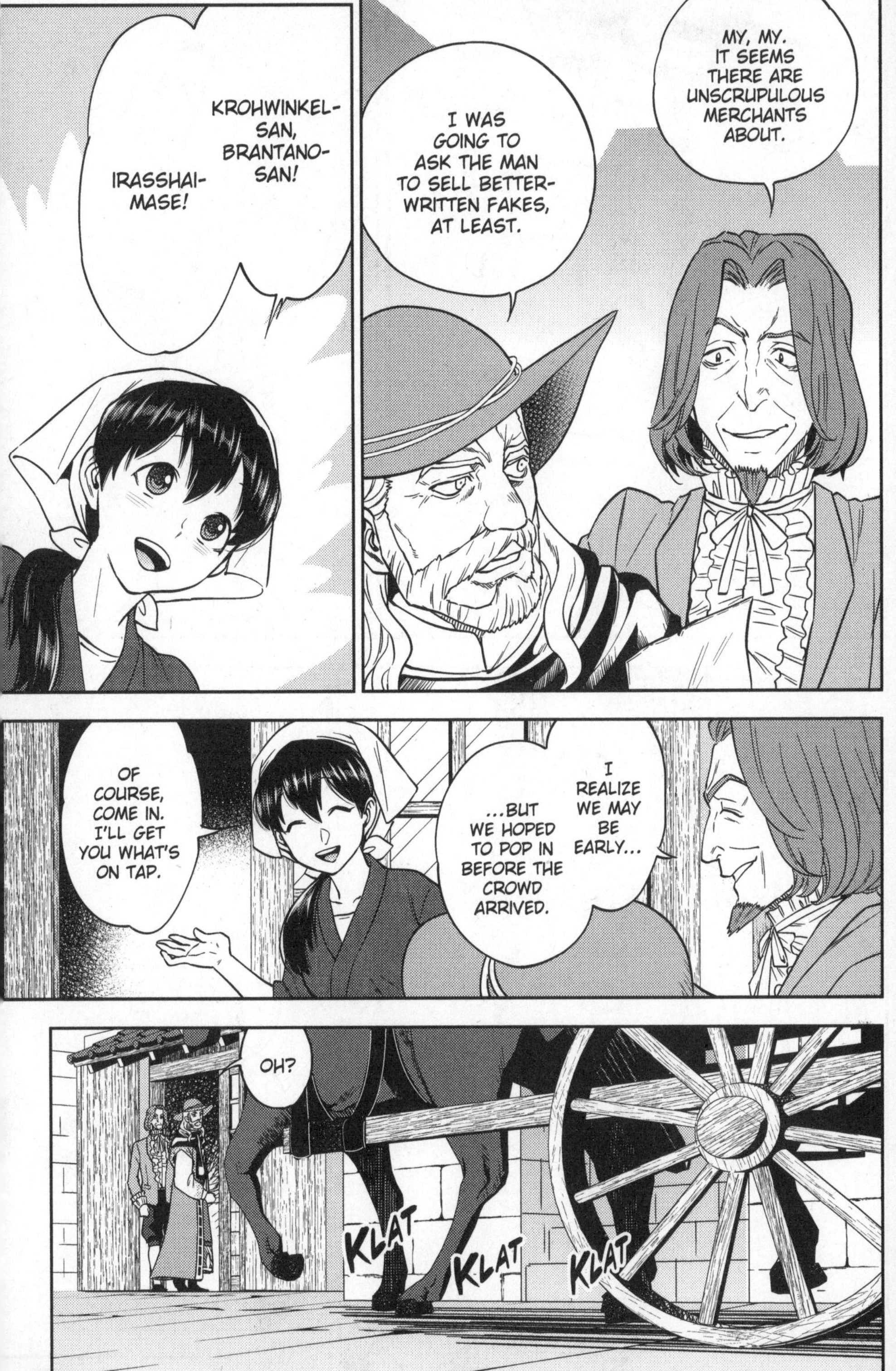
MY, MY. IT SEEMS THERE ARE UNSCRUPULOUS MERCHANTS ABOUT.
I WAS GOING TO ASK THE MAN TO SELL BETTER-WRITTEN FAKES, AT LEAST.
KROHWINKEL-SAN, BRANTANO-SAN!
IRASSHAI-MASE!
I REALIZE WE MAY BE EARLY...
...BUT WE HOPED TO POP IN BEFORE THE CROWD ARRIVED.
OF COURSE, COME IN. I'LL GET YOU WHAT'S ON TAP.
OH?
KLAT
KLAT
KLAT

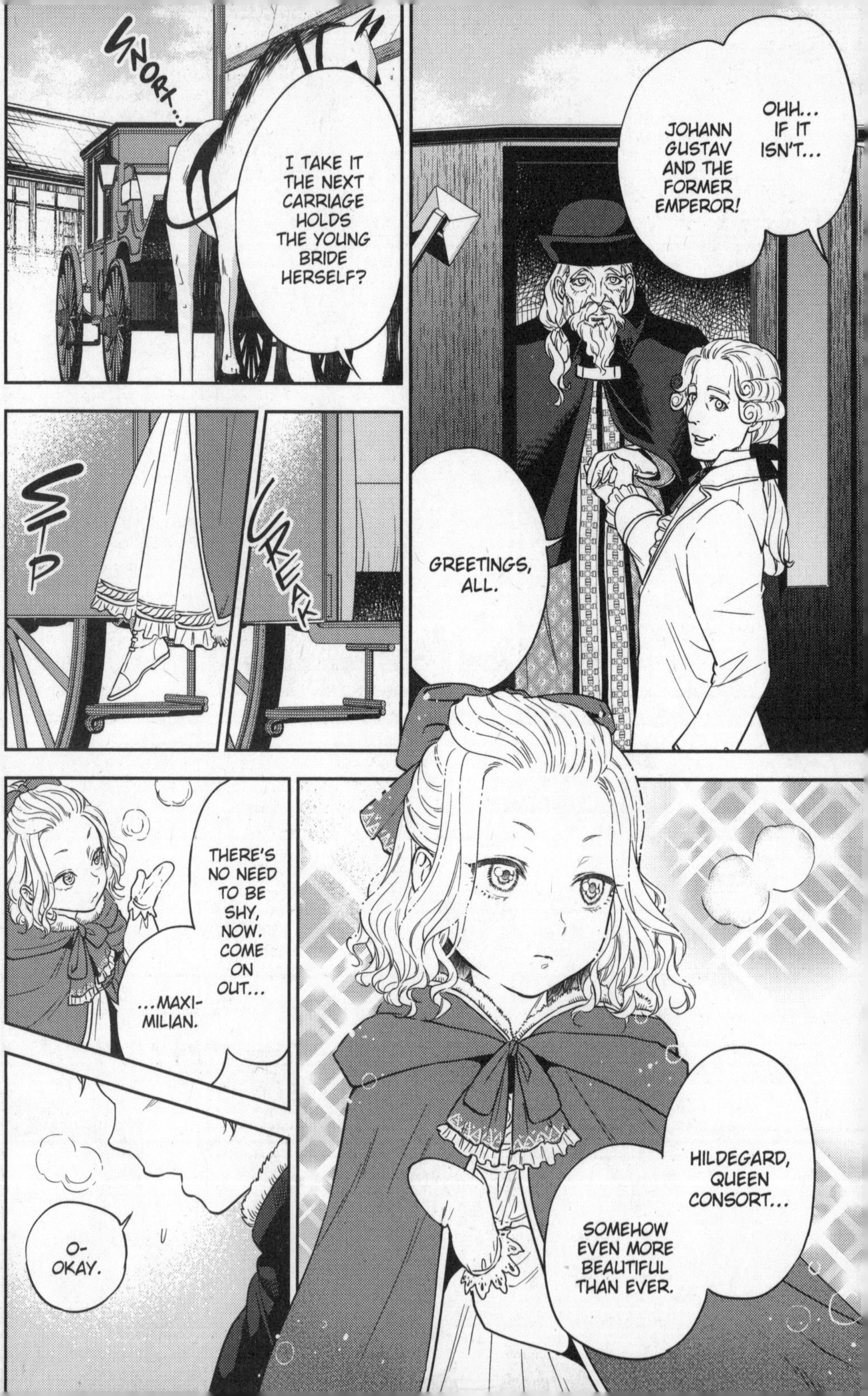
OHH... IF IT ISN'T...
JOHANN GUSTAV AND THE FORMER EMPEROR!
GREETINGS, ALL.
SNORT...
I TAKE IT THE NEXT CARRIAGE HOLDS THE YOUNG BRIDE HERSELF?
CREAK
STEP
HILDEGARD, QUEEN CONSORT...
SOMEHOW EVEN MORE BEAUTIFUL THAN EVER.
THERE'S NO NEED TO BE SHY, NOW. COME ON OUT...
...MAXI-MILIAN.
O-OKAY.

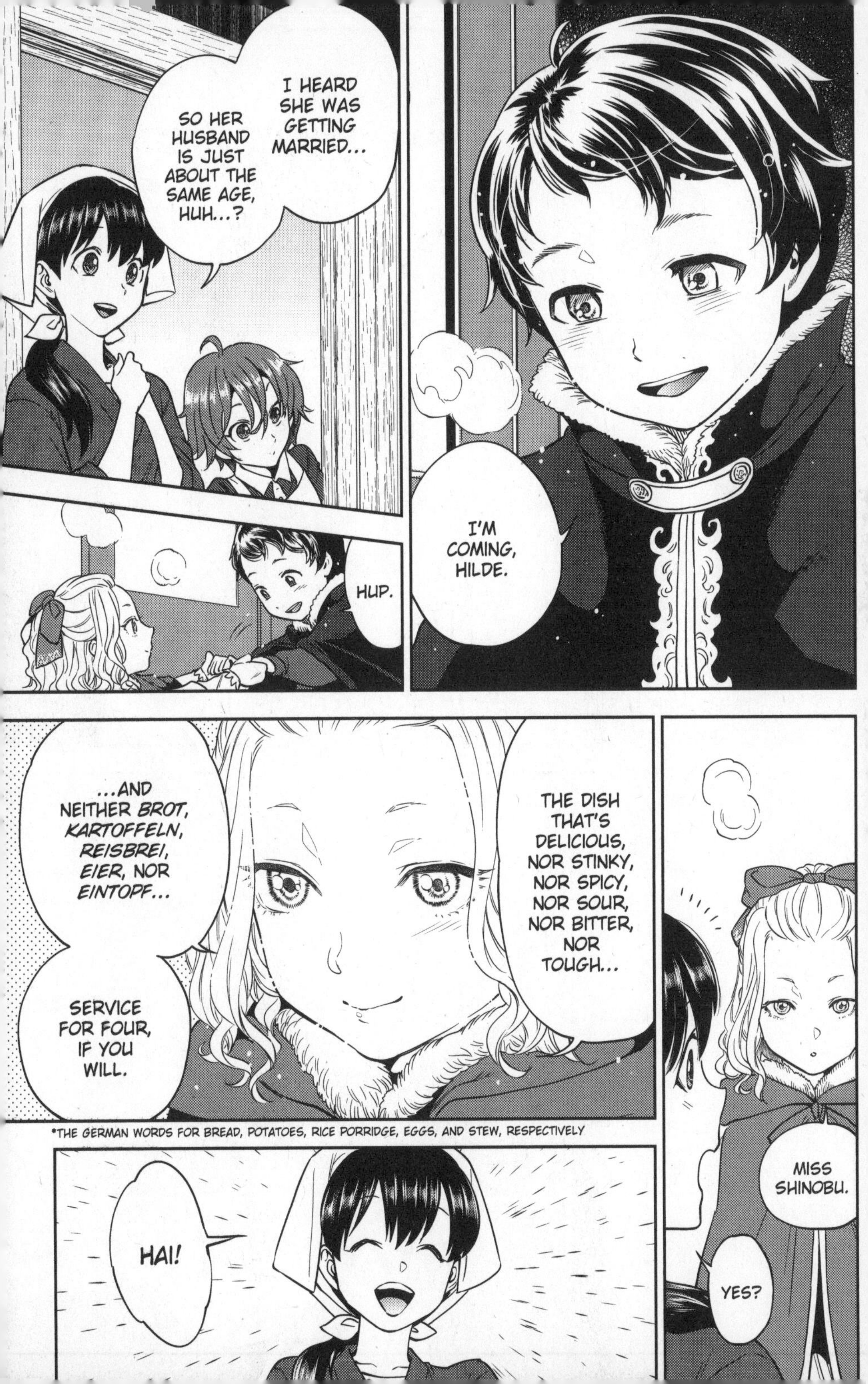
I'M COMING, HILDE.
I HEARD SHE WAS GETTING MARRIED...
SO HER HUSBAND IS JUST ABOUT THE SAME AGE, HUH...?
HUP.
MISS SHINOBU.
YES?
THE DISH THAT'S DELICIOUS, NOR STINKY, NOR SPICY, NOR SOUR, NOR BITTER, NOR TOUGH...
...AND NEITHER *BROT*, *KARTOFFELN*, *REISBREI*, *EIER*, NOR *EINTOPF*...
SERVICE FOR FOUR, IF YOU WILL.
HAI!
*THE GERMAN WORDS FOR BREAD, POTATOES, RICE PORRIDGE, EGGS, AND STEW, RESPECTIVELY

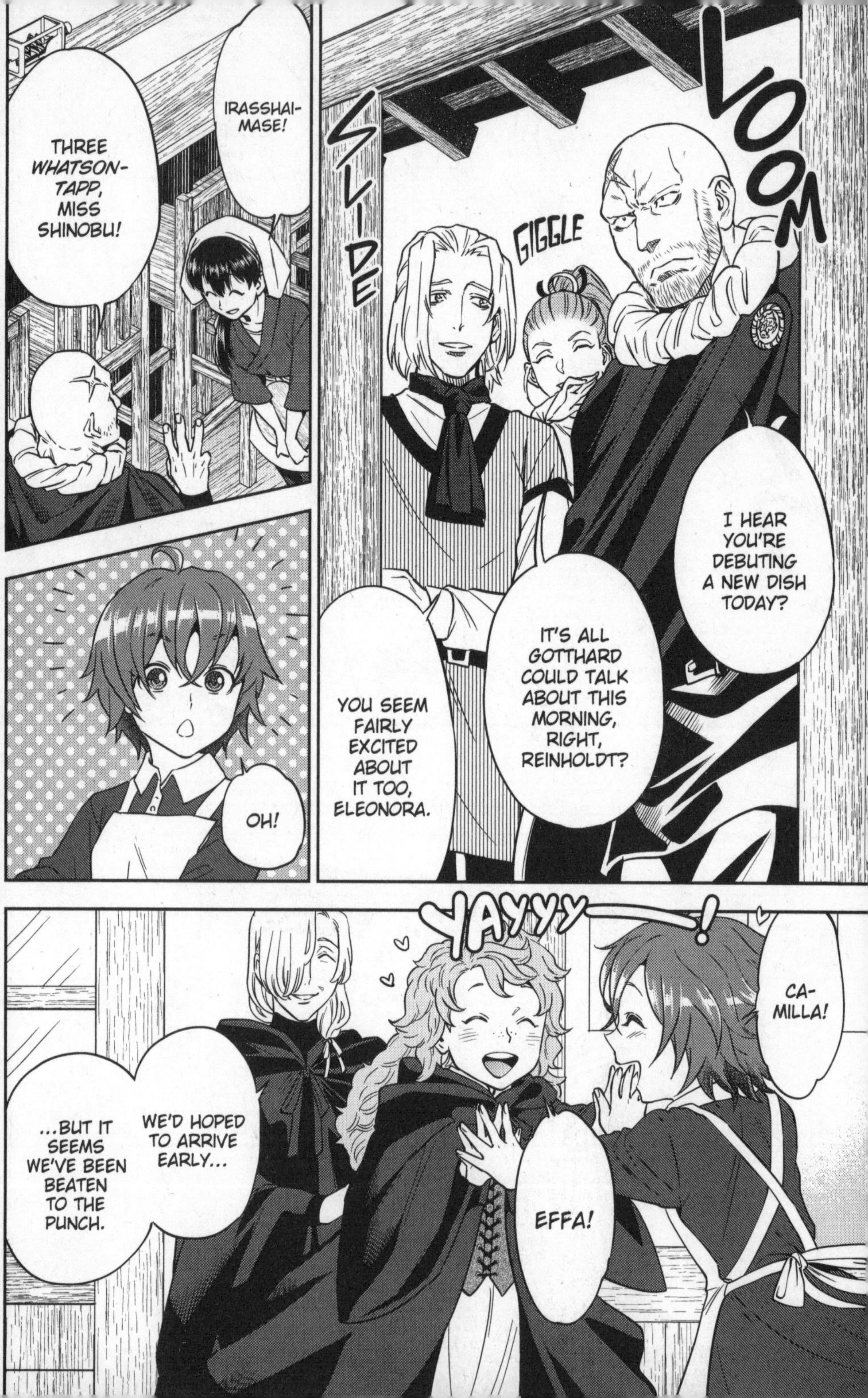
VOOM
SLIDE
GIGGLE
I HEAR YOU'RE DEBUTING A NEW DISH TODAY?
IT'S ALL GOTTHARD COULD TALK ABOUT THIS MORNING, RIGHT, REINHOLDT?
YOU SEEM FAIRLY EXCITED ABOUT IT TOO, ELEONORA.
IRASSHAI-MASE!
THREE *WHATSON-TAPP*, MISS SHINOBU!
OH!
YAYYY—!
CA-MILLA!
EFFA!
WE'D HOPED TO ARRIVE EARLY...
...BUT IT SEEMS WE'VE BEEN BEATEN TO THE PUNCH.

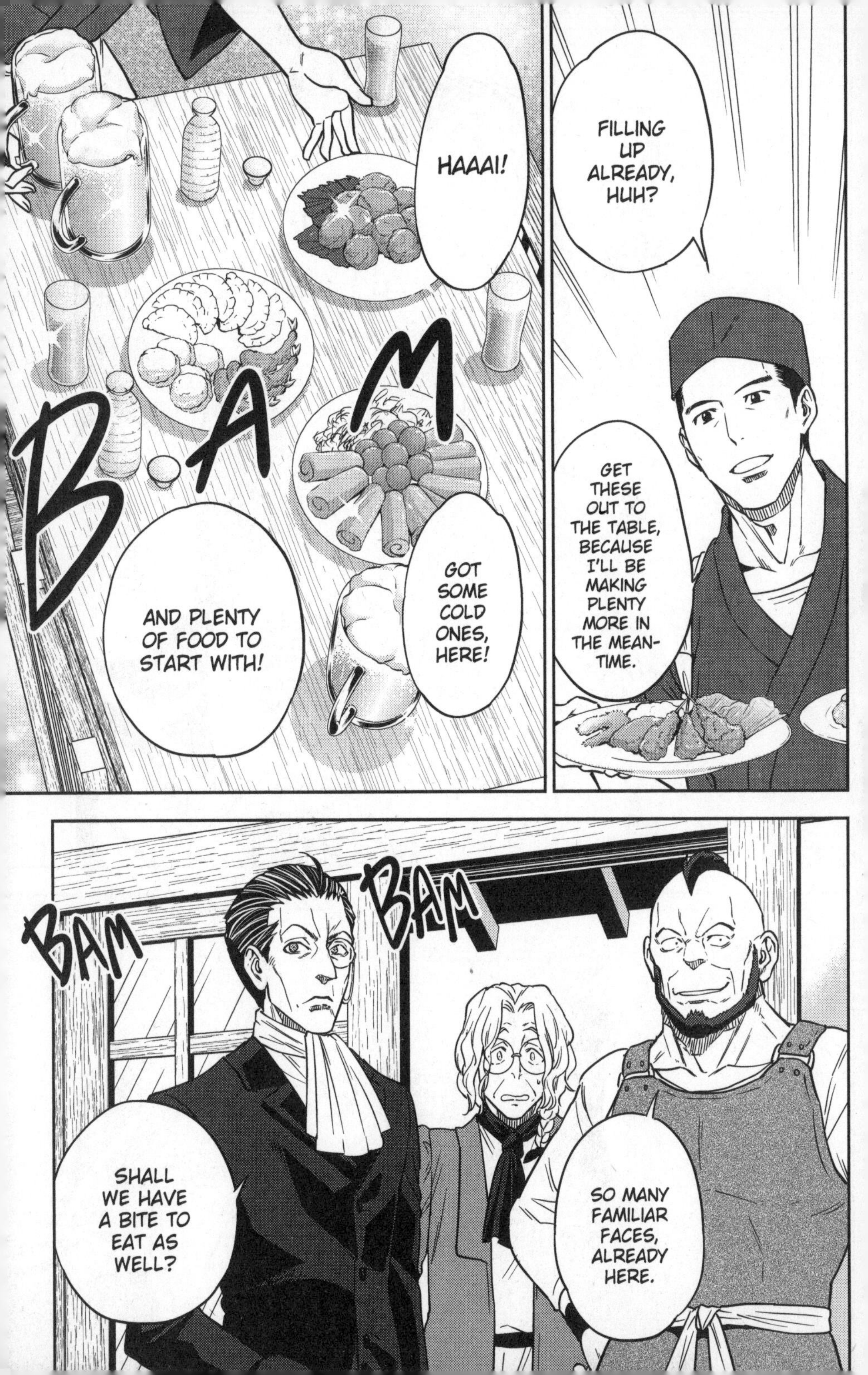
FILLING UP ALREADY, HUH?
GET THESE OUT TO THE TABLE, BECAUSE I'LL BE MAKING PLENTY MORE IN THE MEAN-TIME.
HAAAI!
BAM
GOT SOME COLD ONES, HERE!
AND PLENTY OF FOOD TO START WITH!
BAM
BAM
SO MANY FAMILIAR FACES, ALREADY HERE.
SHALL WE HAVE A BITE TO EAT AS WELL?

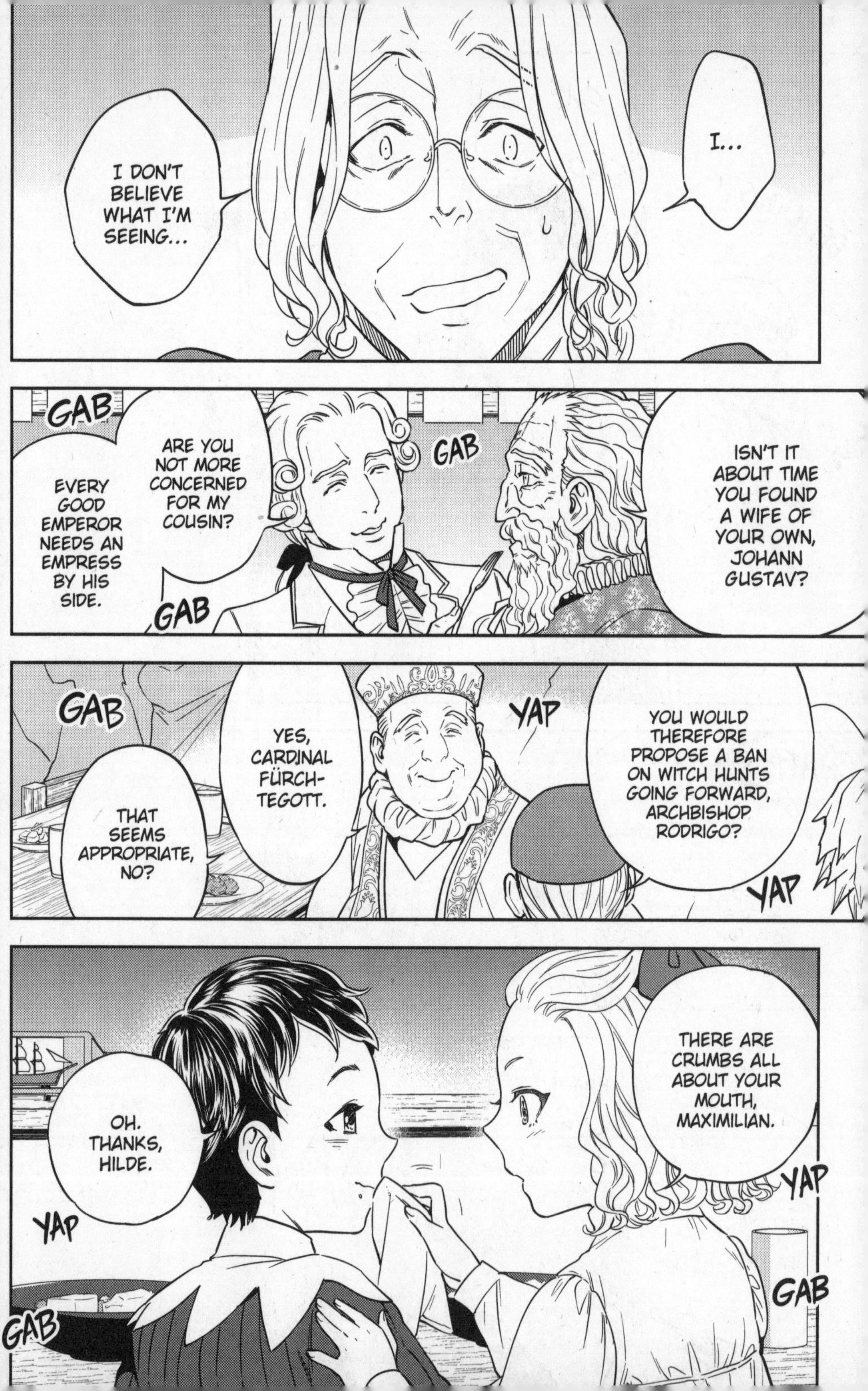
I...
I DON'T BELIEVE WHAT I'M SEEING...
ISN'T IT ABOUT TIME YOU FOUND A WIFE OF YOUR OWN, JOHANN GUSTAV?
GAB
ARE YOU NOT MORE CONCERNED FOR MY COUSIN?
GAB
EVERY GOOD EMPEROR NEEDS AN EMPRESS BY HIS SIDE.
GAB
YOU WOULD THEREFORE PROPOSE A BAN ON WITCH HUNTS GOING FORWARD, ARCHBISHOP RODRIGO?
YAP
YAP
YES, CARDINAL FÜRCH-TEGOTT.
GAB
THAT SEEMS APPROPRIATE, NO?
THERE ARE CRUMBS ALL ABOUT YOUR MOUTH, MAXIMILIAN.
YAP
GAB
OH. THANKS, HILDE.
YAP
GAB

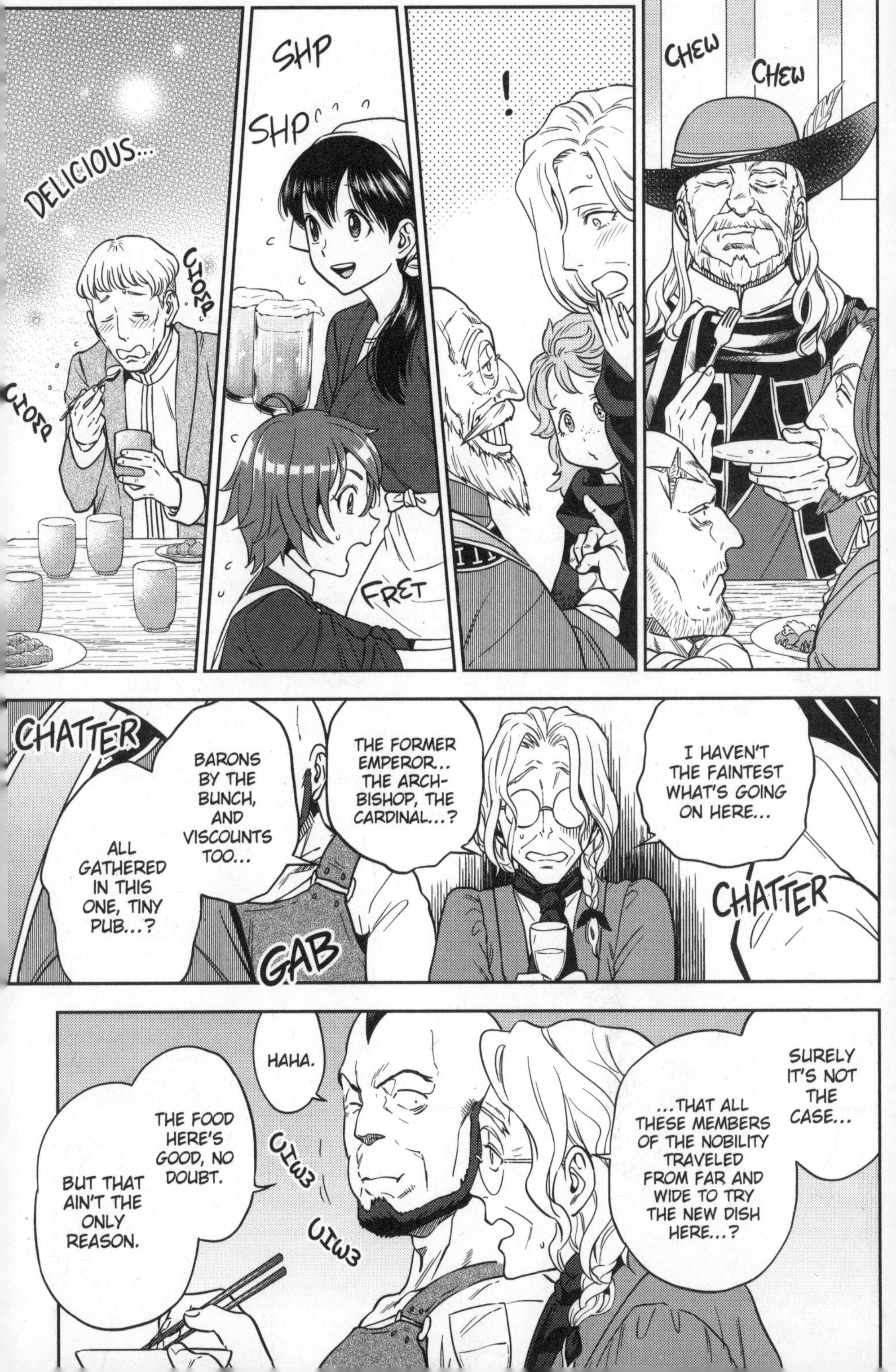
CHEW
CHEW
!
SHP
SHP
FRET
DELICIOUS...
CHOMP
CHOMP
I HAVEN'T THE FAINTEST WHAT'S GOING ON HERE...
CHATTER
THE FORMER EMPEROR... THE ARCH-BISHOP, THE CARDINAL...?
BARONS BY THE BUNCH, AND VISCOUNTS TOO...
ALL GATHERED IN THIS ONE, TINY PUB...?
GAB
CHATTER
SURELY IT'S NOT THE CASE...
...THAT ALL THESE MEMBERS OF THE NOBILITY TRAVELED FROM FAR AND WIDE TO TRY THE NEW DISH HERE...?
HAHA.
THE FOOD HERE'S GOOD, NO DOUBT.
BUT THAT AIN'T THE ONLY REASON.

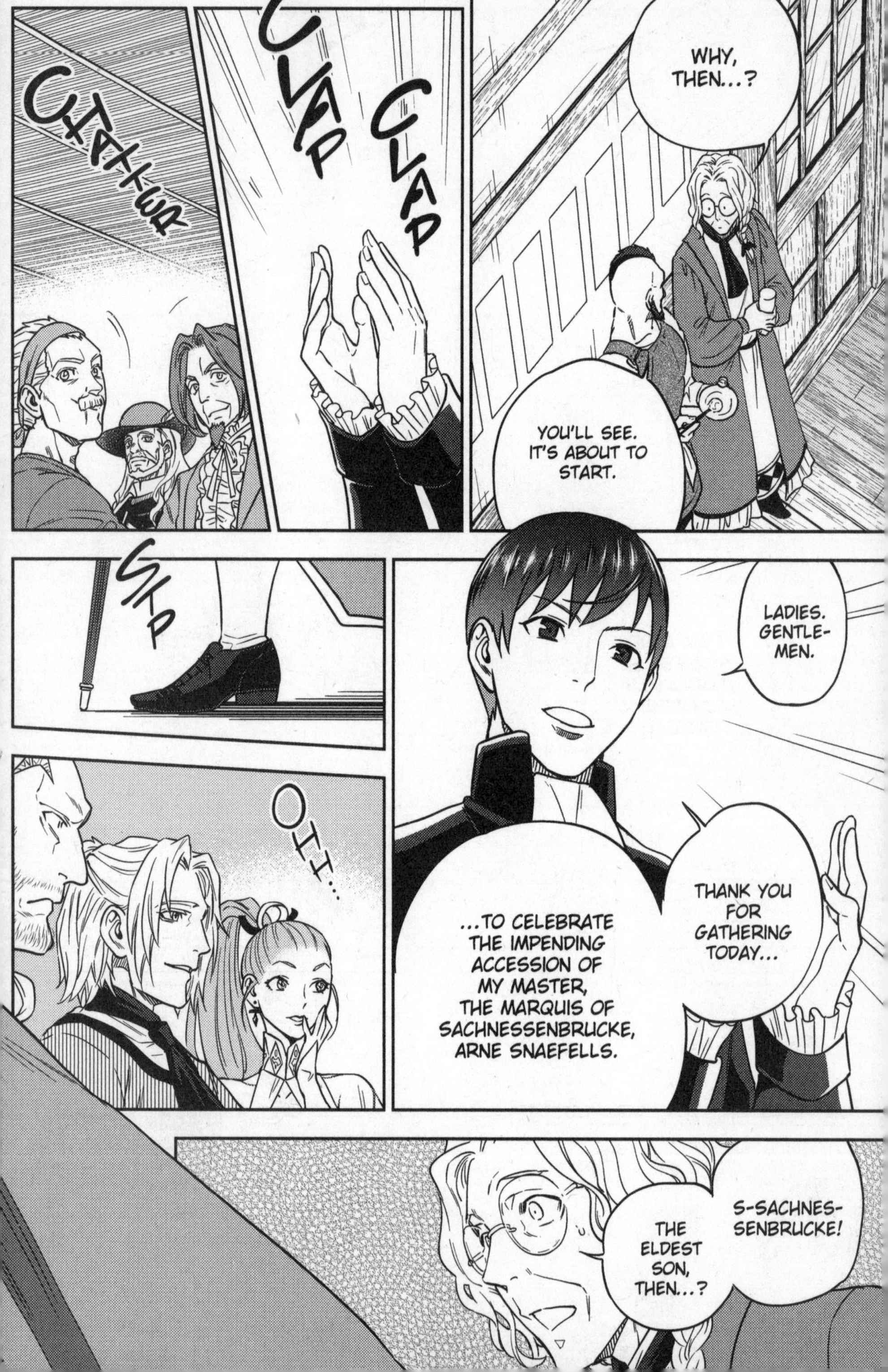
WHY, THEN...?
YOU'LL SEE. IT'S ABOUT TO START.
CLAP CLAP
CHATTER
LADIES. GENTLEMEN.
THANK YOU FOR GATHERING TODAY...
...TO CELEBRATE THE IMPENDING ACCESSION OF MY MASTER, THE MARQUIS OF SACHNESSENBRUCKE, ARNE SNAEFELLS.
SKP
OHH...
S-SACHNES-SENBRUCKE!
THE ELDEST SON, THEN...?

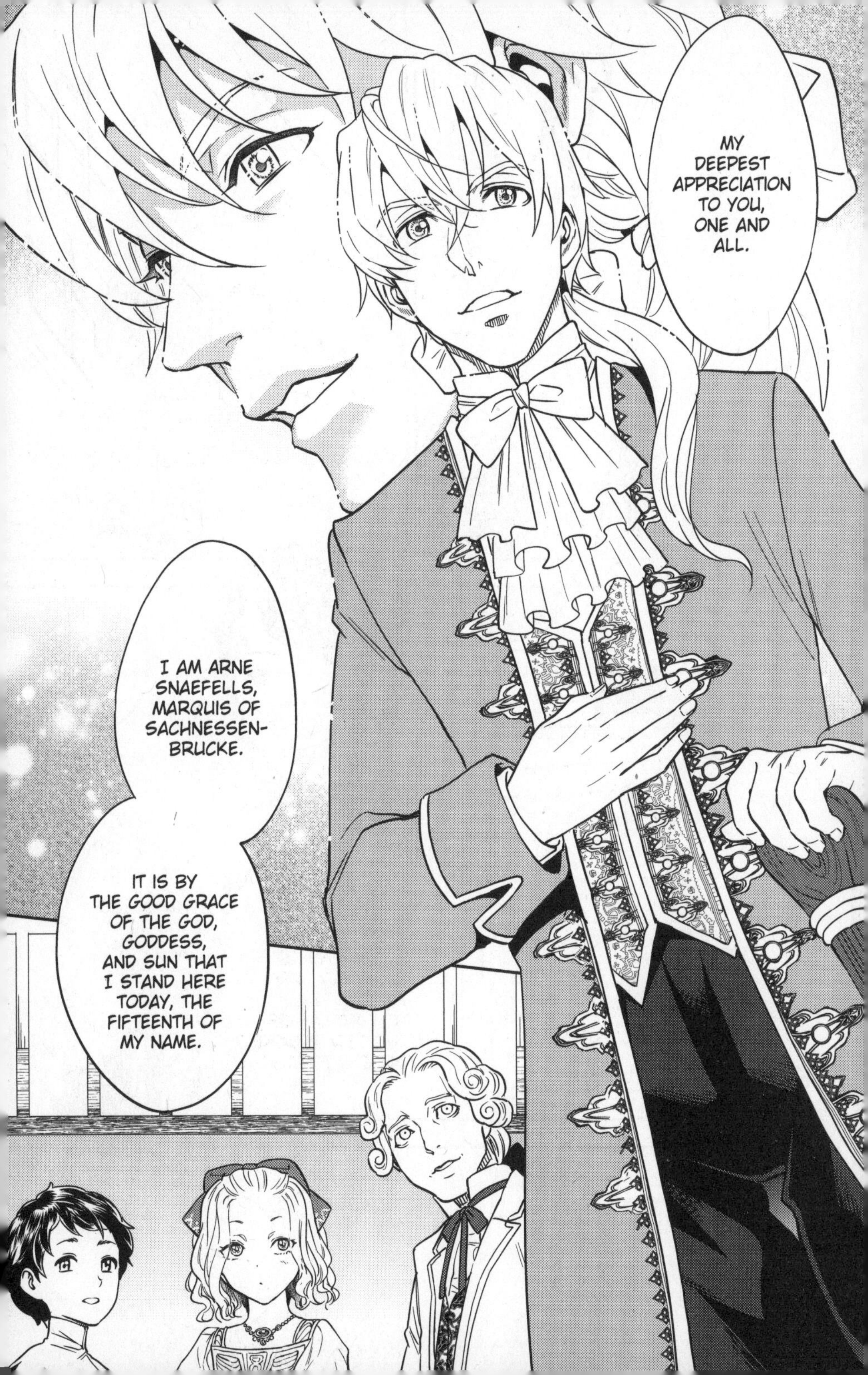
MY DEEPEST APPRECIATION TO YOU, ONE AND ALL.
I AM ARNE SNAEFELLS, MARQUIS OF SACHNESSEN-BRUCKE.
IT IS BY THE GOOD GRACE OF THE GOD, GODDESS, AND SUN THAT I STAND HERE TODAY, THE FIFTEENTH OF MY NAME.

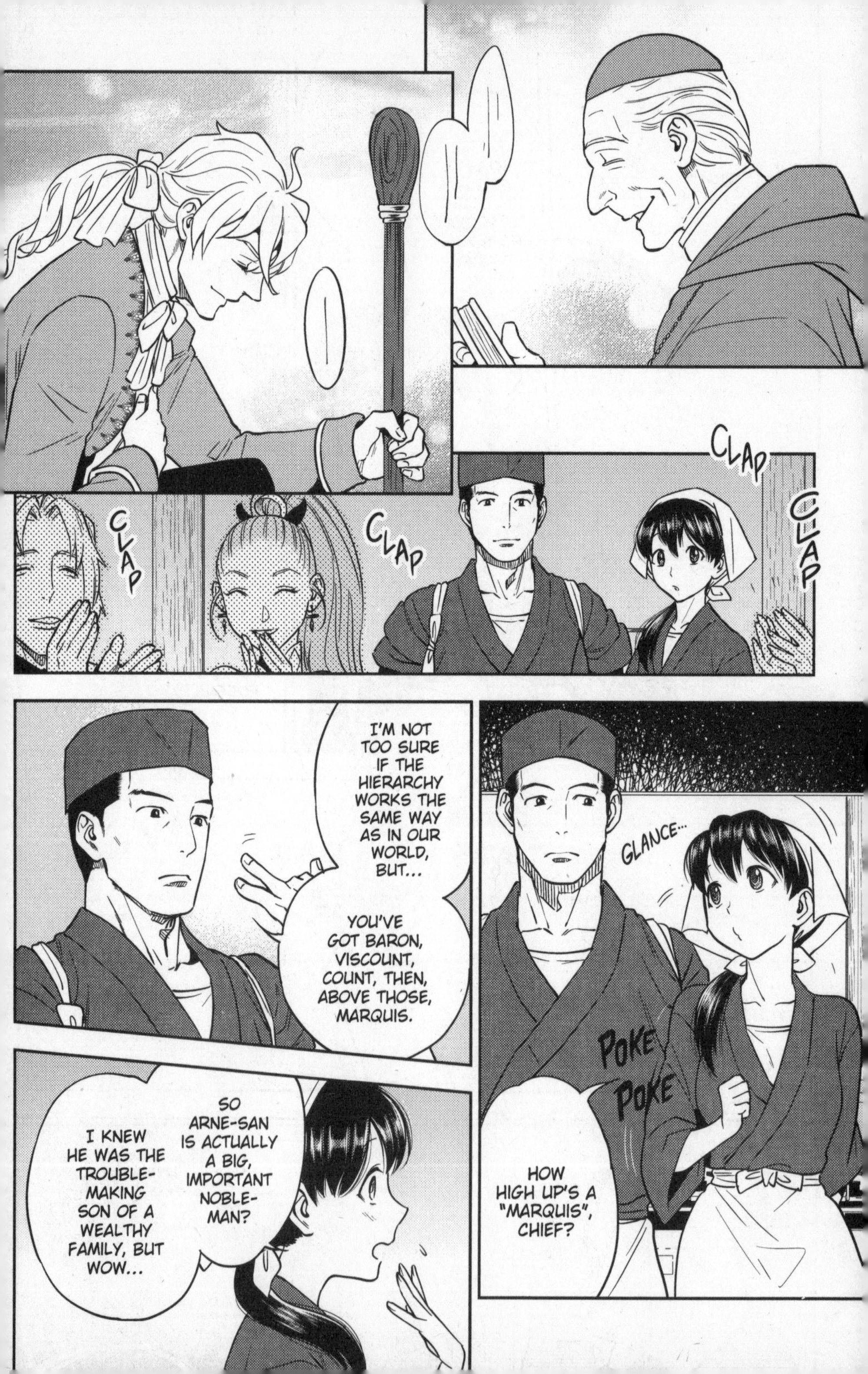
CLAP
CLAP
CLAP
CLAP
GLANCE...
POKE POKE
HOW HIGH UP'S A "MARQUIS", CHIEF?
I'M NOT TOO SURE IF THE HIERARCHY WORKS THE SAME WAY AS IN OUR WORLD, BUT...
YOU'VE GOT BARON, VISCOUNT, COUNT, THEN, ABOVE THOSE, MARQUIS.
SO ARNE-SAN IS ACTUALLY A BIG, IMPORTANT NOBLE-MAN?
I KNEW HE WAS THE TROUBLE-MAKING SON OF A WEALTHY FAMILY, BUT WOW...

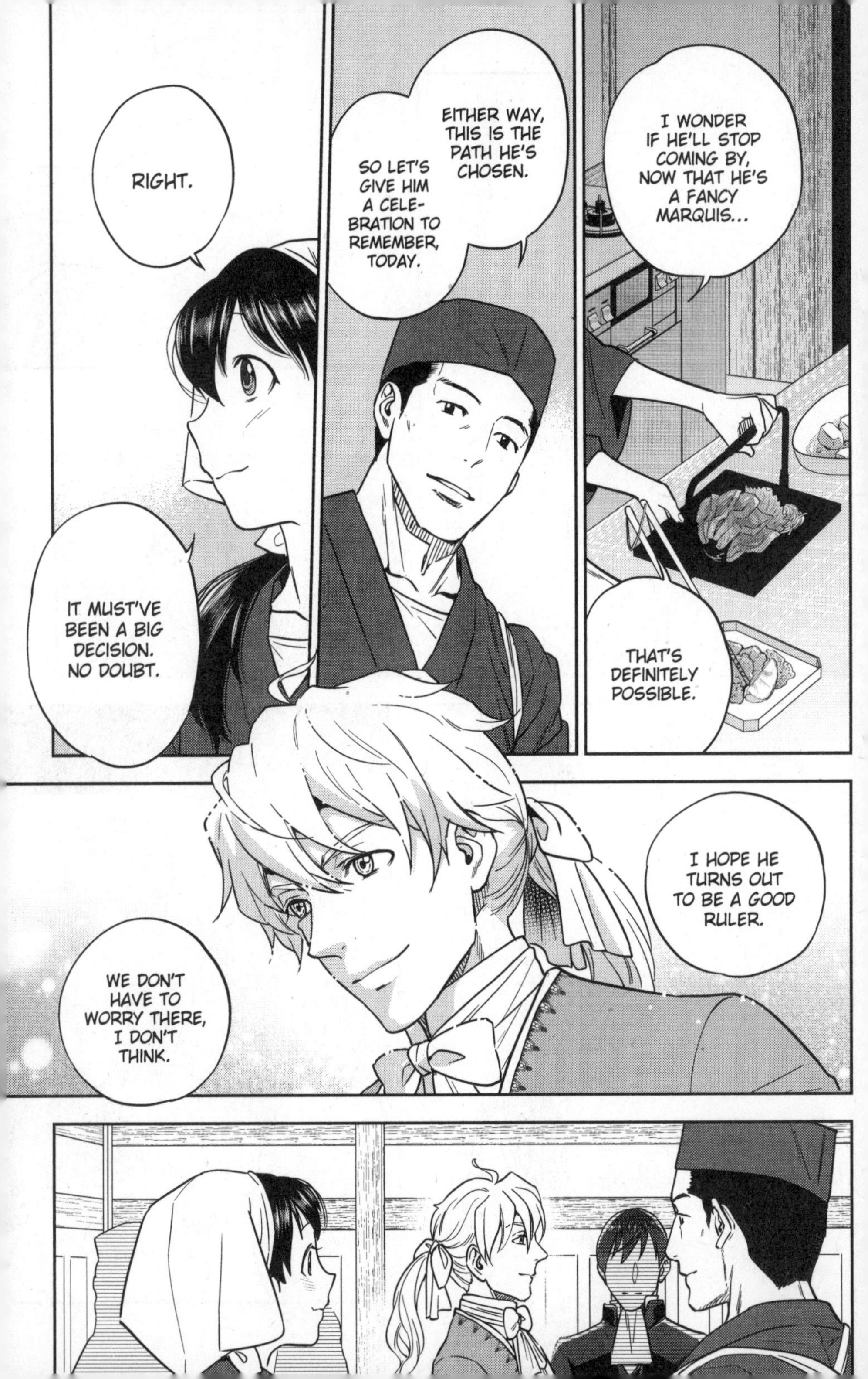
I WONDER IF HE'LL STOP COMING BY, NOW THAT HE'S A FANCY MARQUIS...
THAT'S DEFINITELY POSSIBLE.
EITHER WAY, THIS IS THE PATH HE'S CHOSEN.
SO LET'S GIVE HIM A CELEBRATION TO REMEMBER, TODAY.
RIGHT.
IT MUST'VE BEEN A BIG DECISION. NO DOUBT.
I HOPE HE TURNS OUT TO BE A GOOD RULER.
WE DON'T HAVE TO WORRY THERE, I DON'T THINK.

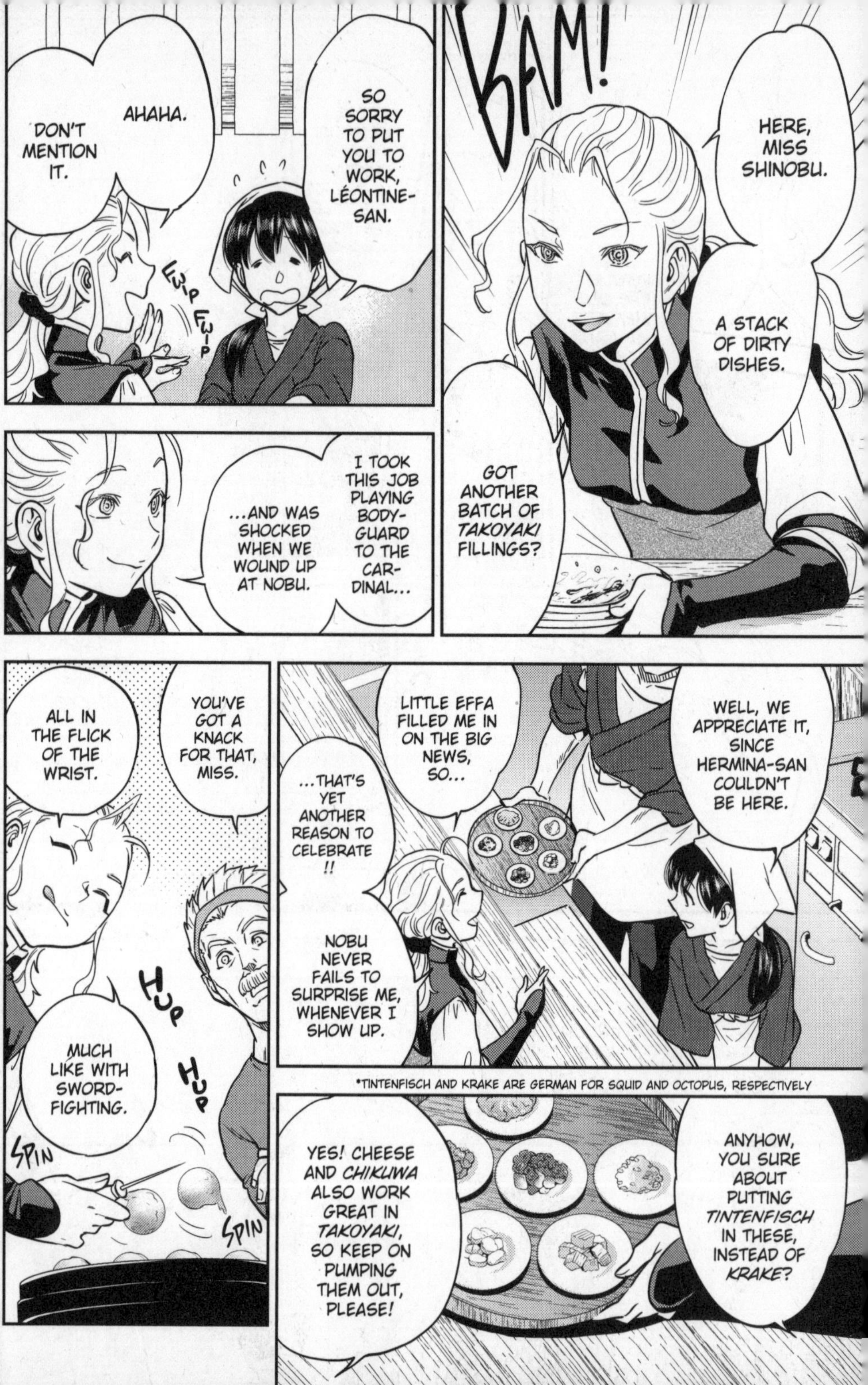
BAM!
HERE, MISS SHINOBU.
A STACK OF DIRTY DISHES.
GOT ANOTHER BATCH OF *TAKOYAKI* FILLINGS?
SO SORRY TO PUT YOU TO WORK, LÉONTINE-SAN.
AHAHA.
DON'T MENTION IT.
FWIP FWIP
I TOOK THIS JOB PLAYING BODY-GUARD TO THE CAR-DINAL...
...AND WAS SHOCKED WHEN WE WOUND UP AT NOBU.
WELL, WE APPRECIATE IT, SINCE HERMINA-SAN COULDN'T BE HERE.
LITTLE EFFA FILLED ME IN ON THE BIG NEWS, SO...
...THAT'S YET ANOTHER REASON TO CELEBRATE!!
NOBU NEVER FAILS TO SURPRISE ME, WHENEVER I SHOW UP.
ANYHOW, YOU SURE ABOUT PUTTING *TINTENFISCH* IN THESE, INSTEAD OF *KRAKE*?
YES! CHEESE AND *CHIKUWA* ALSO WORK GREAT IN *TAKOYAKI*, SO KEEP ON PUMPING THEM OUT, PLEASE!
YOU'VE GOT A KNACK FOR THAT, MISS.
ALL IN THE FLICK OF THE WRIST.
HUP HUP
MUCH LIKE WITH SWORD-FIGHTING.
SPIN SPIN

*TINTENFISCH AND KRAKE ARE GERMAN FOR SQUID AND OCTOPUS, RESPECTIVELY

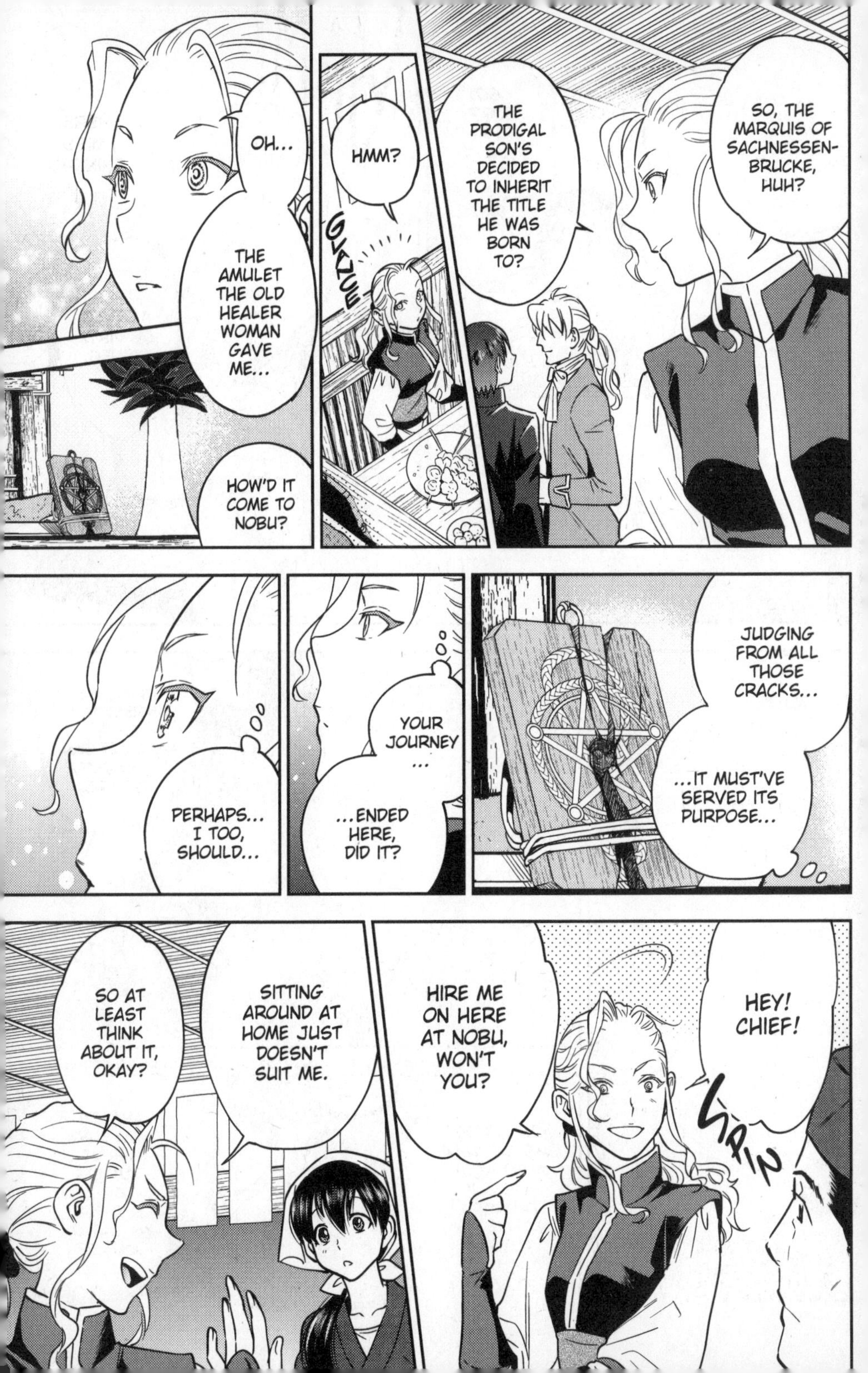
SO, THE MARQUIS OF SACHNESSEN-BRUCKE, HUH?
THE PRODIGAL SON'S DECIDED TO INHERIT THE TITLE HE WAS BORN TO?
HMM?
GLANCE
OH...
THE AMULET THE OLD HEALER WOMAN GAVE ME...
HOW'D IT COME TO NOBU?
JUDGING FROM ALL THOSE CRACKS...
...IT MUST'VE SERVED ITS PURPOSE...
YOUR JOURNEY...
...ENDED HERE, DID IT?
PERHAPS... I TOO, SHOULD...
HEY! CHIEF!
SLAP
HIRE ME ON HERE AT NOBU, WON'T YOU?
SITTING AROUND AT HOME JUST DOESN'T SUIT ME.
SO AT LEAST THINK ABOUT IT, OKAY?

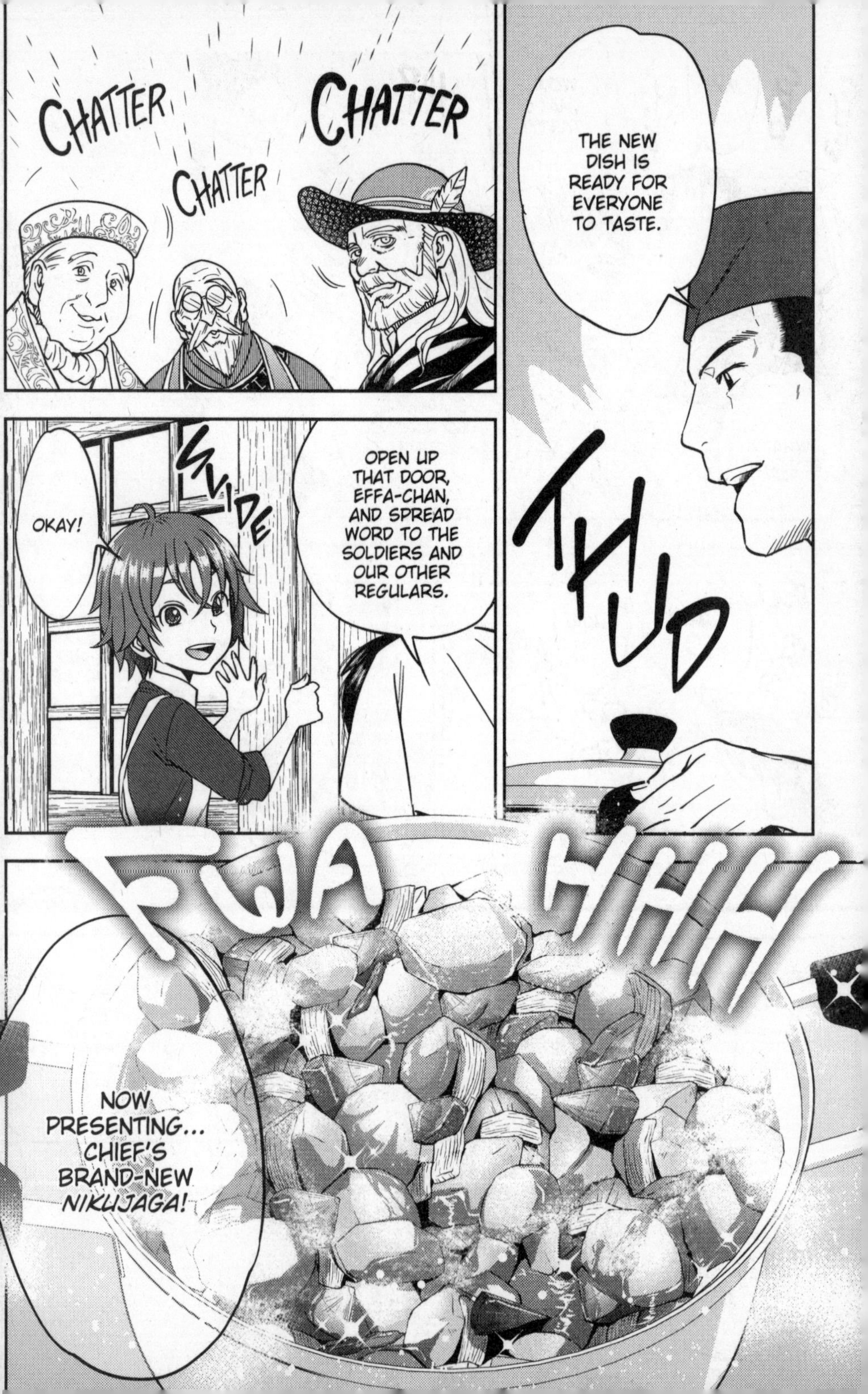
THE NEW DISH IS READY FOR EVERYONE TO TASTE.
THUD
CHATTER
CHATTER
CHATTER
OPEN UP THAT DOOR, EFFA-CHAN, AND SPREAD WORD TO THE SOLDIERS AND OUR OTHER REGULARS.
SWIDE
OKAY!
FWA WHHH
NOW PRESENTING... CHIEF'S BRAND-NEW *NIKUJAGA*!

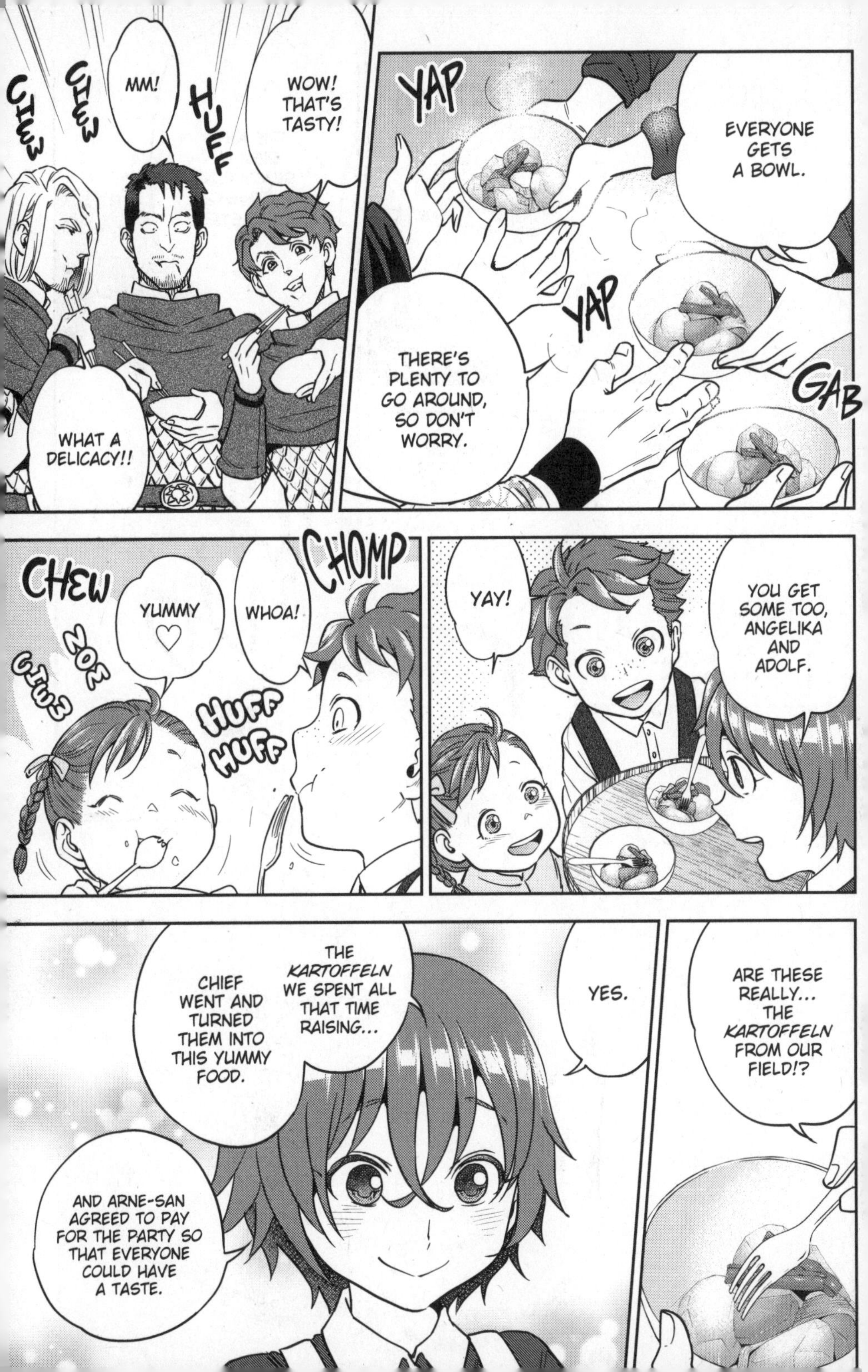
YAP
EVERYONE GETS A BOWL.
YAP
THERE'S PLENTY TO GO AROUND, SO DON'T WORRY.
GAB
WOW! THAT'S TASTY!
HUFF
MM!
CHEW
CHEW
WHAT A DELICACY!!
YOU GET SOME TOO, ANGELIKA AND ADOLF.
YAY!
CHOMP
WHOA!
YUMMY ♡
CHEW
NOM
CHEW
HUFF HUFF
ARE THESE REALLY... THE *KARTOFFELN* FROM OUR FIELD!?
YES.
THE *KARTOFFELN* WE SPENT ALL THAT TIME RAISING...
CHIEF WENT AND TURNED THEM INTO THIS YUMMY FOOD.
AND ARNE-SAN AGREED TO PAY FOR THE PARTY SO THAT EVERYONE COULD HAVE A TASTE.

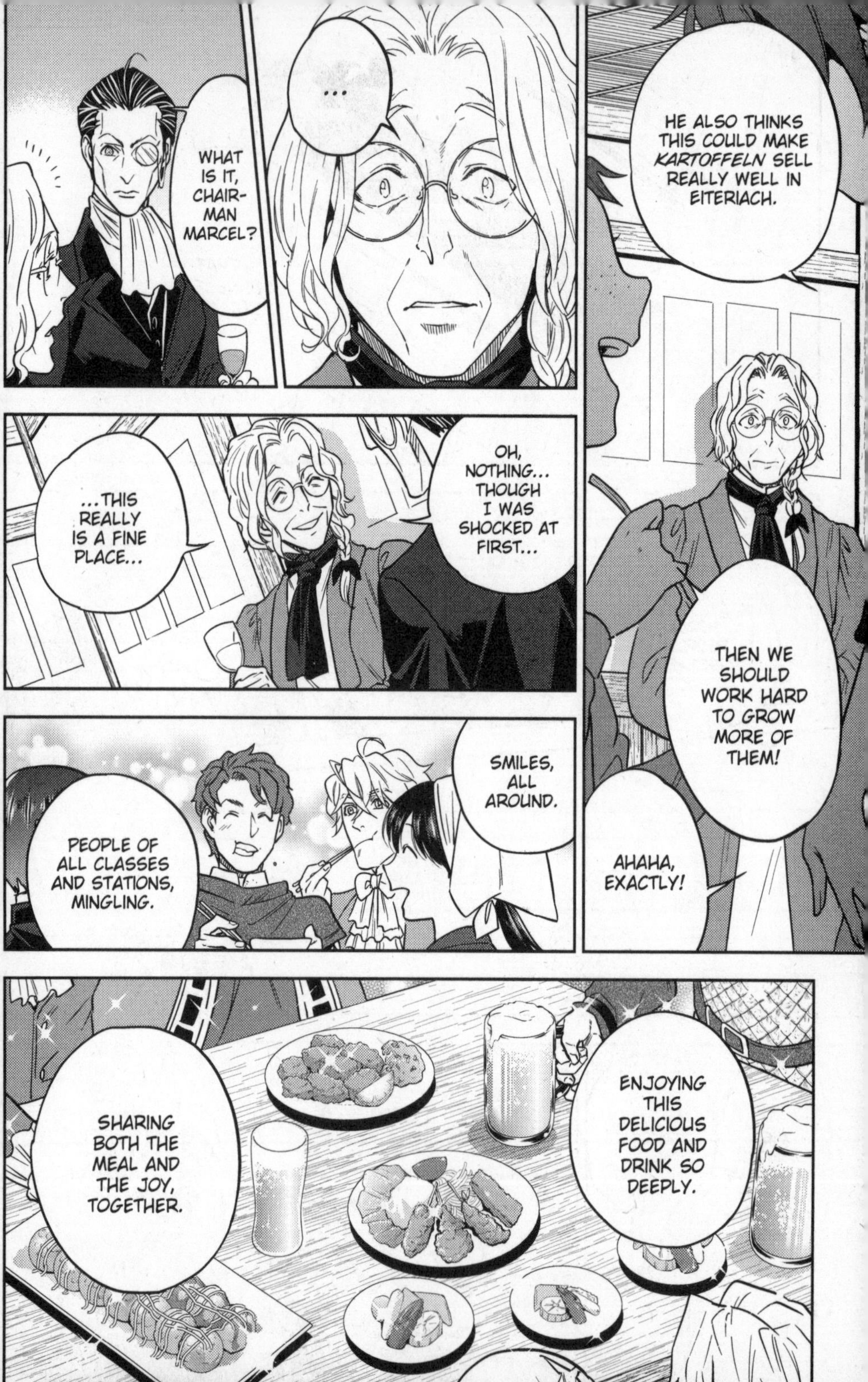
HE ALSO THINKS THIS COULD MAKE KARTOFFELN SELL REALLY WELL IN EITERIACH.
THEN WE SHOULD WORK HARD TO GROW MORE OF THEM!
AHAHA, EXACTLY!
...
WHAT IS IT, CHAIR-MAN MARCEL?
OH, NOTHING... THOUGH I WAS SHOCKED AT FIRST...
...THIS REALLY IS A FINE PLACE...
SMILES, ALL AROUND.
PEOPLE OF ALL CLASSES AND STATIONS, MINGLING.
ENJOYING THIS DELICIOUS FOOD AND DRINK SO DEEPLY.
SHARING BOTH THE MEAL AND THE JOY, TOGETHER.

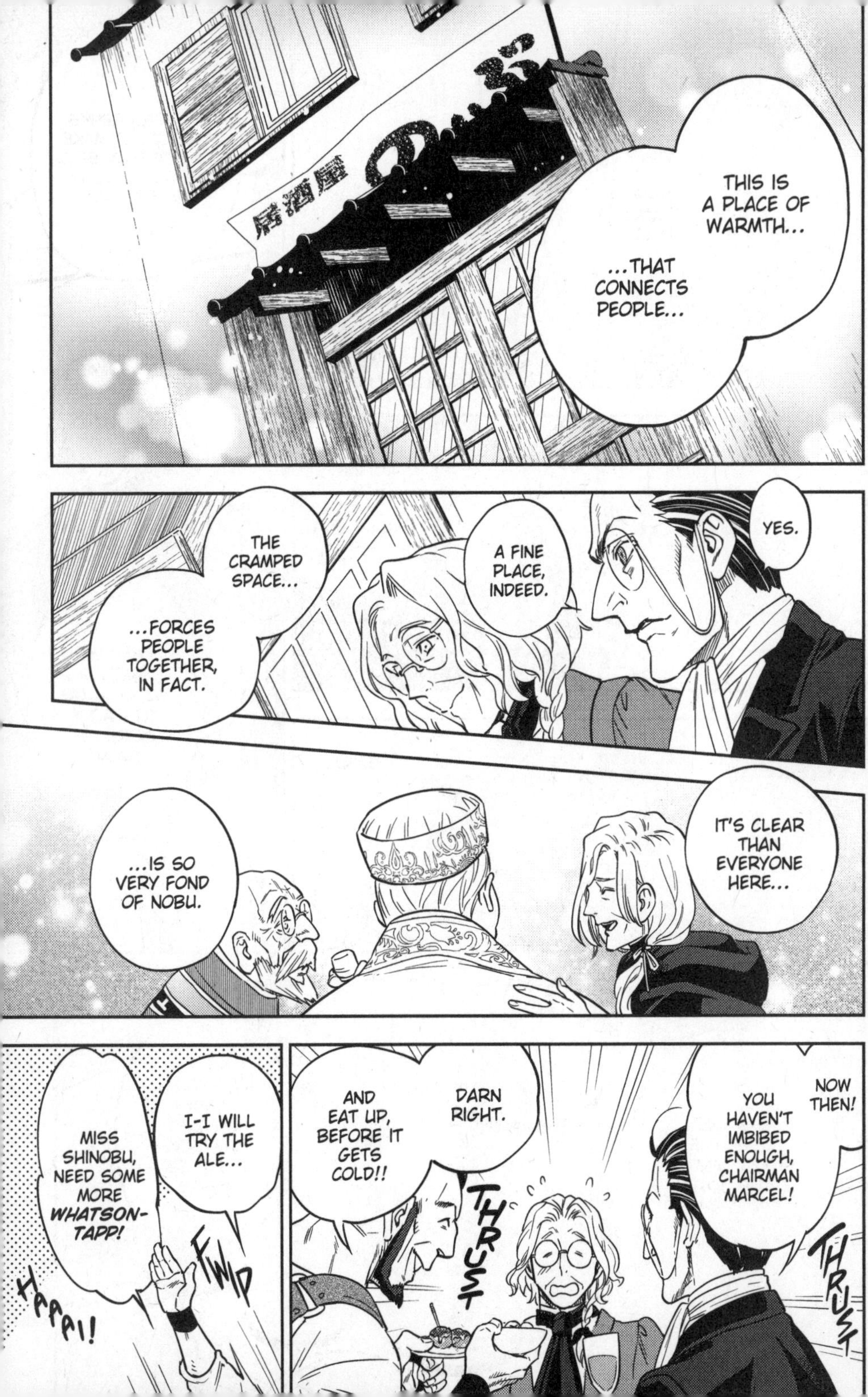
居酒屋
THIS IS A PLACE OF WARMTH...
...THAT CONNECTS PEOPLE...
YES.
A FINE PLACE, INDEED.
THE CRAMPED SPACE...
...FORCES PEOPLE TOGETHER, IN FACT.
IT'S CLEAR THAN EVERYONE HERE...
...IS SO VERY FOND OF NOBU.
NOW THEN!
YOU HAVEN'T IMBIBED ENOUGH, CHAIRMAN MARCEL!
THRUST
DARN RIGHT.
AND EAT UP, BEFORE IT GETS COLD!!
THRUST
I-I WILL TRY THE ALE...
MISS SHINOBU, NEED SOME MORE *WHATSON-TAPP!*
FWIP
HAAAI!

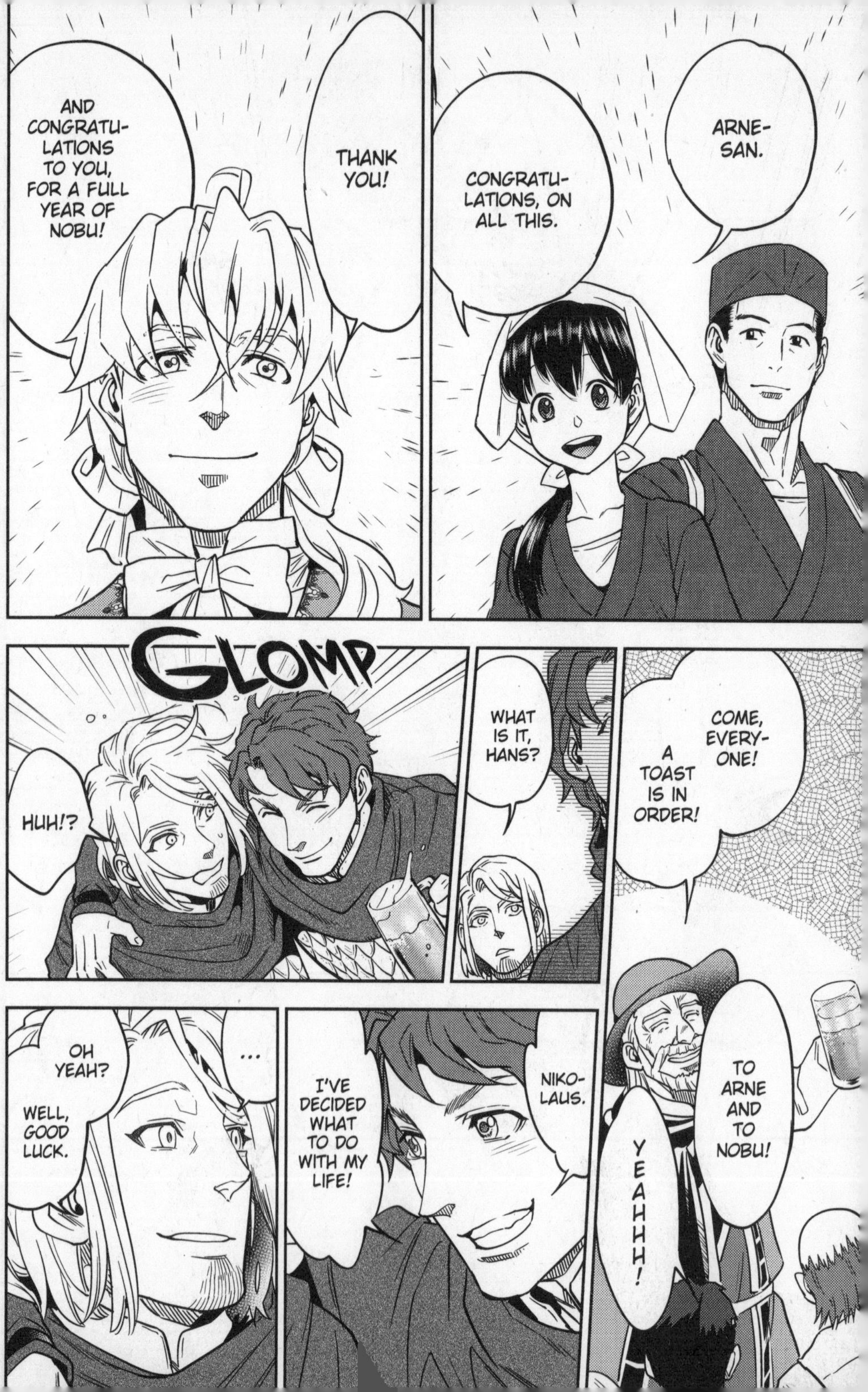
ARNE-SAN.
CONGRATULATIONS, ON ALL THIS.
THANK YOU!
AND CONGRATULATIONS TO YOU, FOR A FULL YEAR OF NOBU!
COME, EVERYONE!
A TOAST IS IN ORDER!
WHAT IS IT, HANS?
GLOMP
HUH!?
TO ARNE AND TO NOBU!
YEAHHH!
NIKOLAUS.
I'VE DECIDED WHAT TO DO WITH MY LIFE!
...
OH YEAH?
WELL, GOOD LUCK.

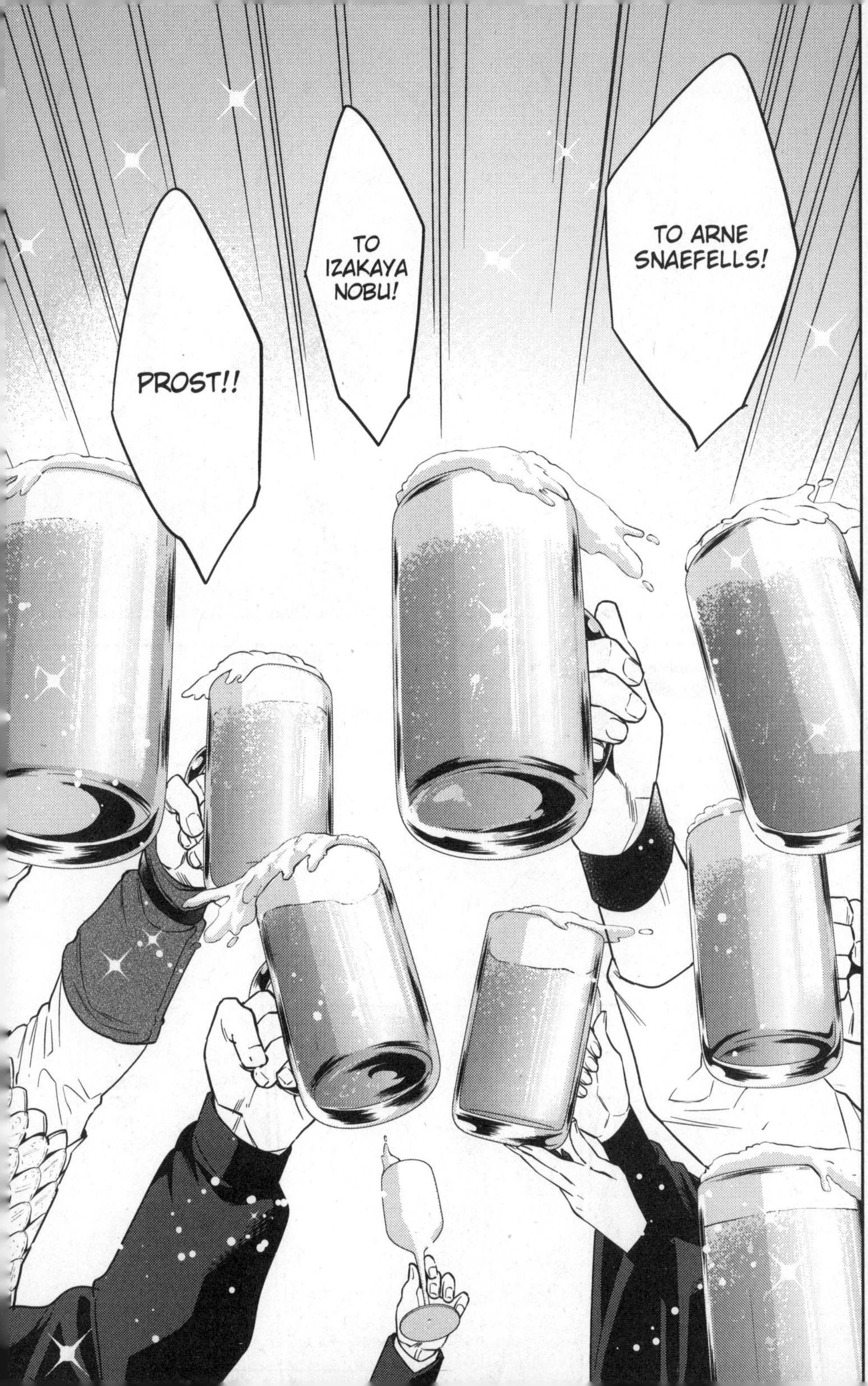
TO ARNE SNAEFELLS!
TO IZAKAYA NOBU!
PROST!!

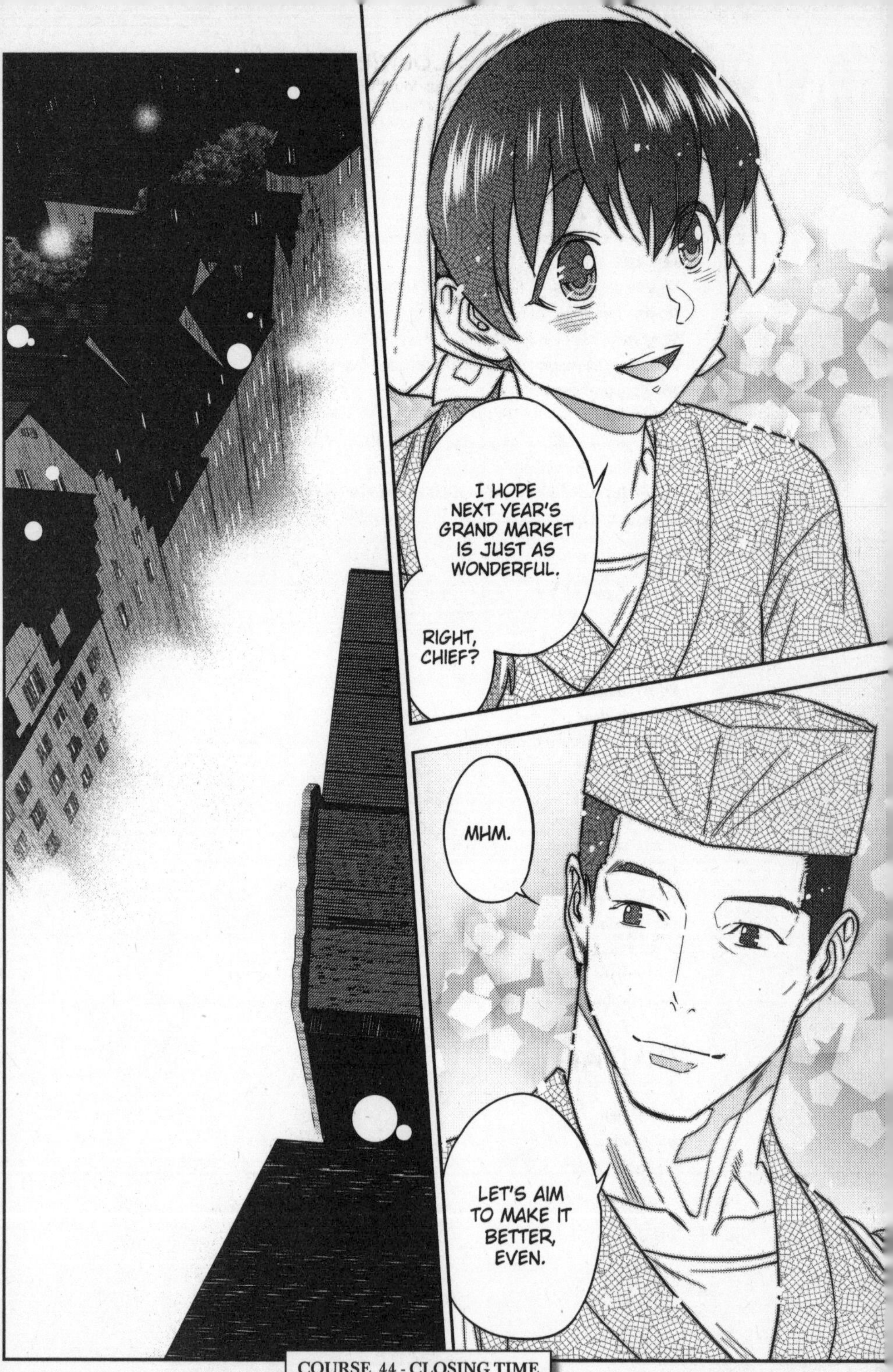
I HOPE NEXT YEAR'S GRAND MARKET IS JUST AS WONDERFUL.
RIGHT, CHIEF?
MHM.
LET'S AIM TO MAKE IT BETTER, EVEN.

COURSE 44 - CLOSING TIME

M
E
N
U

FOOD VOCABULARY ENCOUNTERED IN THIS BOOK:
The fantasy world of "Nobu" brings together speakers of Japanese and German for a delicious cross-cultural exchange. Hans, Nikolaus, Chief, Shinobu, and the gang use a variety of foreign food vocabulary throughout, so here's a quick review of what came up in this volume! Including some Italian!

JAPANESE

Atsukan: hot sake
Chikuwa: processed fishcake, molded into a bamboo-like tube shape
Dashi: Japanese soup broth
Doteyaki: beef tendon stewed in miso, sake, and sugar
Hojicha: tea made with roasted green tea leaves
Nikujaga: meat and potato stew
Oshibori: the hot, rolled towels provided to restaurant customers before the meal
Sakamushi: a dish that's salted and steamed in sake
Satoimo: taro root
Takoyaki: balls made with special batter, typically filled with octopus chunks
Tempura: Japanese deep-frying technique that uses flour and egg batter

GERMAN

Bohne(n): bean(s)
Brot: Bread
Ei(er): eggs
Eintopf: stew
Fisch: fish
Fleisch: meat
Karotte: carrot
Krake(n): octopus(es)
Kürbiskuchen: pumpkin pie
Pilz(e): mushroom(s)
Reisbrei: rice porridge
Schmand: sour cream
Suppe: soup
Tintenfisch: squid
Wein: wine

ITALIAN

Latte: milk
Vino: wine
Vongole: clams

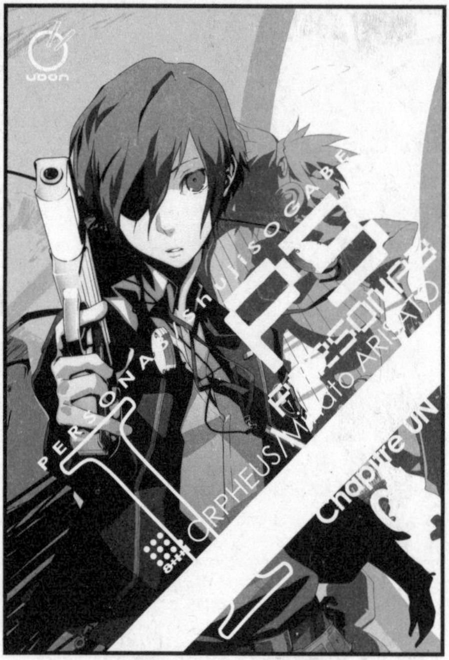
udon
PERSONA 3
Shuji SOGABE
ORPHEUS/Minato ARISATO
Chapitre UN

PERSONA 3 VOL.1
ISBN-13: 978-1927925850

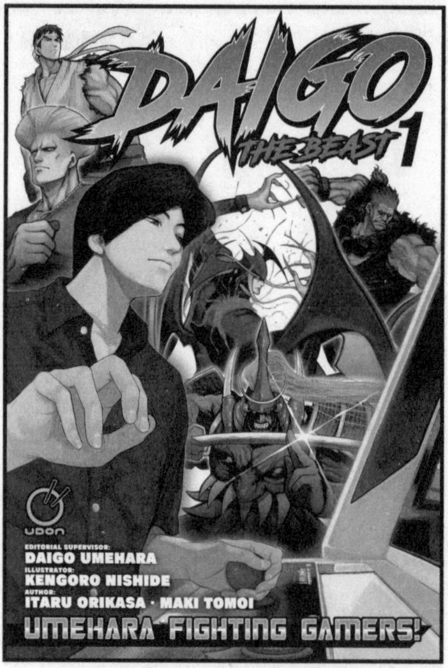
DAIGO THE BEAST 1
udon
EDITORIAL SUPERVISOR:
DAIGO UMEHARA
ILLUSTRATOR:
KENGORO NISHIDE
AUTHOR:
ITARU ORIKASA · MAKI TOMOI
UMEHARA FIGHTING GAMERS!

DAIGO THE BEAST VOL.1
ISBN-13: 978-1772940572

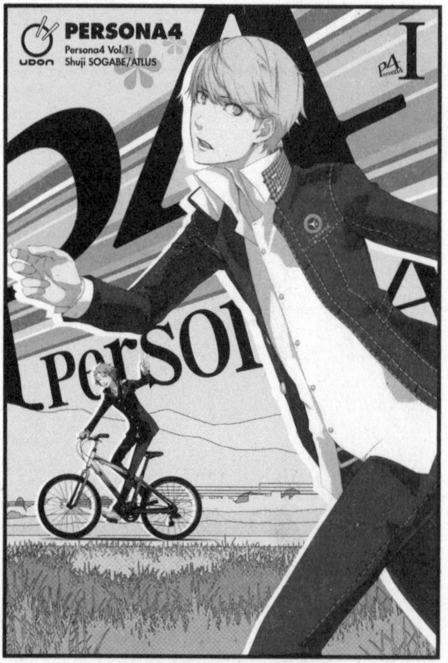
udon
PERSONA4
Persona4 Vol.1:
Shuji SOGABE/ATLUS
I

PERSONA 4 VOL.1
ISBN-13: 978-1927925577

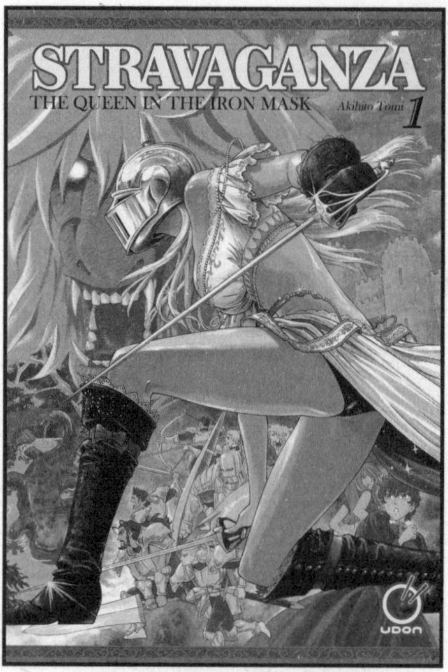
STRAVAGANZA
THE QUEEN IN THE IRON MASK
Akihito Tomi
1
udon

STRAVAGANZA VOL.1
ISBN-13: 978-1772941036

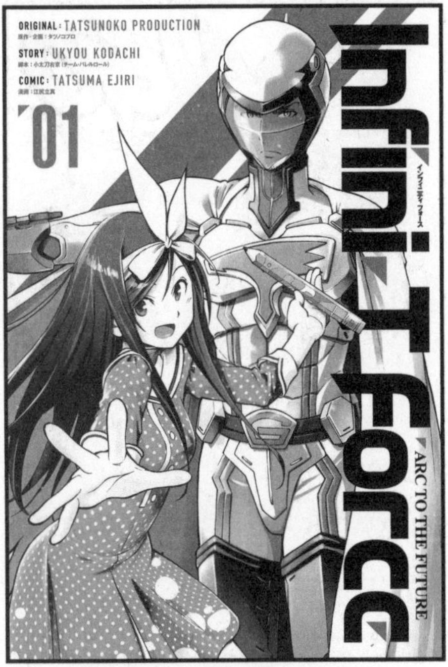
ORIGINAL: TATSUNOKO PRODUCTION
STORY: UKYOU KODACHI
COMIC: TATSUMA EJIRI
01
Infini-T Force
ARC TO THE FUTURE

INFINI-T FORCE VOL.1

ISBN-13: 978-1772940503

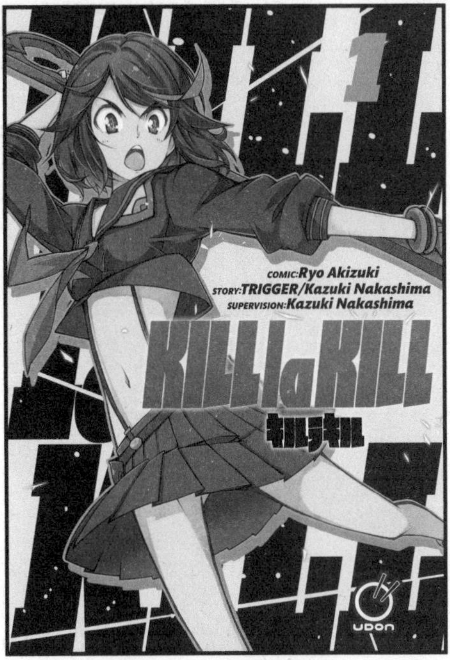
1
COMIC: Ryo Akizuki
STORY: TRIGGER/Kazuki Nakashima
SUPERVISION: Kazuki Nakashima
KILL la KILL
キルラキル
UDON

KILL LA KILL VOL.1

ISBN-13: 978-1927925492

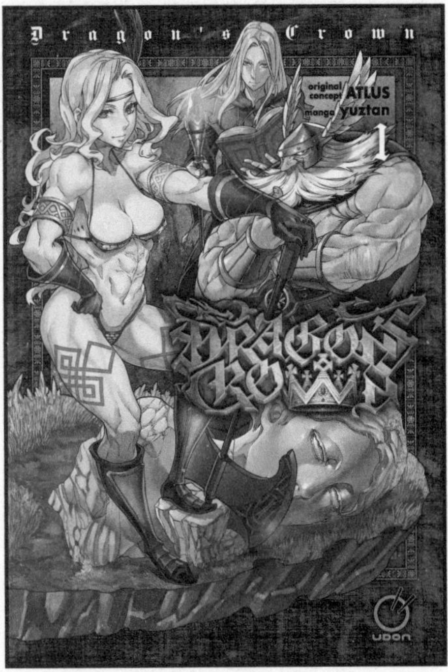
Dragon's Crown
original concept ATLUS
manga yuztan
1
UDON

DRAGON'S CROWN VOL.1

ISBN-13: 978-1772940480

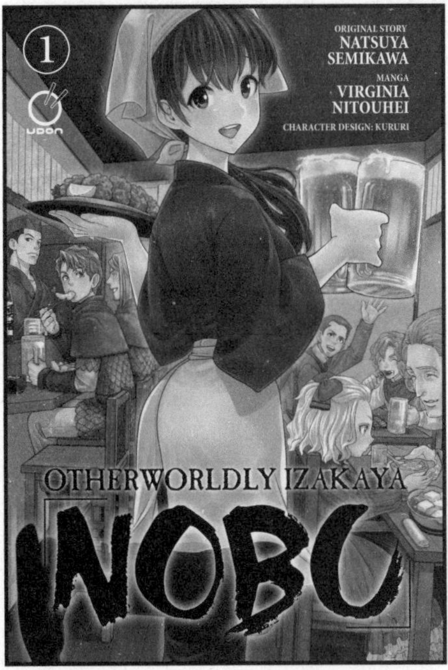
1
UDON
ORIGINAL STORY
NATSUYA SEMIKAWA
MANGA
VIRGINIA NITOUHEI
CHARACTER DESIGN: KURURI
OTHERWORLDLY IZAKAYA
NOBU

OTHERWORLDLY IZAKAYA NOBU VOL.1

ISBN-13: 978-1772940671

OTHERWORLDLY IZAKAYA

NOBU ⑦

ENGLISH EDITION
Translation: CALEB D. COOK
Typesetting: MIYOKO HOSOYAMA
Sound Effects: EK WEAVER
Associate Editor: M. CHANDLER

UDON STAFF
Chief of Operations: ERIK KO
Director of Publishing: MATT MOYLAN
VP of Business Development: CORY CASONI
Director of Marketing: MEGAN MAIDEN
Japanese Liaisons: STEVEN CUMMINGS
ANNA KAWASHIMA

Original Story
NATSUYA SEMIKAWA

Manga
VIRGINIA NITOUHEI

Character Design
KURURI

ISEKAI IZAKAYA "NOBU" Volume 7

©Virginia-Nitouhei 2018
©Natsuya Semikawa,Kururi/TAKARAJIMASHA

First published in Japan in 2018 by KADOKAWA CORPORATION, Tokyo.
English translation rights arranged with KADOKAWA CORPORATION, Tokyo
through TUTTLE–MORI AGENCY, INC., Tokyo.

English language version published by UDON Entertainment Inc.
118 Tower Hill Road, C1, PO Box 20008
Richmond Hill, Ontario, L4K 0K0 CANADA

www.UDONentertainment.com

First Printing: May 2020
ISBN-13: 978-1-77294-110-4
ISBN-10: 1-77294-110-7

Printed in Canada